D1483333

BLACK SABBATH

Also by Mick Wall

Diary of a Madman: The Official Biography of Ozzy Osbourne

Guns N' Roses: The Most Dangerous Band in the World

Pearl Jam

Run to the Hills: The Authorized Biography of Iron Maiden

Paranoid: Black Days with Sabbath & Other Horror Stories

Mr Big: Ozzy, Sharon and My Life as the Godfather of Rock,
(by Don Arden with Mick Wall)

XS All Areas: The Autobiography of Status Quo

John Peel: A Tribute to the Much-Loved DJ and Broadcaster

Bono: In the Name of Love

W.A.R.: The Unauthorized Biography of William Axl Rose

When Giants Walked the Earth: A Biography of Led Zeppelin

Appetite for Destruction

Enter Night: A Biography of Metallica

AC/DC: Hell Ain't a Bad Place to Be

BLACK SABBATH

Symptom of the Universe

MICK WALL

St. Martin's Press
New York

All photographs courtesy of Getty Images, with exception to the portrait of Tony Martin © Simon Connolly

www.stmartins.com

Library of Congress Cataloging-in-Publication Data

Wall, Mick, author.
   Black Sabbath : symptom of the universe / Mick Wall. — First U.S. edition.
      p. cm.
   Includes bibliographical references and index.
   ISBN 978-1-250-05134-9 (hardcover)
   ISBN 978-1-4668-6969-1 (e-book)
   1. Black Sabbath (Musical group) 2. Rock musicians—England—Biography. I. Title.
   ML421.B57W35 2015
   782.42166092'2—dc23
   [B]

                                                              2014040749

First published in Great Britain by Orion Books, an imprint of the Orion Publishing Group Ltd, an Hachette UK company

First U.S. Edition: April 2015

10 9 8 7 6 5 4 3 2 1

For Robert Kirby

CONTENTS

ACKNOWLEDGEMENTS

Linda Wall, Malcolm Edwards, Robert Kirby, Jane Sturrock, Nicola Crossley, Ian Preece, Dee Hembury-Eaton, Lynnette Lawrence, Vanessa McMinn, Wendy Dio, Joel McIver, Harry Paterson, Joe Daly, Paul Clark, Glenn Hughes, Neil Murray, Mark Handsley, Hamish Barbour, Steve O'Hagan, Dave Everley, Jim Simpson, Vivian Campbell, Kathy and Kelle Rhoads, Dana Strum, Holly Thompson, and of course all the various members of Black Sabbath that I have had the pleasure – and occasional pain – of knowing over the years.

PART ONE

Children Of The Grave

ONE
I, AWAKE

They were scum and they knew it. Human debris from the shitty, bomb-cratered streets of a post-war British nowhere named Aston. Black Country misfits with no future they could see and a past they would never escape. Musical interlopers that would always be found out; revealed for what they knew they were: the lowest of the low. A joke no one found funny, least of all the clown that stood at its front. For as Ozzy Osbourne would tell you, not a trace of a smile on his melancholy jester's face, 'We were four fucking dummies from Birmingham, what did we know about anything?'

Their timing would always be bad. Too late for the sky-touching summer of love, too early for the rock'n'roll genocide of glam, they were Black Sabbath and no matter what the musical revisionists would say of them one day, long after it ceased to matter, they were the most reviled rock band on the planet. People whispered of Led Zeppelin, told of their secret magic and insatiable lust for power; others stood in awe of Deep Purple's telepathic musical prowess. Hendrix was still alive and so were Brian, Jimi and Janis. Rock was on high yet Sabbath were oh, so very low. Critics – outsiders, cunts, mainly from London – simply could not relate. The kids, though, they loved them the way only kids can. Like crafty cigarettes in your bedroom, windows cracked open; like stealing coins from your mum's purse when she was out, or finding a porno mag under your dad's bed; like a first glimpse of the cold fires of hell, body oscillating with the feeling of filthy inescapability.

Nobody fidgeted more uncomfortably at a Black Sabbath show, though, almost paralysed by self-loathing, than the four band members themselves. As their lyricist and bass player, Geezer, would later lament, 'For years we went around thinking we were shit – the press hated us, said we couldn't write, couldn't play … other bands hated us, everyone.' Something that could be heard all too clearly in their music: those crucifixion guitar riffs, nailed in with such heavy relish, framed by storm-gathering bass and head-rattling drums, together making a sound like that of a body being dragged from a river. Those eerie singsong vocals: as dramatic and pitiful as the sound of a swan dying. Full of cob-webbed yearning, of self-harm and picked scabs and the shriek of lost souls. The three of them zombie-walking around the stage in their preposterous crosses and moustaches, while the fourth self-combusted at the back, mouldering in his own poisons, the quad combining to ensure a fifth element: the pockmarked face of the most brutally deformed style of rock ever allowed to push its way, stinking and blood-cowed, among us.

Tony Iommi was the leader. Follower of the left-hand path, no noble speechmaker he, no bringer of messages from on high, but a true musical alchemist, the flint-eyed general in whose hands the guitar became both a wand and a war machine. An only child who had always got his own way, never any need to explain, Tony did not take 'no' for an answer, did not waste words nor suffer fools gladly. 'Tony has fists like fucking hammers,' Ozzy would recall, his pained animal eyes still round with the memory of their bruising attentions. 'Somebody had to crack the whip,' Tony responded, typically stone-faced. 'And that was me.' It was Tony's riffs that laid the foundation stone for the Sabbath sound, like a drill burrowing into the underground caves of the tallest mountains, until even they came toppling down, terrifying boulders colliding through the undergrowth, thunderbolts zigzagging across the sky at his command.

After Tony Iommi there was Terry Butler – nicknamed Geezer, after a childhood affectation for calling everyone he met Geezer, which the adults laughed at and found charming, and because of which became the name he retained throughout the stunted growth of his own adulthood, along with everything else from his youngest days: the need to be mollycoddled; to be stroked and petted and constantly reassured, constantly adored. The bright boy of the class, good with words, teacher's pet, good at staying out of trouble, or never being caught out, which meant the same thing to him. Clever Geezer it would be that came up with all of Sabbath's lyrics, because, Ozzy said, 'Geezer's got a great brain.' He could play too, swinging the bass like a guitar, bending the heavy strings, weighing each note, then catapulting it forward, just like his hero, Jack Bruce, he said, 'Who shadowed the riff rather than copying it.'

Then there was Bill Ward, a brilliant if wayward percussionist who loved jazz, especially the crazed Gene Krupa, and who would forever be treated as the joker in the pack. Poor old Bill, the one they set fire to – not just once, and never by accident, but as a matter of habit. The one they laughed at not behind his back but right into his face. Bill, who saw it all from his perch, sweating bullets at the back of the stage, arms flailing, legs spasming, always out of breath, always running to stand still convincingly, always the last to know what even the others, who always knew last, might know first. Poor old Bill, the one who would remain the most honest and would pay the heaviest price for it, kicked repeatedly until he refused finally to get up again.

And of course there was Ozzy – or Ossie, as he was dumbly credited on the first Black Sabbath album. Since *The Osbournes* turned him into a family-friendly, panda-eyed cuddly toy, Ozzy has been denuded of the credibility he once enjoyed as a rock singer. He never had much in the first place, forced to stand at the side of the stage, jumping up and down like a caged gorilla, as Iommi hogged the centre-stage spotlight. Yet there was something about him, for those that tuned in, that spoke of a truly unresolved problem; some echo of rock's original spirit of incoherent, bleary-eyed helplessness that could not be learned or faked; something uncomfortably real. As a fan, you wanted to be Robert Plant or maybe John Lennon. You never wanted to be Ozzy. It was all right to be a tormented romantic soul: a Rod Stewart or even an Elton John. It was an entirely different thing to want to suffer actual pain, to know that you're mad, that you've always been mad. To know, finally, that one day you really might lose your fucking mind.

Yet underneath it all they were so ordinary, so plain, so bleeding obvious. All born within a year of each other – 1948 – all growing up on the same dingy streets, victims of the same dour post-war schooling and slums, there was good reason why they all looked so much alike in person and onstage. Wrought from the same black matter as their music, none of them could have made it in any other band, though they all tried, despairingly, until fate finally forced them together, against their wills, one typically downcast day in 1968, after factory closing time, before the pubs opened, only their cheap pack-of-five cigarettes to warm them.

Growing up the fourth child of six, the mangiest of a pack of strays packed like fresh corpses into the two coffin-sized bedrooms of No. 14 Lodge Road where the Osbourne family lived, John Michael was in trouble from the day he was born. His father, John Thomas – Jack to his mates down the pub – worked nights at the local GEC steel plant, making tools, which meant he slept all day. Forced to tiptoe around the house, lest he wake him 'and receive a belt for my trouble', young John used to fantasise that his dad was dead. 'I'd creep into his bedroom and poke him, to see if he'd wake up,' he later told me. 'Then when he did he'd fucking kill me ...'

A fun-loving, outgoing, easily bored child who left the hard stuff to his mum, Lillian, whom he recalls seeing crying when she couldn't pay the bills, and three older sisters that continued to mother him long after Lillian had gone, Ozzy, as he was quickly nicknamed in the school playground, found his niche early on as the class clown. 'I always worked along the lines of: if you can't beat 'em, make 'em laugh. Do anything you can to keep them on your side. And if they still don't like you after that, burn their fucking house down!' It became a metaphor for the way he would live his whole life. Keep the bad guys happy by appearing to pose no threat, keep 'em laughing as you hid behind a strong woman's skirts. The daft jokes and stupid pranks – the worst of which included stabbing his aunt's cat with a fork, trying to set his sister alight and hanging himself with a clothesline – were also intended to shield the teenager from the sheer monotony of life on the streets of Aston. School was most definitely out; his undiagnosed dyslexia saw to that. Football was for the kids that could afford it, Ozzy instead becoming one of the ne'er-do-wells who would offer to 'watch your car for a shilling' – i.e. agree not to vandalise it in exchange for a bribe – whenever local club Aston Villa played at home.

That left music, something he was immediately turned on by, becoming fascinated by the Teddy Boys: devotees of Fifties American rock'n'rollers like Gene Vincent and Eddie Cochran, and of course pre-army Elvis. Teddy Boys styled their hair in huge pompadours – quiffs – and wore Edwardian-style 'draped' jackets, with shiny winkle-picker shoes, and sharpened the handles of their steel combs to use as shivs. 'I loved hanging round the cafés they went to,' Ozzy would tell me, years later, as we sat together in one such place, its windows frosted over with speckled grease and cigarette smoke, its pinball machine still pinging in the background. Even music, though, would get him into trouble. 'I'd get sent home from school for wearing winkle-pickers and blue jeans instead of their boring grey flannels.'

The same convergence between school, music and trouble would have one, much more significant impact on the early chapters of the Ozzy Osbourne story: his meeting with Tony Iommi. Both boys were pupils at Birchfield Road Secondary Modern School, in nearby Perry Barr, but they were very different people. Where Ozzy was one of a clan of a sprawling working-class family trying to make do, Anthony Frank Iommi was the only child of a family of mixed Italian and Brazilian extraction. A well-to-do middle-class family at the centre of a larger, extended family that owned ice-cream and bakery businesses in Cardigan Street, then the centre of Birmingham's Italian district; a typically hard-working immigrant family that liked to play hard too. 'All my family and relations played accordions and drums. My father played accordion and harmonica, and my aunt and uncles all played accordions and drums.' They would set up big 'accordion bands' in the living room and play all night. 'They would play a lot of weddings, too, my dad and all his brothers.' Young Tony was nine the first time he was encouraged to put an accordion of his own on his knee – a special left-handed piano accordion, 'with the button-bass. In fact, I've still got one.' He had wanted a set of drums 'but nobody would let me because of the noise. So I was fobbed off with an accordion, and basically I learned to play that after a fashion.' Not content to learn the old Italian folk tunes of his father, Tony was soon squeezing out wheezing versions of contemporary hits. 'I'd try different stuff, I'd try Elvis Presley numbers, "Wooden Heart" and things like that.'

It was through his love of Elvis that he first cottoned on to his Fifties' counterpart, Cliff Richard, and in particular Cliff's backing group, The Shadows. Led by bespectacled lead guitarist Hank

Marvin, The Shadows were an instrumental group whose sound was fashioned by Marvin from a then new-fangled device called an echo box and prodigious use of the tremolo arm on his red and gold Fender Stratocaster guitar. It was this slinky, slightly sinister sound that took The Shadows to No. 1 in the British charts with their first single without Cliff, 'Apache', in the summer of 1960. By the time Tony picked up a guitar for the first time, in emulation of Hank Marvin, when he was fourteen, The Shadows had enjoyed another six chart-topping hits, including most recently 'Wonderful Land', which stayed at No. 1 in the UK charts for more weeks than any other single throughout the Sixties. As Tony recalled, 'A lot of people laugh at The Shadows now, but I think they started a lot of guitarists off from my day. Dave Gilmour and people like that were all Shadows fans. Brian May ...'

Unable yet to afford a Fender Strat – Marvin, in fact, was the first guitarist in Britain to actually own one, and his had been imported from America specially by Cliff – Tony's first guitar was a Watkins, marketed in the Sixties as 'the British Strat', bought from a cheap shopping catalogue and paid for by his indulgent mother in monthly instalments. 'Being left-handed, you see, I was very limited to what I could get. And that was a model that they did do left-handed, so I had that one. I mean, in the music shops in them days, it was very, very rare to get a left-handed guitar.' The Watkins was followed by a left-handed Burns Tri-sonic, with a much richer harmonic sound, or as close as the teenager could get to figuring out how to replicate Marvin's Strat and echo box combo. His dexterity on the accordion helped somewhat to learn simple chords. That and the classic Bert Weedon book, *Play In A Day*. He tried seeing a tutor but lasted only one lesson. 'I didn't like it. I didn't feel comfortable. I thought I'd prefer to try and learn myself, and that was it, I never went back again.' Tony became the classic withdrawn teenager, sequestered in his room at home, playing along to his Shadows records. When he felt he'd got good enough he took his guitar to school, and began showing off to kids that had only ever seen an electric guitar on TV. 'I remember at school all the girls fawning over him,' recalled Ozzy, 'I remember thinking, what a great way to pull birds.'

Unfortunately for Ozzy, that wasn't the only thing Tony did that would leave an impression on him. Tony, who was only ten months older than Ozzy but in the year above him at school, and therefore carried all the authority of the older kid, always bullied Ozzy at school. 'I used to hide when I saw him coming,' Ozzy would tell me, only half joking, years later. 'It was just that thing at school,' Tony would say, when I asked him, uncomfortable at my quizzing from such a distance. 'At our school, it was pretty … you had to sort of … keep … um … you know, give the younger kids a clip round the earhole, you know? It was one of those, really. And Ozzy was one of them, you know? He was only a year younger but … you know, at school it was, er … they just used to get beaten up.' He chuckled darkly. 'It was one of them.'

'Tony always intimidated Ozzy at school,' recalled Geezer. Subsequently, there would remain an echo of those early master–servant beatings throughout Sabbath's career. 'When things happen in childhood, you never quite blow it out of your system.' Indeed, years after Ozzy's solo career had far eclipsed that of the band he'd left behind, he still became tremendously agitated whenever Iommi's name came up, referring to him as Darth Vader and other less amusing, more wounding epithets. 'I try not to hate anybody or anything any more,' he told me dolefully. 'But for years I hated Tony Iommi. If you'd have told me one day we'd be back together again I'd have laughed in your face and told you to fuck off.'

Geezer was different again, of course. The youngest of the band members, by eighteen months, Terence Michael Joseph Butler was the seventh of seven children born to Dubliners, recently re-situated to Birmingham, good Catholics in search of good pay for honest hard work. Geezer was the much-cherished baby of the family. 'I was fairly spoiled to death. Me brothers used to give me money, me sisters gave me money and me parents gave me money, so I was richer than anybody else in the family.' He smiled that generous Irish smile, but behind the paddy curls and tufty facial hair were eyes as dark and beady as an old crow's.

Brought up in Aston, just around the corner from the others, Geezer was taken to Villa games as a kid, waving his claret and blue scarf, a season ticket holder, one of the lucky ones. By the time he was a teenager, music began to overtake his interest in football. For one thing, given the way he now looked, it was safer. 'Around the late Sixties, when the skinheads were running rampant, I couldn't go down to the game cos they used to kick hell out of me. Even if you were a Villa fan, if you had long hair it didn't matter what colours you had on, the skinheads would kick hell out of you.' It didn't matter. 'As soon as The Beatles came out, I desperately wanted to be a Beatle.' He'd persuaded his mother to pay ten shillings (50p) for a beat-up two-string acoustic guitar from another kid at school when he was 11. He didn't get good, though, until his brother treated him to a new acoustic with all six strings, bought from the only place in town that sold guitars, George Clay's Music Shop in Birmingham's Bull Ring shopping centre. The price: £8. A week's wages for most workers back then. The baby of the family had got his way again. He began by learning all the songs from the first LP he ever owned, *Please, Please Me*, by The Beatles, then grew more adventurous as he began to build what would become a comprehensive collection of the Sixties' most seminal records. 'I used to buy The Beatles, the Stones, The Kinks. And then when the Mothers Of Invention came out, that was when me musical life completely changed.'

Geezer had already begun growing his hair long. 'I was always a bit of a rebel at school.' By the time he was listening to Frank Zappa at fifteen, he'd become 'the original out-and-out hippy'. His appearance caused a commotion on the streets of Birmingham. 'I was the only one who used to wear beads and kaftans and all that kind of cack. It was like, the more attention the better.' Teaming up with a similarly coiffured school pal named Roger Hope who also fancied himself a guitar-slinging Beatle – nicknamed Dope not just because it rhymed with his surname – Geezer had also begun playing electric guitar – a budget-priced solid-bodied Hofner Colorama, replete with rickety Selmer amp – in his first semi-pro group, the bizarrely named The Ruums. 'It was just a strange word from this science fiction book that the singer read.'

Science fiction stories and novels were something else Geezer and Dope had in common. 'My favourite author when I was a kid was H. G. Wells. I still love all that stuff – *The Time Machine, The Invisible Man*, all the classics. It was so out there. I was like living in Aston, shittiest place on earth, and because I've always had a strong imagination science fiction took me to another place, to things that could be, and inspired me imagination.' Geezer was smart enough to see that the best sci-fi was never ultimately about space travel or seeing into the future, no matter what the supposed time or locale, it was always really about the now. 'Definitely with H. G. Wells, it's all about society. He wrote about [the future] but it was always a comment on the times he lived in then.' One of his favourite Wells' works, *The Shape Of Things To Come*, which postulates a twenty-first-century world state established to solve mankind's problems, 'was definitely commenting on society'.

Along with 'somebody else on bass and his mate on drums', The Ruums started out playing covers in pubs and occasional weddings. 'Then round about '66 we started getting into some Moby Grape and some soul as well, like "Knock On Wood" [and]

Wilson Pickett, some Sam And Dave.' True to the consciousness-expanding spirit of the times, 'If we liked a particular song, we'd do it. It didn't matter if it was soul or progressive or acid or whatever, we'd do it.' They were getting heavier, so they replaced the rhythm section with more musically hirsute players, brought in a new, longer-haired singer who could really wail. Geezer already had the hair and moustache. Now he had the music to go with it. 'It was sort of like the underground kind of thing, which I was very much a part of musically and everything else. It was all love and peace, man.' Or at least it was in the local clubs they would play like The Penthouse and Mothers, rubbing shoulders with other aspirant young psychedelic blues bands like Robert Plant's first band, Listen. 'They were sort of West Coast stuff like Moby Grape and Spirit. We were more sort of Cream and Jimi Hendrix.'

Their stage attire became commensurately freaky. 'I used to go on with my eyes all blacked out so I looked like Satan – exactly like Arthur Brown. But I was unaware of his existence at the time. Then I eventually went to see him and he just blew me mind. Like, that's the way you're supposed to do it, kind of thing.' He would borrow his sisters' mascara and pass it around the band. 'We were all like dressed with stupid big flowers coming out of our heads and stuff like that, and loads of beads, just mental.' It didn't help that Geezer and the rest of the band would be fizzing out of their minds on black bombers – super-strength capsule speed. Geezer would become 'so emotional' they would completely wreck the stage at the end of every performance. 'The drummer would wreck his drum-kit. I'd pick all these beer bottles up and smash 'em up the wall. And that was when we'd get slung out and told never to come back again. So the only way we could ever get a gig was to change the name and go back.' Thus The Ruums became The Rare Breed, and then The Future – then back to The Rare Breed again. 'That's when Ozzy joined.'

Geezer was a student at Matthew Boulton, part of what is now known as the Birmingham Metropolitan College, training to be a cost and works accountant, when he first met Ozzy. Neither of them liked the look of the other. It was 1967: Ozzy was out of his Teddy Boy phase and into being a Mod, about as opposite, musically and culturally, to Geezer's proto-hippy stance as you could then get. The only thing they had in common was a love of The Beatles and a shared love of 'Soul Man' by Sam & Dave – and a growing habit for staying up all night on amphetamines. 'People never believe me when I tell them,' Ozzy smiled. 'But I used to have cropped skinhead hair and a mohair suit. You had to look like that to get into the All Nighters.' The All Nighters were 24-hour dance clubs that stayed open all weekend. The big one Ozzy used to go to in Birmingham city centre was called Midnight City. 'If you were a rocker you couldn't go in there without getting your head fucking kicked in. You'd go in and get your Dexedrine and whatever and then you'd be there from the Friday to the Sunday. You'd have to go home Sunday morning and pretend you were tired with your eyeballs hanging out your head, full of fucking Dexies, you know?'

Ozzy had left school in 1963 without any qualifications and just one wish: 'I didn't care what I did as long as I didn't have to go to school any more.' The only plan he had for the future was to find ways to make quick money as easily as possible, beginning with stealing money from gas meters, quickly graduating to breaking into shops after dark and selling whatever he could get his hands on in local pubs. But he wasn't especially good at being a thief and when he broke into the same women's clothes shop two weeks running, he was caught and arrested. The charge: Breaking and Entering and Stealing Goods to the Value of Twenty-Five Pounds. Unable to afford the £40 fine imposed by the local magistrate, Ozzy was sentenced instead to 90 days at Winsome Green prison, where he would eventually serve six weeks before being released early for good behaviour.

Talking about it years later, his face would assume that pale distant look that has come to define him to the TV generation of the twenty-first century. 'I was terrified all these fucking murderers and whatnot were gonna try and fuck me up the arse! They're not like normal gay guys in there. They're like these lifers who go temporarily gay while they're inside. To them a seventeen-year-old boy was like throwing a fucking juicy bone to a dog.' Attacked in the showers his first morning, 'I walloped him with this big metal piss-pot and ended up in solitary confinement for three days.' In the end, his best defence was his old standby – make 'em laugh. 'I got through a lot of tough situations like that while I was inside.' It was also in prison that Ozzy got his first tattoos; self-administered using a pin and some burnt graphite to scrawl the now immortal letters O-Z-Z-Y across the knuckles of his left hand. He finished off the piece by drawing two smiling faces on his knees. 'To cheer me up when I woke up in the morning,' he added dolefully.

Back on the streets of Aston in 1966, and with all thoughts of a career as a criminal now thankfully behind him, a predictable succession of shitty jobs ensued, from casual labouring on building sites to testing car horns at the same Lucas plant his mother worked at, to, most famously, working in a slaughterhouse. 'I'd do anything in those days. The first day I was there almost did me in, though. It was so vile I was throwing up all day. After a while, though, I really got into it. I loved killing animals! I used to stick them, stab them, chop them, totally torture the fuckers to death.' He laughed. 'I used to take a lot of speed and I would be out of my fucking head all day. I used to kill a minimum of 250 cattle a day and then get on to the pigs and sheep ...'

Always an outsider, in the sense of always belonging on the bottom rung of the ladder, Ozzy's sense of alienation only increased when he realised no one would sit next to him on the bus home each night because of the smell. His luck suddenly changed when a chance meeting with an old school pal led to 'this great big fucking door opening up in my mind'. He told Ozzy about the band he'd formed, called Approach, and how they were all ready to go except for one thing: they couldn't find a singer. 'I'm a singer!' Ozzy announced. He was, of course, nothing of the sort. But this was too good an opportunity to miss. Like seeing an open window on the ground floor of a factory at night. His mate pulled a face and spat into the kerb. 'No, really!' Ozzy brayed. 'I'm a singer! I'm a singer!'

In fact, the only singing Ozzy had ever done had been in family sing-songs, 'when my dad came home with a few beers inside him – old pub songs like "Show Me The Way To Go Home". I used to love all that as a kid.' Knowing he could barely hold a tune, he cemented his position in Approach with the purchase of a second-hand 50-watt PA and two Shure microphones. 'I never really took it serious, you know? I never had any training, it was just, that sounds a good idea, you know?' But while Approach rehearsed regularly enough, they never got beyond the back room of a pub and in frustration Ozzy took the typically chancy step of placing an ad in the window of George Clay's Music Shop, which read: 'Ozzy Zig – Singer Extraordinaire – Requires Band – Has Own PA'.

The same shop which Geezer frequented, and when The Rare Breed needed a new singer – the previous incumbent having grown weary of being banned from local venues and left for a life of cabaret on the *QE2* – he lit on the ad immediately. 'What caught my eye were the magic words: "Has Own PA",' he guffawed. When he saw that Ozzy Zig lived just round the corner he went over and knocked on the door. Ozzy wasn't in so Geezer left his name and address. 'That night I was at home and a knock came on the door, me brother answered, and he came in and said, "There's something at the door for you." I said, "What do you mean, 'something'?" He said, "Well, go and have a look." And there was Ozzy with this bloody big factory gown on, like this big, brown flared smock thing. He's got that on, a chimney brush over his shoulder, a shoe on a dog lead and no shoes on. But the thing that really shocked me was his hair. He didn't have any! He had all this stuff on to try and disguise the fact that he was a skinhead.' Reading Geezer's mind, Ozzy's first words were: 'It's all right, I'm growing my hair.' Geezer thought, 'This bloke's a nut ...'

Ozzy's memories of The Rare Breed are predictably hazy. He'd seen them play at Birmingham Polytechnic supporting Carl Wayne and the Vikings, which later became The Move, and he was not impressed. 'I thought, what the fucking hell was that load up there, jumping round like cunts in fucking blue lights? I'd never heard of psychedelic music before ...' But he didn't have anything else going on and, besides, 'Geezer was really good with a strobe and making it look all weird' so he thought he'd have a go. The experiment lasted for just one gig. It was a working-men's club in Walsall and they were asked to leave after just three songs. Geezer recalled, 'The manager came up and said, "Get off! Here's five quid, now piss off!" And Ozzy said, "Well you can stick your five quid up your arse!" And I went, "I'll have the five quid" ...'

Ozzy had also taken an instant dislike to Roger Hope. 'He was too much riding my ass all the time and I just turned round to Geezer and said, "Fuck this, I ain't doing it."' What Ozzy hadn't bargained for was that Geezer had also become disillusioned. The bassist and drummer had decided to find proper jobs and Hope seemed to want something else too. 'He wrote one song and it was absolutely awful. Can't remember what it was called but it was horrible. So I politely declined to play it.' Geezer announced his own departure from The Rare Breed the next day. Then walked over to Ozzy's to smoke dope and drink tea ...

*

At the same time as Ozzy Zig and Geezer Butler were wondering what to do after The Rare Breed, Tony Iommi was trying to make headway further afield with a four-piece called Mythology. Based in Carlisle, where bassist and founding member Neil Marshall lived, Mythology were well known locally in Cumberland, with regular gigs and a loyal following. Stardom was a long way off but there was money, enough to rent a room in a flat and survive from gig to gig. He didn't look any further than that yet. From his first semi-pro gig five years before, sitting in with a piano and drum combo at the local pub, to joining his first proper band, the Rockin' Chevrolets, at sixteen, Tony had been more concerned with having fun than making it. He joined bands 'as they came' not particularly 'to get somewhere' but because he 'enjoyed doing it'. With the Chevrolets getting regular work on the then bur-geoning Midlands pub and club circuit, bashing out Chuck Berry covers while posing in their red lamé suits, he felt he'd got off to a great start. He'd even found his first girlfriend, Margaret, the sister of the other guitarist. 'The music they played was some Top 20 sort of stuff, some soul-type numbers, different types of rock'n'roll. It was the sort of stuff you'd play in pubs and those sorts of places.' Now he was ready for the next step up: a gig with The Birds & The Bees, who'd actually got a tour of West Germany lined up.

However, disaster struck on the eve of the tour when Tony lost the tips of his middle and ring fingers on his right hand – the fingering hand for a left-handed guitar player – in an industrial accident at the sheet metal factory where he held down a day-job as a welder. He was eighteen when it occurred, on the same day that he was leaving the job to take up music full time. Afterwards, doctors told him he would never play again. He was, he said, 'ab-solutely devastated. My life was over.' Working on the production line, waiting for the operator of the metal presses to send the next

item down to him, on this particular day, because of staff absen-
teeism, Tony had been working the presses as well as welding. 'I
started doing that and of course the fucking machine just come
down on me fingers and had my hand. And the reaction was to
pull your hand back, and as I've done that, I've just pulled the
ends off! Just the bones were left sticking out.'

He was rushed to hospital – along with the broken fingertips in an ice bag – where it was hoped doctors might be able
to sew them back on but it was no use. 'They were all smashed
up. So they snapped the bone off in both fingers and that was
it, really. They said I'd never be able to play again.' He spent the
next month sitting around at home feeling suicidal. Then 'this
guy who used to be the manager at the factory, he bought me a
record of Django Reinhardt, and said, "Here, listen to this."' Tony
thought he was taking the piss; a misguided attempt to get him
listening to guitar music again. But there was method to his manager's apparent madness. Born in Belgium, in 1910, to a family of
Manouche gypsies, Jean Reinhardt grew up in Romany encamp-
ments around Paris, plying a trade as a player of banjo, guitar
and violin. Nicknamed 'Django' – Romany for 'I awake' – he, too,
was just eighteen when he was so badly injured in a fire – knocking over a candle on his way to bed after returning home late
one night after a gig – that he lost the use of his right leg, which
was left paralysed, and two fingers on his left hand. He, too, was
told he'd never play again. But within a year, with the help of his
brother Joseph, an accomplished guitarist himself, he'd learned
to play his guitar solos with only two fingers, using the injured
digits merely for chord work. So distinctive did his work as a
musician subsequently become, Reinhardt influenced all of the
great British rock guitarists of Iommi's generation, including
the unholy trinity of Jimmy Page, Eric Clapton and Jeff Beck, with
the latter describing Reinhardt as 'by far the most astonishing
guitar player ever – quite superhuman'.

Unaware of any of this at the time, however, Tony was aghast. 'I was like, "Oh no, I don't wanna know." But he was like, "Just listen to it." So I did and I was like, "Yeah, what?" And then of course he told me how Django Reinhardt had lost two of his fingers. So that sort of encouraged me to think, "Wow, you know, bloody hell! Maybe I *can* start playing."' In heroic can-do style, Tony began by making his own improvised finger caps out of an old Fairy Liquid dishwashing bottle. 'I melted it down and made a little ball, then I got a hot soldering iron and just kept jabbing it in, just to make it so me finger would fit in this hole, to make these sort of caps that fit over and then I had to glue leather to them so that they'd grip the strings. Otherwise I wouldn't be able to touch the strings without that on. I just sat there for days filing it down with sandpaper, to make it look like a finger. Then I'd stick the other one on and ... play.'

It was a rudimentary solution to an almost unsolvable problem and he had to experiment for weeks before they would work properly. 'I'd jump through the roof if I touched them without the caps on. But it has happened when I've been playing and one of them's come off, and I've pressed down without the cap on and oh dear Christ! It's like getting a hot soldering iron down your neck. Oh, it's painful because the bone's right underneath, you know? The skin's like only a little piece of skin...' The 'new fingers' also had the unforeseen effect of altering the sound Tony was now going to make on the guitar. 'I had to change the whole thing of regular guitar playing. I had to come up with using lighter strings, which they didn't do in them days, so I used to have to make my own, set up from banjo strings. Because otherwise it would hurt my fingers, if you used the regular heavy-gauge string.' Years later, Iommi's sound would become so imitated, so lionised and lingered over, budding young guitar-slingers would talk heatedly of tritones and down-tuning and amp-wattage as somehow possessing the secrets of the uniquely leaden, buzz-saw sound that would come to be instantly identified with Sabbath's quicksand sound. But it was like trying to hold mercury in the palm of your hand. It came down to what he could and could no longer do without those two fingers. How 'some chords I can never play again' and how he worked his way around that obstacle, a river of sound rushing past the dam of impossibilities presented by having only three good fingers to manipulate his ferocious white Stratocaster with.

He knew he'd passed the biggest test of his life when he landed himself in a new band – The Rest. It was 1965. 'They were looking for a guitar player and they came round to my house and we spoke and I thought, "Bloody hell, they've all got AC30s, they've all got Vox equipment and stands – and Fenders!" I thought, "Bloody hell, they must be really good!"' Until then the only other musician Tony knew personally that had a Fender Stratocaster and a Vox amp was himself. 'I just really liked the look of a Strat because, basically, The Shadows had them and with The Rest we used to play a lot of Shadows stuff as well. We used to play instrumentals and Chet Atkins stuff.' Other influences were also making a significant impact on his playing. John Mayall's Bluesbreakers, featuring Eric Clapton, blew his mind. 'I mean, that was *it*.' He'd also become enthralled with The Big Three, a Liverpudlian Merseybeat group whose guitarist, Adrian Barber, was also an electronics whiz who'd custom-built the band their own five-foot-tall amps, nicknamed coffins.

The other truly significant discovery Tony made in The Rest was the band's drummer, Bill Ward. Dark-haired and rugged, like Tony, with whom he shared the same brute determination that could sometimes show itself as pure stubbornness, William Thomas Ward was another of Aston's post-war babies, three months younger than Tony and three times stranger. He had been playing drums in various local bands since he was 15, but had begun 'hitting things when I was about four or five years old'. Unable to afford a drum-kit he'd made his own drums using cardboard boxes, disused cigarette tins, 'you know, anything cylindrical, anything that looked like a drum. I made my own sticks and everything. That's what I would do when I was a kid.' Music was 'just something that came out of the house where I was born, in Grosvenor Road. My mum and dad would have parties all the time pretty much. Mum would play the piano and a friend of the family would come over and play drums, and he used to leave his traps there overnight on a Saturday night, and that's when I just became fascinated by drums.' When the local Boys' Brigade band came marching down the street on parade every Sunday, he could never take his eyes off the drummer. 'Oh man, I just loved all that. And so it was just natural.'

His parents especially loved American jazz music, the big bands led by true musical mavericks like Duke Ellington, Glenn Miller and Count Basie. 'That's where my identification with drummers really began, when I was about ten, with the music of Count Basie and Glenn Miller.' One of his favourite drummers at the time was Joe Morello, the American-born percussionist with the Dave Brubeck Quartet, whose unusual time signatures informed such classics as 'Take Five' and 'Blue Rondo A La Turk'. 'I couldn't work out how he did it at first, then I just sort of improvised my own version.' His single biggest influence, though, was Gene Krupa, whose frenetic, hyperactive style can be heard in all Bill's best work, to this day. 'And of course, Gene Krupa was in black-and-white movies at that time. So I'd watch Gene Krupa and go, "Man, this is just incredible", you know? For me he was really one of the pioneers of rock drumming, when he started to change rhythms. In the late Forties, into the Fifties, he changed some of the styles of certain rhythms in drumming. And basically when one listens to the history of Krupa it's easily identifiable where the crossover with rock took place.' Bill's personal 'crossover into rock' occurred with the release in 1957 of 'Jailhouse Rock', Elvis

Presley's second UK No. 1 hit single. 'Up until that point, I'd been listening to big-band American jazz. The BBC would play a lot of that kind of music on the radio. But when "Jailhouse Rock" came out that was it, I just connected immediately to rock'n'roll. And that's where I've been since. From Elvis came of course The Beatles and the whole early British phenomenon of the early Sixties.'

He was 15 when he first met Tony Iommi. 'I was in a band that was looking for a lead-guitar player and we found Tony through ads. We would change our name every three or four days, you know, but at the time we were called The Rest.' The Rest picked up paying gigs but that didn't prevent Bill's parents from fretting over their son trying for an actual career in music. 'I went through the parental thing, just the same as every other musician. My dad was kind of sticky on it, you know? But my mother was a total support. She was very happy that I was doing what I was doing.' His only sibling, his older brother Jimmy, was also 'terribly influential, in the sense of what I heard. Like he introduced me to the Everly Brothers and all the bands that were playing in Birmingham. See, I was still young, I'm like fourteen years old at this time, and he'd turn me on to bands like The Redcaps, who were a really hot band in Birmingham in the very early Sixties. So I would get all this kind of influential stuff coming to me.'

With the Midlands scene then so active, Bill also crossed paths with some terrific other drummers. He first saw John Bonham play when he was 16, at a pub in Worcestershire called the Wharf. The future Led Zeppelin drummer was then with the Crawling Kingsnakes, whom The Rest had shared bills with. Bill, who would become close friends with Bonham, recalls being impressed as much by Bonzo's drinking skills – 'He had a pint of bitter at his feet throughout, going through glass after glass but never missing a beat' – as his powerhouse drumming. Another good friend was Pete York, then drumming in the Midlands' most popular outfit at the time, the Spencer Davis Group. 'Incredible drummer, Pete York was really supportive of me. I'm like about seventeen or eighteen years old at the time that we're talking about right now, and so having somebody like Pete York, who's got like a string of hits with the Spencer Davis Group, pay special attention to you, that was a major thing to have.'

Bill was already a perfectionist, a trait he would later identify as one of the major strands to his eventual multiple estrangements from Black Sabbath, and his musical connection to Tony Iommi was instant. 'Tony was an exceptionally good guitar player for his age. I'd been working with guitar players that were good but Tony could really play the guitar. So with The Rest we'd throw in a few of the more popular jazz and blues songs, and the rest were cover tunes, stuff like that. We hadn't yet reached the growth period where one can write one's own music. That took about another two or three years before we were actually writing our own music. But we both knew it was coming . . .'

The Rest crossed paths with The Rare Breed on several occasions but there was no love lost between them. They were rivals, not friends. Geezer recalls chatting occasionally to Bill. 'He'd ask me what kind of stuff we were into and I'd tell him and the next week they'd be doing it. So we sort of shared musical tastes at that time.' Tony's memories of Geezer from that time are less charitable. 'He was always out of his brains. He was always like on acid. I mean, you would see him in a club crawling up the wall and stuff like that. They'd do a spot, then we'd do a spot and he always seemed like a bloody nutter, you know.'

Neither band was built to last, though, and when Tony was invited to join Mythology, in January 1968, he leapt at the chance. Neil Marshall had been in Peter And Gordon, whose 1964 single 'A World Without Love' had been No. 1 in Britain and America, the first of several transatlantic hits they would enjoy over the next four years. By the start of 1968, however, Marshall had left with enough money and experience to have his own stab at success. Taking over and reconfiguring a local Carlisle act named The Square Chex, from typically 'straight' mid-Sixties beat combo to longhaired, way-out-dressing psychedelic rock group, he changed their name to Mythology and began rebuilding the line-up. Along with Iommi, he also recruited Rest vocalist Chris Smith, whose actual name was Christopher Robin Smith but he was persuaded to drop his middle name because 'everybody thought we were pissing around'. Within weeks, Marshall had taken Tony's advice and also brought in Bill Ward to be their new drummer.

Big frogs in a small pond, Mythology attracted a strong local following in Carlisle and its surrounds, and were considered the band to open for any visiting chart acts, supporting The Move at the 101 Club, for example, in April. A 'head group' more likely to storm their way through 'All Your Love' by John Mayall's Bluesbreakers, than cruise with regular Top 20 material, it was in Mythology that Iommi and Ward first began turning their endless stoned jams into something more concrete. 'That's when we started to look at the possibilities of adding some of our own things, and so on. Getting away with as much as we could, really – with a lot of guitar solos thrown in.' It was the dawn of the era of monolithic guitar solos, with Hendrix having recently invaded the London scene, and fellow travellers like Jeff Beck, Eric Clapton and Jimmy Page all running to catch up. In Tony's draughty flat at the band's abode – Compton House – in Carlisle, the only one who really penetrated his own playing style was Clapton, whose latest band, Cream, was then changing the face of blues rock in Britain.

'*Disraeli Gears* had just come out and that was where we were all kind of trying to get, or get beyond if we could. That basic guitar, bass, drums format, but which seemed to be able to do anything, you know?' Shrewdly, Mythology also began specialising in covers by bands their audience was unlikely to be familiar with such as Tomorrow and Art. The latter was actually another Cumbrian-born act fronted by future Spooky Tooth singer Mike Harrison, who had released one certifiably 'mental' album the year before called *Supernatural Fairy Tales*; the former was another unsung psychedelic powerhouse featuring future Yes guitarist Steve Howe, and a big favourite on the original John Peel Radio One show. 'They were probably more of an influence than anything, because we felt they were closer in spirit to what we were trying to do in Mythology. Really just playing and soloing for as long as you wanted. And people seemed to like us for it.'

It wasn't just their music that Mythology became well known for locally, though. They were the most high-profile flag-wavers for a burgeoning northern hippy scene that now openly flaunted its drug use – this at a time when properly famous pop stars like The Beatles and the Rolling Stones were being arrested for illegal-drug offences, stories which the country's biggest scandal sheet, the *News Of The World*, championed and turned into endless tabloid 'revelations' – so when the Cumbria Constabulary came under pressure to show proof of its own attempts to 'repel this threat to civilised society', as one magistrate memorably put it, it swooped on Compton House early one morning in the summer of 1968 and promptly busted all four band members for possession of marijuana. Disbelieving police officers singled Smith out as 'the ringleader' when he repeatedly insisted his name was Christopher Robin. The story made the national newspapers, and suddenly Tony and Bill were famous in Birmingham for all the wrong reasons. Mythology, unable any longer to secure regular paying gigs in Carlisle, fell apart shortly after.

'It was awful,' said Tony. Penniless and forced to return home to his parents' house, he recalled his mother 'crying and screaming and shouting, "You've brought disgrace to this house!"' Bill, who had certainly smoked dope more than a few times and was content to continue doing so, shrewdly felt their only salvation was to immediately put together another band, in Birmingham, 'to kind of pick up where we'd left off in Mythology, cos we were really starting to get somewhere, I felt, when it all turned sour'.

Thus the two of them found themselves staring at the same ad in the shop window that Geezer had been; the one for Ozzy Zig and His Own PA. Like Geezer, they immediately went over to Lodge Road and knocked on the door. 'I said to Bill, "I know an Ozzy but it can't be the same one. It can't be him, he didn't sing", because as far as I knew, he didn't. And so we went round to his house anyway, and his mum answered. "John! Someone to see you!" Then he comes to the door and I said to Bill, "Oh, no!" I said, "I know this chap. We went to the same school. It's not gonna work." Because I thought that he couldn't sing, but he'd just put an advert in. We felt ourselves a bit more professional than that, you know, than just starting up again. So I said to Bill, forget it …' Seeing the bully who had beaten him up at school, Ozzy was relieved to see Tony depart. 'You could see it on his face, he thought, "No fucking way!" and so did I!'

According to Geezer, Tony and Bill actually spotted the ad the very same day he did. 'Ozzy and Tony had not got on well together at school. That's why Ozzy came round to my house that day rather than Tony's.' The fact remained, however: Ozzy and Geezer needed a drummer and guitarist to form a new band; Tony and Bill needed a singer and bassist. Geezer, who had his own memories of the two in The Rest who had 'played the same kind of stuff as The Rare Breed', thought they should at least look into it. It had been five years since Ozzy and Tony had been at school. A lifetime ago, surely?

The next day Geezer led a hugely reluctant Ozzy around to the Iommi household in Washwood Heath. The plan, he said, was to try and lure Bill Ward into becoming their drummer, leaving Tony Iommi to stew. Tony recalls: 'Bill had a chat with them and somehow or other we decided to all get together. Because Bill didn't want to split from me and I didn't want to split from Bill. We wanted to stay together as a team, because we'd played together a long time by then.' Neither Geezer nor Ozzy came away particularly happy with the new arrangement. For Geezer it would mean dropping the guitar in exchange for becoming a bass player – by then they had also recently hooked up with a bottleneck player named Jimmy Phillips, and it was either fill the vacant spot for a bassist or walk away completely, something the wily Geezer was never going to do. For Ozzy it would mean returning to the school playground he had loathed so much. But again, it was either that or nothing and Ozzy had already had enough of that.

By the time they were ready to begin rehearsals a sax player named Alan 'Acker' Clarke had also somehow been added to the rambling gang, along with a new name: The Polka Tulk Blues Band. A name filched 'from a Paki shop in Handsworth', according to Ozzy. 'It was on our way to our first gig. We didn't have a name yet then we passed this shop, the Polka Tulk, and I said, "Here, that looks like a good name."'

Travelling to their first gig – at a caravan site in Carlisle, a booking made on the strength of Tony and Bill's old Mythology connections – Tony admitted he felt glum. 'I looked around and thought, Christ, what have I got myself into this time, you know? I thought, this won't last long.'

He was right. It didn't.

TWO
THE DEVIL'S INTERVAL

They were at each other's throats almost immediately. With Tony and Bill having been treated as local heroes in Mythology, Tony, in particular, was aggrieved to find himself returning to Carlisle with what he saw as a distinctly low-grade line-up of chancers and second-stringers. He didn't know where to look when he saw Geezer pull out a borrowed bass with only three strings. 'He couldn't afford the fourth string. And he turned up in like all this hippy-type gear, all white in this Indian thing – like he'd just took a load of acid on the side.' That Jimmy Phillips had turned up 'dressed like somebody out of Robin Hood' made Tony and Bill, dressed down in T-shirts and jeans, even more embarrassed. 'There's me and Bill looking at each other wondering what's going on ...'

Geezer and Ozzy were equally nonplussed. Entirely out of their comfort zone, playing with guys who'd already attained a higher level, as they saw it, they fumbled their way through those early gigs, falling behind as they tried harder to keep up. Yet it was their musical deficiencies that would help define the soon-to-evolve Sabbath sound. Ozzy's sour vocals would not have suited the honeyed burr of conventional blues-rock outfits of the period like Traffic and Fleetwood Mac, but in the context of the barrage of sound Black Sabbath would later build its reputation on, they would become the glinting sheen to the machine-like menace of the sheet-metal riffs and blustering rhythms, baleful, disconnected, uncontrolled. Geezer had spent the previous days of practice, in a draughty room above a pub in Aston, playing his Telecaster, but tuned down to make it sound more like a bass. He still played it like a guitar, though, and instead of countering the rhythm, as did most conventional bass players, he simply followed Tony's riffs, to the letter, adding the occasional fill as he became more comfortable with the song, a trick he'd learned from Jack Bruce in Cream. It seemed ham-fisted, at first, but once he'd perfected it on a real bass – with all four strings – it was what gave Sabbath the heavier sound. 'I used to play with the riff. I liked bending the notes.' Bending minds.

It would be some time, though, before they would convince Tony and Bill of their value. For those first shows, a self-conscious Ozzy, wearing the off-colour kaftan Geezer had lent him in The Rare Breed, was so crippled with nerves he virtually hid at the side of the stage, happy for Tony to hog the spotlight. You couldn't really hear his voice anyway such was the calamitous din being made by the overripe cacophony of guitars, sax and drums, all apparently playing at will. 'It was all twelve-bar blues,' recalled Geezer, 'all covers ... stuff like "Dust My Blues" by John Mayall's Bluesbreakers and Cream stuff, like "Spoonful".' They deliberately shied away from what they saw as the more obvious crowd-pleasers. Even Jimi Hendrix was considered 'a bit too commercial by then'. Even at this embryonic stage, said Geezer, 'It was about totally going against everything that was going on.'

The Polka Tulk Blues Band lasted just two gigs: at a caravan park in Whitehaven and a ballroom in Carlisle. The first show had ended abruptly when the audience of appalled caravaners began to get up and leave after the first number. Even the former Mythology fans that had gathered felt obliged to vent their hurt feelings afterwards. 'What the hell are you doing with that horrible singer, he's useless?' Geezer recalls one fan asking Tony and

Bill. 'And the other pissing bloke can't play bass. Why don't you get the old people back?' The second show also ended badly, after a posse of local townsmen decided the band had been trying to steal their women, and set about them with bottles and chairs as they tried loading up the van after the gig. 'They absolutely killed us!' said Geezer. The police were called and duly arrested the attackers but not before their ringleader – 'A massive, *massive* great big bloke!' – had strangled one of the police dogs. Tony: 'I thought, "Oh fuck, that's it now. We're not gonna get any work."'

They had barely begun the 200-mile journey back to Birmingham when Tony snapped. Fortunately for Geezer and Ozzy, his wrath was aimed squarely at the sax player and second guitarist, neither of whom he'd been convinced by before the shows, both of whom would now pay the price for his humiliation before his former fans. 'They're going. They're on their bikes,' he announced. Nobody argued. Least of all Ozzy, who had learned at school to keep his head down whenever Tony was 'in one of those moods'. But if Ozzy was sad to see Jimmy go ('Me, Jimmy Phillips and a black bass player named Rosko Gee, who later ended up in Traffic, all used to sleep in the same bed, because we had no fucking dough,' he later told me), he was relieved to see the last of Clarke, who was forever playing 'Take Six'. 'To this day I can't stand that fucking tune!'

The other thing to go was the name, now changed to The Earth Blues Band, a mouthful quickly shortened just to Earth. In reality, the changes didn't make much difference to the way the band sounded. Still relying on the same musical stew of blues covers and psychedelic workouts, mixing Howlin' Wolf and John Lee Hooker with Cream and less well-known white-rock contemporaries like Aynsley Dunbar's Retaliation, for the still unconvinced Tony Iommi most nights they were simply 'doing the same song over and over, just varying the tempo a bit'. Fortunately, the mid-Sixties found the Midlands live circuit at a peak, hosting all the big chart acts of the day, as well as many local talents. Unlike the received wisdom that now insists the Midlands was a hotbed for heavy-metal acts, the chief musical influences of all its most significant groups in the mid-Sixties were US soul and R&B. Record deals were few, to begin with, but at a time when only Liverpool was rated seriously outside London as a centre for music, the live scene in Birmingham and the Midlands was thriving. Players like John Bonham and Robert Plant got their first breaks appearing on what was then called the Ma Reagan Circuit – a string of club venues owned by the eponymous Mrs Reagan, including the Oldhill Plaza, the Handsworth Plaza, the Garry Owen club and the Birmingham Cavern – playing in groups like Terry Webb & The Spiders, the Nicky James Movement, Locomotive and A Way Of Life, featuring future Fairport Convention bassist Dave Pegg. Bonham also drummed, briefly, for The Senators, playing on the track 'She's A Mod' from the 1964 compilation album *Brum Beat*.

Beyond the Ma Reagan circuit there were also endless pub gigs and, later on, hipper Birmingham dives like Henry's Blues House and Mothers, a veritable hinterland of venues dotted throughout the Midlands from which many of the key elements in the next generation of post-Beatles bands would emerge: from Roy Wood and Bev Bevan (later of The Move, ELO and Wizzard), who had met in Carl Wayne & The Vikings, to Stevie Winwood and Jim Capaldi of Traffic, both local boys made good (the former in the Spencer Davis Group); Carl Palmer (Atomic Rooster and ELP), Cozy Powell (Jeff Beck Group and others, including, much later, Black Sabbath), Black Sabbath itself, the Moody Blues, Slade and more.

Drugs came in occasional bags of cannabis resin, or more likely, in twos and threes of little blue 'speed' pills. Mostly, says Geezer, 'We would sink a few pints.' Outrageous behaviour was little tolerated. Move drummer Bev Bevan – who also later ended up, briefly, in Sabbath, recalled how The Move were considering giving his job to John Bonham, but 'The Move didn't drink at all in their earliest days and they thought he might be too much of a loose cannon.'

Encouraged, Earth lumbered on, picking up gigs at local hot-spots like Mothers, The Penthouse, and Henry's Blueshouse. It was at the latter venue, run by local scenester Jim Simpson, that they got their first real break. Simpson was also a musician, but ten years older, and had been shrewd enough to branch out into other areas of the music business in order to make a decent living. As a trumpet player in Locomotive (who had earlier featured a young John Bonham, before he was fired for being unreliable) Jim had enjoyed a hit with 'Rudi's In Love'. By 1968 he had branched out into management, agency work and venue ownership, operations all overseen by his Big Bear company. As well as Henry's Blues House he was now managing a heavy rock trio from Staffordshire called Bakerloo Blues Line, and Tea & Symphony, a whimsical acoustic-based act not unlike early T. Rex. When the fledgling Led Zeppelin – still then known as the New Yardbirds – made a tumultuous appearance at Henry's, Tony and Bill had been in the audience. Feeling the connection between the 'psychedelic blues' Zeppelin were then purveying and the frenzied slabs of granite-hard blues Earth were also attempting, Tony approached Simpson about giving his band a shot at the club.

'They struck me as innocent, confused and a bit directionless,' Simpson says now. 'They didn't really know what the next step was.' Arranging an audition at the club one chilly afternoon in November, Jim 'saw enough though' to hand Earth a slot opening for Ten Years After – another local band made good, and now based in London. Fronted by Nottingham-born Alvin Lee, then billed as 'the fastest guitar in Britain', so impressed was he by the young hopefuls opening the show for him at Henry's, Lee invited them to open for Ten Years After at the Marquee club in London, where they had a residency. The Marquee was already on its own way to legendary status as the site where everyone from the Rolling Stones to Led Zeppelin had got a break. As Geezer said, 'That started the ball rolling for us.'

The ball hadn't rolled far though when Earth collapsed back into a hole. Ten Years After were not the only headline act Earth had grabbed the attention of. When they opened for Jethro Tull, again at Henry's, this time it was Tull leader Ian Anderson who gave the invitation to join them in London – only this time the offer was made singly, to Tony. Tull's debut album, *This Was*, had just been released and entered the Top 10. They were hot property. When their original guitarist, Mick Abrahams, walked out on them – coincidentally, the same night Earth opened for them – Tull's need to replace him was urgent indeed. When Tony received a phone call from Tull's management the morning after the show, asking if he'd be interested in joining them, he jumped at the chance. Then began to panic the moment he put the phone down.

'I told the rest of the lads. I said, they've asked me to join them and they were saying like, "Well, you should. You should give it a try. It's a great opportunity" and all that sort of stuff. But I really felt bad about leaving everybody.' Not so bad that he didn't accept the invitation to join Tull in London. He was in for a shock, though. 'I walked in to about fucking a hundred guitar players.' Players that included more established names like Davey O'List, recently of The Nice, and Martin Barre – another Birmingham boy who'd already been making headway on the London scene with a number of different outfits, most recently Noel Redding's Hendrix side project, Fat Mattress. Tony: 'I thought, what's going on? It turns out it's an audition. I said, "Ah, fucking hell! I'm not gonna get this job" so I walked out again.' But not before he allowed himself to be 'persuaded' to go and sit in the café across the road until they called for him. 'So I came over and started playing, and then they phoned me up the next day and said, yeah, you've got the job.'

Delighted and flattered in equal measure, it wasn't until Tony had returned to Aston with the news of his new job that the weight of what had happened began to sink in. 'The others all acted pleased but I knew what they must have really been thinking.' Invited back to London, to begin rehearsing the songs that would surface on the next Tull album, *Stand Up*, Tony was so freaked out he talked Geezer into coming with him. 'Cos I felt like really lonely without everybody. So Geezer came and he'd sit there while we rehearsed. And I'd be looking at him, feeling really bad, you know? And after the rehearsal, I'd say to him, "I don't know, Geezer, it feels funny to me." And he'd say, "Well, just stick with it a bit longer." So I tried it for a few more days and I said, "Ah, I just can't stand it. It's not working for me."'

It wasn't just the company of his friends and band mates back in Brum that caused Tony to have second thoughts. He bridled when Tull's manager told him: 'You're really lucky you've got this job.' He may have had an inferiority complex, being asked to fit in with what for him was a heady new milieu of successful artists and performers, but he'd overcome huge obstacles to become the guitar player he was, and never once thought of himself as lucky. 'That really got on my nerves. I thought, "It's not luck. They have me here because I know how to play – not because I'm lucky!"'

There was also the culture shock of working in London with a chart act with a clear hierarchy of members. Or as he put it, Tull 'worked different to what I knew. Ian Anderson was separate to the other guys. He'd sit on one table and they'd sit on the other. And it just didn't feel like a full band to me. So I talked to Ian and said, "Look, I'm gonna leave ..."' Put out, Anderson tried persuading Tony to 'give it a bit more of a try' but the guitarist's mind was made up. 'I said, "No, I just feel like it's not me and I want to go back to my other band." And he said, "Well, would you just do the film with us?"'

The film in question was the soon to be near mythical Rolling Stones' *Rock 'n' Roll Circus*. An event built around concerts filmed at Intertel Studios in Teddington over two days – 11 and 12 December – the central conceit was that all the acts would be appearing under what appeared to be a seedy big top; hence its title. Headlined by the Stones and involving stellar Sixties' acts such as The Who, Marianne Faithful, John Lennon and his fiancée, Yoko Ono, and an in-house 'supergroup' dubbed The Dirty Mac, comprising Keith Richards, Eric Clapton and Hendrix drummer Mitch Mitchell, with Jethro Tull there to represent the 'next generation' of rock stars, it was to be broadcast on BBC2 – which had become the first European TV channel able to broadcast colour programmes the year before – early in 1969. But when The Who, arriving red-hot straight from an American tour, blew everyone else off the stage – including the Stones, who had not played live for nearly two years at that point – Mick Jagger put a block on plans to screen the programme and the unseen film remained in the vaults, thought lost, for nearly thirty years, before eventually being made available in DVD form – and indeed screened on BBC TV – in 1996.

The last public performance of Brian Jones with the Stones, it was also Tony Iommi's only performance with Jethro Tull, miming to their single 'A Song For Jeffrey'. They had been meant to play live but the shambolic nature of the day left them with no time to rehearse and Jagger had ordered them to mime, while Anderson sang live instead. Their similarly mimed performance of a new Tull track, 'Fat Man', was later edited out of the final footage, again to save time. Adding to the ignominious feeling of the performance, Tony was required to wear a cowboy hat. 'A silly, white Hopalong Cassidy hat.' Thrown in at the deep end, with zero experience of film production, let alone rubbing shoulders with people, as he says, he'd 'only ever seen on telly before', Tony admits: 'I shit myself! It was *terrifying* for me. Cos I was on my own, didn't know anybody, and there I am standing there with a fucking hat on that I've never worn in my life. I found it in the Props Department at the back and they said, "Oh, why don't you wear that?" So I wore this hat, but I was glad because it covered me face up. I could hold my head down, you know, and not be so embarrassed or nervous.'

If working with Ian Anderson and Jethro Tull had been an eye-opening experience for the young, socially unschooled guitarist, playing in the same room as people like Lennon, Jagger and Clapton was revelatory – and not without its funny side. 'We were all sitting there and then suddenly they started arguing about stuff, Brian Jones and Keith Richards, I think it was. I remember Mick Jagger saying something to me like, "Oh, fucking hell! They're off again!" And I couldn't believe all this, seeing this going on! John Lennon would walk in and Yoko would be stuck to his sleeve. Everywhere he went, she went. He couldn't move without her. Then he'd go onstage and she'd sit at his feet, and then she'd start joining in! And quite honestly, it was fucking awful. It was absolutely dreadful. I'll never forget Ian Anderson turning round to me and saying, "Well, what do you think of your heroes now then?"'

He admitted that after taking part in something like that, he began to wonder about the wisdom of his decision to return to Birmingham and the low-rent prospects of Earth. 'I really did think, "I've fucking dropped a right bollock here!" Quite honestly, I thought, well, I've put me foot in it now, after all this. It was such a big build-up, you know. Suddenly it seemed like I was in something that was happening and here I am pulling out of it. But I just felt the urge so strong to get back with the rest of our lads. And so we did, but I tell you what, it changed our career. It changed the whole thing ...' If Ozzy Osbourne had been scared of Tony Iommi and his free-flying fists before he left for London, he would become increasingly terrified of the brutally determined figure that returned to 'crack the whip' and turn Earth into something real at last. Travelling back to Birmingham in the van on Friday, 13 December 1968, Tony told Geezer, 'Let's get back and fucking get some work done and rehearse, and let's do this ourselves, you know, and make this happen. We can become big, like Tull, but let's get cracking.'

Tony would become the undisputed leader from here on in. As Jim Simpson put it, 'Tony had a bit of a fixation on becoming a star. He was the one who spoke most readily.' Not just as the one who wrote the riffs which became their musical signature, but as the one that guided, ordered and manipulated them. Though he was a man of few words, he never let them forget that he was the one who had sacrificed a life of instant stardom and celebrity to come back and save them. He would come back but it would be entirely on his own terms. The others were merely glad to have him back. And soon, as they began to enjoy the fruits of their renewed, more professional efforts, they began to rely on him to keep driving things forward. Tony's word would become law.

'Which is good and bad,' he would muse years later. 'I mean, it's good cos it got us cracking – somebody had to do it. And I think they *looked* for me to lead, you know? But at the same time it did tend to alienate me a bit from the others. Because I had to sort of appear to be the father figure, if you like, you know? Somebody that would say, "Don't fucking do that." So I went back with that attitude, and got everybody together and said, "Look, let's get rehearsing at nine o'clock in the morning. Let's stop pissing around." And I learned all this, basically, from Ian Anderson, because he was Jethro Tull's leader. And I realised that that's what we needed. To get organised, to get into rehearsals early and really put our minds to it. And it did, it really helped. It got us into writing our own stuff. And everybody was pleased we'd got back together so everybody tried harder anyway. And it just worked from then on.'

With Jim Simpson back on board to help, an arrangement was made with the local Community Centre in Aston Park Road for Earth to use its main room to rehearse in. As they only used it during the mornings, the usual ten bob an hour fee (50p in today's decimalised currency) was halved to five. Now acting as their de facto manager Jim also lined up a string of gigs for them, opening for his other acts, like Locomotive and Bakerloo Blues Band, at Henry's, and occasional headliners at places like the Bay Hotel in Sunderland, where support was provided by Van Der Graaf Generator and Radio One DJ John Peel. He also secured return visits to London with another prestigious spot at the Marquee, opening for Jon Hiseman's Colosseum, whose debut album was on its way to the Top 20, and booked them a show in London opening for John Mayall's Bluesbreakers, where Tony and Geezer were so shy about performing before their heroes they could barely look at the audience. 'There wasn't any great emotion about it, the scales didn't fall from my eyes or anything,' says Jim of his gradual takeover of the band's management. 'We sort of slowly oozed into it. I booked them gigs with people who trusted me enough to take on a band without knowing much about them.' But when he followed that with the band's first overseas dates – a headline no less at the Brøndby Pop Klub in Denmark followed soon after by a residency at the same Star Club in Hamburg where The Beatles had cut their teeth as live performers just a few years before – Jim could do no wrong in their eyes. The only one of the four that still doubted their prospects was the one who was nominally fronting them: their singer. Simpson recalls Ozzy 'getting very distraught. His confidence was very low, he needed constant reassurance.'

When Simpson took it upon himself to draw up a professional management contract for the band to sign, he thought that might be the ego-booster Ozzy needed. In fact, it had the opposite effect, putting all of them on the back foot suddenly. Mainly, Simpson now feels, because it also entailed talking to their parents, all of whom saw this pop group stuff as 'just a lark'; something they would soon grow out of. 'I went to meet their parents and I think they all thought that my enthusiasm was misplaced,' Simpson says. 'I knew the band was going to make it. There was no doubt in my mind whatever. But their mums and dads were a bit be-mused by it all, I think. What, our little Tony? How can he be a star?'

What really sealed the deal in all their minds – and the big turn-ing point, musically – came with the first fully fledged original number they came up with, in April. Title: 'Black Sabbath'. 'At the very early part of Earth, we were still doing a lot of improvisation,' Bill recalled. Out of which would emerge the bare bones of their earliest material. 'The first indication of what started to emerge from these improvisations,' said Bill, came from their cover of a song called 'The Warning', originally by Aynsley Dunbar's Retal-iation, to which Earth now added an extended guitar, bass and drums workout. What started out as an extended jam began to take monstrous new shape during the Star Club residency, where they were required to play four 45-minute sets a night. 'We used to have to stretch the songs out because we had to do so many sets every day that we'd get bored doing the same six songs or whatever,' said Geezer. 'For the jam after "Warning" Tony would do this big, long solo and we'd all like join in and eventually that became some of our first songs.' The first to emerge, which they gave a title to, was a bombastic rock Frankenstein they called 'War Pigs'. 'It started out almost forty minutes long. Then we started shaping it into other songs too. Most of the songs on the first two Sabbath albums came out of those jams at the Star Club.'

The defining moment that turned Earth into Black Sabbath, though, occurred one morning back at the rehearsal room in

Aston. 'The way I remember it,' said Geezer, 'I was listening to Holst at the time, the *Planets* suite, and I loved "Mars".' He began to hum the lumbering, dramatic opening stanza. 'And I was playing it on me bass one day and Tony changed it a bit.' He hummed the knife-quivering intro riff to what became 'Black Sabbath'. 'And it went from there. It just seemed to write itself.' This was more than just an accident. The distorted riff that Tony came off with may have begun in seesaw emulation of Holst's masterpiece, but the skeleton of the final riff – E, octave of E, B flat – was based on what practitioners of the black music arts know as the triton, or *diabolus musica*, the most toxic interval in music, equating to half an octave, which so disturbed the church orthodoxy in the Middle Ages that it was instantly branded 'the Devil's interval' and outlawed throughout the land. Tony Iommi has always claimed he knew nothing of this when he first produced it on the guitar to such shattering effect that day, but admits he felt 'something was moving me to play like that'.

The title 'Black Sabbath' – which appears nowhere in the lyrics and was only added later – was lifted from the 1963 Mario Bava film of the same name, aka *Three Faces Of Fear*, starring Boris Karloff. The lyric – one of the few that Ozzy had a hand in – described a particularly 'black' experience Geezer had recently had at his pad late one night, while lying in bed. He was, he later confessed, 'getting into black magic and the occult at the time'. Not participating in actual occult rituals, but overindulging in the prevailing trend of the time towards various aspects of hippy mysticism, from verifiable Eastern religions to the more esoteric works of the most famous English wizard after Merlin – Aleister Crowley. His career underwent a huge renaissance in the late Sixties, a typically solemn image of the occultist making it as far as the cover of The Beatles' *Sergeant Pepper* album the previous year.

'I just like had a morbid interest in it. I was reading every book that came out about it. There were a lot of underground magazines around then, plus I used to go down to London for the weekend, to a place called Middle Earth [in the basement of a townhouse mansion in Holborn]. And there used to be like these occult groups – not musical groups, groups of people. And they used to give out all this literature and they had their own magazines. There was one called *Madness & Magic*, which was like a monthly magazine that you collected that was all about black magic, and I used to read all that stuff.' Describing himself as 'sort of a religious maniac when I was a kid', Geezer had grown up collecting crucifixes, '[holy] pictures, and medals – I wanted to become a priest... I just literally loved God.' By comparison to his strict Catholic upbringing, the subject of the occult 'was all really intriguing – forbidden fruit, kind of thing, and as an impressionable kid, I just got interested in it'.

When, however, he awoke this night to stare aghast at what appeared to be some sort of apparition standing at the foot of his bed – the 'figure in black which points at me' of the lyric – 'It frightened the bloody life out of me! I woke up suddenly, and there was this, like, this black shape standing at the foot of me bed. I wasn't on drugs or anything like that and I didn't drink in those days. And it absolutely frightened the bloody life out of me. And at that time I had like this one-bedroom flat, completely painted black and I had all these inverted crosses all around the place and all these posters of Satan and all that kind of stuff. And this shape ... for some reason I thought it was the Devil himself! And it just frightened the pissing life out of me. It was almost as if this thing was saying to me, "It's time to either pledge allegiance or piss off!" And from that moment on, I just went off the whole thing.'

He was so freaked out he couldn't sleep for the rest of the night. In the morning, he took down all the crosses and posters and later had the flat repainted orange. He also began wearing a cross. When, just a few days later, Tony turned Geezer's thumb-heavy bass rendition of 'Mars' into a genuinely thrilling rock epic, the lyrics he and Ozzy had made up about Geezer's early-hours freak-out fitted perfectly; the new song – the first the band ever wrote together from scratch – becoming a warning against the Satanism and devil worship they would, ironically, be accused of actually dabbling in, time and again over the years, by distressed parents and their gore-thrilled offspring. No one who heard the song's death-rattle guitars, its lightning-forked bass and drums, its trembling vocals, ever asked for an explanation as to what it was all about. They already knew. As Geezer said, by then 'all the love and peace thing had come and gone, the Vietnam war thing was happening and a lot of kids were getting into all kinds of mysticism and occultism. It was just a really big thing at the time. Everybody was getting into it and reading up about it.' They could relate.

The clincher came later that same day they wrote the song, when they performed it live for the first time at a pub in nearby Lichfield called the Poky Hole. 'The reaction was absolutely incredible. In those days when we played everybody would be stood at the bar drinking, not really paying attention. But we played that and everybody just stopped dead ... and listened. The whole place was just like in a trance. We finished the song and it just erupted, they went absolutely nuts! We couldn't believe it. Like, what the hell's going on? And we realised then that we were on to something and it was good.'

Taking the reaction to their new number as their cue, they began trying to write more material in that same gloomy vein. 'We were all totally into different things, even musically. I was into Frank Zappa and the Mothers; Ozzy was into The Beatles. Tony and Bill were into their own things too. But the one common bond we had was a love of horror films and science fiction stuff. And that reflected itself in the sort of music we would now make.' Some of their earliest attempts – like the chattering hyper-blues of

'Wicked World' – were good but were clearly rooted in the Earth era: maudlin repetitive rhythms enlivened by Iommi's tail-flashing guitar. Some of it, though, like the embryonic 'War Pigs', quickly evolved into showstoppers of an even greater magnitude. To cement their new-found direction, within weeks they had also changed the name of the band – to Black Sabbath.

They had been trying to think of a new name for the band since discovering there was another, more established band on the Midlands circuit named Earth. Naming themselves after the first fully formed song they ever came up with was a symbolic choice. Geezer: '"Black Sabbath" was just so different to everything else, we knew then that that's what we were gonna do. Naming the band after it seemed to change everything for us, overnight. I always did love that title. The only problem was all the bloody trouble it caused with the black magic stuff …'

The band made their first appearances as Black Sabbath during a return visit to the Star Club, that summer. They were a completely different band now from the one that had struggled to fill four sets a night three months previously. And not just in name. With a growing catalogue of original numbers and the new-found confidence in their own rapidly expanding abilities that engendered, it was no longer a case of whether they deserved to be there but whether the Star Club, now on its last legs as a viable live venue, was big enough to hold them. 'We were like fucking pirates by then,' said Ozzy. 'First order of the day when you got to the Star Club was you had to get a chick. The reason why, because the fucking accommodation sucked, so you had to get someone to shack up with, you know? And she would give you food and when she'd go to work I'd go rifling through her drawers or try and find if she'd got a gas meter to break into or whatever. They were fun days. We used to smoke dope and get pissed all the time, nick a fucking case of beer off the back of a truck.' The others would keep guard while Ozzy 'had it away. I was the thief of the group.'

Back home, Jim Simpson was also stealing favours where he could. Armed with a newly recorded demo cassette of two original tracks – 'The Rebel' and 'Song For Jim', the latter a hybrid between the kind of emblematic Sixties-style psychedelic blues of Earth, replete with high-pitched backing vocals, and the kind of frayed nerve-endings of what would become the quintessential Black Sabbath sound, the bugling guitar break later being repurposed for use in 'War Pigs'; the latter a catchy, lightweight tune that might have come from a Charlie Christian jazz tune of the Forties – Simpson used his connections to arrange two record company showcase gigs. The biggest of them, at the Marquee in London, found Ozzy sporting a striped pyjama top and a water tap tied around his neck on string; Geezer in lime green trousers with one black leg; Tony in a second-hand buckskin jacket; and Bill shirtless and pouring with sweat. There were no takers among the record company execs and agents Jim had dragged down there.

Running out of options, Jim used the demo tape to persuade a locally based independent producer named Tony Hall to come along to a gig. Hall, who had his own agency, Tony Hall Enterprises, was impressed enough to offer his services in brokering a record deal. 'I just thought they were a great little blues band,' Hall later recalled, 'four good players who deserved to make a record. I would have tried to get a deal for them as Earth [but] they went away to Germany and came back as Black Sabbath.' For the moment, however, it didn't matter what they were called, with the London-based record labels more focused in 1969 on finding 'the new Beatles' than signing a determinedly uncommercial act – read: no obvious hit singles – like Black Sabbath. Hall refused to admit defeat, and offered to 'lend' Jim Simpson £500 – along with the use of a young producer he was also managing, named

Rodger Bain – in order to record a Sabbath album, which they would then 'shop around' to the majors. The first the band knew of it was a phone call from Simpson to Iommi on the morning of their departure for some gigs in Denmark. 'We drove down from Birmingham in an old tranny [transit van]. The manager, Jim Simpson, said, "Oh, you've got to go to this address and record them songs." And we just thought, oh, okay.' Arriving at Regent Sound studios, a mono facility with egg-boxes on the ceiling acting as sound-proofing where the Stones had recorded some of their earliest records, in London's Tottenham Court Road, they began recording their live set on to two four-track machines – the studio's only nod to 'modern' recording technology. Bain, an experienced engineer who saw his job as making these rough diamonds sound suitably convincing, gave them all their instructions – where to put the mikes, when a take was good enough – based more on his experience than on any real connection with the band's music. Though it was Bain that added a telling finishing touch to the final mix which lent the album an extra air of musical foreboding, in the rainstorm and tolling church bells that open the album. 'We got in,' said Ozzy, 'played 'em, and twelve hours later we got back in the van, put the gear in and carried on driving ...'

While Sabbath were traipsing around Europe, Jim Simpson began doing the rounds of the London labels again and, as he put it, 'got another fourteen no's. I was madly enthusiastic – they were madly bored.' Tony Hall thought he had struck oil when he persuaded the Fontana label to sign the band – for one single. A subsidiary of the Dutch Philips label, Fontana mainly specialised in novelty records by artists of no real credibility like Dave Dee, Dozy, Beaky, Mick & Tich, whose 'Legend Of Xanadu' had hit No. 1 the year before, and The Troggs, whose biggest hit, 'Wild Thing', had been three years before. Fontana's main claim to fame at the time the Sabbath deal was done was 'Je T'Aime... Moi Non Plus', by Serge Gainsbourg and Jane Birkin, which reached No. 1 despite being banned by the BBC. Uninterested in issuing the complete Sabbath album, Fontana suggested the group record a cover of a song that had just reached the US Top 40 called 'Evil Woman (Don't You Play Your Games With Me)', written and recorded by a Minneapolis-based band named Crow. Tony and Geezer were appalled at the suggestion, seeing it as 'a sell-out'. But Jim persuaded them that it was simply another rung on the ladder and so they had reluctantly included it during their day at Regent Sound.

They may not have liked the song, but the fact the band had a deal with Fontana led to another of Philips' subsidiaries – the recently launched Vertigo label – getting to hear 'Evil Woman'. Impressed by the record's sound – the muted horns of the original replaced by Iommi's razor-edged new Gibson SG – they inquired further into this, to them, still utterly unknown British band, only to discover they actually had a whole album already in the can. When Jim Simpson turned up at their London office brimming with his usual bonhomie, to play them the album, the bearded, dope-smoking Vertigo staffers couldn't believe their luck. Launched earlier that year in direct competition with EMI's also recently launched Harvest label – set up specifically to promote the coming wave of 'progressive', album-oriented rock groups – Vertigo had already released debut albums in 1969 from Colosseum, Juicy Lucy, Manfred Mann and Rod Stewart. Those had all involved significant outlays of cash. With the Sabbath album already recorded and paid for, the idea of simply distributing it under their own imprint fitted well with Vertigo's own modest aims. Jim Simpson had himself a deal. He ran from the meeting to the nearest red phone box and rang Tony Iommi with the good news.

The real surprise came that Christmas, when Jim Simpson called them over to his house to look at their new album cover. Ozzy thought they would have pictures of themselves on the cover 'like The Beatles'. But he took one look at the now famous depiction of Mapledurham Watermill – a historic mill dating back to the time of the Domesday Book, and situated on the banks of the River Thames in Oxfordshire, before which the graphic designers at Vertigo had positioned a witchy 'figure in black' – and yelped with joy. 'I looked at the sleeve and loved it, with the chick on the front, all that fucking black in the middle. Though I've never read that poem, I thought it was killer, you know?'

The poem was included on the inside of the gatefold sleeve, folded inside an inverted cross – another addition to the package by the record company, which the band only now discovered. Written specifically with the sleeve in mind, it begins: 'Still falls the rain, the veils of darkness shroud the blackened trees, which contorted by some unseen violence, shed their tired leaves ...' And ends: '... by the lake a young girl waits, unseeing she believes herself unseen, she smiles, faintly at the distant tolling bell, and the still falling rain.' Then Jim put the LP on the record player and they were further amazed when it began with the sound of a howling wind and thunderstorm, a church bell tolling dolefully in the foreground, before Tony's guitars come slicing in like a cleaver. Ozzy was beside himself: 'I was like, whoa! Pink Floyd after all!'

What none of them could have known was that their album – such a surprise for them to hear for the first time – was destined to become one of the most influential rock albums of all time. Although it would receive scant praise from the critics of the day, *Black Sabbath* – as they had inevitably decided to call the album, as was the fashion of the day, à la *Led Zeppelin* and *Deep Purple*, both released earlier that year – would become cited, over the decades, as the foundation stone for everything which came after that became known as heavy metal. From pioneering future-shock artists like Metallica – 'Without Black Sabbath, no Metallica', as Lars Ulrich once told me – and Nirvana, whom Kurt

Cobain characterised early on as 'a cross between Black Sabbath and The Beatles', to self-styled emulators like Marilyn Manson and Henry Rollins. As time went by, even hip-hop stars looking for a bump up the authenticity scale like Ice T, Busta Rhymes and even the late ODB (Ol Dirty Bastard) would eulogise Black Sabbath, onstage, in print and even on record. What Sabbath achieved on their first album wasn't just heavy, it was monumental; game changing. So different from what had come before it would become the Dead Sea Scrolls of hard rock and heavy metal.

As well as the monolithic title track, there were other equally statement-making moments like 'Behind The Wall Of Sleep', its title taken from the H. P. Lovecraft short story that concerned one Joe Slater, an inmate at a mental hospital who would erupt from sleep to 'soar through abysses of emptiness burning every obstacle that stood in his way'; its stormy riff taken straight from the opened vein. The band showed their true versatility at the end when Bill Ward's drums ascend towards a deep-space West Coast vibe before Geezer's bass takes over for a solo titled 'Bassically' on the future US version of the album but here on the original presented more opaquely as a tribal-summoning segue into one of the album's other pivotal tracks, 'N.I.B.' Virtually a template for what heavy rock would stand for by the early Seventies, it was built around the sort of freight train blues rhythm Cream were famous for using as a jumping-off point into lengthy improvised solos. Known for years to come as an acronym for 'Nativity In Black', in fact 'N.I.B.' was a typically offhand title for a piece ostensibly about the love of the Devil for a mortal girl, which the band incongruously dubbed 'Nib' after one of many nicknames they used not always affectionately over the years for the undeserving Bill Ward – in this case, after the sharp point his ever-lengthening beard had then grown to. 'It looked like a pen nib so we called it "Nib",' Geezer would snigger. 'I just put full-stops in to make it sound more mysterious …' The song itself betrayed none of this humour. 'It's our kind of knock against love songs. We hated listening to love songs, so I thought I'll write a satanic love song. The line "I'll give you the moon and the stars" – that was like the ultimate chat-up line, cos the devil could do that kind of thing.'

Most impressive of all, perhaps, was 'Sleeping Village', which begins with a minute of eerily brittle acoustic guitar and what sounds like a twanging Jew's harp, Ozzy lamenting hoarsely about a 'Red sun rising in the sky …' and the sleeping village that wakes beneath its toxic rays. Then silence before the track reignites with one of Iommi's guitars leading the band into an instrumental over three distinct parts, from the lugubrious to the dervish-like finale, before dragging everything back to its feed-back-wired segue into the next track, and perhaps the album's greatest display of Sabbath firepower, 'The Warning'. Having used their version of Aynsley Dunbar's track – played to death in the clubs for over a year – as a launchpad for practically every other track in their repertoire, here, finally, on the last track of their debut album, we get to the true bitter heart of the quintessential Sabbath sound as it was first conceived in 1969. Slower, infinitely more ominous than the Retaliation original from two years before, it was also nearly five times longer. The Sixties were the golden era for rock performers taking existing material and reinventing it as their own – from Joe Cocker's powder-fingered version of The Beatles' 'With A Little Help From My Friends' to Jimi Hendrix's raising-sand version of Bob Dylan's 'All Along The Watchtower'. But what Sabbath did on 'The Warning' was more than just breathe new life into an old song as reconfigure the whole hard rock and heavy metal universe: from writing their own nearly four-minute intro, in 'Sleeping Village', to rolling right past the point where the original version faded from view and on to new, cloud-gathering horizons, Tony, Geezer and Bill seemingly taking it in turns to outdo each other in the improvised-solo stakes. Listened to separately, the final eight minutes of 'The Warning' could be an improvised jazz outfit along the same lines which Miles Davis was also then exploring on the sessions that would become *Bitches Brew*. Only this wasn't the cream of New York jazz stylists slugging it out for pole position in the told-you-so stakes – this was Ozzy's 'four fucking dummies from Birmingham' playing out of their heads, unstoppable, even by producer Rodger Bain, who gave up giving them the signal to halt after the first half an hour, leaving Tony to solo for a further 18 minutes. When it was over the band didn't even acknowledge each other. They simply packed up their gear and took off, as if ashamed of the mess they'd left behind in the studio.

Even the album's lighter moments – like 'The Wizard', a staccato psychedelic rhythm-and-blues, bound over from Earth days, featuring Ozzy on siren-like harmonica and a lyric from Geezer based on his over-indulgence in J. R. R. Tolkien, with Gandalf as the wizard in question, and 'Evil Woman', which had flopped as a single but was included here to try and win back some money for Fontana in the unlikely event that anyone actually bought the album – still sound like something different going on, something, yes, heavier. It took Bain the whole of the next day to edit down and mix what they'd done into what became the finished album. So cleverly did he manage the feat that the very last explosions of noise which ended side one also ended side two.

If the four band members had been stunned when they finally got to hold their first album in their hands and actually listen to it, they were in for an even greater shock. Released on Friday, 13 February 1970 – a PR stunt that caught the eye of no one at the time but has been remarked on ever since as though the date really was a portent – *Black Sabbath* jumped straight into the UK charts at No. 28. It hadn't been reviewed yet, it had only been heard so far on British radio courtesy of that stalwart of the underdog, John Peel, and hardly anyone south of Birmingham had even heard of the band. Yet such was the strength of the band's follow-ing everywhere but London that at a time when album sales had suddenly outstripped those of singles, Black Sabbath had almost by accident positioned themselves at the forefront of an emerg-ing rock audience that only bought 'album-oriented' bands. Led Zeppelin had enjoyed similar success just a year before, as would Uriah Heep just a few months after the Sabbath album. The fash-ionable music press were caught on the back foot – and would never really forgive those bands for putting them in that position. If the fans that attended their gigs in the Midlands and elsewhere were ahead of the curve, in terms of the London media, it must be because the bands themselves were intrinsically worthless. Or so the twisted logic ran. Meanwhile, Black Sabbath kept on selling, and suddenly their club gigs were becoming bigger.

'Jim Simpson rang me the night before and asked me if I'd heard the news,' said Ozzy. 'I go, "What news?" He says, "Your album's entered the British charts!" I go, "Fuck off!"' Ozzy stayed up all night waiting to buy the music papers, which carried the national album charts. 'It was a Wednesday night and *Melody Maker* and *NME* came out on a Thursday, and I couldn't sleep cos I had to see it in black and white, and from six o'clock in the morning, every few minutes I was like, "Have the papers arrived yet?" When it finally arrived my knees went to jelly and I sat on the fucking doorstep and there it was in the paper, "*Black Sab-bath*, new entry ..." I was speechless, I couldn't fucking believe it! And from that moment on, my life totally went off like a rocket!'

Geezer, who appears not to have read the same music papers as Ozzy, has his own distinct recollection of hearing about the album reaching the Top 30: 'I remember to this day the first time we heard it on the radio. We were driving up to do a gig at the Manchester Polytechnic, and in those days the album charts used to be on Radio One on a Saturday afternoon and we always used to listen. And so we had it on in the van, and it says, "And in at twenty-eight this week, Black Sabbath!" And we were like, "WHAT?!?" We all nearly *died*. We just couldn't believe it! We were shocked, just driving up to Manchester on the radio!'

Within weeks, *Black Sabbath* had climbed as high as No. 8. But if the band and their followers were delighted, the London-based music press were confounded, even hostile. 'The London press absolutely hated us when we made it,' said Geezer, 'cos they'd never written an article about us, they didn't know of us. When our album, the first week, went straight in the charts, the London press went, like, what the hell's going on here? And they've hated us ever since.'

It wasn't all bad. *International Times*, then Britain's most cutting-edge music and culture paper, while bridling at, as reviewer Mark Williams put it, Vertigo's 'press statement spiel about the band's black magic interest' which he not unjustly branded as 'hype, rather adding to the initial plasticity of the total thing', did conclude, however, that 'Black Sabbath have found a fairly uncomplicated formula of straightforward melody lines and counterpoint, added a lot of weight and fire and they execute the whole thing with instrumental excellence (Tommy Iommi's guitar work meriting special attention) and compulsive gusto.' The band cared but pretended they didn't care, not while the success kept on building and the five-quid-a-night gigs turned into £20-a-night. They knew they'd really made it, said Geezer, when they turned up for a gig at The Boat Club, in Nottingham, in March, 'and we went there in a car instead of the van, and we found an ounce of hash in the dressing room. It was like, "Yes! This is the life!"'

By the summer the £20-a-night gigs had turned into the hundreds. This achieved with no hit singles, no sustained interest in the music press, very little radio exposure, no TV whatsoever, and only a thin crust of self-belief among themselves. The speed of their ascent was so astonishing it left them all agog. Once they assumed the Black Sabbath name and musical identity, reaction at their earliest gigs had always been positive. But not so full-on that it prepared them for how quickly word spread about their debut album. As Bill said, 'I was surprised because I'd been used to living in this kind of like "nothing will ever work out" kind of frame of mind, you know? I was used to being on the poverty line, as were we all. It was wonderful, but totally unexpected.'

'It felt just great,' said Tony, still smiling at the thought decades later. 'Everybody was just so excited with the whole thing. I personally felt incredibly high on the whole thing, you know, because it was such an achievement, such a thing that you never, ever thought would happen. And you have to remember that these were the days when fucking everybody hated us, so we never got any sort of good press at all. I don't know why. Probably because we were different at that time, I think. And maybe, um ... maybe we just weren't sophisticated enough, I don't know.'

THREE
BRINGERS OF WAR

The name Black Sabbath may have meant nothing before the album of the same name burst like an uninvited guest through the doors of the Top 10, but now though, in the spring of 1970, the rest of the world was making up for lost time. Within weeks Jim Simpson had been contacted by the then executive vice-president of Warner Bros. Records, Joe Smith, about putting out the *Black Sabbath* album in North America. Smith, a fast-talking former promotions chief from New York, had been at the forefront of the company's recent attempts to contemporise its catalogue. As the recording offshoot of Warner Bros. Pictures, the Warner Bros. Records label had enjoyed considerable Stateside success in the early Sixties with acts such as Petula Clark, the Everly Brothers, and Peter, Paul & Mary. It wasn't until Smith became their A&R chief in 1967, however, that the label first embraced the new album-oriented 'longhaired generation' of music artists. His first breakthrough signing had been The Grateful Dead, whose self-titled debut album had gone gold. But Smith's relationship with the Dead had never run smooth. When, soon after becoming vice-president of the company, Smith gave a speech at a party for the band in San Francisco, in which he announced 'what an honor it is to be able to introduce The Grateful Dead and its music to the world', Dead leader Jerry Garcia quipped sarcastically: 'I just want to say what an honor it is for The Grateful Dead to introduce Warner Bros. Records to the world.' When the second Dead album, *Anthem Of The Sun*, took over $100,000 and six months to make, then failed to crack the US charts, Smith washed his hands of them. When his next major project, Van Morrison, whose first album for Warner's, *Astral Weeks*, recorded in just three days, was hailed as a classic and sold several hundred thousand copies, Smith felt he knew the way forward: low-maintenance UK-based acts looking for their big break in America and prepared to work hard for it. An idea further reinforced when Morrison's next album, *Moondance*, again recorded relatively quickly and cheaply, broke into the US Top 30, eventually selling over three million copies.

It was while basking in the critical and commercial heatwave of *Moondance*, in March 1970, that Smith, leafing through the British trade magazine *Music Week*, glanced at the album charts and espied a group he had never heard of riding high in the Top 10: Black Sabbath. He picked up the phone and began making some calls. Discovering that the band had no US deal, nor any heavyweight management behind them, Smith pounced at once, offering Simpson a deal with the dice all loaded in Warner's favour: i.e. a modest cash advance against 'standard contract' royalties (rarely more than a few cents per record sale). The only request Smith made, in terms of the music, was that 'Evil Woman' be omitted from the US version of the album, as it was already well-known in America and not, Smith correctly divined, entirely representative of what Sabbath was about. Instead it was replaced by a track recorded in London at the original day-long session but left off the finished record, 'Wicked World'. One of many songs the band had come up with while 'lying on our backs in the studio smoking dope and listening to Led Zeppelin', according to Geezer, they would be more than happy to have it replace 'Evil Woman', which they hated, on the US album.

The only other change to the Warner Bros. version of *Black Sabbath* was in the way the tracks were listed on the label and sleeve. Concerned that there would be no single released upfront of the album, Smith had come up with the idea of breaking up the lengthier tracks, title-wise at least, to make them appear more easily accessible for American radio – and to make potential buyers feel they were getting value for money. Again, the band, over the moon simply to have a record out in America, were happy to acquiesce, though their choice of titles hardly reflected the seriousness of Smith's request. Thus 'Behind The Wall Of Sleep' was listed as actually two tracks, its witchy acoustic intro given its own title: 'Wasp'. While Geezer's forty-second bass intro to 'N.I.B.' became 'Bassically'. Similarly, side two's centrepiece tracks, 'Sleeping Village' and 'The Warning', were now listed as being hinged together by a newly named intro, 'A Bit Of Finger'.

'We were still living in the van, so it didn't mean much at the time,' Ozzy recalled. When, however, *Black Sabbath* was released in America in June 1970 and began to instantly climb the charts, Jim couldn't wait to tell the boys the news. 'We were absolutely flabbergasted!' Not as flabbergasted, though, as the rest of the London-based UK music business, whose key players were now beginning to take the name Black Sabbath very seriously indeed. 'No one had any idea who they were,' their future manager, Don Arden, would tell me years later. The self-styled Al Capone of Pop, as a headline in Britain's most scurrilous Sunday tabloid, the *News Of The World*, had described him, in 1969, Don Arden was then the most notorious mover and shaker in the London biz. A former song and dance man and physical fitness fanatic from Manchester who had graduated in the 1950s to becoming a promoter, shrewdly booking then emerging new American rock'n'roll acts like Bill Haley and Jerry Lee Lewis, Arden had quickly expanded his business, in the Sixties, to become manager, agent and, eventually, even record company chief to a string of huge international acts, beginning with Little Richard and Gene Vincent, before moving on to oversee the careers of the Animals, the Nashville Teens, Amen Corner, the Small Faces and The Move.

Don's modus operandi, he explained to me, was 'to get in there at the first bell and knock hell out of the other guy'. This had resulted in some infamous adventures that have since become part of rock'n'roll folklore, from the time he balanced budding pop impresario Robert Stigwood from a balcony window, threatening to drop him over its side for daring to try and steal the Small Faces from him, to less well-known but equally disturbing occasions like the time he held down former Move manager Clifford Davis with one hand while grinding out a cigar in his face with the other hand. As Don famously warned investigative reporter Roger Cook, who took him to task in a 1979 radio documentary, 'I'll take you with one hand strapped up my arse.'

At the time Black Sabbath first registered on the Arden radar, in 1970, Don was in the middle of 'persuading' Capitol Records to spend fortunes marketing and promoting the debut album, *Scorch*, from another of his upcoming stable of acts, called Judas Jump. Comprised of ex-members of Amen Corner and The Herd, purveyors of the same brand of college dorm boogie and progressive rock then doing so well for fellow travellers like Deep Purple and Jethro Tull. So far, however, no cigar. When Don saw another group with roughly the same musical template, Black Sabbath, jump into the charts with absolutely no promotion whatsoever, he looked on with frustrated envy. The next time the band played in London, at the Marquee, in May, he was there, as were several other leading music biz figures. Following his maxim to 'get in there at the first bell', Don moved quickly, pointedly telling anyone within earshot what 'a complete waste of time they were, how they didn't stand a chance', while positioning himself close to the entrance to the dressing room, to ensure he was first through the door to greet them as they came offstage that night. He told me, 'Ozzy looked like a genuine mental case, but he never stopped moving, never stopped communicating with the crowd, getting them going. He may not have been the greatest singer in the world but as a performer he walked away with everything. I decided there and then that Black Sabbath would be my next signing.'

In the tiny Marquee dressing room afterwards Don introduced himself by announcing: 'You are superstars and I am going to make you a million dollars.' But the band just looked at him dolefully. 'They were just kids from the sticks that had never seen a ten pound note let alone a million dollars and I scared the living daylights out of them.' Nevertheless, Don insisted they meet with him at his office the next day. There waiting to show them into Don's office was his eighteen-year-old daughter Sharon; someone who, though none of them could have known it yet, would have a profound and lasting impact on all their lives and careers.

In showbiz parlance, Sharon Arden had been born in a suitcase. The youngest child of professional showbiz people – her mother, Hope, aka Paddles, had been a dancer in Ireland before the war, under the stage name Paddy O'Shea, her father Don (real name: Harry Levy) then starring in the *Black & White Minstrels* TV show – her earliest memories revolved around various hotels and train stations, as her parents moved from gig to gig. Born in 1952, Sharon had grown up a daddy's girl. But while her elder brother David would spend most of his life working for their father, Sharon was too much like the old man to take orders for long. Privately educated, later becoming a student at the Italia Conte stage school, she had aspired to being a dancer like her mother. But as well as his brains and his temper, Sharon had also inherited her father's short stumpy legs and puberty saw her dreams vanquished as she became a binge eater, gaining the weight she would spend the rest of her life then fighting to lose. 'Cake, fried food, cheeses, anything and everything. Any time I felt a pang of fear, I ate,' she remembered.

Don, whose own career as a performer had 'been up and down like a toilet seat' – headlining the London Palladium one year, opening up a boarding house for travelling Variety acts the next – believed that 'money breeds money'. It wasn't enough just to be successful; one had to be seen to be so. Once he'd made it as the most notorious entrepreneur in the music business – a kind of Sixties Simon Cowell, but one who liked to carry a gun into meetings – he made sure that he and Hope were always be-decked in the most expensive clothes and jewellery, that his children were ferried to and from school in one of the fam-ily's three Rolls-Royces, and that they only ate out in the most exclusive restaurants. It wasn't unusual for him to splash out several thousand pounds on a whim – a piece of antique furni-ture perhaps or a painting – and give his children anything they wanted. Seventeen-year-old David was allowed to hold lavish parties for all his less well-off friends at the house and have an account for gambling at a bookmaker's. Sharon would also invite her school pals to the family mansion, where she made sure she was always the best-dressed, most fashionable-looking girl in the room.

After school and a couple of fainthearted attempts at a 'proper job', she followed David into working for her father, starting out as the receptionist at their Mayfair office. She was eighteen, clever and mouthy on the outside, insecure and easily hurt on the inside. Her first sexual encounter – with the good-looking young guitarist in one of Don's bands – had left her pregnant. Her furi-ous mother had told her she would have to 'get rid of it'. Giving her the name of a local abortion clinic, she sent her there alone the very next day. 'I was terrified,' said Sharon. 'It was full of other young girls, and we were all terrified and looking at each other and nobody was saying a bloody word. I howled my way through it, and it was horrible. It was the worst thing I ever did.'

Throwing herself into her new job at her father's office, she had accompanied him to the Black Sabbath show at the Marquee. 'I was like, "What the fuck is this?" It was like nothing else.' When the band showed up at Curzon Street the next day, she virtually hid from them. 'I knew they had something from having seen them at the Marquee but in person I just thought they were these awful smelly hippies,' she told me. 'I remember they all sat on the floor smoking and they all had really long hair. I was more used to the sort of well-groomed American artists my father usually dealt with. This lot just looked mad to me! The only reason I noticed Ozzy was because he looked like a complete nutter, I really did think he was a lunatic or something.'

She got to know him better, though, a few months later, when she bumped into him at a New Year's Eve party at the London home of one of Sabbath's new managers, Patrick Meehan Junior. Still wary of this strangely dressed young hoodlum, she found him surprisingly shy and actually very funny. High on champagne and each other's company, there was clearly a sexual chemistry between them. Only one problem: for the naive Brummy still on a weekly wage despite his band's roaring success, a girl like Sharon – scary Don Arden's daughter, no less – was way out of his league and, drunk as he was, he knew it. For overweight Sharon, whose need for approval from the opposite sex was even stronger than Ozzy's, there was a more clear-cut reason why they shouldn't get together: the knowledge that Ozzy had a fiancée back in Birmingham named Thelma Mayfair. Having met in the Birmingham nightclub where she worked as a cloakroom attendant, they had been together ever since and were due to marry later that year. What's more, Thelma already had a five-year-old son, Elliot, from a previous marriage, and not even Sharon was prepared to start tiptoeing across that minefield. Convinced Ozzy saw her purely as a one-night stand she wasn't about to take matters any further, no matter how much he made her laugh. It would be another three years before their paths crossed again and by then both their circumstances had altered drastically.

What neither Don nor Sharon Arden knew in the summer of 1970 was that two of Don's most trusted lieutenants, Patrick Meehan and Wilf Pine, were plotting to steal Black Sabbath away not just from Jim Simpson, but Don himself. Something Don would never forgive them for – or himself for not having seen it coming. Not that either Meehan or Pine made it easy for him. Having learned from the master, they both made their moves for control of Sabbath as stealthily low-key as possible. Meehan was the first to go, announcing his 'retirement' from the business. As Patrick was already in his fifties – ancient by Seventies music biz standards – Don was unsurprised. When, just a few weeks later, however, Wilf Pine also announced his departure from Arden's employ, Don's suspicions were well and truly aroused. Wilf Pine 'had some good boys working for him – characters like Canadian Dave, Jinksy and Big Arnie'. Don had looked after them all for years, putting them up in the top-floor apartment of his former offices in Denmark Street, keeping them on the payroll through thick and thin. Where would they go without him? And why make the move now, when things were going so well? He soon had his answer.

The four members of Black Sabbath, meanwhile, were working through their own swings and roundabouts. Released in the first week of June, the *Black Sabbath* album repeated its remarkable straight-out-of-the-box success in Britain by sailing straight into the US Top 30, where it hovered like a cloud of flies for several months, peaking at No. 23. Joe Smith at Warner Bros. was ecstatic, and immediately moved to get the band signed to America's top booking agent, Frank Barsalona, who had recently overseen the trailblazing breakthrough of Led Zeppelin. Sixteen shows were swiftly arranged, beginning with three consecutive appearances in July at the prestigious Fillmore West in San Francisco, the same venue Zeppelin had made such a mark with when they kicked off their own American success there the year before. The band were already packed and ready for the drive down to London's Heathrow airport when Jim Simpson took a phone call late that night from a distressed Joe Smith. The American tour was cancelled. Not through lack of ticket sales, as might have been expected – in fact tickets for all three Fillmore dates had sold out as soon as they had gone on sale – but because Warner Bros. feared a public relations disaster after it had been pointed out that Sabbath's shows would coincide with the start of the trial of a real-life Satanist named Charles Manson.

Eventually convicted for the multiple murders of Roman Polanski's actress wife, Sharon Tate, and several others, over two nights in August 1969, Manson and his psychotic followers had made headlines across the world not just for the apparently motive-less murders, but the gruesome manner in which they were carried out. Tate, then eight and a half months pregnant, was stabbed in the stomach sixteen times, before her blood was smeared over the front door to her house to make the word 'Pig'. When Manson turned up at the first day in court, on 24 July, having carved an X into his forehead, it ensured more headlines, speculating on his occult intentions. When it then emerged that Manson had embarked on the slaughter of his innocent victims after receiving 'secret signals' from the Beatles song 'Helter Skelter', the whole area of occult rock music became so charged with new meaning that the idea of launching a US tour by a band named Black Sabbath whose show highlight was a song titled 'War Pigs' was considered in extremely bad taste, to say the least. When Manson stood up in court and proclaimed 'Why blame it on me? I didn't write the music', it sealed the deal for Warner Bros. The Sabbath tour was off – for now, anyway.

What couldn't be put off was the Black Sabbath Parade, planned to take place along Folsom Street in San Francisco, the same week the band were to have appeared at the Fillmore West, and organised ostensibly by Anton LaVey, self-styled head of the Church of Satan, with the backing of the Warner Bros. promotions team before the decision to cancel the dates had been made. The shaven-headed LaVey, who arrived in character as the Black Pope, dressed in a long black robe with an inverted crucifix hanging from his neck and wielding a tall sceptre, looked on solemnly from atop the main float as the rest of the gathered freaks below put on their own show: a mixture of glamorously dressed drag queens and gay fancy-dress freaks, alongside several grinning passers-by, none of whom looked like they knew what was going on. There were also groups of black men who may have misunderstood the group's name entirely, standing around looking incongruous beneath a large white banner proclaiming: Warner Bros. Records Welcomes Black Sabbath – The Dawn Of The Aquarius. The parade eventually got underway, led by a white Rolls-Royce, draped in black for the day, and followed by various floats depicting astrological scenes, strange Kennedy-like open-top limos peopled by yet more drag queens and numerous other bizarre presentations, from what looked like a Mexican mariachi band to a wolfman in a red dress. There was also a flatbed truck with a pick-up band playing horrible chicken-wire versions of Sabbath songs. The scene, mildly amusing in a cringe-worthy way, was picked up by local TV news crews and brief clips made the evening news in several states. When the band, still back in Birmingham, were later shown pictures, they were aghast. 'I thought, "How stupid",' said Geezer. 'It just seemed bizarre to me. Ridiculous.' Ozzy took it more seriously. 'I remember going, "That can't be for us, man." But it was the Black Sabbath Parade and it was held on this certain fucking astrological day or something. I mean, I got scared, I wouldn't go out my room for fucking weeks. It was like cockroaches and pizza for fucking six months!'

Tony Iommi had more serious things on his mind, though. With the band forced off the road while the US dates were being rearranged, he looked on with astonishment as their new single in Britain, 'Paranoid', suddenly began to rocket up the charts. Recorded over five days in June, back at Regent Sound with Rodger Bain again behind glass in the control booth, the plan had been to release the second Sabbath album after the band had returned from America in September. Releasing the single on 29 August, more in hope than expectation, Vertigo were as astonished as the band when it rose to No. 4. Suddenly things were moving fast again. But while the rest of the band were simply happy to be on *Top Of The Pops*, then Britain's most popular weekly music TV show – 'Your single's pissing up the charts!' Geezer was amazed to be told by the show's famous presenter, Jimmy Savile – Tony Iommi was already looking to the future, and especially susceptible to the approaches now being made to him by the newly formed management team of Patrick Meehan and Wilf Pine. Along with Patrick's eager-to-succeed son, Patrick Junior, who would quickly assume the day-to-day control of the band, and under the company name World Wide Artists – chosen, specifically, it seemed, to make Jim Simpson's operation seem even more parochial and small-time – initially Tony reacted cautiously to the phone calls he began to be bombarded with. His attitude quickly changed, though, when presented by Simpson with a list of tour dates for September that included such dives as the Spa Hall, Bridlington, and the Greyhound club in Croydon. With the second Sabbath album due for release in Britain the same month, Tony felt the band should be aiming higher. The boys from World Wide Artists agreed, promising to rectify the situation the minute the band signed a management contract with them. Exactly two weeks before their second album was released, Jim Simpson received a lawyer's letter informing him that he no longer represented Black

Sabbath, nor was he allowed to contact them directly any more. An old hand at the 'music biz game' as he calls it, he was nevertheless devastated by the news. 'What really got me, the letter said they were leaving because I hadn't been doing my job right. Yet when they left me they had an album in the charts in Britain and America, and a single in the UK Top 5. And I hadn't been doing my job right?'

Jim wasn't the only one put out by this latest development. When Don Arden – still trying to make his own backdoor move on the group via their mutual friend Carl Wayne, formerly of Brum favourites The Vikings, latterly of the Arden-affiliated The Move – found out it was two of his own recent employees that had plotted behind his back to snap Sabbath up, he was furious. Issuing threats of retribution to both Meehans, senior and junior, he also offered financial assistance to Simpson, whom he encouraged to sue for damages. With Don's backing, Jim did exactly that, but the outcome was unnecessarily protracted, and resulted after several years in a meagre court-appointed award of £35,000. Jim shakes his head and sighs. '£8000 was paid to us on the day – of which Legal Aid took £6000, [my lawyer] took £1000 and I took £1000. It took fourteen years to get the balance. I did what I could [but] it costs money to enforce a judgment.'

By the time the matter was finally settled Black Sabbath had broken with Ozzy over five years before, and their career as a top-selling act was considered all but over. Nevertheless, Jim says he feels no lingering bitterness against the four young 'chancers' he helped when they needed it most. 'I liked Ozzy and I still do. He's very honest, very loyal, very straightforward, and he was the one who didn't want to leave me when the push came. I've got a lot of time for Ozzy, I've seen him a couple of times and he's been absolutely great. I've encountered Tony a couple of times and it's been very formal but friendly. We've both been very dignified, polite and pleasant to each other – there's no need to be anything else after all these years. I bumped into Geezer at House Of Fraser in Birmingham and he scuttled away. And I haven't seen Bill.'

Setting a pattern for the way in which they would view all such 'awkward moments', as Tony put it, throughout their career, Black Sabbath simply carried on as though nothing had happened. Yet it was that second album – written and recorded while they were still very much under Jim Simpson's influence – that would become the first stone-cold classic of their career. With one hit album now under their belts, Jim had leaned on Vertigo to provide them with a significant budget for the next album. The result found them moving into Rockfield Studios, in Monmouth, south Wales, for a week of intense rehearsals, with producer Rodger Bain. 'The building we were in was a fairly old barn. The whole of the roof actually did move.' Returning to Regent Sound in London to lay down the basic tracks, they then had the added luxury of taking the bones of the new recordings into Basing Street Studios, Island Records' plush new 16-track facility in Notting Hill Gate – the same studio where Led Zeppelin had just put the finishing touches to what would be their landmark fourth album – in order to complete the overdubs and final mix.

They began with the track that would open side one, and which was originally intended to be the title track of the album, 'War Pigs'. One of the first monsters to emerge fully formed from the primordial swampland of their earliest, 40-minute jams onstage at the Star Club, from which so many of their other earliest classics also acquired a life of their own, 'War Pigs' was staggeringly powerful. At over seven minutes in length, it was also a monumental statement to kick off an album with. 'Like a lot of the tracks on *Paranoid*, it had been around since the first album,' says Geezer. 'But we only recorded them for the second album cos that's all we had time for.' Lyrically, it was a genuine anti-war protest song that spoke directly to a generation of young Americans then facing the draft to Vietnam, with its incendiary lines about bodies burning in bullet-strafed fields, 'As the war machine keeps turning/Death and hatred to mankind/Poisoning their brainwashed minds …' 'The whole "War Pigs" thing came from when we used to play American military bases in Germany,' explained Geezer. 'They were like halfway houses. They used to come from Vietnam and have a couple of weeks at these bases in Germany before they went back to America, you know, just to get back to reality kind of thing. And I used to talk to them and they'd tell me these *horrendous* stories about Vietnam and about all the heroin and how people used to be on drugs just to get away from it all over there because of how horrible it was. And that's where the lyrics for the song "War Pigs" came from.'

Most of the other tracks came from the same murky source. Equally titanic was 'Iron Man', which until they came to record it had laboured for months under the working title 'Iron Bloke', after Ozzy said the slow, clomping riff 'sounded like an iron bloke walking'. But that was to undersell its considerable menace. Destined like so much from the album to become a cornerstone of the Sabbath and Ozzy live show for decades to come, 'Iron Man' came straight from Geezer's sci-fi-obsessed, comic-devouring mind, and, he later claimed, was meant as a warning to mankind about the dangers of letting technology get out of human control, but was more likely the product of a late-night 'loon' smoking weed and fantasising about the interior life of original power-suit wearer Tony Stark. Smoking dope was great for coming up with lyrics, said Geezer. It was just a pity not everyone got the joke. 'As far as I'm concerned all the lyrics we ever wrote were always misinterpreted.' Also in that mould was 'Fairies Wear Boots', a hard-driving riff sweetened by a beautifully baleful melody, that Geezer later claimed was based on an incident in Birmingham when a gang of skinheads attacked the band. A story belied by the final line of the lyric, in which the protagonist goes for help to the doctor only to be told it's too late, he's already gone too far: 'Cos smokin' and trippin' is all that you do.'

More affecting were the truly serious tracks like 'Hand Of Doom', as spikily accurate and gruesome a depiction of heroin addiction as anything penned by Mick Jagger or Lou Reed. 'First it was the bomb/Vietnam napalm/Disillusioning/You push the needle in …' Musically, it is as momentous as 'War Pigs', as long and as explosive, but with even more daring in the way it snakes from deathly slow to bushfire fast, before collapsing back into an electrical blaze of flickering static. Similarly, 'Electric Funeral' could make the hairs on a dead man stand: the robotically de-tached tale of a post-apocalyptic half-world of radiation-smothered beings trying and failing to cling to their humanity. If 'War Pigs' spoke out directly against the American war in Vietnam, 'Electric Funeral' was a message from the grave to all governments of the world: nuclear war was no longer a threat, it was a prophesy.

Ironically, however, the two tracks that most distinguish the second Black Sabbath album from the pipeline glut of other self-consciously heavy rock albums released in 1970 were the two least like the signature heavyweight sound of the band in their earliest, greatest days: 'Paranoid' followed on side one by 'Planet Caravan'. The latter was a shimmering piece of metal-sheened whimsy where 'stars shine like eyes' and 'black night sighs', a surprise showcase for Iommi's jazz guitar touches and even a piano. According to Tony, 'The others were like, "Well, where is that gonna go?" I tried to explain, "Well, it's good to do that, be-cause then it makes the heavier tracks sound [even] heavier." And it gives a bit of strength to the album …' Quite so. The former was the hit that almost never was. 'Paranoid' had been the last track to be recorded for the album, 'a bit of nonsense', said Tony, 'that we were amazed when [Rodger Bain] said let's record it'. The producer later recalled: 'They said, "You're joking. We're just pissing around. We just made it up." I said, "Well that's great, let's do it!"'

Geezer, for one, was dead against it. 'I said to Tony, "It's too much like Zeppelin, we can't do that." I thought it was "Communication Breakdown". I thought it was so much like that we couldn't possibly get away with it. But everybody else just couldn't see it. To me, ["Paranoid"] is like a remake of "Communication Breakdown" and I just didn't want to do it.' Geezer had already looked the other way, he felt, when the second from last track on side two was given over to 'Rat Salad', a short instrumental showcase for Bill Ward that in every respect echoed 'Moby Dick', the equally short and ferociously powerful drum showcase for John Bonham that had been the second from last track on side two of the *Led Zeppelin II* album released earlier that year. 'They were our favourite band by that time. It was *all* we listened to,' said Geezer. 'And I used to know Planty and Bonham from Birmingham, and we were like so glad that they'd finally done something. But that's who we used to get stoned to together, you know, lying down on the floor, smoking our dope and listening to Zeppelin.'

Tony, though, aware of Zeppelin's own nasty habit of 'borrowing' other people's best material, had no such qualms. He was also a friend of both Bonham's and Plant's, becoming especially close to the young tearaway drummer, but barely knew Jimmy Page or John Paul Jones, other than as illustrious names on the London session circuit – an alien world to the socially ill-at-ease guitarist in those days. (Iommi would only become friends with Page long after both their bands' heydays were over.) Recorded in just two takes with Ozzy wailing Geezer's hastily thrown together lyrics – the word 'paranoid' not even mentioned in the song – it not only became Sabbath's first – and only – household-name chart single, it became their anthem in the same way 'Whole Lotta Love' had now become for Zeppelin, or 'All Right Now' had that same summer for Free. So much so, when Warner

Bros. in America objected to the proposed title of the album –
War Pigs, named after what the band felt was the best number on
there – on the same grounds that they had cancelled their first
US tour, fearing blowback this time from record chains sensitive
to anything that referenced the Vietnam war, which had notched
up record casualties in 1969, in a critical or controversial way, the
band chose *Paranoid* instead.

According to Tony, 'I don't think any of us even knew what
"paranoid" really meant. But it was a word you heard a lot then,
and it kind of summed up the time in other ways too.' It was too
late to change the album sleeve – a bafflingly blurred figure in
a pink leotard wielding a shield and sword, meant to represent
a 'war pig' – but they were rewarded with their first British No.
1 album. Released on the same day news broke of the death of
Jimi Hendrix, once again Black Sabbath were denied the same
acreage of newsprint from the music papers that Led Zeppelin,
who they now saw as their nearest rivals, were granted when their
second album also became their first No. 1 earlier that year. As
Rob Partridge noted in *Record Mirror*, 'The Black Sabbath album
Paranoid slipped into your record shops a couple of weeks ago.
No ballyhoo. The release was as quiet as it was for their debut
album earlier in the year.' 'We never got any good press, not even
when we went to Number One,' lamented Ozzy. 'We thought,
well, if they ain't gonna come round after that, they never will.
And they didn't . . .'

Indeed, it was now that the name Black Sabbath became synonymous among the so-called serious rock press for everything
they considered 'wrong' about the latest generation of heavy-duty
British rock bands, including Led Zeppelin, who would hide their
hurt by simply refusing to co-operate any further with the music
press. 'I think Zeppelin were glad we were around,' mused Tony,
'cos we got the brunt of it.' The same week the *Paranoid* album
was released in Britain, *Rolling Stone* in America ran its belated

review of *Black Sabbath*. Written by fabled rock writer Lester Bangs – who, conversely, would later eulogise the band for the same 'elemental virtues' he scolded them for here – it summed up the prevailing view, describing the album as 'a shuck – despite the murky song titles and some inane lyrics that sound like Vanilla Fudge paying doggerel tribute to Aleister Crowley, the album has nothing to do with spiritualism, the occult, or anything much except stiff recitations of Cream clichés that sound like the musicians learned them out of a book, grinding on and on', before delivering the coup de grâce: 'Just like Cream! But worse.'

It would be their first and last review in *Rolling Stone*, who pointedly refused to even acknowledge them, except in jest, for years.

But if the band didn't feel much like stars at the time – Geezer remembers walking from their hotel in Shepherd's Bush to the BBC studios down the road when they did *Top Of The Pops* and being astounded to see Engelbert Humperdinck pull up in a chauffeur-driven Rolls-Royce. Also appearing on the show were Cliff Richard and Cilla Black. 'I always remember, I got Cilla Black's autograph,' he laughingly told me – things began to change when they finally touched down in America for the first time the last week of October 1970. With their new management structure in place, and Joe Smith at Warner Bros. insisting that all posters and advertising for the dates bear the promise: 'Louder Than Led Zeppelin', they began with two warm-up shows at Glassboro State College in New Jersey and the University of Miami in Florida, opening for Canned Heat. Few people at either show were familiar with the *Black Sabbath* album, even less with the five numbers they performed from *Paranoid*. But the following night – Monday, 1 November 1970 – they flew into Staten Island for a massively important showcase gig before Joe Smith and the rest of the Warner Bros. top brass at Ungano's Ritz Theater. It was not a good gig.

Ungano's was 'the smallest place I've ever played in me life', complained Geezer. A small, rundown basement club, miles from New York, 'It was the biggest shit-hole you've ever seen,' remembered Tony. 'I thought, fucking hell, this is America? A little farty club! A piss-hole downstairs! This is it?' It was too late to turn back now though and, despite a succession of power failures mid-set – 'Our roadies knew nothing about the difference between English and American electrical systems,' Ozzy recalled – the band got through the set and just hoped they hadn't blown it. Afterwards, though, news of Britain's latest heavy rock sensations began to spread. Sabbath may not have had the backing of the print media behind them, but they had the full support of an even bigger network in America, as word of mouth passed among the groupies and the hard-core fans. Suddenly they could do no wrong. 'Zeppelin had already been there and kind of opened up the gates for us,' said Geezer. 'But it was like they'd just never seen anything like us before. They just went mental!' Several more high-profile shows were hurriedly added to the itinerary. On 10 November, they opened for the Faces at the Fillmore East, where, according to Tony, they went down so well the headliners 'got bottled off! When we went on the crowd went absolutely mental! Then Rod Stewart came on and they began throwing things at him. It was just incredible. And from then on, we became like *the* underground band in America.'

Between 11 and 15 November, they completed a five-night residency (doing two sets a night) opening for Alice Cooper at the Whisky A Go Go in LA. They followed that with four nights at the Fillmore West, in San Francisco, opening for the James Gang. By the time they'd reached Detroit, on 25 November, however, they were now able to headline two shows of their own, at the East Town Theater, supported by Savoy Brown and Quatermass.

This, according to Bill, was 'the turning point' in America. Taken aback at the lack of reaction to the opening of the set, Ozzy began swearing at them. Then Bill lost his temper and threw part of his drum-kit into the audience, then walked off. The rest of the band followed him sheepishly. 'And it caused a rumble across the audience, you know? They were going, "What the fuck is going on here?" Anyway, after a little while we returned to the stage, just stormed into the audience again, very loud and gradually the whole thing turned around. By the time we finished playing our set, we went back and did seven encores that night. News of the East Town Theater gig just spread like wildfire across America. The next time we were there we were playing arenas.' The tour ended on 27 November, when they headlined again, this time at a club in New Jersey called the Sunshine, supported by local band Steel Mill, fronted by a young Bruce Springsteen.

The *Paranoid* album was duly released in the US on 1 January 1972. Already a No. 1 album in the UK, it quickly became Sabbath's first Top 20 American hit, reaching No. 12. Within weeks they were back for their second tour, kicking off on 19 and 20 February with two sold-out headline shows at the Fillmore East. Two nights later they headlined the massive Forum arena, in LA, with Grand Funk Railroad supporting. By now the name Black Sabbath had become synonymous with something new and important, though still decidedly distasteful to mainstream media like *Rolling Stone*. The band affected not to notice. They had too much else going on. 'I didn't know the prestige of places like the Forum,' Bill admitted. 'I just thought, here we go, this is a nice gig ...' For Ozzy, America was a vast adventure playground where he half expected to see Machine Gun Kelly walking down the street. 'I remember when I eventually got on a plane to go to America, we flew on our very first flight with Stevie Winwood and Traffic, and it was like, whoa! I thought all big rock stars flew on the same plane. I thought it was the Rock Star Express, you know? And then I remember flying for about six hours and thinking, "Fucking hell, this thing's gotta stop for gas soon!" I was amazed that thing could fly that long without stopping for petrol. I remember coming out the airport, and it was a warm evening, very humid. And this airport limousine drove past with about twelve doors on, a big yellow thing. And we went, "Fuck me, man, the cars are big here!"'

America was also the place where, despite his impending marriage to Thelma, 'I had my first experience of silicone tits.' They were back in New York in February 1971 for two headline shows at the Fillmore East, supported by the J. Geils Band. 'We went to the hotel, a shit-hole of a place on 8th and 48th Street. But it was the first time we had single rooms. And the manager had got a load of these slags around the room and they were fucking Dobermans, I swear to God. But we took 'em inside and banged 'em. I remember knocking on the adjoining door to Tony's room and going, "Fucking hell, Tony, you want to see this fucking thing I've got in bed, it looks like the 3.30 winner from Kelso",' he guffawed, referring to one of Britain's most famous horseracing tracks. 'Tony said, "You think that's bad, look at the fucking thing in my room!" And they all had these giant tits! But that was it then, we were off. We were like, rape and pillage wherever we went.'

Later, Ozzy would joke: 'Other bands' roadies got better-looking groupies than we did. They would be so bad you'd have to put a bag over their heads. The really bad ones we called Two-Baggers. One bag for her head, to stop you seeing what you were doing, and one bag for your head – in case anyone came in, so they wouldn't know it was you.' But that was just part of his well-developed clown act, to put Thelma and the other wives off the scent. 'I mean, the whole thing in England in them days, if you wanted to fuck a chick you'd wine her and dine her and you'd take her to the pictures and maybe fucking three weeks later you'd pop the question. Forget it, baby, they ain't got the time for that in America. It's like, the chicks would walk up to you and go, "I wanna ball you" and I'd think, "What the fuck does that mean?" Like a dummy, I'd go, "Oh, yeah, so do I." I didn't realise what it meant. It meant they wanted to fuck you. And the chicks would come out of nowhere and say that to you!'

Over 25 dates that would end with them headlining the Spectrum Theater in Philadelphia on 2 April, supported by Humble Pie and Mountain, for Bill 'everything about that second American tour was mind-blowing and that was when I realised we were involved in something big.' Things only became more so when they got to LA and found themselves booked to headline two nights at the 15,000-seater Inglewood Forum. 'We were just taken away with the whole thing,' said Tony. 'I don't think we probably grasped exactly what we were doing. It just seemed to be happening around us so quick and we didn't know what was really going on. We didn't realise how big and how powerful we were becoming. We were just out there playing, you know?'

There was also the band's 'occult' image to live up to. As Tony put it: 'We attracted unbelievable amounts of nutters from Satanists to acid casualties – you name it, we had 'em.' Ozzy frowned: 'I got scared. You'd get people walk up and go, "Man, we know that you know that we know that you know." And we'd go, "Yeah, well, keep on knowing, man." There was every Satanist you could ever imagine, every Jesus freak ...' These were the days before laminated passes, when almost anybody could wander backstage or into a band's hotel at night. At first the band found it funny. Tony laughingly recalled one gig on the tour where 'we had three women turn up all in black, and they were at the front. And apparently they were witches, or we were told they were witches. And when we went onstage in crosses, they all ran out! So we never saw them again ...'

At another show on the tour, they received a visit from the head of the American Hell's Angels 'I can't remember where it was,' said Geezer, 'but it was like the pissing President of the United States coming into the gig. About fifty bodyguards came in, all these bikers. Straight into the dressing room, throws all the security out – they're all going, "Yes, sir, no, sir." Then he told us who he was, says I'm from whatever chapter of the Hell's Angels and I give you my approval. And you'll be all right wherever you go – whatever that was supposed to mean. And that was it. I mean, it's like a dream now. They stayed and watched the show and then they went, all in a big cavalcade.' He chuckled nervously. 'I think it was just their way of saying, "American Hell's Angels like Black Sabbath – official."'

America was also the place where 'we discovered the old waffle-dust'. They all have different memories of how it began, but the result was the same, to a greater or lesser extent in each case: almost instant addiction. According to Tony, the first time he did coke was before a show at Madison Square Garden later in 1971. 'Somebody said to me – one of the crew I think it was at that time – "Would you like a little something for the gig?", you know? And I'd never had it but he was like, "Oh man, just try one, it'll perk you up and help you concentrate" and all that stuff. Anyway, I was like, ah, no. But he was like "Go on, go on!" So I did, and I went onstage and I convinced myself it was fucking brilliant, you know? So ever since that it was like, "Let's try one of them again at the next gig", and then another one and it sort of went on from there, you know?' For Bill, it had happened during those two nights in LA. 'Ozzy and myself were probably the worst offenders of drug abuse. I discovered cocaine the night we played the Forum. I immediately took to the drug. I'd been using speed, like pills and stuff like that, since I was about sixteen. And I'd been smoking marijuana since I was about sixteen. But the real hard-line narcotics came in once we got to America in 1971.' Ozzy maintained he first got into cocaine a few nights after the Forum shows, after being turned on when the band opened for Mountain at the Denver Coliseum. 'It was Leslie West, the guitar player from Mountain. He gave us this big rock and I went, "Ah, no. Is that coke? I don't wanna touch it. Apart from pot and beer, I don't wanna touch it." But then he says, "Try one." So I did and it was like ...' He sniffed loudly ... 'and ding! "Oh, it's not so bad ..." And I hopped all through the night!' Bill sighed. 'Ozzy and I, we got into a lot of trouble. We would get pretty bent out of shape.' They would stay that way for years to come. 'Once we discovered the wonderful white powder,' said Ozzy, 'we never looked back again.'

Not until it was too late.

FOUR
POPE ON A ROPE

The next three years flew by in a blizzard of dope, cocaine, booze, sex and the best music anybody in Black Sabbath would ever make. The music they have been living off ever since. They also made money – multimillions of dollars – but none of them would ever see much of that. Not until long after their best days were behind them and the name Black Sabbath lived on only in the fumes of its shattered past. Returning from America, in April 1971, as bona-fide rock stars, blinded with success, satiated in sex and drugs and the unnerving adulation of a generation of post-war baby boomers, the only thing the four Sabbath members were now intent on was doing it all again. Only better, if that was possible. For a while, it appeared it might be.

Work on the third Sabbath album, *Master Of Reality*, had begun back at Basing Street Studios in early February, again with Rodger Bain at the controls. But the band no longer had a backlog of material to draw from their club days. What they had instead was the enormous confidence two international hit albums give you. In Britain, where they completed their first headline tour of major venues, in January, they had even had a Top 5 single and were recognised as a force of nature even by those who only knew the name, or had just seen them on the telly. 'I felt like I was involved in something very big now,' said Bill. 'I had accepted the fact that we were making hit records and that we were playing to audiences that were about as big as one can get. And yes, for me it went really quickly. From the first record, we were out on the road for about three years solid.'

At the end of January they had headlined the Myponga festival in Adelaide, Australia. Staged in the hills just outside the small dairy-farming town from which it took its name, Myponga was Australia's first major outdoor rock festival and billed as 'the Australian Woodstock'. Sabbath headlined over a bill of largely domestic stars like Daddy Cool, Billy Thorpe & The Aztecs, and a young heavily bearded roots rock outfit named Fraternity, fronted by future AC/DC singer Bon Scott, whom Ozzy would later befriend. According to a review in the local *Sunday Mail*, Sabbath's appearance was marked by what it characterised as 'Ten thousand heavy rock fans … settled firmly in their garbage-strewn pop paddock for a night of love, peace, banshee rock music and booze, booze and more booze.' Adding, 'There are about 2500 girls at the festival and there does not seem to be a bra between them.' Not that that prevented Ozzy, who was developing a habit for always seeing the shite side of life, from complaining when he got back: 'We flew in, wrecked the hotel, drove four cars into the ocean.' What not even Ozzy knew was that Tony Iommi and Patrick Meehan Junior were in the next room trying for a threesome with one of the dozens of female fans that had turned up after Tony had complained he was 'lonely' during a local radio interview. When the girl passed out Meehan freaked out. 'She's dead!' High as a kite, Tony joined in. 'Christ, she's dead. She's dead! We got to get rid of her!' They would throw her off the balcony and say she had fallen, he told the panicking guitarist. They were still trying to drag her inert body to the window when she awoke. 'We could quite easily have just tossed her off there and I would have become a 22-year-old murderer,' he later recalled. He was stone cold sober as the band took the stage that night. Not so Ozzy, though, who could barely remember the show the next day, he said. Just that on the flight back to London, when the plane stopped off at Perth to refuel, Ozzy had sat on a wall outside for half an hour, where 'I got sunburnt like a son of a bitch. Then I had to sit for thirty-six fucking hours in one of the old 727s in economy, fucking frying.' As usual, the others just laughed at him. Then went back to whatever Tony said they should be doing.

Arriving at Basing Street the next day bereft of finished material but bursting with ideas for 'weird' new riffs, Tony Iommi began by making things easier for himself. A star now, he began to mould the Sabbath sound even more in his own stone-faced, monosyllabic image. Endless nights on the road over the past year had left his shattered fingertips in almost constant pain. He now down-tuned his already murky-sounding guitar a further three semi-tones, reducing string tension and making it easier for him to bend the notes of his mongrel one-string riffs. With Geezer also forced to down-tune his bass to match Tony's guitar, the Sabbath sound took a dramatic new plunge into even greater darkness. Bereft even of reverb, leaving the sound as dry as old bones dug up from some desert burial plot, the finished music's brutish force would so alarm the critics they punished Sabbath in print for being blatantly thuggish, purposefully mindless, creepy and obnoxious. Twenty years later groups like Smashing Pumpkins, Soundgarden and, in particular, Nirvana, would excavate the same heaving-lung sound to delineate their own scorched-earth policy to a music scene even more elaborately formulaic than the heavy rock scene of the early Seventies – and be rewarded with critical garlands, heralding a whole new genre they called 'grunge'. In 1971, however, Sabbath and their new, planet-heavy sound were simply dismissed as dimwitted, offensive, beyond redemption.

For the band, though, these were groundbreaking musical times. It became a signature component of Iommi's oeuvre, the ability to incorporate more neat riffs and sudden, unexpected time-changes in one song than most bands would contemplate on an entire album. Mostly, it developed from a combination of influences, from his early love of jazz, to being forced to develop long, extended solos to fill in the gaps in those interminable mind-altering Star Club shows. And, of course, things were just going there anyway – the extended, 'free form jam' – from Hendrix and Cream to Zeppelin and Pink Floyd, and back again in more self-consciously virtuoso form to Deep Purple, Yes, and musically gargantuan dragon slayers like Vanilla Fudge and Iron Butterfly. None though, including Jimmy Page, his nearest musical neighbour then, struck out quite as deliberately, some might say perversely, in the direction of multi-riff darkness as Tony Iommi. Years later, when relations between the two were at their lowest ebb, Ozzy still referred to his former guitar-master as King Riff.

For Tony, though, there was really no other choice than to play like that. 'It was something that just seemed to knit into place for us. It seemed to be an easy thing to do for us, to change tempo right in the middle of something. Where most people would go, "That's not gonna work, you can't *do* that!" We'd make it work. It just seemed the natural thing for us to do that. It became a regular thing – right, up-tempo, or change it into a different riff – and we'd make it work. Sometimes we'd do it more with jamming, other times I'd do stuff at home. I think around about the third album I started doing things at home. Because I'd need to try and get something ready I could play to the others for when we went into rehearsals. Instead of waiting and everybody looking at you going, "All right then, what you gonna come up with?" Which often happened, you know?' Once the riff had been nailed down though, the rest was down to chemistry. 'Everyone was as important as each other – it made that sound. Geezer's sound, the way he played, the style, matched my sound and style perfectly. And Bill's playing as well. He was such an unorthodox player, yet it all gelled. And then the way Ozzy would put it over with his unusual voice and stuff, I mean, it just really gelled together. It really made that thing happen.

Finishing off the album in early April, just days after their show at the Philadelphia Spectrum, and with both *Paranoid* and *Black Sabbath* on their way to gold status in the US for a combined sale of over a million copies, for the moment Sabbath were no longer trying to second-guess the critics nor please their managers and record company executives. They simply went for it. The result was another future classic. From the stoned persistent cough that erupts into the yawning, spastic riff of 'Sweet Leaf', on side one, to the finale of side two with the jolting electric shock ending of 'Into The Void', the album spinning off into echo-heavy obliteration, though it never quite reaches the heights of its astonishing predecessor, *Master Of Reality* joined the first two Sabbath albums in setting the template for every determinedly heavy rock outfit that has tried to follow them.

The rest of the album was laden with similarly unapologetic metal-brained monsters. Tracks like the romping, sneering 'After Forever', with its for the time shocking lines of religious irrev-erence, written straight from the heart of the unreconstructed Catholic schoolboy, Geezer: 'Would you like to see the Pope/On the end of a rope/Do you think he's a fool?' And another time-less musical headstone in 'Children Of The Grave', a glimmer of hope in a world where the odds are impossibly stacked against you, with a final warning to those 'children of today' to be brave enough to spread love, lest they become 'children of the grave ...'. The rattling, machine-like sound that accompanies such homi-lies, and Ozzy's almost monotone white-light delivery, meant Sabbath would compare unfavourably to the new back-to-the-garden sensibility of 1971 and new critics' darlings like Joni Mitchell, Crosby, Stills and Nash, The Band and James Taylor, to name the most prominent, next to whom Black Sabbath sounded positively oafish, unschooled and ultimately unwelcome. Not even when Tony Iommi insisted on including such detour moments as 'Embryo', a weird medieval-sounding instrumental, Tony plucking with his leather fingertips at a tune as old as time before ascending into the heads-banged-together riff of 'Children Of The Grave'. Or 'Orchid', another of Tony's 'Greensleeves' instrumentals, its chestnuts-on-the-fire ambience allowing rare breathing space before the plodding, cloven-hoofed 'Lord Of This World' roars into life, Ozzy decrying the 'evil possessor' who becomes 'your confessor' for choosing 'evil ways' instead of love. That word again.

Even Led Zeppelin, still being scolded as equally derivative heavy metal dogs of war, were considered cultured and not without charm compared to Black Sabbath. It became one of the reasons why, just five years later when the new wave of punk rockers broke out of Britain like a sudden rash, one of the very few 'old wave' rock bands that lived on in the imaginations of people like Johnny Rotten and Rat Scabies was Black Sabbath. Even with tracks like 'Solitude' – this album's 'Planet Caravan', all burnt-offering melody and speed comedown vocal – there was nothing flowery or hippy-dippy about the Sabbs, not to their fans at the time, nor to the take-no-prisoners punks that soon followed, sparing Sabbath the eager evisceration dished out to their one-time contemporaries. When Sabbath sang of the efficaciousness of pot, as on 'Sweet Leaf', they didn't summon up beautiful worlds full of flower children, but visions of life on the dole where the only escape was through a cloud of cheap dope. 'My life was empty, always on a down,' Ozzy bellows, 'until you took me, showed me around ...'. If The Beatles had set the benchmark for mind-expansive pop music, Sabbath now did the same for rock's underclass, creating an utterly uncompromising sound, which, when examined closely, featured bleak, heavy-duty lyrics that reflected the band's genuine 'no future', working-class roots. Not that it looked like that from inside the eye of the storm. 'Our music, it felt totally natural to me,' shrugged Bill. 'I wasn't conscious that there was any image taking shape. I think that was naiveté on my part, and possibly everybody else's part, too. But in the early days, the writing was so natural and almost instant, so it felt completely good and wholesome to me. It just felt like, yeah, this is great.'

Keeping with the habit of their first two albums, Warner Bros. issued the US version of *Master Of Reality* with an unnecessarily elongated track listing, turning its eight tracks into twelve by giving the intros to 'After Forever' and 'Lord Of The World' their own titles (respectively, 'The Elegy' and 'Step Up'), deciding the coda to 'Children Of The Grave' should also have its own title ('The Haunting') and halving 'Into The Void' into two segments, the first part titled 'Deathmask'. Not so much gilding the lily as ladling on the cheese, while it satisfied Joe Smith's desire to try and make Sabbath's albums more attractive to radio, it also had the knock-on effect of making them appear more two-dimensional, as though sci-fi and comic-horror was the best they aspired to. Given that the Seventies were the heyday of FM radio in America, which specialised in playing long album tracks, it did nothing to service the band's underground credibility. Early US pressings also bore the hallmark of injudicious planning when the title appeared in the plural as *Masters Of Reality*. The mistake was soon spotted and those pressings withdrawn from circulation. But it only further fostered a perception of Black Sabbath that would persist throughout their career: that they were the runt of an unholy triumvirate of British heavy rock goliaths, always placed last behind Led Zeppelin and Deep Purple.

Even the few friends the band did have in the music media now deserted them, in the wake of their astonishing success. A charge led by John Peel, whose proclivity for forsaking artists once they had successfully infiltrated the mainstream would later become part of his own legend, but whose sudden about-turns were seen by the artists that he had so recently championed in the early Seventies – Marc Bolan and T. Rex had been the first, Black Sabbath were now the latest – as inexplicable betrayals. 'We got on really well with John to begin with but something seems to have upset him,' Tony told *Record Mirror* in 1971. 'It's very difficult to say what gets into these people.' In fact, Peel was expressing a common bias held by most self-styled tastemakers at the time for albums over singles. By having a huge hit with the 'Paranoid' single, Sabbath had compounded their earlier error of becoming famous without any support whatsoever from the British music press – they had committed the ultimate hate-crime of having a hit single. Instead of being something to celebrate, as it would become with the advent of MTV in the 1980s, a decade earlier Tony Iommi found himself having to defend the band against their hit. 'The single was just one track taken from the album by the recording company because they thought it would sell and was representative of something we did,' he protested in *Record Mirror*. 'We don't specifically record singles and the decision to release them rests with the record company.'

The band told themselves it didn't matter. But when *Master Of Reality* was released in Britain in July – purposefully without the benefit of a single to precede it – and only reached No. 5, they began to seriously wonder. In America critical opinion was now split between the guardians of rock-as-poetry-and-art, exemplified by the Mount Rushmore of American music critics, Robert Cristgau, who described the album in *The Village Voice* as 'dull and decadent ... a dimwitted, amoral exploitation', and more street-level rock writers like Metal Mike Stone, who reviewed the album for the short-lived but ultra-hip San Francisco underground magazine *Rags*, concluding, 'If you've ever liked crude rock and roll noise, whether the early Kinks and Who or the Velvet Underground or the Stooges, there is definitely something going on here worth listening to.' But press reviews counted less in America than radio and radio counted less than the true gold standard for heavy rock royalty in the early Seventies: word of mouth. At the time *Master Of Reality* was released in America, in September 1971, Black Sabbath had better word of mouth than anybody except Led Zeppelin, and the album shot into the Top 10, spinning like a plate on a pole at No. 8 for several weeks – the highest chart placing any of their albums would achieve there.

The third Sabbath American tour had begun on 2 July 1971, with a massive outdoor show at the Michigan State Fairgrounds in Detroit. With the album pronounced gold on pre-release orders alone, this was their longest US tour yet: 57 shows supported by, variously, Yes, Humble Pie, Poco and Black Oak Arkansas. The only band they opened for now was Led Zeppelin, whom they played with on the same bill at the Onondaga War Memorial Auditorium in Syracuse on 10 September, and again the following night in Rochester, at the Community War Memorial Auditorium. As a result, *Master Of Reality* became their biggest US chart hit yet. Indeed, all three Sabbath albums were on the charts at the same time throughout the US tour that year. At the urging of Patrick Meehan, they again emulated Led Zeppelin, who made a point of not co-operating with the press, refusing interviews, and Tony and the band decided the press could now go fuck themselves. When *Rolling Stone* finally deigned to interview them, for a piece published in October 1971, the band simply sent them up. In it, Geezer claimed to be the seventh son of a seventh son, with the ability to see the Devil, while Ozzy predicted he would be the first member of the band to die. 'It'll be me, definitely,' he insisted. 'I'll die before I'm forty, I know I will ...'

Meanwhile, back on the road, things just kept getting freakier. At an after-show party in LA, legendary producer Kim Fowley told Ozzy he should go to Mexico and buy a corpse, then take it onstage and stab it. Even the audience was now becoming out of control. As a wide-eyed Ozzy told a reporter from *Creem*, 'One concert in America, after the show, on the floor there was about a thousand fucking syringes! I was amazed, I felt sick, I really felt ill to think I had just performed to people that were that one step nearer to the hole ...' Sick or not, they had begun to take the weirdness for granted. 'We got all sorts of letters, all sorts of things in blood. You name it, we had it.' When they arrived in Memphis and discovered someone had drawn a large cross in fresh blood across their dressing room door and nailed it shut, they simply kicked it open and ordered a roadie to scrub it down. 'We got so used to it,' shrugged Tony, 'we didn't know it was blood at first, we thought it was paint.'

When the tour finally ended on 28 October, they had two weeks off before the start of a 30-date UK and European tour that would carry them right through Christmas and the New Year. But by now serious cracks were starting to appear and the first 12 dates were cancelled when it was reported that three of the band – Tony, Geezer and Bill – had become 'ill'. A press release was issued to the effect that the band were suffering from 'nervous exhaustion', with Geezer's gallstones given special mention. But as Bill Ward would later tell me, 'It was partying for us, definitely. It was just like getting loaded and having a good time. We were just getting high, having a party, you know, partying twenty-four hours a day, actually.' In that respect, said Bill, 'The *Master Of Reality* album was a turning point.'

Any thoughts that Christmas back home in Birmingham might have helped them recuperate though were swiftly dispelled once they were let off the reins, parading around at old stomping grounds like Henry's and Mothers like the conquering heroes everybody now saw them as. Five days after the rescheduled British tour finished at a packed St George's Hall in Bradford, in February 1972, they began another US tour: 31 shows in just 33 days that would leave them clinging to their sanity like ship-wrecked passengers to a life raft.

'In America, we were just out of our minds!' Ozzy cried. 'We wouldn't sleep for fucking days! Me and Bill were the worst, we were like the Drug Commandos – never come through the door where a plate-glass window will do!' Setting fire to Bill became another on-tour pastime. 'We'd wait for him to pass out and put lit matches between his fingers and toes.' Too drunk and stoned to care, Bill never batted an eye. When they set fire to his beard he merely inhaled the fumes and proclaimed it 'good stuff'. Tony went too far one night though when he squirted lighter fuel over Bill's legs before setting fire to them. Bill couldn't put out the flames and ended up being rushed to hospital. 'We thought, oh fuck, we've gone too far this time,' chuckled Tony. 'But no, he was more worried that we'd ruined his new jeans.' Ozzy nodded. 'As long as he had his cider and his drugs, Bill was all right. He was such an easy-going bloke, always surrounded by liggers. At one point it got so crowded with liggers at Bill's house [in England] he moved into the garden shed with a little night watchman's fire. I remember once asking him if he'd brought all his luggage to the airport, and he said, "Yeah!" and held up four flagons of cider! That was Bill ...'

When the band stayed at the Edgewater Inn, in Seattle – famous for being built on stilts by the water's edge, making it an ideal spot for fishing from your hotel room window, and scene of the now infamous Led Zeppelin shark episode, as related by countless scribes and, most famously, Frank Zappa, on his 1971 *Live At Fillmore East* album, on the track 'The Mud Shark' – where Zeppelin drummer John Bonham and tour manager Richard Cole had reputedly tied-up a willing groupie and forced the snout of a dead shark into her vagina, Ozzy took the shark he caught and simply put it into his bathtub, then filled it with water. When, unsurprisingly, he returned after the show to find the shark dead, he began disembowelling it with a knife, leaving blood and fish entrails all over the walls. Tony, meanwhile, who had also caught a shark, managed to hurl it through Bill's hotel room window, where it landed on the bed. 'He was very surprised,' Tony deadpanned. 'Not pleasantly ...'

The band were given a long weekend 'off' at the end of the US tour, a three-day gap before flying to Japan for two shows back-to-back at the same venue, the Koseinenkin concert hall, in Osaka, where Deep Purple would make their Japanese debut just three months later, taping the shows for release as the *Made In Japan* double album. Sabbath could have beaten Purple to it. Except that they were denied entry visas, because of their various criminal convictions: Ozzy for theft. Tony and Bill for dope. The same problem would occur the following year, before a frustrated Patrick Meehan was able to persuade Warner Bros. in Tokyo to hire lawyers influential enough to arrange temporary waivers for the band. In fact, the break worked in their favour. Sabbath were now in pieces, heads awhirl, bones creaking: fucked. The Japanese shows were cancelled, as were dates in Australia, while the band flew back to London, and then on home via chauffeur-driven limos to Birmingham. Geezer had been the first to crack, complaining of terminal tiredness, as one show blurred into another. 'The trouble was in them days it wasn't, oh, have a few weeks off until you feel better,' he would moan. 'It was, "Here, have a line of this or a smoke of that. Take these pills, they'll keep you going." It wasn't about getting better, it was just about keeping going on the road. Until suddenly one day I knew I'd had enough – and just had to stop. The others weren't happy but there was nothing I could do. I thought, I'm cracking up here, you know?'

When Bill was diagnosed with serum hepatitis, they knew they were in trouble. 'We were still only about twenty-two, twenty-three years old,' Bill told me, 'but we were already pretty much veterans, you know? Then I got hepatitis, and I came pretty close to dying. The alcohol level in my body was that bad I was jaundiced for about three months. I was on my way out ...' Hepatitis B, as it's also known, is not an infection that can be contracted from casual acquaintance, but a serious virus almost always caused by using infected syringes – or 'dirty needles' in the vernacular – to inject drugs. Or as Bill put it in an interview for BBC Birmingham Radio in July 2011, 'I got serum hepatitis from narcotic abuse and alcohol abuse.' Until then, he said, 'I thought I was invincible ... I didn't feel so invincible after that.' Despite doctors' warnings, though, as soon as the jaundice subsided, he went straight back into doing what he was doing. It was 1972 and that was simply 'what you did'. He paused, grimaced and added, 'I'm pretty lucky to be alive, to be honest.'

Within weeks, however, Black Sabbath were back at work on their next album. Or rather, Tony was. For the first time, they were al- lowed to take their time coming up with material. Rehearsal time was booked locally and for the first time since Tony had returned from Jethro Tull, laying down the law about coming in on time and getting down to serious work, the band were expected to give serious attention to what they were doing. No more albums re- corded on the run, between tours. This was the big time, they had a lot to live up to suddenly, and like Zeppelin's momentous fourth album, released six months before, a great deal was expected of Sabbath's next album. There was just one snag: a pub situated less than a mile from their Birmingham rehearsal studio. Most days, after a cursory plod through a few 'warm-up' numbers, mostly just loose jams, Tony would be left to work on coming up with some of his trademark riffs while the other left him to it – by strolling down the road to the pub. Hours later they would return and ask him, 'Got anything yet?' Tony began to get the hump. A week into this routine he'd had enough. When Patrick Meehan suggested they record the next album in Los Angeles, partly as a tax avoidance scheme, and partly because studios were cheaper to hire in LA than in London, Tony jumped at the idea. The others dragged themselves away from the pub long enough to follow.

It had now been a year since they had recorded *Master Of Reality* – a lifetime ago in Seventies rock terms, when artists were largely contracted to release two albums a year. But then most rock artists weren't as big as Black Sabbath had now become, still cold-shouldered by critics but increasingly adored by a mistrustful public that had begun to see their exclusion from the mainstream media as a badge of honour. They were also rich – or thought they were. 'As long as we had a few quid in our pockets and a new car to drive around Birmingham and pull a few tarts, that's all it was to us,' recalled Ozzy. 'We never realised the full potential of what we were earning and what the deal was, because our management would always keep us on a [short string].'

Just how short was spelled out for Ozzy when he went to Patrick Meehan and asked for money to buy his first house, an upscale property in Welford-on-Avon then on the market for £15,000. At the time he was living with Thelma in a flat in Birmingham city centre. The couple's first child, a girl they would name Jessica, was due and 'I just wanted to buy a house. I'd never lived in a detached house. So I went to this beautiful village near Stratford, it was this really old Tudor cottage, and I phoned and said, "Patrick, can I have it?" He said, "No, it's too much money." I ended up buying a house a bit further up the road for £20,000. But I didn't know what you made off a fucking record. From having nothing to my first record royalty advance, which was £105, I thought, "Fuck me, man, I've got a hundred quid!" I never ever thought I'd own a hundred quid. Then at the end of the first American tour, which we worked I think it was for two months, two shows a day, he gave us all a cheque for a thousand pounds and we thought, "Hey, baby, we've fucking made it, man!" And we thought that was it, you know? We never thought about what he was getting.'

By 1971, 'The whole thing [had] changed for us,' Tony recalled. Once they'd made it in America, 'We were travelling in private jets everywhere. Any time we wanted anything we would just phone [Meehan] up. "I want to buy a new car." He'd go, "Oh, okay, what car?" In my case a Lamborghini. "Where is it?" I'd tell him where it was. "How much is it?" I'd tell him how much it was. "I'll send them a cheque and I'll arrange to get the car over." And that was it. If I wanted to buy a house. "Where is the house? How much is it?" And I got the house. That's how we lived.'

Geezer was still taking his laundry home for his mum to wash when he passed his driving test – and bought a Rolls-Royce. Or rang Patrick and got him to 'send a cheque'. Bill also bought a Rolls-Royce, filling the back seats with crates of cider. Ozzy, now a husband and father – though mainly by long distance – also moved his young family into a house. The only thing none of them ever really saw was cold, hard cash. There were wages put into a bank account for them all every month, and as Tony says, 'coming from what we came from, a few hundred quid in the bank was brilliant'. Or as Ozzy put it, 'He was taking us to the fucking cleaners, and we never knew.' They were all just glad that 'we were stars and we didn't have to go on the prowl for a bit of in-and-out'.

By June 1972 they were living in Los Angeles, sharing the same Bel Air mansion that quickly became notorious. Rented from John Dupont, millionaire scion of the Dupont family, who owned the multinational Dupont chemicals corporation (one of the key players in America's development of atomic and chemical weapons, an irony entirely lost on Geezer, writer of 'War Pigs' and other anti-nuclear diatribes, who was too busy snorting spoonfuls of coke to care), the house came with an enormous ballroom overlooking a swimming pool, which the band used to jam and work on material in. Meehan also set up office there, along with two French au pair girls, included in the rental agreement. Recording, meanwhile, took place at the nearby Record Plant, one of the first state-of-the-art recording facilities to offer rock musicians the kind of relaxed vibe they worked best in. As such, the Record Plant had lately become the go-to studio for high-decibel rock bands. The perfect environment, Sabbath decided, to produce the album themselves, which they had decided to call simply *Black Sabbath Vol. 4*, another idea inspired in no small way by the fact that Zeppelin refused to give their albums titles (a habit they then broke for their remaining albums). No more Rodger Bain to answer to – or look for help from – this would be all the band's own work, a situation which both contrived to make the sessions the longest the band had spent on an album (over two months eventually) and also the most hectic. What also helped the process along was the enormous quantity of cocaine the band were now getting through.

'We were all fucked-up bad,' Ozzy remembered, 'dealers coming round every day with cocaine, fucking Demerol, morphine, everything coming round the fucking house.' Iommi: 'It became a ritual. Every time we'd do an album we'd get a load of dope and then some coke and whatever else, and off we'd go. I never used to want to leave the studio. That's why we enjoyed making *Vol. 4* so much, because we had the house and it was a great vibe we had. But it did become insane …' The cocaine would be delivered in a sealed box, as large as one of their speaker cabinets, and filled with wax-covered phials of the drug. The wax would be carefully peeled off to reveal the strongest, purest cocaine then available anywhere in America. The band would start to drool with anticipation as huge mounds of the white powder would be carved out on one of the mansion's large dining tables, from which the band would take whatever they wanted, which was a lot. Word soon got around and Sabbath's Bel Air mansion became one of the trendiest places in LA to hang out that summer. Crowds of drug dealers and groupies would gather at the house night and day. There were so many that the band would make the girls queue outside on the lawn. Going to the studio and actually working was 'the downer part' said Geezer. Not for Tony Iommi, though, who now began to spend longer and longer at the studio, as the cocaine nights flitted by like the lights of a train. 'You'd always read about bands like Deep Purple or the Faces going off playing football together but we took our music much more serious than that. Or I did, anyway. Once I got in the studio, that was it, I wasn't coming out again till it was over.'

One night, Ozzy was so stoned he accidentally sat on the button for the alarm, rigged to alert the local police station. As two squad cars drew up and armed officers began banging on the ornate front door, the band freaked out and began trying to flush several ounces of grass and dozens of phials of pharmaceutical cocaine down the mansion's various toilets. 'It was like a mad dash,' Geezer recalled. 'We must have flushed like 10,000 dollars' worth of cocaine [and] grass.' Convinced they were being busted, when finally they got one of the au pairs to answer the door and discovered the cops were simply responding to a false alarm, there was another crazy scramble to see if they could unclog any of the toilets and recover their drugs. It was too late.

Geezer claims it was also at the house in LA that they first experimented with LSD. 'I'd done acid in England but unknowingly; I didn't really know what it was in England. And I hated it, man. Never wanted to do it again. I just had a terrible, really bad experience with it, *really* bad. I almost topped meself. The girlfriend that I had at the time had to literally lie on top of me to stop me from jumping out the window, it was so bad, and killing meself. So I swore I'd never do it again. Then we got to California and we were at this chick's house, this massive place on the beach, in Laguna. And she give us this stuff, psilocybin. I'd never heard of it, didn't know it was another name for acid, and just took it – me and Ozzy and these girls. It was mental. Ozzy went for a swim – at least he thought he was swimming in the ocean but he was still on the beach, flailing away in the sand.' Ozzy shook his head: 'At that time in America, too, people were very fond of lacing your drinks with acid. I didn't care. I used to swallow handfuls of acid tabs at a time. The end of it came when we got back to England. I took ten tabs of acid then went for a walk in a field. I ended up standing there talking to this horse for about an hour. In the end, the horse turned round and told me to fuck off. That was it for me …'

Despite or even because of the mayhem surrounding its genesis, *Vol. 4* became another absolute classic Black Sabbath album. Opening with the eight-minute-plus epic 'Wheels Of Confusion', what jumps out is Iommi's wolverine lead guitar, a lightning leap on from the muggy sound of *Master Of Reality*. Intent on proving the band's critics wrong, desperate to somehow catapult their musical credibility into the same starry stratosphere that Led Zeppelin now inhabited, the emphasis was on versatility, musicianship, craft. Tony sat down to play piano while Geezer operated the mellotron on 'Changes', their most sophisticated ballad yet, and their first fully formed love song. It might have been an American hit single, too, if they had taken the advice of the Warner Bros. radio promotion team, but Tony wasn't far gone enough yet for that. Keeping with their policy of not releasing more than one single per album, they plumped instead for 'Tomorrow's Dream', a stolid mid-tempo rocker that could have been an offcut from *Master Of Reality*, and as such one of the least exceptional tracks on the new album.

Elsewhere though it was first class all the way. With its ferociously funky rhythm and needle-sharp single-string riff, 'Supernaut' was like a white metal version of Isaac Hayes' 'Theme From Shaft', a huge hit the year before, Ozzy's voice like mercury pouring over the silver spoon of the guitars and drums, Geezer's lyrics, which he now claims to remember very little about writing, yielding to the new era of debauchery the band were now fully embarked on, of wanting to 'touch the sun' and the 'need to fly'.

There is not even a guitar solo, just a hail of percussion that takes over halfway through, before finally allowing the twisted riff in again through the back door.

The subject matter – their very inspiration for an album they would not so subtly thank in the sleeve notes with the words: 'We'd like to thank the great COKE-Cola company of Los Angeles' – was addressed even more directly in 'Snowblind', Ozzy balefully singing of his dreams being 'flaked with snow' as the band pounded down on the lumbering rhythm, lashing out the icy riff like a razor blade chopping white lines on a gigantic cracked mirror. Again the melodrama is expanded with the surprise addition of a string quartet over the last minute or so, as Iommi weaves his way through a frenzied guitar solo. Even the lighter moments that Tony always insisted on, as contrast to the frosted darkness of the showstoppers, were somehow more malevolent. Of the two instrumental interludes, the first, 'FX', was simply Tony, fuelled by too much coke and grass, standing naked in the studio control room, distractedly fiddling with his electric guitar, as if sending signals out into space, which is in effect exactly what it was, hence its title. 'He took all his clothes off in the studio,' recalled Geezer, 'and he was hitting on his guitar strings with the crosses that he wore around his neck.' The second, 'Laguna Sunrise', came fully formed from his childhood imagination, a lush acoustic instrumental, almost flamenco in style, accompanied by a soaring, blissfully romantic string section. This was music to watch the Californian sunrise by – but only after you had been up all night getting wasted on the moon and stars first. There was also another hit that never was in the surprisingly short and catchy 'St. Vitus Dance', its irresistible tunefulness belied only by the mercilessly brutal chords Tony punctuates each verse with.

The true voice of *Black Sabbath Vol. 4*, though, was captured on its finale track, 'Under The Sun'. A perfectly executed bookend to 'Wheels Of Confusion', it's another journey track, long, convoluted, and as hard to hold on to as the tail of a great white shark. Moving through three discernible musical sections, it was tracks like 'Under The Sun' that would become the sonic signpost for those bands that would follow Sabbath in the years to come; groups like Iron Maiden and Metallica, whose entire careers could be traced virtually to the last two and a half minutes of 'Under The Sun'; self-important, pained, almost repellent in their insistent magnetism; over-involved and desperately serious; epic right down to its last inglorious nail-hammering chords.

Final mixes for *Vol. 4* took place back in London, but only Tony was there to oversee them. Ozzy had gone back to Thelma and the family in Birmingham, Geezer had retreated to his new pad in the countryside and Bill was, as he put it, 'leading a Sid and Nancy lifestyle', with his latest girlfriend, who travelled back with him from LA, 'living in hotels [and] loaded all the time'. He added: 'That was the first album where I nearly got kicked out the band.' It was one thing for Bill to be zonked out all the time on cider, dope and cocaine; quite another for him to raise any objections to the 'more sophisticated' music, as Tony saw it, that presented itself on the new album. When he suggested they forget the mellotrons and string quartets and 'do some blues jams' Tony turned his back on him. After that, 'There was kind of a cold eeriness in the studios and I realised I was under the gun.'

British music paper reviews of the new album, when it was released in September, were, again, universally snub-nosed – Max Bell described it in *Let It Rock* as 'a monumental bore'. In America, however, the critics seemed to be coming round to them at last. Even Lester Bangs, who had eviscerated their first two albums, now performed an unashamed about-face, describing Sabbath in *Creem* as 'moralists' and comparing their lyrics to those of Bob Dylan and the books of William Burroughs. 'We have seen the Stooges take on the night ferociously and go tumbling into its maw, and Alice Cooper is currently exploiting it for all it's worth, turning it into a circus,' he wrote in *Creem*. 'But there is only one band that has dealt with it honestly on terms meaningful to vast portions of the audience, not only grappling with it in a mythic structure that's both personal and universal, but actually managing to prosper as well. That band is Black Sabbath.' Paradoxically, however, just as the media spotlight was finally swinging their way, Sabbath experienced the first reverse of their career, with *Vol. 4* only getting as high in the US charts as No. 13 – their lowest chart placing since their first album. In Britain it was the same story, getting to No. 8, the same spot *Black Sabbath* had peaked at in 1970. These days, ironically, it is one of the Sabbath albums mainstream critics cite as their favourite, yet at the time Tony Iommi looked on *Vol. 4* as a comparative failure. Iommi blamed the pressures the band were under to come up with a follow-up to their biggest American hit. He also blamed the rest of the band for, as he saw it, 'leaving everything up to me'. He was determined that their next album would be different.

None of which stopped fans flocking to their latest American tour, where Sabbath's reputation as monolithic doom merchants now preceded them. By the start of the *Black Sabbath Vol. 4* US tour, in the first week of July, they had their own coke dealer travelling with them. 'He'd just turn up,' Ozzy said, 'and he had a suitcase full of fucking kilos of this shit. Then one day I was in his room and I opened his bag and there was bags of uncut coke, cut coke, different grade coke. And I picked up one of these bags and there was a revolver underneath! I thought, "This smells like bad news!"'

That was also the tour, according to Ozzy, that 'the groupies knew more about our tour itineraries than we did'. One morning he was awakened by a voice on the phone telling him: 'I'm the Blow Job Queen. And who are *you*?' Wary, Ozzy said he was Geezer and gave her his room number. Ten minutes later Geezer was on the phone to Ozzy complaining bitterly that he's got some crazy chick in his room and he can't get her out. When he stopped laughing, Ozzy called Tony and Bill and got them to accompany him to Geezer's room. 'So we all go over and say, "Please leave" and she says, "No! Why? I give the best blowjobs in the west. Don't you believe me?" We don't want to hurt her, we don't know fucking what to say or do, so finally we all threaten to piss on her if she doesn't leave, and she does.' Ozzy looked forlorn. 'Gigs, bars, hotels, radio interviews … they were everywhere we went. We suffered the results as well. We got clap, crabs – all sorts of diseases. Then we'd have to go through the cures, big painful shots of penicillin in the arse …'

There would be many more US tours, and a great deal more posterior pain of one sort or another, but the 1972 shows were the last before the rot set in as a combination of money and drug problems eventually robbed the band of their original spark. For all their misadventures on the American road, they would never be quite so innocent again. Critics now routinely referred to Sabbath as 'downer music'; the perfect soundtrack to the Quaaludes-and-red-wine generation of Vietnam draftees-in-waiting that attended Sabbath's US shows in the early Seventies. It was an image their increasingly volatile American audience seemingly did its best to live up to. Onstage at the Hollywood Bowl, in 1972, Iommi, whose gear was playing up, became so irate about his malfunctioning equipment that he strode over and kicked over a large speaker cabinet. 'As I walked off there was this guy behind me, that I'd never seen, with a big dagger! He was about to stab me! He'd got past security and he was all in black. And it turned out he was one of these like Satanists or religious freaks or whatever he was, and he was about to bloody stab me. And I'd never even seen him. I'd walked off and they jumped on him and he was on the floor and I still never seen him! And I got into the dressing room [afterwards] and they says, "Fucking hell!"

and I went, "What?" I did feel uncomfortable about it, but I think in them days we was doing so many drugs that it just flowed into one, you know? "Oh, somebody went to stab me? Oh bloody hell! Give us another line!"' More deep chuckles from the bottom of the well.

The band would try to rationalise the effect their music was having on their audience. Speaking with Mike Saunders of *Circular* magazine the week before the new album's release Geezer claimed: 'People feel evil things, but nobody ever sings about what's frightening and evil. I mean the world is a right fucking shambles. Anyway, everybody has sung about all the good things … We try to relieve all the tension in the people who listen to us. To get everything out of their bodies – all the evil and everything.' The evildoers it seemed were back to stay. Another time, Tony recalled with a straight face, 'We had all these Satanists and witches and whatever come to a show, and they all actually went back to the hotel. We had one whole floor at that time always booked for the band. And we got back to the hotel and fucking hell, there's about twenty people sitting in the corridor all in black [and] all holding black candles, all sitting down chanting. And they were all in front of our rooms, you see, and we thought, "Bloody hell!" Anyway, we all said good night to each other then went into the room – you know, bent over them, stepped over them and shut the door – and then phoned each other up. "What we gonna do with all this crowd outside?" So we synchronised our watches and what we did was we all went out at the same time, blew the candles out and sang happy birthday to them. And they got so fucking pissed off that they just left! I mean, they left so quick! But it was either that or get security up.'

The perennial outsiders, too nervous and uptight in that undereducated English underclass way – never knowing which knife to use in which back – to make friends, they just took more drugs to get them through the whole boring ordeal. Tony: 'We just weren't that type of band – you know, oh, we're going out for dinner with the fucking president of So-and-So [record company]. And of course we'd end up at these things and half the time we wouldn't wanna go. And so you'd go and do drugs. And of course everybody else would be doing them too, which you never knew at that time, but they all would be! We [met] all sorts of different people we found out later were doing it, it was unbelievable.'

They were much more at home letting fireworks off in hotel corridors, or just drinking and drugging themselves into oblivion. Nevertheless, even amongst the four members, dividing lines were now starting to appear. In their room-sharing days on the road, Bill and Geezer had occupied one room, while Tony and Ozzy occupied the other. Now they were all able to afford separate suites, it was Bill and Ozzy – the stoners of the group – that gravitated together. While Tony and Geezer, the principal writers of the band, formed their own special alliance.

Ozzy: 'It was because me and Bill were both stoned, drunk fucking pirates going round the place, doing all kinds of fucked-up things.' Tony and Geezer, he said, 'would do their own drugs and their own booze but in their own private space. I mean, I could write a book on Ozzy Osbourne and Bill Ward episodes. He saved me from choking thousands of times,' he quipped, referring to their latest on-tour craze, swallowing handfuls of 'reds' – a heavy-duty barbiturate named Seconal then popular. 'They were wonderful things,' he added sarcastically. 'Just gonna do some reds and …' His head dropped as he feigned unconsciousness. 'You'd wait for the thump [of the head]. You'd be drinking then someone would say: "Fancy a red?" And of course you'd be like, "Oh, great!" Then thirty minutes later you'd be out for twelve hours straight. I was taking four and six of the fucking things at a time. Big 100 milligram pills.'

Metrospan, a popular anti-depressant of the time, was another pill Ozzy began to take handfuls of, whenever the mood took him, which was usually after the show each night. 'They really give you a hit on the head,' he took the trouble to explain to one American writer. 'A doctor gave them to me for depression a few days ago. [But] they make me crazy.' He grew morose. 'I'll be okay as long as there is me and my wife and my kids and my group. But sometimes I start to wonder if my family's going to wait for me. I wonder if she'll get pissed off while I'm running around, recording and all. I don't know what I'd do without her.' Again, this was all smokescreen talk for the little ladies back home to read and feel sorry for them. Ozzy and Black Sabbath knew exactly what they were doing without their wives and families.

As Ozzy would later recall: 'I remember one occasion, we did Virginia Beach. I've just spoken to my wife [Thelma], put the phone down and the door knocks. This beautiful chick comes in, and "Fuck, I'm happening tonight!" I get her on the bed and I fuck the ass off her. She goes. Knock-knock-knock on the door comes. I think she's forgotten something … it's a different chick at the door. Beautiful as fucking God! I swear she looked like an angel. And I fuck the ass off this one. She goes. Knock-knock-knock, and I'm thinking, "I can't believe this." Three – five chicks come in, and I fucked [them]. Where are these chicks coming from? I start walking the corridors and thinking, "What the fuck?" …' He went on: 'When you're a kid and you come from Aston to the States and you see all these fucking cunts wanting to be fucked, you go like a bull at the gate. You're like a fucking lunatic – I was having perverted scenes … all kinds of crap was going on with my sexual life. It's bizarre, it was wild.'

The big offstage pastime now though was cocaine. 'You know,' said Ozzy, 'cocaine is an amazing substance. You're never alone with a bag of coke. You could be on a desert-fucking-island with an ounce of coke and I guarantee you that about ten people will knock on your door before the night's out. I guarantee you. People that you don't know and at the end of the night you know 'em but the next morning when you've come down you go, "Who the fuck are you?"' By the end of the US '72 tour, he said, the band were getting the coke 'mailed to us through the post, cos it was hard to get here [in England]. It was like speed and fruit-powder over here. So we used to get it mailed to us.'

He paused, then added gloomily: 'By then it didn't matter anymore what country we were in or what we were supposed to be doing as a band, it was all just blurring into one, really. I look back now and I think of them days as the best we ever had. It's funny though how quickly that feeling passed and suddenly they turned into our worst days ever. And there wasn't anything we could do to stop it turning that way. We were just fucked...'

FIVE
KILLING YOURSELF TO LIVE

17 March 1973. The Rainbow Theatre, in London's Finsbury Park; the twenty-fourth of 25 shows across Britain and Europe that Black Sabbath have completed in a 32-day period. Everyone is exhausted, physically, emotionally. Everyone propped up on speed, coke, dope, acid – anything they can get their hands on to keep going. This is the band's second of two shows at the Rainbow. Their last night in London, there will be a party afterwards. But then there is a party after every show these days. The following day they will all lie comatose, flopped across the tiny seats of a small propeller plane as it wafts them low in the skies, north to Newcastle, for their next tour-stop at the City Hall.

Right now, though, Ozzy only knows the Rainbow spotlight and what it's doing to his head. Holding the mike stand with both hands, to stop himself from falling, he yells into the darkness.

'Are you high?'

The crowd respond with a muted 'Yeeaaahhhh ...'

He tries again. 'I said, *are you high?*'

Same response, only a little louder this time. Still not good enough, though.

'ARE YOU HIGH?' he screams at the top of his voice.

This time the place erupts.

'Good!' he tells them. 'Cos so am I!'

At the same moment, Tony swipes at his guitar and the gargantuan riff to 'Snowblind' explodes into life. Geezer and Bill thrumming as the building seems to shudder and quake. This is the Black Sabbath experience at its apotheosis: dark, inward-staring, blinded by the merest pinpoint of light, as clammy and all-embracing as a giant cobweb into which the audience are glued like fatally compromised flies. This is what it's all about in 1973, man. Not all that glam stuff you see on TV but the real hollowed-out shell of what rock music – hard, vicious, unstoppable rock music – has finally become, now The Beatles are dead and the Stones are past it. The splendid view from the rotten underbelly of so-called civilised music, of so-called modern longhaired culture. The very top of the very bottom, baby ...

What no one knows yet is that this will be the last time Black Sabbath will tour for nearly a year. There will be no big headline-grabbing speeches, like the one Bowie will make from the stage just three months later, no melodramatic exits amid anguished cries for more-more-more. There will simply be a phone call, made a few days later, after the last fan has gone home clutching their tour programme, quietly cancelling what should have been Sabbath's next American tour. Promoters will be furious, the record company in a panic about how to prolong the shelf-life of *Vol. 4*, already gold but a sure-fire bet for platinum on the back of another three-month tour. But it is not to be. A festival appearance in Germany scheduled for July is also cancelled. Eight months on the road all over the world has nearly killed them. Now all Tony Iommi wants is to get back into the studio and produce the masterpiece that will, finally, he is determined, prove that Black Sabbath are as important, as deep and worthy of press attention, as the bands they are now outselling, like the Stones and Deep Purple, like anyone you would care to name with the sole exception of Led Zeppelin, who are now bigger than everybody. The others want it too but not nearly as much as Tony does. The others still feel their place, ultimately, is at the back of the class, sneering at teacher. Not Tony. Tony wants Black Sabbath to have their own hallowed place in the pantheon, for the name Tony Iommi to be up there, where it belongs, he feels sure, alongside those of Jimmy Page and Ritchie Blackmore; Jeff Beck and Eric Clapton.

As he complained to Keith Altham in an *NME* interview that year: 'On drawing power and album sales we can compare with groups like Zeppelin and the Who, although we seldom get recognition for the fact.' He wasn't just a heavy rock guitarist, he said. There was more to his musical tastes than that. 'I've got a few tapes of Deep Purple in the car but I prefer to listen to things like Peter Paul and Mary, Sinatra, the Moody Blues and the Carpenters.' He was an artist and should be treated as such. 'I want to move to a bigger house,' he said. To get completely away from people so he could work, create. 'I mean, I have a big house with a swimming pool now, but I want one with tennis courts and a studio so I have everything in the house and don't have to go out at all ...'

His personal life followed a similar arc. Earlier that year he had met Susan Snowdon, a 'posh' friend of Patrick Meehan's that Tony fell for. Susan had presented herself as an aspiring singer; Tony had offered to write for her. But the first time they got together it was clear Susan couldn't sing – and Tony hadn't written anything for her. Instead they went out for dinner and Tony became smitten by her air of self-confidence and easy charm. They were worlds apart; opposites that attracted. But it was clear from the day they got married in November 1973 that they were destined to remain strangers throughout the eight years they would eventually be together. Susan's father invited the newlyweds to move into his own 200-room mansion on several hundred acres of grounds halfway between Birmingham and London, and Tony had his house with 'everything' including his own studio and didn't have to go out – ever. Susan was in for a shock though when she realised he meant it literally. Between tours, while the rest of the band took their wives and girlfriends on long holidays, Tony stayed behind to work alone in his new studio, snorting coke and carrying on long into the night. Perhaps Susan should have read the signs early on when Tony chose Zeppelin's notoriously rambunctious drummer John Bonham as his best man at their wedding, and nearly derailed the reception when it became clear that after the champagne toast there was only apple juice to drink. Tony had visions of 'antiques going through the walls' before his mother saved the day by inviting Bonham and the equally thirsty Ozzy back to her house for drinks.

Most of all, Tony Iommi wanted the one thing money couldn't buy: respect. And he was now willing to do almost anything to get it – even if it meant calling off tour dates and dragging the band back into the studio for weeks on end. Anything to put Black Sabbath up where they should be: at the very top. They had been going to release a live album, à la Deep Purple, whose live double, *Made In Japan*, released in December 1972, had been a colossal international hit – and had cost virtually nothing to make; an idea which excited all of them, not least Patrick Meehan. But when Tony listened back to the tapes from the London and Manchester shows once he'd finally got off the road, he was aghast. This was old school Sabbath, heavy as hobnailed boots trudging through snow, obnoxiously loud and overbearing. Exciting for the audiences that were there for the actual shows perhaps, but utterly enervating on record, draining as a coke comedown, and as a signifier of where Tony now intended Sabbath to go, completely off-message. He binned the idea. Now it was Meehan's turn to be appalled, seeing potentially millions of dollars disappearing in the space of a phone call. He would get his revenge eventually, and it would cost the band dear, but for now Tony Iommi still called the musical shots and so it was that Black Sabbath found themselves back in Los Angeles, in the summer of 1973, working on their fifth album.

The band duly set up camp again in the same Bel Air mansion where they'd conceived *Vol. 4,* immediately calling up the same drug dealers and groupies that had made their time there the year before so inspiring. But while the rest of the band thought they were merely making what would effectively be *Vol. 5,* Tony had other, much bigger ideas. Unlike previous Sabbath albums, most of which had been recorded on the run, between tours, this time things would be markedly different, Tony decided. Instead of simply conjuring a mood and going with it as they might a live jam, they would step back and take time to consider what they had and how they could improve it, worry later about how they would or wouldn't be able to reproduce the new material live, and build something the fans and the critics could begin a whole new con-versation about, alter perceptions so that Black Sabbath no longer laboured under the imprimatur of a loud, clanking heavy rock band and butterflied into something more exciting and nimble on its feet, something where the music really did come first, the image put to one side, where it could be allowed to rehabilitate itself into something more in line with new headline-makers like Yes, whose daring new double album, *Tales From Topographic Oceans,* would ostensibly feature just one track per side, and Pink Floyd, who had left their own earlier image as psychedelic prophets behind to metamorphose into a progressive rock goliath with the release that same year of *The Dark Side Of The Moon.* Concept albums were now de rigueur for the rock artist looking to be taken seriously. Tony listened to The Who's double album, *Quadrophenia,* and felt like Sabbath were being left by the side of the road, pushed out of the way by the new cognoscenti that had arrived in the early Seventies who considered David Bowie and

Roxy Music cutting edge; and acts like Mott The Hoople and The Sensational Alex Harvey Band as a very different, more stylised and thought-provoking and therefore more genuinely challenging form of heavy rock than anything the still considered brutish Sabbath might come up with.

There were also commercial pressures to consider. For all their satisfaction with the way *Vol. 4* had come out – the first of the Sabbath albums not to be made under the gun of budgetary considerations – it had essentially been more of the same, musically, albeit with a more polished sheen than before. Something its dithering performance in the world's charts put into sharp relief. Although it had gone gold in America, *Vol. 4* had only reached No. 13 in the chart, lower than either *Paranoid* or *Master Of Reality*. It was the same story at home in Britain, where it stalled at No. 8. Suddenly Sabbath's previously upward sales trajectory had ceased. They still sold tickets, their tours still sold out, but their fan base had given a clear indication that it already had enough Black Sabbath albums to be going on with and probably didn't need any more. Meanwhile, bands that had once supported Sabbath on tour, like Yes, were selling more than double the amount of records. Even Deep Purple, who had always lagged behind Sabbath in terms of worldwide sales, had now overtaken them too. In just four years, Black Sabbath had gone from being the biggest new noise on the block – instant chart stars on both sides of the Atlantic, seemingly without even trying – to chart also-rans. Unlike Purple or Zeppelin, Sabbath had stood still musically. If you owned two Sabbath albums you owned them all. With the advent of progressive rock giants like Yes and the rise in popularity of glam gods like Bowie and Roxy Music, Sabbath were increasingly seen as one-trick ponies. Hard-core munchies purely for hard-core fans. With their heads buried in booze and coke, Ozzy, Geezer and Bill might not have noticed it, but in the summer of 1973, as the guitarist struggled to come up with what he was determined would be genuinely new and startling music, Tony Iommi was painfully aware that it was now or never for Black Sabbath.

The problem was Tony just couldn't quite manage it, no matter how much coke he shovelled up his nose in his now rou- tine 36-hour shifts at the Record Plant. 'It became a ritual, you know, "Oh, right, we're in the studio, get us an ounce." It sort of went with the part of what you did. Every time we'd do an album we'd get a load of dope and then some coke, and off we'd go, you know? We'd be there all bloody night writing stuff and I never used to want to leave the studio. I'd be in there all night every night.'

This time though, no matter how long or how hard he tried in the studio, Tony simply could not conjure into being anything like the music he was now hearing in his head. The glorious sound of a band reborn, eluding him every time he refocused his eyes and picked up the guitar to play. He recalled: 'We thought we'd go back to LA, get the same studio. Do everything the same, get the house and rehearse there and write. And of course we did, but we couldn't think of anything and nothing happened. We just dried up. Nothing was happening … it all just fell to pieces for us, and we were all despondent. "Oh, that's it, you know, we can't think of anything" …'

He began to get furious, then desperate. One day, in a fit of angry gloom, he walked into a hairdresser's on Hollywood Boule- vard and ordered them to cut his hair – short. When he got back to the Bel Air mansion, he also shaved off his moustache. He became unrecognisable even to his own band; even to himself. Yet still things would not fall into place in the studio. Arriving back at the house one night after another long jag in the studio, he found Ozzy and Geezer, drunk and rolling around on the floor fighting. Finally, in June, he threw in the towel and ordered the band back to England, where they would take a break – in order to try and re-establish some sense of normality – before beginning again.

Ironically, the place where Sabbath decided to achieve a clearer idea of what it was they needed to do was even stranger than the demented atmosphere they thought they'd left behind in LA.

Clearwell Castle, an eighteenth-century neo-Gothic pile in the Forest of Dean, in Gloucestershire, had been built for the Member of Parliament Thomas Wyndham in 1728 to replace an older house which had occupied the same site. Constructed of local stone with battlements and an ornate gateway formed by two huge towers, it had been restored to its former glories in the 1950s by the son of the former estate under-gardener, Frank Yeates. When Yeates died in 1973 he left behind a newly built rehearsal room and basement recording studio. Having noted the burgeoning number of large countryside properties now being occupied at no little cost by the new generation of album-oriented rock artists, he was determined to cash in on the trend, and the rest of the decade would see the dark, atmospheric basement of Clearwell Castle become temporary home for a number of high-profile artists, including Mott The Hoople, Bad Company, Deep Purple and Led Zeppelin. The first band to rent the property out for such purposes – somewhat fittingly, given the subterranean aspect of the facilities – was Black Sabbath.

'We had to rehearse in the dungeon of all places,' Geezer laughingly recalled. What they did not find out until they were actually sleeping there was that the castle was reputedly haunted by a mischievous female ghost whose modus operandi was apparently to enter locked rooms and leave them a mess, as though a strong wind had blown through the room. She was also said to sing lullabies to her ghost child on the landing at night while playing a tinkling musical box. The band were not told any of this, lest it should discourage them from hiring the place. But they certainly felt the vibes. The first few days they were there, rehearsing new material in the former dungeons, they saw a figure in a long black cloak hurry past the door. Wary from so many previous experiences of black-robed Sabbath fans making their almost always unwelcome presences felt on the band, Tony stopped playing and, with a roadie, ran after the rapidly retreating figure.

'They saw him go into this other door at the end of the corridor,' said Geezer. 'They were shouting at him, because they thought he was some lunatic that got into the castle. They went into the room where he had gone and there was nobody in there; he totally disappeared.' Sent to inquire about any other visitors that may have been staying at the castle, the owner told them: 'Oh, that's just a ghost.' The castle was full of ghosts, he said.

With everyone now doing so much coke it felt like they already had a million ghosts inside their heads every time they played, the band shrugged it off, as they always did. Tony had long been convinced of his own growing occult powers. 'The whole group communicates on a very close level,' he solemnly informed one interviewer. 'Like, we have what you could almost call a third eye. We can sense with each other what is going to happen. We've had actual experiences. One I remember – Geezer was asleep and he must have astral travelled. I was stuck in the lift. He dreamt this and when I woke him up he said, "I'm glad it's you cos I just dreamt you were stuck in the lift." These are quite regular occurrences. They used to frighten me at first till I got used to it.'

Desperate to meet Tony's demands for something – anything – new to add to the Sabbath sound, the band tried everything to find different sounds and textures to utilise on the new album. Continually coked out as they were now, paranoid about ghosts and bad dreams, intimidated by Tony's increasing perfectionism, often this resulted in hours more lost time. 'We'd spend all day farting about and end up with nothing usable,' Tony glowered. Gradually, though, things did begin to happen. 'We'd end up making things, making all these cabinets and coming up with all these brilliant ideas,' said Tony, 'like trying things going off the piano, into the piano and then miking up the piano strings to hear different sounds.' At one point, Bill took an anvil he'd found while poking around the castle's outhouses, and recorded himself dropping it into a barrel of water. Tony also brought in unusual instruments that he felt went well with the castle's permanent midnight ambience: violins, cellos, even bagpipes for what would become the album's big sign-off epic, its very own 'Stairway To Heaven' moment, called 'Spiral Architect'.

For all the intensity of their new, much more self-conscious approach, there would be a lightness of touch to the new material too. With Tony now in full control of production, the Sabbath sound became far less about thuggish riffing and brutal rhythms and much more about a newly mellifluent style that could embroider even woolly-mammoth riffs like the heavyweight track that became the title of the album, 'Sabbath Bloody Sabbath', its unexpected sideways turns, jazz-like, awash with zinging electric and acoustic guitars and Geezer's pulsing new fuzz bass, making it as good as, possibly even greater than, all-time classics like 'War Pigs' and 'Iron Man'.

Once they'd accomplished the trick with the title track, which would open the album, the rest of the tracks fell quickly into place. So that when the next number on side one, 'A National Acrobat', does begin to twist the sound into a more recognisably malevolent Sabbath territory, even then the shift in gear is so smooth, so full of space and time, Iommi really is leading the band into a whole new sonic galaxy. Lyrically, the band were also now having more fun. Ozzy singing 'When worlds collide I'm trapped inside my embryonic cell' might sound like it's straight from the H. G.

Wells-obsessed mind of Geezer Butler, but in fact 'A National Acrobat', he told me, 'is about wanking, not that anybody got it'. Or more specifically, it is a song about wanking told from the collective sperm's point of view.

Indeed, the only droopy moment on the album is the now seemingly obligatory acoustic instrumental, titled 'Fluff'. Named after Alan 'Fluff' Freeman, who became the voice of rock on Radio One in the Seventies and was, in effect, the only DJ left in Britain still regularly playing Sabbath tracks on the radio, his Saturday afternoon shows famous for their letters: 'Dear Fluff, more Sabbs, more ELP ...' The novelty of such moments, however, had long since begun to wear off. Tony was insistent Sabbath continue with them, as part of his attempt to demonstrate how much more there was to them than blunt-instrument metal. Utilising steel and acoustic guitars, augmented by piano and harpsichord, this though was a case of too much sugar on the pill.

The rest of the new material, though, really did find Sabbath touching new heights. 'Sabbra Cadabra' was pure, bounding rock'n'roll, its 'Lovely lady make love all night long' lyrics made up on the spot by Ozzy, based on the laughably cumbersome English voiceovers on some German porn films the band had been watching. Geezer cohered them into lyrics and Rick Wakeman of Yes was brought in to add some cheerfully ebullient honky-tonk piano and cathedral-like synthesiser, the vocals and guitar run through a processor, giving them a futuristic sheen. Rick, said Iommi, 'was wild back then'. Certainly too wild for Yes, who had opened for Sabbath in America some years before. 'Rick used to travel with us, and not Yes, for some reason,' he added disingenuously. When the beer-and-curry quaffing Wakeman left the brown rice-eulogising and Sanskrit-reading Yes later the same year, there was some discussion about bringing him full-time into the Sabbath fold. But Rick had had enough for now of the over-the-top rock'n'roll lifestyle. When a few months later he suffered the first of what would eventually be three heart attacks, his decision not to join Sabbath just as they were reaching the nadir of their own 'health issues' seemed prudent.

The four tracks on side two of *Sabbath Bloody Sabbath* were similarly musically inspired, similarly lyrically playful, if not unhinged. On the rousingly rock-steady 'Killing Yourself To Live' they gave an autobiographical hint that all was not well behind the scenes, its crunching bass and neat drums given a bed of synthesised vocals and guitar that lend it an air of real drama, Ozzy issuing his entreaty over the lost-in-space bridge, 'Smoke it … Get high!'

It's the same feeling of artificial highs amid the self-administered lows on 'Looking For Today', the days of meat-hook riffs long gone as the band pick up a new buzz that isn't quite generic rock – not with those flute and organ sounds flickering like candles in the dark – but is so catchy it could have come from The Beatles' mid-period, had they been on heavier drugs at the time. The classic Sabbath air of cobwebbed mystery had not been lost, just refurbished for the Seventies. On 'Who Are You' the piercing synthesisers again lend an atmosphere of insomniacal paranoia as Ozzy rages: 'Please I beg you tell me, in the name of hell, who are you?' before the ascending Bolero-like piano brings the whole deranged monstrosity full circle.

The other highpoint of *Sabbath Bloody Sabbath* though – the gothic bookend to the tremendous opener – is its finale: 'Spiral Architect'. More like The Who than Led Zeppelin, going from heart-tugging acoustic guitars and pale-sky orchestral strings one moment – name-checked almost apologetically on the sleeve as The Phantom Fiddlers – to full-on epic rock with a capital 'R' the next. And amid Geezer's typically oblique lyrical futurisms the final message is reassuringly universal: 'I look upon my earth and feel the warmth and know that it's good …' the tacked-on sound of applause at the end lending it an extra level of just-for-fun grandiosity.

Did they know what they were doing or were they just making it all up as they went along? It didn't matter. As Geezer would recall: 'It was a whole new era for us. We felt really open on that album. It was a great atmosphere, good time, great coke!' It was, as he rightly put it, 'like Part Two of your life … Right before that we were in a terrible slump. We were all exhausted from touring. We weren't getting on very well. Then Tony came up with the riff for "Sabbath Bloody Sabbath" and everybody sparked to life.'

It was a false dawn. As Ozzy would later tell me: '*Sabbath Bloody Sabbath* was our final record, as far as I was concerned. Then it started to go and drift around all over the place. See, our idea of making a good record was to run and find some new location. We thought, if you travel somewhere new, it's kind of like a new adventure. So you'd get there and for the first few days you'd jam about a bit and then you'd be back to your own. You'd be locked in your own heads. Someone would come in with another ounce of fucking powder and you'd be up there talking bullshit for three weeks, you know?'

The distress signals were already being sent by the time *Sabbath Bloody Sabbath* was released in Britain on 3 December. It became Sabbath's biggest chart album since *Paranoid* three years before, eventually plateauing at No. 4. In the US, where it was released a month later, it also reversed the downward chart trend, reaching No. 11. What it didn't do, for Tony Iommi, anyway, was quash the doubters and naysayers that he felt now made it their mission to unfairly trounce everything Sabbath did. In America, where *Rolling Stone* reviewed it in February, Tony was surprised to read something good about one of their albums at last. 'Black Sabbath's major contribution has been to successfully capture the gist of specifically Seventies culture through their music,' wrote Gordon Fletcher. 'They relate to this impersonal, mechanical

decade much as Delta bluesmen and their Chicago spin-offs related to their eras – by synthesizing collective feelings and giving
their contemporaries hope by revealing the disaffection that
unites all of them. In that remote but real sense, Black Sabbath
might well be considered true Seventies bluesmen.'

But such praise felt faint and belated, compared to the sav-
aging the band had already received in the British music press.
When *Melody Maker* star writer Allan Jones came to do a piece on
the band, he used them as a punch bag for his verbal dexterity.
'Musically Black Sabbath are an Irish joke,' he began, adding that
onstage they 'looked like Mott the Hoople groupies masquerad-
ing as gay Cossacks', and even going so far as to mock their Black
Country accents: 'That comical accent that so afflicts those un-
fortunate enough to have been born in the colourful vicinity of
Birmingham.'

As Tony said: 'It's only the bad press you ever remember.' In
Jones' case, this was particularly true and Tony would eventually
get his revenge some years later. For now though, despite delivering what he was convinced was 'as good an album as any we
ever made', Tony felt Sabbath had been condemned without a
fair trial, perverting the cause of musical justice, leaving Tony,
locked away in his various hotel rooms, working his way through
another ounce of coke, thirsting for revenge. Something would
have to give or someone would have to pay. As it turned out it
would be the band that had to pay; their career that was about to
give. For if they thought before ghosts had haunted them, they
would now discover that evil comes in many guises, not least as
a smiling face holding out a helping hand. Or perhaps a straw or
rolled-up dollar bill ...

Black Sabbath performed just 52 shows in seven countries between December 1973 and November 1974. The highlight in
America, where *Sabbath Bloody Sabbath* had already gone gold,

was a headline spot at the first California Jam, before nearly 200,000 people at the speedway track in Ontario, east of Los Angeles. (And where the band first met newly installed Deep Purple bassist and vocalist Glenn Hughes, someone who would figure more seriously in the Black Sabbath story a decade later, when both bands were seriously down on their luck. 'There was the gig, which I just about recall, but mainly I recall spending the rest of the night going crazy back at the hotel with Ozzy and Bill,' says Hughes now, 'just bags of coke and what have you for days. Me and Ozzy were made from the same thing. We both just liked to rage all night every night.')

There was also a headline-grabbing 14-date UK tour with latest American sensations Black Oak Arkansas in tow, whose frontman, the indefatigable 'Big' Jim Dandy, rivalled even Ozzy when it came to on- and offstage madness. (Three years earlier he'd received a suspended sentence of 26 years for grand larceny and now lived each day like it was his last.) In November there had been a triumphant seven-date tour of Australia, where they were supported by new dicks on the block, AC/DC, and another British survivor from the late Sixties, now also reborn as a heavy rock denim-clad success, called Status Quo.

There might have been more but the band were no longer in any shape to manage months on end on the road. For 1974 was also the year when their whole world came crashing down around them. The year when they discovered the truth about just where their money was going – and not going. The year when their management company, World Wide Artists, went to the wall.

According to Ozzy, doubts had begun to creep in during the *Sabbath Bloody Sabbath* sessions. 'It suddenly occurred to me when I went to the office [in London] one day and [Patrick Meehan]'s got this whole fucking block of offices and Rolls-Royces for days and all this shit and fucking different agencies and whatever. And it doesn't take a cunt to go, "Hang about, he's got four

Rolls-Royces now and I'm still in a VW", or whatever.' For Tony, 'The situation with Patrick' had already become 'unworkable' even before they began to question his business dealings. 'We could never find him when bills had to be paid and apart from one girl in the office, there was no one we could talk to about anything. It was a nightmare and eventually I was left with no option but to walk away and try to pick up the pieces.' Ozzy was more forthright. 'You know, he would get coke for us – whatever you wanted. If we wanted money, he'd give it to us. He wouldn't give us like twenty grand or fifty grand [but] if you wanted like a thousand quid or five thousand quid, he'd give it ya, you know? But he'd always have control over you. So when the axe did fall, who was the first to go under – it was us. Not him, he saved his own arse.' The band had long suspected things weren't quite as they thought they should be, he said, but had been too scared to openly question the way their affairs were being handled. 'It went on all along the way, but it was like, "I don't know what I'm doing, so what if I open Pandora's box and I unleash something that I don't really know how to control at this level, so how can I hope to control it once I open the lid and it all comes flying out?"'

The answer, as they learned over the summer of 1974, was that they had no control whatsoever over what happened next. 'It was like the more you found out, the less you wanted to know,' said Geezer. 'It was horrible.' Sabbath had been snared the same way countless other acts had in the music business of the Sixties. 'The way he had us tied up in his contracts, we had to pay him to get away from him. We didn't have lawyers or anything when we signed the contracts, because we didn't know.' The band spent a fortune in legal fees only to discover that, in effect, they had no real money of their own. The cars they drove, the houses they lived in, all were owned on paper by their management company. Most excruciating and potentially fatally damaging of all, they didn't even own their own music.

'We never actually sat down and went, okay, we've got this problem,' said Ozzy. 'What do you think we should do about it? You'd start off like that maybe, and then somebody would say, "Fucking hell, you know what happened to me this morning…?" And it would be off. "You got any powder?" And then the meeting was fucked. I'm not blaming [the rest of the band] and I'm not blaming me, that's the way it was for all of us. We never knew how to tackle the problem head-on, because we weren't reared that way. We didn't have the capability of dealing with it, we didn't know about law. We didn't know a contract was a binding piece of law. We just thought it was a bit of paper so you could make a fucking record.'

'That was why we called the next album *Sabotage*,' said Geezer. 'I think he took all the money and bought a hotel chain. We were potless, absolutely broke. If the band had finished there, we would have been totally destitute, but thankfully we went on and made a few quid back on tour. I think we were totally away from him by the end of the *Sabotage* album.'

It would, in fact, be years before Black Sabbath were free from the legal manacles of their WWA contracts; a situation that would blight their career throughout the Eighties and Nineties as Meehan and co. continued to make money out of a string of lowly compilation albums of Sabbath's most recognisable material, mismanaging their back catalogue at a time when such things were becoming the wellspring from which the future prospects of all classic Seventies rock bands now flowed – like their old heroes, Led Zeppelin, who, by contrast, managed their back catalogue throughout the same period so well it actually redeemed their reputation among critics. The precious gold of Black Sabbath's cargo, however, would be so haphazardly slung around the marketplace it nearly destroyed the band's long-term prospects.

Ironically, their would-be saviour happened to be one of the most infamous gangster managers in the music biz: Don Arden. For any other major rock artist of the period in a similar situation, this might have been out of the frying pan, into the fireplace. But Tony had remained friendly with Don, despite turning down his original offer of management in 1970. Arden, for his part, did not take kindly to being turned down by anyone. He made an exception, though, for Sabbath. For one thing, they were still one of the biggest-selling rock bands in the world, not least America, where Arden's previous artists had never enjoyed such sustained success. 'America was always the dream,' he told me. 'Until I'd made it there, I couldn't rest.' Then there was the satisfaction he derived from, as he put it, 'taking back what was rightfully mine', from Patrick Meehan, whom he loathed.

When, in early 1975, Tony Iommi came to see Don, pleading for help in sorting out Sabbath's own disastrous dealings with Meehan and World Wide Artists, Arden didn't need to be asked twice. Urged on by Sharon, Don agreed to take the band under his wing.

From a business point of view, it felt like a triumphant moment for Tony and Sabbath. Now 50, Don Arden was reaching the apex of his own, long career in the music business. By the mid-Seventies he was managing Roy Wood's Wizzard, who had enjoyed two No. 1 singles in Britain in the past year; and Jeff Lynne's Electric Light Orchestra, who had also enjoyed a string of hit singles and had now recently made their own breakthrough in America with *Eldorado*, the first of six US Top 10 albums. He was also, most shrewdly, in the process of setting up his own record company, Jet Records, whose first release, the single 'No, Honestly' by Lynsey De Paul, had made the Top 5 of the UK charts.

Sabbath, though, would be something else, he decided. 'My number one priority was to get them some money. That meant going to the record company – Vertigo in the UK, Warner Brothers in America – and making them understand that the band were still viable and now in good hands. I told both labels to forget about the previous mess, to leave everything to me. This was exactly what they wanted to hear and I got a nice big advance from them and used it to put the band back in the studio to make another album.' Don correctly identified the need for the band 'to stop worrying about money and start thinking about music again'. He also, shrewdly, realised that the only money they could rely on coming in from now on would come from whatever they did next. 'I wanted something new out there that they *did* earn royalties from.' And by extension, of course, that Don could earn money from too.

It sounded like an eminently sensible plan. But even with the formidable figure of Don Arden behind them, the fallout with Meehan would continue to cast a deep shadow over Sabbath in the Seventies. After months and years of litigation between the two camps, the band were eventually forced to seek an out of court settlement; the final straw of which saw them agree to pay Meehan an unspecified sum for breaking their contracts with him, as well as agree to give up their rights to the catalogue released while Patrick was their manager; most of the best work they would ever produce.

Talking to me about it more than 20 years later, Ozzy tried to be philosophical. 'The beauty of the management thing is that once you sign the yin-yang [contract] they can sit on their arse for ten years and fight legal and civil actions. But you [the artist] haven't got ten years to spare. In ten years you've been and gone, you know? That's always the gun to your head, so you end up settling out of court just to get it out the way and what happened to Sabbath is instead of the management ripping us off, the fucking lawyers were now charging us for everything, from fucking tips at the airport to fucking 10p for a shit in a public toilet – everything was going!'

It wasn't just about the money, though. Sabbath now began to lose sight of the most important thing of all, the one thing that might have saved them: the music. The next Sabbath album, *Sabotage*, released in November 1975, would be the last Ozzy-era Sabbath album of any significance. Recorded at Morgan Studios in London, in February and March, it was a case of same old drugs, very different expectations. Any thoughts for what their legacy might be, what the critics might think, or where Sabbath now stood in the rock pantheon were subsumed by the extremely urgent need to simply make money.

There were many fine moments, nearly all fuelled though by sheer rage. The opening track, 'Hole In The Sky', has the kind of door-slamming riff that wouldn't have been out of place on *Paranoid*, as Ozzy rants and raves about going through a hole in the sky, 'seeing nowhere through the eyes of a lie.' The sheer anger of the song is emphasised by its abrupt, look-twice ending, segueing instantly into what appears at first to be another of Tony's sultry acoustic rambles, 'Don't Start (Too Late)', but which also dies young, overlapped by the snarling, dumbbell intro to 'Symptom Of The Universe', another of the best tracks on the album but, again, so far removed from the considered finesse of *Sabbath Bloody Sabbath* as to be positively Neanderthal. A year later groups like the Sex Pistols and The Damned would make such a virtue out of such angry, snub-nosed riffing and thuggish drums they would be credited for inventing a while new genre: punk rock. But this was Black Sabbath, and in their hands, in that otherwise listless year of 1975, a time of milque-toast 'rock', when everyone from Rod Stewart to David Bowie was flirting with disco, what they did sounded unnecessarily disruptive, anti-everything, self-harming. Then, just as things sound like they really are careening out of control, with two minutes to go Tony leads the band into the kind of left-field move which did harken back to where they thought they were going on *Sabbath Bloody Sabbath*, before the shit hit the fan: a wonderfully percussive acoustic section, jazzy and spaced-out, yet propulsive and a weird blend of hate-love, Ozzy's voice cracking as he sings of 'love's creation' and 'riding through the sunshine' while sounding like he's getting ready to throw dirt on a coffin.

The remaining tracks all followed suit, veering from straight-ahead iron-handed riffing to Raven-calling, Edgar Allan Poe-like melodrama. The titles alone are enough to induce a choking sense of claustrophobia, of paranoia and obsession that can't all be explained by coke-psychosis. The nearly ten minutes of the body-dragging 'Megalomania', all bat-swooping mellotron and killer robot guitars; the back-arching rhythms of the sarcastically titled 'Thrill Of It All', swaggering like a zombie puckering its rotted purple lips as Ozzy sneers, 'Won't you help me Mr Jesus ... When you see this world we live in, do you still believe in Man?'; the sound of chanting monks over the spear-chucking intro of the instrumental 'Supertzar', the only over-contrived track on an album almost doubled over with heavy-handed meaning, the kind of mock-horror movie thing future shock-metallists like Slayer and Megadeth might reach for in their more doped-out moments, but which Tony, in his coke-induced isolation, felt so strongly about it became the tremble-tremble intro tape to Sabbath shows for years to come. The only other wincingly off moment is the track released as the solitary single from the album, the drearily titled 'Am I Going Insane (Radio)'. Understandably, cynics assumed it was the band being cynical by adding the word 'radio' in parenthesis. In fact, it was just another of their typically daft Brummy jokes, like 'N.I.B.' had been for them years before: radio being short for 'radio rental', rhyming slang for 'mental'. Not that it mattered in the long run. Sabbath, who had only released one single per album since 'Paranoid' had never had another hit 45. 'Am I Going Insane (Radio)', with its second-hand riff and baleful vocal, maintained that achievement. The final track of the album,

however, 'The Writ', was of a different, much higher order. Inspired by the fact that Patrick Meehan had actually issued them
another writ while they were in the studio, 'The Writ' became
another bile-filled, near nine-minute epic, built on a bubbling-
cauldron riff, the band war-dancing as Ozzy screams of 'Vultures
sucking gold from you', wondering self-pityingly, 'Will they still
suck now you're through?'

'We were getting ripped all over place,' said an exhausted
Iommi when it was all over, 'that was a terrible period for us.'
There was one final, jokey, coda, a bit of drab nonsense that belies
the very seriousness of everything that has just come to pass,
which they unnecessarily gave the title 'Blow On A Jug' (Ozzy
and Bill pissing about in the studio, ha, yeah) and which the
album would have been much better without. But everything else
about *Sabotage*, from its title to its contents, to its frankly hideous
sleeve of the band standing with their backs to a huge, ornately
framed mirror, seemed to self-prophesise Sabbath's impending
doom.

Once again, the British music press twisted the knife. 'This
isn't psychodrama,' wrote Mick Farren in the *NME*, 'it's an
amusement park ghost train. It has the same cheap, lowest
common denominator, dubious thrill quotient while totally lack-
ing the kind of gaudy innocence that might make it redeemingly
charming. It's also highly successful, and probably causes brain
damage. Can I please take it off now?'

In order to keep the money coming in, Don had Sabbath back out
on the road before the album was even released, and the latter half
of 1975 found them on the road continuously in America, Britain
and Europe. When *Sabotage* was released in the late summer, it
did a good job of keeping the band in the UK Top 10, where it
reached No 7. But in America it was their least successful album
to date, barely scraping to No. 28. They were still doing boffo live

business though and when they returned for their latest dates in New York – at Madison Square Garden on 3 December and the War Memorial in Syracuse a week later, supported, respectively, by Aerosmith and Kiss – they did so to sold-out crowds.

Behind the scenes, though, things continued to unravel. Just as Sabbath felt they had begun to work free of the mess they had found themselves in after breaking with Patrick Meehan, their former manager struck another blow, authorising the release in December of a double-album compilation entitled *We Sold Our Souls For Rock'n'Roll*. Featuring all their biggest hitters from their first five albums, and released to coincide with the Christmas-present-buying market, the band didn't know whether to be pleased or not when the album – from which they would make no money whatsoever – barely scraped the UK Top 40. It might have stymied their former manager's posthumous efforts to turn a buck from the band he probably thought would collapse without him, but it also said something for where even the best of Black Sabbath now stood in the public mind.

Don Arden told them to forget about it; to finish the tour and get on and make a new album they could sell, one without Meehan's fingerprints on it. But whatever was left of the best of them after the prolonged battles with their former manager was now being fully eroded by their monstrous drug habits. The final night of the *Sabotage* world tour was at the Hammersmith Odeon, in London, in January 1976, a show originally scheduled for the previous November that had been called off after a drunk and stoned Ozzy crashed his motorcycle, injuring his back. It wasn't serious and he spent his week off out for the count for most of it, he said, on prescription morphine and painkillers. Now, on the eve of the rescheduled show, while rehearsing in Willesden, it prompted a long overdue discussion among the band about how far their reputation had slipped over the past two years – and why.

'We said, look, we've got to put this fucking drug thing behind us. It's fucking us up. When we started, all we had was a few beers and a smoke of wonga and that's all we needed. Now we've got this fucking powder everywhere we go and everybody's fucking talking their mouths off and talking bullshit. Let's stop the coke. So we've got a gig at Hammersmith Odeon and I'm thinking, "Fucking hell, how am I going to get on after the gig?" Cos after the gig, it was like your sugar lump at the end of the race, a snort of coke. So we go on the stage and I'm all depressed because there's no blow about and they're playing 'Hole In The Sky', and the band are playing like fucking demons, you know? And I'm going, "You know what, I am right, it is better without coke! We don't need this shit!" But the second song, it starts to slow down. All the music starts to come to a stop. Third song it's like ...' He droned a slow tail-off riff. 'And I'm going, "What the fuck's going on?" Then I look at them and they're all going ...' He mimed rubbing his nose and staring eyes. 'Before they went on they'd all had a couple of lines! And like a cunt, I'd never had any!'

The next year would see a rapid decline in the band's fortunes, personally and professionally. As if to sound the death knell the latter half of 1976 saw the arrival onto the British music scene of the first wave of releases by new self-styled punk rockers like the Sex Pistols ('Anarchy In The UK') and The Damned ('New Rose'). By the start of 1977, The Clash, The Stranglers, The Jam and the hordes that followed had also released their first records and the face of the British music scene had changed for ever. If Sabbath had always felt out of kilter with prevailing rock trends in the first half of the Seventies, they now felt utterly left behind. 'Paranoid' may have been a favourite of Johnny Rotten's, but Sabbath's image of long hair, flares and those outsized crosses which they all still wore onstage and off fingered them as The Enemy. Not least, of the even more fashion-conscious music papers, the most cutting edge of which, like the *NME* and *Sounds*, now threw in their lot with the new dawn punk promised. Even hard rock and heavy metal were undergoing a radical reinvention. As the *Sounds* editor at the time, Alan Lewis, says now: 'Suddenly bands like Sabbath and Purple were seen as old-fashioned, out of touch, even by rock fans who were now becoming far more interested in newer bands like AC/DC, Van Halen and Kiss. For a while it really did seem like Black Sabbath and the rest had had their day. That there was no way back for them, except perhaps in America. And even there they were now being supplanted by this next generation of heavy rock bands that had come along.'

Just as Britain was undergoing its changing of the guard – musically, culturally – Black Sabbath became even further removed from what was going on by literally moving themselves away. At Don Arden's urging, they had now become tax exiles; ironically, trying to stave off the injurious claims of the British Inland Revenue at a time when their income streams were at their lowest since they'd actually started selling records five years before. Tony Iommi's response to all this was to simply bury himself ever deeper in the recording process. Working on material for their next album at Criteria Studios in Miami – the studio du jour for British tax exiles looking for sun, sea and relaxation as a backdrop to recording, while at the same time avoiding the pitfalls of working in the hangers-on hotbed of another Hollywood studio – oblivious to the new direction the rest of the rock world was now heading in, Iommi began to conceive of a new, even more grandiose Sabbath sound. Programmed to allowing Tony to take the music wherever he wanted, after years of letting him have his own way, the others didn't even turn up at the studio any more, waiting to be summoned to play their parts.

'I must admit it,' Tony would later say, 'it did become insane. If I'd walk in the rehearsal room and couldn't think of anything, we'd end up probably not doing anything [that day]. So it got to a stage where you *had* to come up with something and if I didn't I used to feel so bad I'd get really frustrated inside. I just felt that they sort of looked to me, like, "Oh well, he'll come up with something." And it did become a strain in the end.'

It was the beginning of the end of the original Black Sabbath as a creative force on record. The longer they spent in ever more lavish and distant studios, the more cocaine and smack and dope and beer and cognac and whatever else they fancied to 'aid' the creative process they took with them, the worse their final albums became. The only way the coke now worked for them was to further fuel their sense of paranoia and insecurity, and cripple the music. Discipline was not part of the rock lifestyle in the Seventies, but now the band were out of control, almost beyond saving. These were the last days of Rome and Black Sabbath were burning down while Tony Iommi continued fiddling amid the flames.

These days, Tony told *Circus* magazine at the time, in a classic example of coke-immersed delusion, 'We have more control over what is happening ... having to think about sides of the business which we didn't concern ourselves with in the past. It gives us a broader outlook, because we can do whatever we want now.' You could almost hear the razor blade chipping away at the mirror in the background. 'Any decisions are taken by all four of us and we all have to be fully behind them.' Ozzy's memories of Miami were markedly different. 'The golden period of Sabbath, for me, was *Master Of Reality, Volume 4* and then right at the pinnacle for Sabbath, in my opinion, came *Sabbath Bloody Sabbath.*' Of the albums that followed, 'There are some good tracks but there was an emotion that's missing there because we were fighting the fucking world. And we were so used to fighting the system.'

To make matters worse, the band were now beginning to feel

like they'd slipped from Don Arden's radar. Just as Sabbath's sales graph was in decline, ELO's had begun to rise steeply. Their 1975 album, *Face The Music*, had been their first to reach the US Top 10. Work on the follow-up, *A New World Record*, was taking place in Munich just as Sabbath were straining to rediscover their mojo in Miami. ELO were enjoying massive worldwide hit singles now, too; something Sabbath had never managed to achieve. There was another crucial difference: Jeff Lynne and ELO moved quickly and were now in huge demand. While Tony Iommi struggled to complete a new Sabbath album from which their label now expected only relatively modest returns, advance orders for the new ELO were enough to ensure a platinum album on release. Needless to say, Don was now spending more time on the other side of the world with ready-to-go ELO than he was with the slowly disintegrating Black Sabbath.

When, halfway through recording in Miami, Sabbath ran out of money, and with Don nowhere to be seen, Ozzy recalls the band sending Warner Bros. a telex. 'We said, "Look, you've gotta send us some dough, we're living in this Thunderbird Hotel in Miami recording and we're broke. They sent [a telex] back saying four McDonald's are on their way over to you. They were joking but do you know what I mean? It was like, fuck, we've sold you all these records and you're taking the piss out of us?'

All the signals were getting crossed. But still the band members did nothing to help themselves. When Warner Bros. did eventually advance them some money, said Ozzy, 'We'd have coke dealers over, we'd have stuff on the drip, you know. Cocaine had got a hold of us bad. It got a hold of me. Then comes the time when you think, "How can I do it without it?" You get used to that euphoria, which at the end has gone up and down. You didn't last as long every time you were doing it.'

The fact was, though, said Ozzy, by then, 'The music was paying for the lawyers' bill and the whole good idea that we had was so fucking raped by not just Patrick but everybody involved, you know?' Did the others share the feeling of falling apart? Geezer: 'Yeah, in their own way. I mean, Tony's the one who's always kept everybody together musically, he always believed in it and he was the one who always used to give everybody a kick up the arse when we'd get despondent. If it wasn't for him we'd probably have broken up in '75, '76. He's the one that kept the flag flying when everybody else was starting to disbelieve.' But not even Tony Iommi could drag Black Sabbath back out of the creative hole they found themselves in as they worked on their seventh album, the wince-inducingly titled *Technical Ecstasy*.

Released in September 1976, just as punk was gathering momentum in Britain, *Technical Ecstasy*, with its swirling keyboards, more generic guitar sound, and distinctly oddball moments like the track 'It's Alright', a substandard Beatles-esque ballad featuring Bill Ward on vocals, wasn't just the wrong album at the wrong time, it was, by some stretch, the worst album Sabbath had ever made. From its bizarrely bright cover – supplied by rock sleeve designers du jour Hipgnosis, and looking like something even Pink Floyd had rejected for being too anonymous ('It was supposed to be two robots screwing,' said an exasperated Ozzy, 'but to me it just looked like shit') – to its cringe-inducingly under-par songs, *Technical Ecstasy* was a long way removed from the band that had once sounded like no other. The biggest hit of the summer in America that year had been Boston's 'More Than A Feeling'. On tracks like the nerve-shredding 'Gypsy', it sounds like Tony has bent over backwards to make Sabbath fit onto the same radio formats. But where Boston's Tom Scholz was a gifted genius that had played all the instruments on his record bar drums, Tony Iommi was now a drug casualty on the commercial rebound. Instead of leading the way, as Sabbath had done with their earliest albums, creating a sound so indifferent to critical bon-mots it made them almost invulnerable to passing fads, now – even on the better *Technical Ecstasy* tracks like 'Back Street Kids' (exceptional for a Kiss collection, perhaps, decidedly second-rate for a Sabbath album) or 'All Moving Parts (Stand Still)', a plodding nod to Alice Cooper, perhaps, with its ho-hum lines about teachers not sticking to rules but which Geezer now says is about 'a female transvestite who becomes President of the United States because America was such a misogynistic society at the time' – Sabbath sounded like they were trying to catch up.

On tracks like the frankly embarrassing 'Rock'n'roll Doctor', with its sub-Stones riff and sixth-form lyric, or the equally disastrous, 'She's Gone', with its laughable cinematic strings and clichéd tinkling acoustic, Ozzy actually reduced to issuing cries of 'Ooh, my baby', Sabbath begin to sound a joke. On the dreadful final track, though, the seven-minute dirge 'Dirty Women', a paean to prostitution with such finely wrought observations as 'Dirty women, they don't mess around', the album reached an even more dire, even offensive level of stupidity.

Iommi's commercial instincts may have been correct – future 'soft rock' squillion-sellers *Hotel California* and *Rumours* were just around the corner – but to try and force that sound on Black Sabbath was like trying to put lamb's wool on a suit of armour. It just didn't work, pleasing nobody. Not even the rest of the band. And certainly not the fans, most of whom had the good sense to steer well clear. In America the new Black Sabbath album was dead on arrival, not even penetrating the Top 50. In Britain, it was also a flop, reaching No. 13, before disappearing from the charts completely after just six weeks.

'Personally, I like *Ecstasy*,' Tony told Steve Rosen in *Sounds*, in another article almost comically immersed in self-delusion and emotional denial. 'Most people that have heard it thought it was a big step from *Sabotage* and a lot of people say it's totally different from anything we've done before. I think it's probably the type of album you have to listen to a few times before you really get into it. I don't think it's sort of an instant thing.'

And so it remains.

SIX
BORN TO DIE

The four, always nervous, members of Black Sabbath may have been freaked out by the disastrously poor sales of *Technical Ecstasy*, but they were able to assuage their fears, at least for a while, back out on the road in America, where their 1976 autumn and winter tours were largely a sell-out. In this, though, they were helped immeasurably by the addition to the first leg of the tour of support band Boston, whose self-titled debut album and hit single, 'More Than A Feeling', were then burning up the charts. Don Arden, who'd pioneered package tours in the Sixties – multi-band bills aimed squarely at the mainstream consumer – now drew on that expertise to ensure everywhere Sabbath went they had 'support' acts capable of selling at least half the house for them. Hence additions to the bill that year of Boston, Black Oak Arkansas, Tommy Bolin, Bob Seger, Ted Nugent and Journey, all of whom were on the threshold of headlining their own US tours.

Back in Britain for a ten-date tour in March 1977, which culminated in four sold-out shows at London's Hammersmith Odeon, the band were back in their cups. Arriving home just as debut albums from The Damned, The Clash and The Stranglers were hogging headlines in the British music press, Tony simply glowered from his ivory tower. If this was what the press thought was good then maybe Sabbath were better off no longer being part of the conversation. 'I admit, I didn't see it coming at all,' Iommi would later tell me. 'The punk thing for me was just a passing fad in the music papers. They hadn't started talking about it yet in America and these bands were still club acts. We thought they'd have a long way to go to catch us.'

Geezer, always the most sensitive to new trends, and the most fearful of change, instantly grasped what a threat to the band's continued prosperity this new generation of rock bands posed to Sabbath, and how limited their future now appeared. 'We lost direction. I think the punk thing damaged us a lot. I thought, well, that's Sabbath old hat now, once I heard the Sex Pistols. Even though our stuff has easily outlasted their stuff, and the punk thing only lasted a couple of years anyway, it just sounded so ... fresh to me. And it sort of reminded me of how we used to be. I just thought, well, we've lost it now, just lost all that anger and energy. And it was hard [to accept] because we'd sold millions of albums, we'd been through these horrific management fights.' The whole double-whammy of punk and Meehan 'just left a big dent in us'.

The rest of them were so confused by the new reality of punk, when they agreed to have AC/DC open for them in Europe in April, they thought they were punks simply by dint of their shorter hair and schoolboy uniform-wearing guitarist. With their ingrained sense of inferiority, they looked on with mounting horror as AC/DC all but destroyed the stage after just twenty minutes at the first show in Paris. They didn't know the band were reacting with fury to malfunctioning equipment. They thought it was all part of their act. It didn't matter that their singer, Bon Scott, another frontman over-fond of drugs and alcohol in any order you cared to name, became a frequent visitor to the Sabbath dressing room, hanging out with Ozzy. Tony regarded them all with suspicion. When, after a show in Gothenburg, Geezer jokingly pulled a toy flick-knife on Malcolm Young, which the fiercely combative AC/DC guitarist and leader mistook for the real thing, he was rewarded with a punch in the face for his trouble. Realising his mistake, Malcolm offered his apologies but Geezer threw a fit, insisting AC/DC be thrown off the tour forthwith. They were and the final four dates of the tour were cancelled.

It was in this cocooned atmosphere that Tony Iommi seethed over ways to make his band matter again. More than any previous Sabbath album, *Technical Ecstasy* was, as Ozzy sneeringly put it, 'a Tony album'. Given free rein for the first time to do what he pleased, Tony had delivered the worst-selling Sabbath album ever. Rather than doubt himself, which the coke would not let him do, he blamed others. All the others. The record companies that had not promoted the album properly; the radio stations that had not given it a fair crack of the whip. Most of all he blamed the music press, who he felt, justifiably to an extent, had systematically undermined Sabbath's reputation over the years, to the point now where their credibility lay at an all-time low.

The only one who escaped his ire was keyboard player Gerald Woodroffe, formerly of jazz fusion outfit Matibu, regulars of the Brum club circuit, who had been hired to play on the *Technical Ecstasy* album and tour as a session man. Jezz, as he was known, became the first of two Sabbath keyboard players who would tour and record as band members but were in effect hired hands, playing at the far side of the stage, behind curtains or amps for the first few years, before Jezz's eventual replacement, Geoff Nicholls, was eventually allowed a berth in full view on the stage. What they also had in common was a willingness to sit up all night working on material with Tony. The others had long since given up on that, but Tony now found a more equitable 'work mate' to write and try things out with. Not that Woodroffe or Nicholls would be credited with many of the songs they co-wrote with the guitarist.

Even immediate peers like Led Zeppelin and Deep Purple, neither of whom had enjoyed an easy ride from the music press, seemed to be held in higher regard than Black Sabbath. Sitting in his hotel suite alone each night after the show, glugging orange juice and helping himself to the mountainous quantities of cocaine he was now ingesting every day, a heavy metal Scarface surrounded by traitors, fools and fakes, Tony began to moulder over Sabbath's fortunes. Where they had gone wrong, what they needed to do now to right the ship, how they could claw back some credibility in the eyes of the press and the serious critics. How to prevent Sabbath becoming even more of a joke?

It didn't help that Ozzy was now in free-fall too. 'By that stage, we were all just fucking out of our minds! We wouldn't sleep for fucking days. Several times I'd set myself on fire with a fag, lying in bed pissed. And I'd wake up and me chest would be blazing.' Other times Ozzy would wake up in his own urine – if he woke up at all. Most nights he was simply picked up where he lay and thrown over the shoulder of a roadie who carried him to his bed. Tony, who'd always thought of Ozzy as a clown, now began to see him as a liability. Worse, he began to channel his frustration at the band's diminishing record sales directly onto Ozzy, comparing him unfavourably to Robert Plant, the troubled but still golden god that fronted Zeppelin, and Deep Purple's David Coverdale, another good-looking powerhouse vocalist who didn't let his drug habits rob him of his dignity – certainly not in public.

Tony, who'd always seen Ozzy as a necessary evil – happy to put up with his stupid antics while the band's star was rising – now began to resent the fact that his band, Black Sabbath, had a buffoon for a singer. At least with Bill, whose drug and alcohol problems were the equal of Ozzy's, you knew he'd come up with the goods onstage or in the studio. Bill was also the butt of Tony's many 'pranks'. Like the time, during the recording of *Technical Ecstasy*, when Tony and a roadie hid a large lump of Gorgonzola cheese under Bill's bed. Knowing Bill's habit of rarely changing clothes anyway, plus his reluctance to allow maids in to clean his room more than once a week, within days the smell was so horrendous you could smell Bill coming round the corner. Or the time Tony ordered the crew to dress a hopelessly drunk Bill up as Hitler, using gaffer tape to hold down his hair – then discovered the only way to remove the tape without pulling out his hair was to cut the hair extremely short and jagged. Or the time Tony ordered an unconscious Bill to be carried down to the side of a lake, placed in a rowboat and pushed out onto the water – then walked away. Bill was a hopeless drunk and coke fiend, but he was 'a laugh'. And he rarely missed a beat.

As for Geezer, he still played great, wrote great lyrics and did what he was fucking told. But Ozzy . . .

Paul Clark, who began working for the band around this time, first as a driver, then later tour manager, recalls how 'Tony always used to encourage me to stay away from Ozzy.' Clark, who'd met Iommi in 1973 while working as a bouncer at the Rum Runner nightclub in Birmingham, had been 'in and out of prison all me life, you know what I mean? Borstal, detention centres and shit like that. That's how I was. But it straightened me out [being with Sabbath] and I made a career of it. I learnt such a lot from it and I did put a lot into it.' Even the unshakable Clark was taken aback though when Iommi warned him off the band's singer. 'Ozzy would ask me to pick him up or something. "No, don't do anything for him," Tony would say. "He'll have you running all over the place." But I treated everybody the same. I remember Ozzy, if I was driving him and somebody in another car had pissed us off, he'd go, "When he stops, I'll shit on his bonnet!" He'd be getting out the car and I'd be like, "Fuck off, Oz." He'd be, "No, I'll shit on him!" He could shit at the drop of a hat, Ozzy could. Fucking funny.'

'Because I didn't play an instrument,' said Ozzy, 'I felt like just the singer. Like not really involved a lot of the time.' A situation not helped by Tony's now complete control of affairs onstage and off. 'So, you know, you would have confrontations – I thought I was better than him, he thought he was better than me and he thought he was better than him. But really I'm no better than Bill and Bill's no better than me. None of us are any better than anybody else. Just as long as we all had a bag of powder and a fucking block of dope and a bottle of booze in the boot and a car to drive and a nice hotel to stay in and do waffle-dust all night, we were happy.'

All, that is, except for Tony.

Finally, Ozzy couldn't take it any longer. None of them could but Ozzy, who'd always been terrified of Tony, who'd always flinched whenever Tony even came near him, was the first to bail out. The latter part of 1977 had been especially hard for Ozzy. His father Jack was dying of cancer. His band no longer felt real. His marriage to Thelma was unravelling. Ozzy was either out of control on the road, or out of luck off it. When he went out, surrounded by the usual posse of old friends and hangers-on, he felt like a circus freak, stared out or started on, the best way he knew how to deal with it, snorting more coke and drinking more booze, smoking more dope and shagging more 'tarts'. Nothing was off limits. 'I did it all,' he told me. 'The only one I never got into was smack. I tried it a few times but it just knocked me out and I already had the booze and the downers for that. I'm lucky, I suppose, cos that really would have been the end of me.'

Instead, the end would find him all by itself. Back at Rockfield studios, near Monmouth, for the first time since *Paranoid* seven years before, the band were supposed to be writing and rehearsing new material for their next album, scheduled to be recorded, once again for tax reasons, in Toronto, in the new year, the feeling in the room where they played was the worst it had ever been. Feeling more pressured than usual to come up with the goods, Tony could not find the right vibe. Even Geezer, normally so tuned in as long as he had a joint and a drink in his hand, struggled to come up with anything useful. For Tony, this was unacceptable. He was used to Ozzy and Bill being useless, but Geezer was his co-songwriter, his fellow guitarist, the only other one in the band who was supposed to know what the fuck Tony was trying to do. Tony sacked him.

'There was just an air around the band that somebody had to go,' Geezer would shrug and say years later. 'First it was me. They all had a meeting, then Bill came over to my house and said I was fired. There was no reason. It was just that I was out the band, everybody else thought I wasn't into it and that I should just go. So I was a bit pissed off but, you know, I didn't want to argue about it. And I wasn't really that bothered to be honest. I'd lost interest by then.

'Then about three or four weeks later I get a phone call from Bill again, saying the band wants to meet me at the Holiday Inn, in Birmingham. So I thought, what the hell's this about now? So I went and met them and it was like, we want you back in the band and I wasn't doing anything else so I said all right. It was just an upheaval in the band. It was like, somebody's gotta go, kind of thing, but who's it gonna be? And the first person was me. So I went back to the band, and then like obviously that caused bad feeling. No matter how much everyone tried to disguise it, there was [now] bad feeling in the band.'

A week later they received a visit in Wales from their accountant, Colin Newman, who worked for Don. 'I knew there was something very bad gonna come down,' said Ozzy, 'in the fact that we'd never paid tax, because Patrick Meehan used to say, "Don't worry about that, I'll take care of that." Everything was taken care of, you know? And then we left Patrick and Colin Newman came to Monmouth and he spent four fucking hours telling us the ins and outs and whatever. And basically, he was saying, "Look, you ain't paid tax since fucking zero, day one. You gotta pay some tax." And after all this, Bill was pissed and he says, "Can you repeat that, please?" And I says, "Oh, for fuck's sake, Bill! This is hope-less!" So I just got up and walked out. And I was drunker than they were but I drove my car like that from Monmouth in Wales to Staffordshire. I didn't even have a driving licence. I just had to fucking get away ...'

Tony went insane. How dare he, the lowest totem on the pole, run off and leave the band in shit? Geezer and Bill were more fearful. Ozzy was the singer of the band. As Geezer said: 'You didn't just go out to the shop and buy another one.' Would his leaving mean the breaking up of the band? But Tony was ada-mant. As Paul Clark recalls: 'Put Tony with his back to the wall and he's a fighter, he'll always come at you. His attitude was, like, fuck that. We'll get a new singer. And that's what he tried to do.'

The singer Tony turned to was indicative of the kind of counter-intuitive moves he would consistently make over the next 20 years whenever it came time to find Sabbath yet another singer. Instead of searching for someone whose voice might easily suit a now extremely well-known back catalogue of mate-rial, he went for someone that was as far removed from Ozzy – personality and voice-wise – as he could possibly get. In this case, former Savoy Brown frontman Dave Walker. Dave could sing all right, but in that generic, bluesy style endemic among singers of his generation: rough-edged, throaty, vibrato-led and earnest. Someone for whom the words 'Ooh baby' would come naturally. But who would tie himself in knots trying to sing something like 'Iron Man' or 'Children Of The Grave'.

Tony didn't care. Although he now lived in San Francisco, where he'd washed up after a brief, unsuccessful period in Fleet-wood Mac, Dave was another local Brummy boy that Tony and Bill had known since their days in Mythology. He was a little older than the others – 33 in January – but he had always looked up to Tony, who had helped him get his gig with Savoy Brown years before, and the guitarist knew he would be no trouble. Certainly no more, surely, than Ozzy. What's more he was available to fly back immediately – and he could write. One, brief, mumbling phone call from Tony later and Dave was in.

But if Walker imagined he was walking into a dream job with a supernova rock band, he was in for a big surprise. Arriving at Monmouth on a bitterly cold, rainy day just before Christmas, 1977, he was not reassured by the scene he found himself walking into. Tony seemed glad to see him – at last, someone he could write with that was happy to be there. But Tony was not a big talker. You were meant to simply know what he was feeling at any given point. Dave could handle that, Tony's guitar doing his talking for him. The singer quickly set about working up new material, including three songs that would eventually be recorded for the next Sabbath album. Geezer, who had never met Dave before, was quiet, though, standoffish, put out, Dave guessed, at the prospect of a new lyric writer joining the gang. While Bill ... Bill only spoke to Bill these days, it seemed, when he was sober enough to do so. Looking back years later, Dave seemed to pinpoint the absence of Ozzy as something that hovered over everything still, making an already shaky ambience even stranger and more dissolute. He recalls Ozzy joining them for a drink in a nearby pub one afternoon. 'I felt really sorry for him because he was just going through some awful crap, I think, at the time. I felt then, you know what, Ozzy's really not quite sure about what he's doing. He's not really quite sure if he did the right thing quitting Black Sabbath.' Working with the rest of the surviving band was 'Like going home and not knowing where you were.'

Maybe so. But it didn't stop him 'writing a shit load of lyrics' for them while he was there. New band photographs were also taken, in lieu of an official announcement in the music press.

Ozzy was quick to respond, giving a tearful interview the same month to Tony Stewart of the *NME*. Sequestered by a roaring open fire in the palatial lounge of his Staffordshire cottage, he told the wide-eyed writer that if he hadn't quit Sabbath 'I would have been dead in two or three years [and] I don't think anything's worth giving your life up for.' He spoke of being on a 'two-year binge' and of his guilt at letting the fans down, 'because it's never going to be the same again for the people who liked Sabbath then'. But he had no choice. 'I wouldn't say the band screwed me up. But there were a lot of personality clashes.' He admitted he had not liked *Technical Ecstasy*, yet was bored with playing the same old songs every night on tour. He drew parallels with classic early Sabbath and the new emerging wave of punk bands. 'I'm not saying we were before punk, but in our own way we were what the punk groups are now: a people's band. I don't want to play it, but I'm into the new wave because you don't have to be a brain surgeon to listen to it. It's just a simple, down-to-earth music that people can tap out on a tin lid.' Mostly, he decided, it was the business that was really destroying Sabbath. 'The business,' he declared, 'is like a rosy red apple at the front, with a big crab at the back.' He also, prophetically, as it turns out, announced he was forming his own band, to be called the Blizzard Of Ozz. 'I'll do it again,' he shrugged, 'but I'll do it comfortably. I won't ever let myself be prostituted again.'

In January 1978, the 'new' Sabbath marked the new year by performing live on a local Birmingham Friday lunchtime TV show called *Look Hear*, hosted by Toyah Willcox, blasting their way through 'War Pigs' and a new track co-written with Dave called 'Junior's Eyes'. Friends and co-workers from Don's office and the record company said it was marvellous and predicted big things for the new line-up. Behind the scenes, though, Don was not amused. But he waited to make his move and when he did it would be decisive.

Two weeks later, Ozzy's father died. It was 20 January, the same date his eldest daughter Jessica had been born on seven years before. Ozzy later told the writer David Gans how during his father's last days in hospital he had been moved out of the main ward into a side room, where the mops and buckets were normally kept. 'It was too distressing for the rest of the patients so they put him in a cot, sort of a crib thing, a giant crib. They strapped him ... like a boxer, fucking bandages on his hands, with a glucose drip going into his arm. He was stoned out of his head. You know, the most amazing thing he said to me. I told my father one day, I take drugs. I said to him, before you go, will you take drugs? He says, I promise you I'll take drugs. He was on morphine. Totally out of his mind on morphine, because the pain must have been horrendous. They had the operation on a Tuesday, and he died on Thursday ... I haven't got over it yet. The twentieth of January, I'll go freaking like a werewolf. I'll cry and I'll laugh all day long, because it's the day my daughter was born and the day my father died. Like a fucking lunatic.'

A month after that Ozzy was back in Sabbath, and they were in Toronto making a new album. In the end, money prevailed, as it always would with Ozzy and Sabbath. Don read them the riot act, how they couldn't expect to draw the same level of advances from their record companies or concert promoters with what he uncharitably but not inaccurately called 'this fucking nobody' fronting the band. Especially not now Ozzy wanted back in. Or as Ozzy later told me: 'I didn't know what I fucking wanted. All I knew was I was on my way to being skint if I didn't get some-thing else off the ground but I was still so fucked up I knew that was never gonna happen. So when they said, "Oh, we're going to Canada, do you want to come too then or what?" I thought, well, what else am I gonna do?'

Nobody was any happier though. Least of all Dave Walker, who was given his marching orders but at least felt his time would be compensated by having some writing credits on the new album. But when Don nixed that too – 'People were only interested in Ozzy singing Ozzy's lyrics,' he told me, in that typically double-think way of hardened old music biz pros like him, disregarding the fact that Ozzy hardly ever wrote any of the lyrics anyway – Walker became but a footnote in the Sabbath story. A true sign of things to come, now and into the future. For Sabbath's history would be long and often painful, but so often rewritten that today the four original members agree only on what is most circumspect, depending on who is paying the bill. An attitude that began with what was effectively the true end of Black Sabbath: the ironically, yet, in retrospect, all too aptly titled *Never Say Die*.

According to Don Arden's famous music biz maxim, 'You can't polish a turd.' Never was this more clearly demonstrated than on the abysmal *Never Say Die*. Even Tony Iommi would later confess that this was an album that 'nobody in the band even liked'. A compendium of half-baked ideas processed through a prism of cocaine, booze, dope and a slackness of vision that led them to believe all they had to do to contemporise the Sabbath sound and bring it in line with the new, bleeding-edge punk musical ideology was speed up the riffs, as exemplified by dire tracks like 'Johnny Blade' ('the meanest guy around his town') and 'Hard Road', which sounds more like a throwback to their Sixties blues past than a grasp of the new punk present.

Rehearsing from nine every morning at a disused cinema where the heating was not working, they would stand and jam in their coats and mufflers, huffing and puffing life into dirge-like rock-by-numbers like 'Shock Wave' and 'Air Dance', then break for dinner during which they hardly spoke to each other before shuffling in ones and twos across the road to Sound Interchange Studios, to record whatever they had just come up with. As if to emphasise their change in fortune, 'the studio turned out to be crap', said Tony. He blamed himself. He had only booked it, he said, because he'd been told the Stones had recently recorded there. 'But the sound was dead as a doornail.'

And on the seventh day … Black Sabbath circa 1970. L–r: Terry
'Geezer' Butler; Bill Ward; John 'Ozzy' Osbourne; Tony Iommi.

A beautifully posed picture of Ozzy pretending to play keyboards, at Island studios, London, early 1971.

On tour in America 1972.

'We used to get the coke mailed to us from America,' says Ozzy, London 1971.

'Smoke it! Get high!' The band plus rubber friend, London 1971.

The Al Capone of pop. Sabbath manager
Don Arden on his way to court (again). 1968.

'Geezer's got a great brain.'
Onstage in Manchester,
England, March 1973.

Four men in a leaky boat, on the Hudson River, New York 1971.

Like punk is not about to happen. Madison Square Garden, December 1976.

Symptom of the universe: onstage in Copenhagen, 1975. Ozzy still marooned to one side.

Bill Ward, in the library bar, Plaza Hotel, Copenhagen, October 1975. The final straw was when he realised, 'I was now incapable of being on stage' without drugs and alcohol.

'We were the drug commandos,' says Ozzy of his destructive on-tour relationship with Bill Ward. 'We would never come through a door where a plate glass window would do.' America, 1977.

They tried rolling up the carpets to bring some life to the air-less acoustics but when that didn't work they simply grinded it out, hurrying to get done as fast as they could. It wasn't all bad. Several of the tracks, including 'Over To You', 'Junior's Eyes' and 'Swinging The Chain', had been written while Dave Walker was in the band. But Ozzy 'refused' to sing any of Walker's lyrics, forcing Geezer to provide hasty rewrites on 'Over To You' and Bill being pushed to sing the lead vocals on 'Swinging The Chain'; while the band simply pulled the wool over Ozzy's eyes for the other – 'Junior's Eyes' – telling him they'd rewritten them when they hadn't, at least they had a musical framework to build on. Yet another Walker-era track, 'Breakout', simply became an instru-mental, with a phalanx of saxophones brought in to add colour, simply because it was easier than trying to think of anything else to do. The whole thing, said Tony, 'was doomed from start to finish'.

According to Ozzy, 'What happened was, eventually we were writing the music for the wrong reasons. We were tired. The drugs and the alcohol were taking their toll and it's true to say that the things I [later] said about Tony were somewhat unjusti-fied because we were all fucked up and expecting him to pull us out of the shit. For which he would spend days in the studio, and he was out of his box anyway. But we left it upon his shoulders to make us a good record and if it wasn't good and we didn't like it we condemned him for it secretly, in our heads.' Geezer agrees. 'It was horrible. I hated that album. I hate that album so much. Even to this day I can't stand the bloody thing, because it's just so false and fake.'

The only bright spot was the title track, a frantic thrash that really wouldn't have sounded out of place on the Sex Pistols album. There wasn't even a guitar solo, just a superbly cartwheel-ing riff that came in, did its business, and left again, leaving the listener breathless and impressed. When they were persuaded to release it as a single, 'Never Say Die' became their first hit single in Britain since 'Paranoid' eight years before. They even paid a return visit to the *Top Of The Pops* studio, in May, to mime it. By then they were halfway through a 29-date UK tour, including five shows in London and four in Birmingham. With the album peaking in the charts at No. 12, it seemed the home fans still loved them, no matter how hard the four band members tried to tarnish the legend.

Nevertheless, said Geezer, 'There was horrible vibes in the band by then. Ozzy really was only there because he didn't have anything else to do. None of us really liked the songs that we were doing but we couldn't come up with anything better. And we just sort of did it, and put the album out for the sake of putting it out and then [did the tour]. The tour was great, but we were on with Van Halen and Ozzy just completely lost it. He thought Van Halen was ten times better than we were.'

Offstage, they did at least try to have fun. Paul Clark recalls one running gag that involved trying to convince Geezer that his driver and personal roadie, nicknamed Concorde because he had a big nose, 'was nothing but a smelly farm boy. He was a lovely kid, but we used to take the piss, saying to Geezer, "Fucking hell, he smells! Has he shit himself?" And Geezer would be like, "I can't smell anything, leave me alone."' In a twist on their previous gag on Bill, after the show one night Paul and Tony shoved a huge wodge of Gorgonzola into the heater of Geezer's car. Geezer, who was then living in the upmarket Midlands town of Clows Top, had taken to having Concorde drive him home each night. 'The next day,' says Paul, 'Geezer comes in and he's got a handkerchief over his nose. And he's got all those danglers hanging from the rear-view mirror, to make the car smell nice. Literally, dozens of them. He says, "You've got to sack him! Get me another driver! I can't breathe in the car!" Me and Tony were fucking dying trying not to laugh.'

It was, as ever, Bill though who bore the brunt of Tony's 'humour'. Just before they were due onstage at the Ipswich Gaumont, in May, Bill pulled on what he thought of as his new 'punk gear' – camouflage trousers and jacket bought earlier that day from a nearby Army & Navy store. When he asked Tony what he thought of his new stage clothes, Tony told him: 'Fucking shit.' Bill pleaded: 'No, come on, Tony.' Tony tutted: 'Shocking.' Then Tony went out and got a bucket of water and threw it over Bill. 'How can I go onstage like this?' wailed Bill, but Tony had already gone, staggering down the corridor laughing ...

Things took a decidedly less funny turn, though, when the tour arrived in Glasgow and Tony discovered there was an 'old friend' from the *Melody Maker* there: Allan Jones. Tony had never forgiven the larger-than-life writer for the pasting he had given him years before. He decided it was time to exact his revenge. Getting Paul to invite Jones backstage 'to say hello' again, Tony was taking off his expensive wristwatch as Jones entered the room. As he stuck out his hand to be shaken, Tony delivered what he later described as 'a finely judged left hook' to the writer's jaw. Naturally, it made headlines in the *Melody Maker* and elsewhere the following week, and threw the band into even more disrepute with an ever more militant punk audience, but Tony didn't give a fuck. This wasn't about music. This was personal.

Recalling their earlier meeting, Tony explained how he'd met Jones at the station then driven him back to his house in Leicestershire, where they had dinner together. 'It was fine,' said Tony. Except that later, Jones had committed the cardinal sin, as the guitarist saw it, of criticising and making fun of his lifestyle. 'He expected me to live in a cave. He ran it down because I collect antiques and paintings.' Jones mocked his growing collection of artworks 'that most people wouldn't have the room to put in their homes'. The final straw, though, was when, according to Iommi, Jones made fun of his large German Shepherd dogs, which he claimed 'attacked him'. Sooner or later, Tony decided as he chopped out yet another monstrously large line of cocaine, Jones would have to pay. In Glasgow, in May 1978, he did so. Eventually, Tony decided, they would *all* have to pay. And by the end of the same year, they would. Beginning with Ozzy. Before moving on to the rest of the band and anyone else who now stood in his way ...

By the end of the year, Black Sabbath were a burned-out husk. They had spent most of the year on tour with Van Halen, a new Warner Bros. signing that threatened to do more to destabilise Sabbath than any number of the best punk bands could ever do. With the Seventies coming to their inglorious end, no rock band better summed up the changing of the guard than the lightning-fast Van Halen. Fronted by David Lee Roth, another clown with limited vocal ability but convincingly believable street appeal, Roth was nearly seven years younger than Ozzy and ten times more athletic, his marshal arts training and mountaineering skills making him appear almost as if he was flying onstage. Their guitarist, Eddie Van Halen, was even more impressive. A world apart from the kind of blues-oriented feel of Iommi's classic playing style, Eddie had taken rock guitar to a whole new level, introducing the style that was to dominate the sound of rock-to-come in the 1980s: shredding. A genuine virtuoso, he also brought a completely fresh bag of tricks to his game, including the finger-tapping, though that wasn't what he called it, that would also come to dominate the way the Eighties generation of guitarists played their instruments, right up to the present day.

Their self-titled debut album, instantly hailed as a classic, had been released earlier that year and was already on its way to platinum in the US when *Never Say Die* arrived, undercooked and under-loved, in record stores in America. When Sabbath's album barely scraped the US Hot 100, it wasn't just the critics that were now comparing Sabbath unfavourably to their flash new support act. For fans, there could scarcely be a more stark contrast between the rapidly fading old and the brand arse-spanking new.

Predictably, the band began bitching about their 'upstart' support act. Paul Clark tried to console the band by telling them they had 'paid for Van Halen to be famous'. But behind the scenes, Tony Iommi knew the truth. Enamoured of Eddie Van Halen's startling new technique, he befriended the younger guitarist, taking him back to his room, where they would spend the night ploughing through Tony's seemingly endless supply of cocaine. As if by becoming friends, he might develop a mentorship that would rub off on Sabbath's own credibility. As if they were merely two sides of the same coin. Yet the truth was plain for all to see. It wasn't just that Sabbath now relied on their support act to sell their tickets for them – they were routinely being upstaged every night. Any other time, they would have sacked the band from the tour, but this time they couldn't afford to. Not unless they wanted to cancel the tour and go back to playing theatres and clubs.

Nobody, though, least of all Ozzy, befriended the outlandish David Lee Roth. A college dropout and son of a millionaire eye surgeon, Roth had an IQ that was off the scale and his over-exuberant personality balanced on a hair-trigger. He was, in fact, everything that the four Sabbath members were not: born wealthy, intelligent, upper class. Worst of all, he seemed happy.

'We did start having problems,' said Tony, 'and with that and the drugs and everything else, it made the band start coming apart. We probably should have stopped before we did.' Instead, Sabbath ploughed on until the bitter end, which came, finally, mercifully, with two shows at the inauspiciously named Tingley Coliseum in Albuquerque, New Mexico, two weeks before Christmas, 1978. They didn't know it yet but it would be Ozzy's last show with the band.

*

When the tour was finally over they all went home to England but any hopes of an extended break were soon dashed when Don Arden, now living full-time in Los Angeles, where ELO were at the dizzy peak of their American success, insisted that Sabbath, too, join him permanently in Hollywood. It would ease their tax burden to become non-domicile British residents again, and it would relieve them of the odious task of being within reach of the UK music press, who were now gunning for all the old 'dinosaurs' of Seventies rock. More important, it kept the band within earshot of Don, whose empire had expanded to such an extent he felt able to fix anything – even Black Sabbath's increasingly charred recording career.

Now living in the vast mansion house and grounds formerly owned by Howard Hughes – 'Which I paid for, cash!' – close friends with the New York Mafia chief Joe Pagano, contributor to the Republican Party, along with his other good friend, Tony Curtis, and making money hand-over-fist managing ELO, Air Supply, Sabbath and several others he was now repositioning on his own Jet Records label, Don no longer saw himself as the gun-toting gangster of the British music biz but a major player in the American entertainment business. He knew Tony and Sabbath were in bad shape. No problem! He would install them in one of several spacious properties on his own grounds and fix everything, wait and see. Beginning with a new, disproportionately steep advance for their next album from Warner Bros., all Tony and the band had to do was write it.

There was another, darker reason why Sabbath now received favourite-son status from Don: Tony had recently begun a not-so-secret affair with his daughter Sharon. 'It was crazy,' Don would tell me years later. 'She was mad, passionately in love with him or so it seemed to me. But he didn't want to know. He was a musician. He had a wife and kid back home. To him it was just a fling. When she realised he didn't feel the same, she went insane.'

He laughed but his eyes remained cold and hard as he said it.

In fact, Tony and Sharon had a lot in common. Both were vulnerable people – he with a rapidly disintegrating career and ever-worsening drug habit, she with the same issues of low self-esteem she'd suffered from since she was a kid – both the type to disguise such insecurities by putting on a bold, seemingly impregnable front. Two needy people in search of short-term fixes that, ultimately, would satisfy neither of them.

Sharon Arden was Don Arden's daughter, and someone who had earned her music biz spurs years ago working with many of her father's major acts. During the coming years and decades, Sharon took Ozzy and turned him into a bigger star than Tony Iommi could ever have dreamed of becoming to the point where Iommi would eventually return, cap in hand, virtually, happy to revive the Ozzy-led lineup of Black Sabbath that did entirely as Sharon Osbourne, as she had now become, bid it.

Tony, for his part, felt trapped into keeping Sharon happy while her father still held the keys to his renewed success. He liked Sharon. She was lively, adventurous, intelligent and funny. But he didn't really fancy her.

Around this time Tony met Hollywood's own notorious Dr Feelgood – the dentist Dr Max Shapiro. Shapiro had been Elvis Presley's preferred dentist at the time of the singer's controversy-shrouded death eighteen months before. Known for his round-the-clock 'house calls', Shapiro would later be named and shamed as one of the several doctors that regularly wrote Presley prescriptions for heavy-duty drugs, including liquid cocaine. Clark says Dr Shapiro would now routinely write Tony prescriptions for vials of pharmaceutical cocaine, delivered in large pill form.

'One [pill] would have been like a gram of powder,' he reckons. 'And they would come in these vials with about fifteen pills in them. In fact, Tony had a thing, I thought it was a pencil sharpener, but he'd put [a pill] in this machine and grind it down.' Then snort it. Clark recalls Shapiro coming out to the studio where Sabbath were supposed to be working. 'The guy was covered in scabs.' He would disappear into a side room with the guitarist, perform a desultory 'examination' of his mouth then write him a script, for which Tony would pay cash.

Not even Dr Shapiro's magic pills could lift the guitarist's mood, though, as he struggled to come up with new material for another Sabbath album. Every week or so Don or the record company would inquire as to how it was going and Tony would lie and tell them everything was going well. But in reality he didn't even know where the rest of the band were, much of the time. Then when they did put in an appearance, it only added to the frustration as none of them seemed to have any ideas left at all. Ozzy, in particular, now began to bear the brunt of Iommi's anger.

Tony would sigh when I asked him, some years later, if he blamed Ozzy for the band's troubles at this time. 'I suppose, in some ways. You would at that time. I suppose we all blamed each other, because we were all going through funny stages of . . . Whether it was the drugs or what but it was definitely . . . mooted. Because of Ozzy going and coming back, and we all had all these traumas going on. It was very difficult to deal with. And I think you just get annoyed with the situation, with the way it's going.' They had been in LA for months, 'and we done, basically, fuck all, really – apart from loads of drugs. We were rehearsing, nothing was happening, and Ozzy, I think, was going through a lot of stuff then. He was getting more and more into drugs and we were getting more and more into drugs and it really just came apart. It just fell apart, and we just had to do something.'

According to Geezer, the final straw came when they all arrived at the studio one day, only to find Ozzy lying unconscious in a pool of his own piss. 'Tony just went, "I can't work with him any more. He's just not into it, so let's just admit it. Ozzy's not into it, so it's either just spoil it or get somebody else in."'

According to Tony, though, when I spoke to him, it was Geezer and Bill that laid down the ultimatum. 'Bill and Geezer came to me and said, "Look, you know, we've got to do something. Either get Ozzy sorted out or we're gonna leave." I went, "Oh, thanks, leave it to me", you know? So it just came to a situation where we had to tell Ozzy, "Look, if you don't do something we're gonna have to find somebody else." It really got to that situation, which was awful. But the band was gonna break up and so ... that's what happened, really.'

In fact, they all have their own versions of just how and why Ozzy was fired from Black Sabbath. According to Geezer, he had been so distraught at what he suggests was Tony's decision to fire Ozzy that he himself also walked out on the band shortly after. 'I cried me eyes out for two days. Cos I always said like, "Sabbath is four people – Ozzy, Tony, Bill and me. And if any of us ever leave or are fired, it's not Black Sabbath any more."' And it wasn't. Geezer was so upset that 'a couple of weeks after Ozzy went, I left. I had personal problems as well and I just couldn't get into it without Ozzy. So I pissed off for about three months.'

Bill, whom the others coerced into being the one to actually give Ozzy the news, now claims that he, too, was so utterly devastated by the decision that he never really recovered – a situation that led to his own messy departure from the band barely a year later. 'I felt lousy about the circumstances that surrounded the whole thing about Ozzy and being asked to leave, and I've never really stopped feeling lousy about it.' Even Ozzy would put his own spin on the story at times over the years, once claiming he went out of his way to deliberately get fired, after receiving advice from an unnamed lawyer who warned him that if he left of his own accord he would forfeit any pay-off.

The first Ozzy knew of it, though, was when he was told he'd have to leave the house they were all sharing in Beverly Hills. A maid came in and packed his things, and a driver was summoned to deliver Ozzy instead to the Le Parc hotel in West Hollywood, where a small apartment had been reserved for him. 'I was thinking, hey, I don't really like what's going on here but what if I jump out of the frying pan into the fire? And when I did get fired, I was devastated! Because I thought, now that's it, it's all over, I'm back on the dole, I've lost it all. And so all I did when I eventually did get fired in California ... I think Bill told me they'd all had a meeting and that I'd gotta go ... And I was just fucking gutted, you know?

'And so I'd locked myself into an apartment in Le Parc. I never used to go out my room. Never opened the drapes or let the maid in for three months. I just used to order Dominos pizzas and my coke dealer would come round every day and I'd order beer and booze from Gilson's on Sunset because they said they would deliver it. That's the beauty of California, if you want anything, it's delivered, you don't have to fucking go out for a piece of arse paper. It's just delivered if you want it. I was thinking, oh well, I might as well have one last fling and then get ready for the fucking big bang. In fact, the most money, at that point, that I'd had was when I did my settlement, with selling my part of the name to Black Sabbath. I think I got £96,000, and I was like, "Fuck, man! Ninety-six grand! I can't believe it!" It was the first time in my life that I'd owned so much cash.'

Don was outraged, seeing Ozzy's sacking as coming at the worst possible time for the band. Already struggling to convince the industry that Sabbath was far from a spent force commercially, this sent out decidedly the wrong signal. But Tony was adamant. Either Ozzy went or he did. And even Don was not arrogant enough to believe he could rebuild Black Sabbath without its chief songwriter. What he was convinced of, though, was that if Ozzy really was to be ousted, there was still a career for him to be had as a solo artist. As such, and as part of the singer's parachute out of Sabbath, he was signed – for a modest advance, which essentially consisted of his day-to-day living costs – to Jet Records. Always one to find a silver lining in any financial cloud, Don reasoned that the breakup might even be a good thing – if it left him managing two potentially successful rock acts. All would depend on who exactly Sabbath got to replace Ozzy. It would not be easy, Don knew, but he could already think of several possible replacements that might do the job.

Before he could even discuss them with the band, however, Tony had already made up his mind.

'A fucking midget!' Don was still crying with scorn when we discussed it over twenty years later. 'A fucking midget, that's who they wanted! I told them, "You can't have a fucking midget fronting Black Sabbath. You'll be a laughing stock!" But that's what they wanted so I fucked them off. I thought, I'm too old, too successful, too fucking smart for this shit. And that was it.'

The midget in question was, in fact, one of the most totemic singers in rock in the late Seventies. Someone short in height but tall in stature already with a voice like a lion roaring and a drive and ambition – and songwriting talent – that would achieve what had seemed all but impossible that long, hot, cocaine-confused summer of 1979, and actually bring Black Sabbath back, bigger and better than before.

His name was Ronnie James Dio and he meant business. Whether Tony, Geezer and Bill liked it or not ...

'It's not just about being able to sing,' Ronnie James Dio would tell me later on, when the blood had scabbed over and the fires damped down. 'It's about being able to form a bridge between you, the band, and the audience. Somewhere all that energy can meet – and explode!'

Unlike Ozzy Osbourne, whose sad-clown act was partly down to character, forged through a misspent childhood of hopeless poverty and grim gallows humour, and partly down to the collective weight of Black Sabbath's own constantly low expectations of themselves, and others, Ronnie James Dio saw himself as a dragon slayer, an alchemist of dreams who could turn the dourest situation to advantage by sheer force of his iron will. Like Ozzy, he enjoyed a joke; unlike Ozzy, you would never dream of laughing at Ronnie – not to his face anyway. And where Ozzy seemed to just drift along in his career, either falling at the first hurdle or somehow leaping to the top of pile through sheer luck, Ronnie took every step of his career extremely seriously. He wasn't as tall as Ozzy, wasn't as good-looking or easy to love, but he could get inside an audience's mind and stay there like a mental wormhole, like a force of nature, like the very wind and rain he seemed able to summon every time he opened his mouth to sing and that incredibly powerful voice came out, reborn again, the sun that always rises, right after the coldest part of the darkest dawn.

A product of that original, irony-free era of utterly earnest rock frontmen, he told me: 'When I stand onstage and sing I like to imagine I'm looking into the eyes of every single person in the audience, that I'm singing specifically for them. Even when I'm just talking to them introducing a song, I never shout, I simply speak to them as though we were having a private conversation. Partly, it's because I've always hated frontmen that simply shout and leer at an audience, treating them as though they were one big blob. I've always thought that was so rude. And mainly, it's because I take what I do *very* seriously. Don't get me wrong, I like to have fun up there. But I really do mean every word I sing or say. And I want people to know that ...'

Born Ronald James Padavona on 10 July 1942 in Portsmouth, New Hampshire, the only child of an immigrant Italian family, Ronnie grew up in Cortland, upstate New York. He was raised a Roman Catholic, but his real religion was always music. Having learned bass, piano and trumpet at high school, he joined his first band, the Vegas Kings, as a fifteen-year-old. Starting out as the bass player, by the time the band changed its name to Ronnie & The Rumblers (later Ronnie and The Red Caps) he had graduated to being their singer. But only, he insisted, 'because no one else wanted the job. It wasn't my plan at all to lead the band.'

The first time he sang, he said, 'I knew I had something. Unlike learning to play an instrument, it just seemed to be something that was there immediately – a gift.' Nevertheless, it was his skill as a trumpeter that initially gave him his edge as a vocalist. 'It was partly to do with knowing how to breathe, partly to do with the fact that the trumpet has its own voice, its own way of phrasing. I learned a lot about singing just from being able to play the trumpet.'

When the line-up changed again, he also changed his name – deciding Padavona simply 'wasn't catchy enough, this was the Sixties, don't forget' – to Ronnie Dio, after an infamous local mafia figure, Johnny Dio, 'which just sounded cool', the band becoming Ronnie Dio and the Prophets. It was the Prophets that, in 1967, would metamorphose into his first proper rock outfit, The Electric Elves – later shortened to Elf. 'It was the first band we had which tried to make it with its own original material.' It was also the first band he'd been in that enjoyed a degree of success. When they were signed to Deep Purple's own newly minted label, Purple bassist Roger Glover became their producer and Elf were invited to open for the band on their legendary *Burn* tour of 1974 – which was also where Ronnie met the man who would single-handedly transform his career: Purple's own moody guitarist and leader, Ritchie Blackmore. 'It was quite a compliment for us because Purple were one of the biggest bands in the world then.'

It came as an even greater – and unforeseen – compliment when Blackmore invited Ronnie and Elf to effectively become his backing band on what was ostensibly his first solo album, in 1975, but to all intents and purposes they became his new post-Purple band, the guitarist having become disaffected by the increasingly funk-oriented direction Purple's music was taking by then. The resulting album, *Ritchie Blackmore's Rainbow*, Ronnie would always make a point of telling you, 'should really have been called Ritchie Blackmore and Ronnie James Dio's Rainbow'. He had a point. Enraptured by the startling voice and untapped songwriting talents of his new singer – not least on what would become cornerstone metal classics like 'Man On The Silver Mountain' – if it hadn't been for the potential of his new partnership with Dio, it's doubtful Blackmore would have been courageous enough to quit Purple, who were at the height of their commercial success, when he did. As Blackmore later admitted: 'I left because I'd met up with Ronnie Dio, and he was so easy to work with. He was originally just going to do one track of a solo LP, but we ended up doing the whole LP in three weeks, which I was very excited about.'

It was their next album together, though, *Rainbow Rising*, that would catapult the band into the annals of rock history. Released in 1976 and featuring what is now considered the quintessential Rainbow line-up – all Dio's former Elf sidemen replaced by rock veterans: drummer Cozy Powell, bassist Jimmy Bain and keyboardist Tony Carey – *Rainbow Rising* set the benchmark by which all heavy metal albums would be judged throughout the rest of the Seventies. Certainly, it was one of the best albums Dio would ever sing on. 'Yeah, I'd agree with that,' he said nonchalantly.

Unfortunately, with the line-up fracturing again (neither Bain nor Carey survived the cull) before the recording of a follow-up could begin, the potential of the band was never fully explored. 'It was a shame but that's the way Ritchie liked to work, in order to keep things fresh,' Ronnie told me straight-faced. His cold, hard glare said the rest. Within a year, Dio was also on the receiving end of Blackmore's pointy black boot. They broke up because 'I didn't want to make the kind of music he wanted to make. He wanted to be a pop star and I don't write that way. I wanted to still have roots in intelligence and he wanted songs about love affairs.' That said, *Long Live Rock'n'Roll* in 1978 was a far better album than Black Sabbath had made in years. Again, Dio co-wrote all the songs with Blackmore (and occasionally Powell) and by the time they toured it looked like their worries were over. They weren't. 'People still tell me how surprised they were when I left the band shortly after. The truth is, I was kinda surprised myself,' he added sarcastically. 'Ultimately, it was Ritchie's choice, yes. But it was also mine in that I knew I couldn't give him what he wanted. The answer lies in what the band did after I left, which was singles like 'Since You've Been Gone'. It's a great song and it was a big hit for them but it's not one I would have written or sung with them. It was mainstream pop-rock and that's where Ritchie wanted to go. If I'd wanted to go there too I'm sure we could have continued working together. But I didn't.'

He was getting ready to start writing and recording his first solo album, he said, when a chance meeting between the singer and Sabbath guitarist Tony Iommi one night at the Rainbow club in Los Angeles, changed everything. 'It was fate,' he told me. 'It really must have been because we connected so instantly.' When Iommi invited him up to the band's studio for a late-night jam, 'I certainly didn't see it as an audition for a job. It was just two musicians having a blast.'

This particular blast, however, resulted in the track – 'Children Of The Sea' – that would eventually form the template for the next Sabbath album, *Heaven And Hell*. 'Tony had this great riff he played me but nothing to go with it. I said, "Gimme a minute" and went into the corner and started writing down the words. Then we recorded it. When we played it back it was obvious to both of us, we really had something here.'

They certainly did. *Heaven And Hell*, released in the summer of 1980, was not only the band's most commercially success- ful album since their early-Seventies heyday; nor was it merely one of the greatest Sabbath albums ever, with or without Ozzy; quite simply it was, and remains, one of the greatest heavy metal albums of all time – official. 'If I was asked to name one album that I'm really proud of in my career, that would be it,' said Ronnie. 'Of course, there have been others I've loved equally, but there were so many elements to that – from travelling the world to record different parts of it, to how pleased we all were with the music on it, to the huge success it had – that make *Heaven And Hell* special for me.'

If only the rest of the band had felt the same way.

PART TWO

Unlucky For Some

SEVEN
NEON NIGHTS

February 1980. The George V hotel in Paris. It is one o'clock in the morning when Paul Clark answers the door of Bill Ward's suite to admit the hotel plumber. Bill, who is 'sick', has been throwing up for hours and now every toilet, sink and bath is clogged with his vomit. The plumber throws up his hands in disgust but Paul takes a roll of dollar bills from his pocket, peels off a couple of hundreds and stuffs them in the guy's overalls pocket. It will take Monsieur Le Plombier several days to unblock all the drains, by which time Bill will have checked out. For now, though, he has convened a little salon in the extravagantly spacious living area of his suite, comprising Paul, myself, Bill's American wife Misty, and a hapless journalist from *Sounds* magazine who looks like he would rather be any other place on Earth.

As the band's newly installed London PR, I have been assigned the job of 'taking care' of Black Sabbath. Unlike some of the acts I work with though – Journey, REO Speedwagon and the like – I am intimately acquainted with Sabbath's music, having been a fan since school days, when the *Paranoid* album became one of the first I ever bought. Already, at twenty-one, I am a veteran of tours with Thin Lizzy, Dire Straits, Motörhead and Hawkwind, and I feel I am more than qualified to deal with whatever vicissitudes Black Sabbath might care to throw my way.

I was wrong. Unaware of just what a knife-edge their career was now precariously perched on, I had been greeted by what appeared to be chronic apathy on the one hand – after years of being kicked around in the UK press, Tony and Geezer had simply given up, it seemed, blissfully unconcerned about who I was or what my plans for their forthcoming press campaign might be – and an over-zealous lust for glory that put me permanently on the back foot, in the shape of their over-eager new singer, Ronnie James Dio, who wanted things to be so right there could be no wrong. Ever.

And then there was Bill. When Bill didn't show up for any of our initial meetings, no one batted an eye. Bill was sick, they said, when I asked. Or Bill was simply off somewhere else. No one knew where. They said.

He would, however, definitely be there for the photo session I had arranged at the Sacré Coeur, Paul assured me. When he was, I was surprised, then dismayed, as I got a closer look at him. Dark panda-eyes, hair untamed, full druggy beard, beer belly hanging over his ungainly, studded rock star belt.

I went over to introduce myself. 'What the fuck are we doing here?' he asked despairingly, his eyes peering through me.

'We're getting some shots done, Bill, for your press photos …'

'I don't care about that,' he interrupted, almost pleadingly. 'I want to know what we're doing poncing around in the freezin' fuckin' cold when we should be in the studio working on the album.'

'Never mind Bill,' Paul told me, leading me away. 'Let me take care of Bill.'

'Paul!' pleaded Bill. 'What the fuck are we doing?'

Somehow we got through the photo session. Later, when we got the shots back, I was just pleased we had got enough that we could use. Then when I took the pictures to the band's hotel to show them, I discovered Geezer and Bill had shaved off the bushy beards they had had in Paris, and that we would need to do another photo shoot.

Meanwhile, back in Bill's suite in the early hours of a Monday morning, none of us entirely sure why we had been summoned there, it was like a scene out of some old-time vampire movie. The windows to the large expansive balcony had been left open, giving a view of the Eiffel Tower, the cold winter's night air cooling the room, where the heating appeared to have been turned to its maximum. Bill and Misty were in bathrobes, Bill's hanging open at the gut, making you wince every time he sat down and crossed his legs or bent over to fill his glass. Misty was more done up but her face, puffy from drink or maybe crying, or maybe both, and her eyes, like two black bruises, her hair limp as soiled sheets, gave her the appearance of a patient at death's door. They were a most sickly couple.

'I've got a treat for you,' Bill announced as we all found somewhere to sit and not look too closely at either of them. There was a smell of puke in the air. Puke and cigarettes and booze and … something else. Ozzy would recall how, by then, 'We were all fucked up bad, cocaine was coming round and fucking Demerol [a synthetic morphine-like opioid], morphine, everything was coming round the fucking place.' There was more even than that going on here. You could feel it. The sense of quarrels, outbursts, things being busted up in the night. Misty was standing in the shadows on the balcony, looking as though she might throw herself off it. You wondered what had happened, how they had got like this? Later, Paul told me how when Bill first met Misty a couple of years before, 'She was just partying with Bill. When she first was on the scene she was a laugh, in fact. She was so thin, a skinny bird. But she was no good for Bill cos she was drinking as well. They were both as bad as each other. At some of the shows, the festivals, we'd have the dustbins full of ice and beer. And when they'd come offstage, I can always remember Tony going, "Where the fuck's the beers gone?" and she'd have drunk 'em. Soon she was really fat. Her brother used to come to the gigs sometimes too. They were just a bunch of booze hounds.'

'I've got a surprise for you,' Bill said, getting to his feet and tottering over to where a studio-size hi-fi system was set up. He was going to play us the new *Heaven And Hell* album. Only one proviso: 'It hasn't got the vocals on it yet,' said Bill, 'but at least you'll get an idea.'

Oh, we were getting an idea all right. We sat slumped in our chairs, while the music blared out of two custom-built speakers Bill had specially set up in the room. No vocals, but a heck of a lot of very loud drums and guitars. At the end of each track, Bill would bellow at us: 'What do you think? Fucking brilliant, right?' We would nod and smile and try to look enthusiastic. Every now and again I snuck a look at my watch. The time crawled by. Then I would sneak a look at Misty. She didn't look any more pleased to be there than I was. She and Bill were living in a parallel world to the one the rest of Sabbath lived in. Later, once the tour began, I got used to being summoned to the dressing room after the gig each night, so Bill could dictate his own press release to me. Whatever happened to Bill during the course of a gig, from breaking a drumstick to missing a cue or anything else that he felt needed some explanation, he wanted it all put down on a press release, he said, and sent out urgently to the local media in whatever town we happened to be in. He would sit there, a sweat-drenched mass of blubbery white flesh, completely cuckoo-faced, and make me write it all down and then read it back to him. 'Now make sure that cunt goes out on the wire tonight!'

Then, as I made my way out of the dressing room again, Paul Clark would be waiting at the door. Sometimes he would take the paper, fold it up and put it in his pocket. Other times he would wink and say: 'Just chuck it in the bin, all right?'

*

By the time Ronnie James Dio agreed to team up with Tony Iommi in 1979, Black Sabbath was already a ghost ship. Had Dio joined Sabbath even one album earlier, the story might have been different for all of them, including Ozzy. Indeed, it could so easily have happened. By the summer of 1977, just as Ozzy was on the verge of leaving the band for the first time, Ronnie had begun making an album with Rainbow that he already knew deep down inside would be his last. Had Ronnie bumped into Tony then, instead of two years later, Sabbath might have been spared the ignominy of *Never Say Die* and instead relaunched their career with the kind of music Tony had always dreamed of making: melodic, high-end rock, the kind of deal other musicians of the age would have more easily admired than the mongrel riffs and spastic rhythms of the Ozzy line-up. Rainbow guitarist Ritchie Blackmore would also have got his plans underway a lot earlier to take his career in a more chart-friendly direction. The only one who in all probability would have lost out was Ozzy. As he would tell me a thousand times over the coming years, without the eventual intervention of Sharon Arden 'I'd be sleeping on a park bench.'

Instead, by the time Tony Iommi began 'jamming' with Ronnie James Dio in LA, in the latter half of 1979, both men were now searching intently for ways to resuscitate their ailing careers. Emboldened by that suit of emotional armour heavy cocaine use lends all its victims – at least, at first – Tony acted as if firing Ozzy was the shot in the arm Sabbath needed. Behind closed doors, however, he feared the worst. Geezer and Bill, never the strongest personalities, now cowered behind Tony's pharmaceutical shield. Besides, they both had more to think about than songs for a new album. Geezer's marriage was in disarray. While he fully expected his wife to turn a blind eye to any on the road 'shenanigans' he'd been involved in with female members of Sabbath's fan base, particularly in America, where out of sight really was expected to be out of mind, when he suspected she had been having a secret affair with a musician friend; Geezer would not recover easily and now fell even more heavily into his own drink and drugs hell.

When Tony finally put his foot down about Ozzy, and suggested they bring in Dio to work with, Geezer was flummoxed. His immediate reaction was to side with Ozzy. 'Tony told me that he'd met Ronnie Dio and he wanted to do an album with him. Me and Ozzy were gonna do an album together and Bill was undecided whether to go with Tony or with me and Ozzy. So eventually we were having meetings all the time with each other, and there was always backbiting and talking behind each other's backs kind of stuff.' In the end, Geezer simply ran and hid. Like Bill, he had become so entangled with his own problems he could no longer see straight. He was also suffering from an as yet undiagnosed depression, which would dog him for years.

'I didn't even know I had it until I had proper tests and got pills to sort it out,' he confessed to writer Joel McIver in 2005. 'People used to think I was just being miserable, but it was actual depression.' In those days, though, 'People just didn't ever talk about it.' If you did, 'you were literally a nutcase. I used to get told to cheer up all the time. You just think that it's part of boozing or whatever, but it's not, it's a clinical thing, something in your brain.' At the time of Ozzy's sacking from the band, the only help at hand was cocaine and, eventually, briefly, but painfully, heroin. 'I couldn't explain what the mood was, but there was nobody to talk to about it at the time. They used to tell you to go and take your dog for a walk or something.' Unlike Bill, however, Geezer had the sense to step back from the brink. But not before he'd sunk into his pity pot for several weeks.

As for Bill, with Ozzy gone and Geezer shunted to one side, this was now an endgame Sabbath were playing and he wanted no part of it. 'There are things that are blacked out for me, which shows how numb I was on the inside by then. So I have very little memory of the latter part of our career. But Ozzy being fired ... I thought it was the wrong thing to do. In 1984, when I got truly sober, I looked back at those events and everything made sense to me. In the way I had kind of withdrawn and gone inside myself. I just felt lousy that Ozzy was not with the band any longer.'

Bill was now so low in the Sabbath pecking order he figured somewhere beneath the roadies, somewhere down near where the groupies and dealers lurked in the collective band conscious-ness. When they cut the leg off one of his trousers one night, for a lark, he simply came down the next morning wearing them with one bare leg. When Tony tried to set fire to him – again – another night in the studio, and Bill actually kicked up a fuss about it, he was so repentant he came back an hour later and apologised to Tony before inviting him to proceed. 'We had it down, like a little show we would do,' Bill would insist, as if he was really somehow in on the joke. This time when the guitarist did so though – grab-bing a bottle of the highly inflammable fluid used to clean tape-heads and squirting it over Bill's jeans before throwing a lit match at him – it nearly ended in disaster.

As Bill rolled around on the studio floor, his body on fire, Tony, laughing, squirted yet more cleaning fluid at him. Bill's jeans melted against his legs as the flames increased in intensity, now lapping at his arms and head, and he began to scream. 'We got him to the hospital,' Paul Clark recalls now, 'and he had third-degree burns all over his body. Bill's mum phoned up and threatened to fucking kill Tony. Said Bill was dying and he was having his legs amputated. Tony was shitting himself.' It was as if Black Sabbath had finally become what their critics had long accused them of being: the walking brain dead. Rock'n'roll bottom-feeders.

Ronnie James Dio was no drug casualty. But his career pros-pects were certainly no better. His then wife, Wendy Dio, recalls how after Ronnie had been fired from Rainbow they were flat broke. How it was only a small inheritance from her recently deceased grandmother that was keeping them afloat. 'We had no money, nothing.' In Rainbow, Ronnie had been provided with a house in Connecticut, a car and a weekly wage of $150. All of which they forfeited when Blackmore sacked the singer in 1978. 'We came out to Los Angeles, because that's where we knew there were people that we might get something going with, but we had no money whatsoever. And we struggled really hard. We had hard days, and quite honestly when Ronnie went into Sabbath he was saying, "I don't know if I want to do this or not." I said, "Ronnie, we've got eight hundred bucks in the bank, we've got to do something." We went through struggles. We did what Ronnie called paying your dues.'

At the time he first met Iommi, Dio had been talking up a prospective solo career, working with old friend and former band mate, former Elf and Rainbow keyboardist Micky Soule, but without a record deal they would be starting from the ground up. Instead he was spreading his bets across several different musical projects, including writing with British guitarist Paul Gurvitz, most recently of power trio Three Man Army. He was also jamming on the side with former Steely Dan and Doobie Brothers guitarist Jeff 'Skunk' Baxter, whose own career was now at a crossroads. (When Dio joined Black Sabbath, Baxter would go on to become one of the premier session players of the day.) There was talk also of collaborating with former Rainbow bassist Bob Daisley (who, ironically, would then become the bassist in Ozzy's solo band).

When Tony suggested they simply rebuild Black Sabbath together, now that Ozzy had been shoved out of the picture, Ronnie initially bridled at the prospect of joining someone else's band again, despite Wendy's pleadings about their rapidly dwindling bank balance. But Tony assured him that it wouldn't be like Rainbow, where Blackmore was always boss, free to hire and fire at will. Ronnie would co-front the group, with Tony, musically and in every other way. There were not – as yet – any details that needed working out in terms of who would write the lyrics. With Geezer now absenting himself from the band, possibly for good, and Bill now so out of control on booze and, his latest thing, smack, it didn't matter what they thought. Geezer had grown to 'hate' writing lyrics. 'I used to write these lyrics and give them to Ozzy. He'd say, "I'm not singing that." So you'd have to rethink the whole thing again.' The way Tony sold it to Ronnie, it would be their show to run as they saw fit. Equal partners, come what may. 'That was the way we talked about it at the time,' Ronnie would later tell me. The way Ronnie saw it, '[Sabbath] had just come off the back of a couple of terrible albums, they were finished. Me getting together and working with Tony was what was gonna bring them back' – and Ronnie, of course, with them.

Tony thought so too. 'I'd never seen Tony so excited,' recalls Paul Clark. 'Ronnie was like a breath of fresh air to me. He was on time, totally together, and he had this unbelievable fucking voice! He also wrote really great lyrics. Tony must have been like a dog with two dicks. After years of having to work pretty much alone, he now had a singer who could really take a lot of the weight off his shoulders.'

Warner Bros. in America and Phonogram in London didn't care either way. With the band's sales trajectory on a steep decline, they had all but given up on Black Sabbath ever regaining a commercial foothold. It was only later, once they'd heard the brilliant initial demos, that they woke up to what they had. They became even more enthused after they met Ronnie, and realised they might finally have someone in Black Sabbath they could do business with; someone who actually enjoyed giving press and radio interviews, who was bright and articulate and grasped immediately what the needs of the record labels were when it came to promoting and marketing the band. Above all, someone who wasn't going to punch the journalist or fall asleep drunk and urinate over themselves during meetings. 'The band had got to the stage where they wouldn't even do interviews,' says Clark. 'People would show up and Tony would send me out to tell them he was sick or had to be somewhere else. Then Ronnie joined and he was a grafter. He would work the press and radio all day, in person, on the phone, whatever it took. He was also really good with the fans. The band had got it into their heads they should be like Led Zeppelin – aloof. Talk to no one. But Ronnie would go to the stage door after gigs and be out there for hours, chatting to the fans and signing autographs. Word went round and they started following him everywhere. He'd walk out of the hotel in the morning and there'd be a crowd waiting for him. He didn't mind. We'd end up having to drag him away so we could get to the airport or wherever. It got on the band's nerves but the fans loved him for it.'

The only one who didn't like what he saw was Don Arden. He was absolutely adamant: Tony was making a big mistake. If it was a risk getting rid of Ozzy, expecting the public to welcome this elfin-like American as a credible successor was simply insane. When it became apparent that Tony wasn't going to budge Don pulled the plug. First on the house where they lived, then on the band itself. On the one hand he still had Ozzy under contract; Ozzy who had no clue and would do what he was told or else. On the other hand he had Tony Iommi and the others; Tony insisted on bringing in some utterly unsuitable replacement for Ozzy. 'Fuck 'em,' decided Don. 'If they wanted to commit career suicide that was up to them but I wasn't going to be part of it.'

Don sold the management contract to Sandy Pearlman; someone he considered 'not fit to tie my shoes as a manager'. In fact, Pearlman was already a successful figure in the music biz, most famously with Blue Öyster Cult, an American rock band clearly influenced by early Sabbath. The son of a successful pharmacist from Smithtown, Pearlman had graduated in philosophy and carried a virtual library of books around with him. He was an expert on ancient mythology. He had been a rock journalist for *Crawdaddy*, a BOC lyricist, then producer and manager. He was also now manager of New York punk-metallists The Dictators, and upcoming French band Shakin' Street, fronted by a beautiful Tunisian former model named Fabienne Shine, and whose 1980 album, *Solid As A Rock*, would attract significant attention in the music press that year. He had also recently produced the second Clash album, *Give 'Em Enough Rope*. In short, Pearlman was nothing like the rock manager stereotype. Perennially dressed down in a baseball cap and denims, he would turn up for meetings with a backpack instead of a briefcase, and was always happier talking French symbolist poetry than nuts-and-bolts rock management. As Blue Öyster Cult bassist Joe Bouchard once put it, 'Sandy doesn't feel that he has to retain a normal vocabulary, and it's that way if you ever talk to him. He will come out with some good ones; he feels that words are to serve *him* and to hell with everyone else ...'

Other new faces on the scene included another young, Birmingham-born-and-bred musician named Geoff Nicholls, whom Tony had first met in local Brummy rockers Bandylegs, who had opened for Sabbath on tour some years before. The same age as Tony, Nicholls was a talented guitarist, keyboardist and singer who didn't have the face or personality to make it on his own but who had the kind of pliant me-sir attitude which would endear him to the domineering Tony Iommi for years to come. He was also a useful foil for Tony to write with. 'He was like Tony's shadow,' says Paul Clark. 'Geoff was into coke, and he'd sit with Tony all night, every night. And he would wear a little Black Sabbath medallion that he'd had made. Then he'd have his jacket with Black Sabbath on, and even if it was a hundred degrees outside he would carry that and have it wrapped around his arm, so you could see the words "Black Sabbath". But he was a good writer. Though he never got the credit for it, he definitely helped write some of that stuff on *Heaven And Hell*. Him and Tony in LA.'

Ronnie also brought in another old Elf and Rainbow pal, Craig Gruber, to play bass while they waited to see where the cards fell with Geezer. It was this conglomeration that flew out to Criteria Studios in Miami in the late summer of 1979 to see if they could at least start to make another Black Sabbath album.

For Tony Iommi, working with Ronnie James Dio was a revelation. A schooled musician, he didn't merely sing with the riff, which is what Ozzy largely did, but his vocal melody would work in contrast to the main riff, 'singing across the riff', as Tony put it, 'which musically opens a lot more doors ... a new way for me to think'.

Certainly, the *Heaven And Hell* album would be a huge departure for the band. 'I wouldn't say we were glad to see the back of Ozzy. [But] when Ronnie came in, he was a different person altogether. He sang different, he was more enthusiastic. Because obviously with us, we'd got through so many years all together, and when you get out of it all the time it's hard to be enthusiastic about anything. So we needed that break. With Dio being there, it opened another door for us to write music with somebody singing on it in a different way to what Ozzy was doing. So it enabled me, in particular, to be able to write in a slightly different, more melodic style.'

By the time Geezer had been coaxed back, the songs were all written. By the time Bill was summoned to the studio, he simply had to do what he was told. Neither man liked it but that was their problem, Tony decided. This was a new Sabbath and no one was going to spoil it for him and Ronnie. From the production by Martin Birch – a veteran of all Deep Purple's best albums, and several highlights from Fleetwood Mac, Wishbone Ash and

Rainbow – brought in again at Ronnie's suggestion, to lift the burden from Tony, and also, though Ronnie didn't say it out loud, specifically to ensure that this Sabbath album did not sound like any of their previous ones with Ozzy. As to the actual songs, this was to be by far the strongest, most confident thing they had done since *Sabbath Bloody Sabbath* seven years before.

Opening with 'Neon Knights', their hookiest track since 'Paranoid' and an instant rock classic in the making, the rest of the album was defined by similar musical highs. The next track, 'Children Of The Sea', the first song Tony had written with Ronnie, was another arrow-through-the-heart classic. Full of light and shade, building to the kind of epic climax the band would never have pulled off with Ozzy. Gone were the days, it seemed, when Sabbath's music was head-bent-backwards, roaring metal, or languid acoustic instrumentals. Now they could do both equally convincingly in the space of one track. At last, they were coming close to the ideal Tony and Geezer had until then thought of as the true domain of Led Zeppelin. Suddenly Black Sabbath didn't just have power, didn't just have hate and anger, they had soul, they had emotion, they had joy.

All of which was captured most perfectly in the title track itself. An epic, heartbeat-paced mission statement, this was Black Sabbath at their most glorious. Anthemic, depth-charged, a crowd-pleaser that worked equally well listened to alone, just you and the lyric sheet and the turntable with the volume turned to maximum, or blasting out from the stage to a transfixed audience of thousands, 'Heaven And Hell' belonged in the same pantheon of stone-cold forever Sabbath classics as 'War Pigs' and 'Iron Man', as 'Snowblind' and 'Children Of The Grave'. In many ways, it was better than all of them. They had been one-offs, messages from some distant passing ship hurtling to the earth, broken down, burning up as it crashed through the atmosphere. Dying stars that flared most brightly as they exploded into space. 'Heaven And Hell' was a rocket moving in the opposite direction: outward-bound, heaven-sent, hell-raised, a vehicle to take the listener with it in its warm and all-embracing afterglow. The old Ozzy-borne Sabbath had always been an inward-looking, misfitting, dysfunctional head-trip for outsiders and no-gooders. The new Dio-led Sabbath was one fit for heroes and merrymen, for lovers and fighters of the good fight. It was life-affirming and true and utterly unlike any other rock band of the time. Even on hell-for-leather rockers like 'Die Young', this was a Sabbath from the future, bringers of hope through musical alms. Best of all it rocked with a vengeance. Something the Ozzy-era line-up hadn't done for so long the generation of fans that now flocked to buy the new Sabbath album could not even remember anything good about the old. Even filler tracks like 'Lady Evil' and 'Walk Away' sounded good to go; the perfect fit for a band that hadn't had anything new played on American FM radio for years. There was even a ballad, of sorts, in the closing track, 'Lonely Is The Word', though even there the cavernous power of the track was such that it could blow out your candles at a hundred paces.

'This was an album where they had a lot to prove,' Ronnie later reflected. 'This band had died a severe death three albums before … then suddenly came this album. It made Sabbath important again. It showed that these guys were not a bunch of musical fools. That Tony and Geezer and Billy were really good players and that they could do things nobody thought they could do. And it started heavy metal up a little bit again. This was a great album. It took a long time [to make] but it's one of the albums of which I'm most proud.'

Suddenly, whether Bill and Geezer fully understood it yet, it was a great time to be in Black Sabbath again. Even Tony could finally allow himself to enjoy the ride, unworried what his singer might do next to upset the applecart, or how well his new album was selling. *Heaven And Hell* was an immediate hit in Britain, where it reached No. 9, their highest chart placing for five years, and in the US, where it put them back in the charts, becoming their first million-seller since *Sabbath Bloody Sabbath*. With Ronnie there to front the whole deal, it seemed they couldn't miss. A born leader, as Wendy points out, 'He had a band when he was ten years old. He stole cars when he was eleven or twelve. He'd always done things.'

A truly American story of sheer will overcoming adversity, Dio was not without his own deep-rooted insecurities. Thirty-seven at the time he joined Sabbath, he took to shaving seven years off his age in interviews; a habit he maintained for years to come. He was also acutely conscious of his height – or lack of it. Just 5 feet 4 inches in his cowboy boots, he became so sensitive about it he would later get Wendy, who took over his personal management in the mid-Eighties, to fax *Kerrang!* magazine, requesting their writers desist from referring to him as 'diminutive' – something the staff scoffed at and which merely ensured they always referred to him by that or some equally pejorative term for years to come. What he lacked in feet and inches, however, Ronnie more than made up for in sheer force of personality. I recall walking into a room backstage at Madison Square Garden where Ronnie was taking Sandy Pearlman to task over something, and being shocked at the scale of the singer's anger, as he literally pinned Pearlman to the wall in his fury.

Ronnie was one tough cookie, and he let you know it as soon as he could. 'Ronnie might have been small but he was definitely in control,' says Wendy. This latter quality would eventually bring him into direct confrontation with Tony Iommi, but for now, at least, it provided the spark that had been missing since Sabbath's early-Seventies heyday. For Ronnie was smart, too. 'He was very, very intelligent,' says Wendy. 'He had a pharmacy degree from Buffalo University, which he could have followed but didn't. It was just something he did for his parents. He was very, very bright. He used to read a book a day, just to make sure he was on top of things.'

Above all, Ronnie knew just how to handle Tony and the other Brits around the band. 'Even though he was from upstate New York, Ronnie had always been surrounded by British people. Even in Elf he had some British road crew. And he always liked British humour and he always felt comfortable with Brits.' There was more to his Anglophilia even than a penchant for Monty Python, Indian curries and strong dark ale. 'He liked the way British musicians thought about music more than the flashy American kind. It was more melodic, and I think that's why later he wanted to have British players [in his own band]. It was almost like he'd been a Brit at one time in another life.'

And there was something else Ronnie James Dio brought to Black Sabbath – and which he bequeathed to the world of heavy metal ever after.

'I wanna ask you something,' Ronnie said the first time we met. 'What do you think of this?' He held up his right hand, making the shape that now, 30 years later, the world knows as the devil horn salute. I stared in puzzlement. I had never seen anyone do that before. He held up the other hand, and did it again, this time with both arms held aloft, as though addressing a crowd. He stood up and strode purposefully around the room, arms held high, making the signs, as though sending out a message of the highest importance. Which, of course, he was – or soon would be, when he made his first appearance onstage as Black Sabbath's new singer.

It was in Paris, at Studio Ferber, where he and the band were finishing the *Heaven And Hell* album. The feeling behind the album was strong, thoughts of how Sabbath could possibly replace Ozzy Osbourne rapidly fading from view. 'The only thing worrying me now,' he said, was how he would be received by

Ozzy's fans when the band went on tour; of how 'to connect with' Ozzy's audience. 'I know they're gonna miss him,' he confided. 'So I've been trying to think of something that says, look, I'm not here to try and be like Ozzy, but I am respectful of what he did with the band. And I thought of this ...'

He did the devil horn thing again, both hands held high.

'What is that?' I asked.

'Something my Sicilian grandmother used to do, to ward off the evil eye. I figure the peace sign thing belongs to Ozzy. I can't do that. Maybe I can do this instead.'

At last, the penny dropped. Ozzy was known for flashing 'V' peace signs throughout Sabbath's shows. This would be Dio's highly personalised version of the same thing. Sure enough, by the end of the first date of the tour, the whole crowd was doing them back at him. Within a few years it became a common sight at all metal concerts; a cultural signifier of something specific to that experience: brotherhood and rebellion, all wrapped up in one beautifully executed piece of physical graffiti.

On tour for the first time with Dio, in the spring of 1980, Sabbath were suddenly taken seriously again. For once their timing was spot on. In Britain, *Sounds* magazine had begun championing a new musical phenomenon it dubbed the 'New Wave Of British Heavy Metal' – a very definite reaction against the so-called death of hard rock and heavy metal heralded by the arrival of punk. Suddenly the UK music press was awash with new full-on rock bands like Iron Maiden and Def Leppard, Saxon and Diamond Head. Rock with a capital 'R' was also back in the charts in a big way, after the post-punk lull, with established pillars of the community like Motörhead, Judas Priest, Gillan and AC/DC all scoring their biggest-selling albums that year. The reborn Black Sabbath, with their glistening new sound, incomparable new singer and top-drawer new album, were seen as part of a widespread revival in rock fandom. No longer a throwback to the pre-dawn Seventies, they were now viewed as the coming wave of rock in the 1980s.

When Sabbath arrived in London in May for the first of four nights at the Hammersmith Odeon, the whole town came out to greet them, including members past and present of Rainbow, Thin Lizzy, Pink Floyd and, most sensitively for Bill Ward, Zeppelin drummer John Bonham. Both men had come up through the shitholes of the Midlands scene in the 1960s, both had made it to the big time, somewhat improbably, playing the kind of music they both loved best. Both now held identical badges of honour: farms in Worcestershire and raging drug habits. There had been other famous drummers from the Midlands – Bev Bevan of ELO, Cozy Powell then of Whitesnake – but Bill always held Bonzo in particularly high regard, as did they all. During downtime, they would all congregate at Mick Evans' Drum Shop in Birmingham. 'We all went down to Mick's place and talked bullshit and it was great. And always, Bonzo was right there. He was always in the thick of it, in the centre, just like the main pin on the wheel, if you like. I always regarded him as like the boss. His technique and especially his tempo and his balance are second to none – to this day. There's never been anyone like him, not even close, you know? He had so much good stuff to give, as a drummer and as a person, too.'

Not on this particular occasion, though. Bonham was then rehearsing for what would be Zeppelin's first tour since their disastrous 1977 American jaunt, which crashed to a halt after Bonham and band manager Peter Grant brutally assaulted a backstage crew member, in Oakland, California. Two days later singer Robert Plant received a phone call informing him of the death of his young son, Karac, from a viral infection. Since then – their two mixed-emotion shows at Knebworth the previous summer notwithstanding – Zeppelin had been on ice. The prospect of

Bonham, like Bill now a heroin addict and full-blown alcoholic, returning to the road filled the outwardly bombastic drummer with anxiety. To which his response was to behave in public even more obnoxiously than usual.

Paul Clark recalls how, that first night at the Odeon, Bonzo had asked to sit behind Bill during the gig, in the spot where Bill's drum tech, Graham, would normally be perched, out of sight but well within reach to aid Bill, should he need to. Bill agreed – then regretted it when, midway through the set, Bonham began pulling at his legs, trying to stop him playing. 'Bill played like a mother-fucker that night,' says Clark. 'It was incredible. It was like a fresh Bill Ward, because he had John Bonham sitting where his roadie was.' Clark was incensed, though, when he saw how 'Bonham kept grabbing his legs, fucking him, cos he was all screwed-up seeing Bill play so well.'

Further trouble ensued when Bonham, despatched to the side of the stage to watch the remainder of the set, was overheard by Ronnie to remark: 'He's a really good singer – for a fucking midget!' Ronnie turned on his heel and marched over to where the burly drummer was standing. 'You cunt!' he screamed in his face. Bonham went to react but Tony intervened, tried to cool the drummer out, telling Paul to take him backstage and get him another drink.

In the Sabbath dressing room afterwards, I watched as Bonham taunted Bill endlessly. 'What did you think, Bonzo?' Bill asked in his weepy voice. 'You were fucking shit!' Bonham told him then growled with something approximating laughter. 'It was just fucking terrible,' agrees Clark. 'Geezer got the needle and said to me, "Get him out of here." I said [to Bonham], "Right, you, out!" He said, "Who do you think you're talking to?" I said, "I'm fucking talking to you. I want you out of here now! I've asked you once nicely, now get the fuck out – now!" He was with his minder but I told them both to fuck off. They don't want you here. And they left.' (Later that year, they were on tour in America when they heard Bonham had died. Paul recalls the promoter coming into the dressing room to give them the news. 'He said, "I've got some bad news for you guys. John Bonham's died." Geezer went, "Good." I'll always remember it.')

Nobody, it seemed, could bring Sabbath down during that long, rosebud summer of 1980. 'Ronnie was flying high because he really felt like this was his band now,' Wendy Dio recalls. When the band arrived for their first tour of Japan, Ronnie was treated like royalty because he had been there so many times before with Rainbow. Unlike in Rainbow, however, where Dio co-wrote the songs but always felt lost in Ritchie Blackmore's shadow, 'Being in Sabbath was totally different. The time that Ronnie was with Ritchie, just going in there, it was his big opportunity. So he was very much into yes, sir, no, sir, three bags full, sir – in the beginning. With the Sabbath situation it was more of equals, because he did have things under his belt by then ... Ronnie felt more in control.'

Tony was also back on his throne, turning every day into night. In every hotel suite he stayed in, he would have the spare blankets taken out and draped across the windows to keep out the light. Black candles would be burning night and day and gallons of iced orange would be placed in the refrigerator, next to the metal boxes filled with pharmaceutical cocaine. 'We called it the Bat Cave,' says Clark. 'You'd go in to see Tony and he'd be, "Have a line." And that was it; you'd never get out again. I once had a bird sitting waiting for me in reception for twenty-four hours. Because I was stuck in Tony's room and this silly bitch sat there, waiting. You didn't realise the time had gone, you know? He'd be sitting there with his orange juice and his Charlie. And it weren't fucking shit gear. It was like top shelf ...'

The other happy camper was Geoff Nicholls. Not yet a fully endorsed member of the band, he would play keyboards each night from behind a side stage curtain, or so far back by the drums as to be almost invisible to most of the audience. Paid a weekly salary of $750, plus expenses, Geoff nevertheless enjoyed all the other perks of the job. During a brief tour break in LA, he boasted to me of scheduling different girlfriends in at various times for 'hotel visits', waving goodbye to one at 2 p.m., then resting before the arrival of his 4 p.m. Most of the time, though, he stayed close to Tony. Tony and his crosses and black candles and his seemingly endless supplies of the best coke. 'Me and Ronnie used to bet how identically Geoff would be dressed to Tony,' says Clark. 'We'd be sitting in the lobby waiting for them to come down to go to the gig and we'd put a couple of dollars on the table. Sure enough, the elevator doors would open and here would come Tony – followed by Geoff in exactly the same clothes.'

Geezer, who had sworn off heavy drugs after his emotional collapse the year before, still liked to drink, still liked a toke and a toot and a poke and a root when the fancy took him, but now kept himself to himself; still unsure of what to make of the all-new Sabbath that Tony had forged ahead and built without him, for now he was simply along for the ride, wondering what the hell would happen next. He wouldn't have to wait long.

Two years before, when the band played the Checkerdome Arena in St Louis, they were driving from the airport to the venue when a Porsche drew up alongside them on the freeway. Inside were two chicks that Tony had spied earlier picking up their bags from the same airport carousel as the band. When the girls began waving at the tour bus, Tony ordered the bus to slow down and for Paul to give them passes for the show, passing them through the car windows. One of the girls, a pretty, curly-haired cutie named Gloria, ended up that night with Tony, while her friend was in bed with Albert, one of the crew. Two years on, when the band, now with Dio, returned to play the same venue, Gloria was again in attendance. This time, though, she ended up with Geezer, still down and forlorn after a year in which his band had fractured and reconfigured itself without him, and his wife had had an affair which he still could not forgive her for. Or as Paul puts it, 'Somehow Geezer's now fallen in love with her [Gloria].' By tour's end, he will have bought a house in St Louis and moved in with her. Meanwhile, 'Every fucking minute of the day he was playing "Three Times A Lady". I had to room next to him and coming through the fucking walls it was.' When it appeared that Gloria was an habituée of the local music scene, fond of hanging out with the bands that headlined the massive local arena, it didn't faze Geezer one bit. 'He was madly in love with her,' says Paul. 'The fact they've been together ever since says it all.'

Tony, whose own marriage was now in tatters, would also meet the new love of his life on tour that year. Her name was Melinda, a part-time model from Modesto, whom he met when Tony and Geoff went out one night in Dallas, after the band's show at the Convention Center. Melinda was dark, pretty, slim but shapely – exactly Tony's type – and he fell for her big time. But while Melinda would accompany Tony on the road for the remainder of the tour, behind the scenes Paul Clark was aghast. According to some of the American members of the band's crew, Melinda was well-known to various sets of roadies, including those of Journey, whom Sabbath played two festival shows with a few weeks later. 'One of the guys knew her and said she'd been blowing all the Journey crew,' says Clark now. 'So as a mate I passed it on to Tony. And we became unfriends. He just completely changed. We were fucking inseparable up till then, closer than brothers, but he didn't want to hear that about his new bird and that was it.'

When, during a short break back in LA, in October, Tony, out of his head on Quaaludes and coke, asked Melinda to marry him, the ceremony was held in the hotel room at the Sunset Marquis. When the Justice of the Peace asked who the witness would be,

Tony pointed to a giant teddy bear he had bought Melinda and said, 'That's your fucking witness!' The JOTP shrugged and the ceremony concluded. Paul Clark, who had the adjoining room to Tony's, was pointedly not invited. Nor even informed for weeks afterwards, until Tony told him to drive Melinda to the passport office, to get the name on her passport changed to Melinda Iommi.

Paul used to dread it when all the wives and girlfriends were coming on the road. 'By the end of the tour, they had Wendy, Melinda, Gloria ... all on the road, asking for chairs so they could sit at the side of the stage, fighting over who got the good spot. It was, "Paul, I want to sit on the other side of the stage tonight and I want her off that side of the stage." So I had all that shit. Then I had, "I'm gonna go out to the front tonight, Paul, to stand at the board, I'm gonna need some security." They got fox fur coats on and god knows what else. I'm like, for fuck's sake ...'

After years of being seen as out of touch, at best, on the way out completely, at worst, for the members of Black Sabbath everything that year had been a huge and unexpected turnaround, and they all revelled in their rediscovered fame and fortune. All, that is, except for Bill, whose problems were only just beginning ...

In an effort to maintain some sort of equilibrium, Bill, who had long since decided he simply couldn't stand flying to gigs any more, not even on the band's own private plane, now travelled everywhere in America on his own tour bus. That way he could have Misty with him, and their dogs, and not worry about getting in the way of the others. It also meant he could do his drugs in peace, without interference or comment. He was now injecting – jacking up – and not even playing the shows seemed to satisfy his soul any longer.

On 20 August, after a show the night before at the Metropolitan Sports Center, in Bloomington, Indiana, Bill Ward could stand it no longer and walked out. He had done so before – most recently, during rehearsals in London, during which the band were shown the finished 'Neon Knights' video, and Bill stormed out of the room, screaming 'Beautiful! Just fucking beautiful!' He turned over some tables and threw a glass. There was a brief hush as he left, then the sound of tittering. 'Is he all right?' I asked somewhat pointlessly. 'He's Bill,' said Geezer. I later found out that Bill's beloved mother had died just days before, and that Bill had been on a bender ever since. But it seemed to me that Bill had been on a bender for far longer than that. You wondered if he would ever come back.

This, though, was different again. 'We got to Denver,' Geezer recalled, 'it was the night before we were playing the McNichols Arena, which is an 18,000-seater which had been sold out for weeks. And Bill decided that's when he was gonna leave. He just got in his bus and he was gone. And I was so used to Bill saying things that he didn't mean, I thought, oh, he'll be back tomorrow, and he wasn't.'

Forced to cancel the show, the promoter threatened to sue them for $100,000. When it became clear that Bill really wasn't coming back, though, the promoter took pity and the next four shows were all rescheduled for later in the year. Fortunately, the next shows were in Hawaii and there had to be a short break to fly the equipment over, and the band took the opportunity to hastily draft in a replacement: 22-year-old New Yorker Vinny Appice. The younger brother of former Vanilla Fudge drummer Carmine Appice, then part of the Rod Stewart band, Vinny had earned his spurs backing guitar hotshot Rick Derringer, and in his own band, Axis. Ironically, Vinny had just turned down the chance to join Ozzy Osbourne's first solo band ('My brother warned me he really was crazy,' he says now) when he agreed to join Sabbath, temporarily, in 1980, to replace Bill.

'I went down to meet them and Tony walked in and he had

my Axis album, and said he really liked it. Then I went down the next day and that's when I met Ronnie and Geezer, and had my audition. After we played for about an hour everybody went to the pub and decided I was in the band till Bill came back. But as the tour went on Bill didn't return and then it was time to do another album – and Bill never returned. So I thought, this is good. Good for me, not for Bill.' He says that 'Musically, it was like a machine. We played great together. I don't have any luggage with me and we just focused on the music.' Equally important, 'Ronnie took me under his wing right away. Cos I had to learn all the songs and this and that. Then we started talking. He's Italian. I'm Italian. He's from New York, upstate. I'm from Brooklyn, New York. So we had a lot of things in common.'

Always smiling, always positive, always, as he says now, 'very aware of who was in charge in that band', after Bill's midnight tantrums Vinny Appice was a breath of fresh air. 'Bill was on another planet by then,' said Geezer solemnly. 'Of course, you couldn't tell him. You can't tell a drunk that he's on another planet cos he just goes nuts. And so you just couldn't talk to the bloke. It just wasn't Bill any more, he'd become this lunatic.'

I had last seen Bill just a few weeks before he finally did a bunk for good. It had been down in Brighton, where the band played a rescheduled show at the end of June. When he spoke it sounded like he was weeping. It wasn't just his braying Brummy accent. It was the tears in his voice put there by the alcohol and cocaine and the knowledge that Ozzy was gone and so was his youth and so were the good times. Gone for ever. And that soon, with all the prophetic self-knowledge of the true junkie, it would be his turn to go, too. Maybe it had already happened. Maybe Bill had already gone and just didn't know it. There had been no roadie to tell him, put him straight for the gig. Now he was permanently gone to wherever it was he would need to go to recover from this strange hell that he inhabited.

We didn't speak again for over fifteen years. When we did, he said this: 'I think alcoholism and drug addiction played a great part in the breaking down of the union of Black Sabbath. I don't think that can be overlooked, that has to be acknowledged.' Nevertheless: 'One of the reasons why I had to leave the band was because I just couldn't accept a Black Sabbath without Ozzy. That was the beginning of the end for me, of Black Sabbath. It was very difficult to play any original Sabbath stuff with Ronnie. I have no axe to grind with Ronnie. I had a good relationship with him at that time. However, it was not Black Sabbath to me. I could not accept Oz not being there. So that was really the beginning of my downfall, if you like. I knew then, it was a question of how many more days I could exist in the band.'

The final straw, he said, was when he realised 'I was now incapable of being onstage. The [drugs and alcohol] had gripped me in such a way that I was basically incapable of walking, let alone playing. My drug and alcohol problems worsened after Oz was asked to leave the band. I couldn't bear to see the changes in the band. I saw Geezer disappear as a songwriter. I've always relied upon a lot of his lyrics ... See when I play music with Sabbath, I listen to Tony's playing and I listen to Geezer's lyrics or Ozzy's phrasing or whatever, and I work inside their movement. It's almost like I react to a note, I'm not a drummer in the sense of playing notes or anything. I react to them. So when Ronnie came into the band, he had all his stuff intact, you know, he writes his own lyrics, he does his own melodies, so I was out of a job, in some sense. And Geezer was out of a job, too. And I'd look up at Geezer and think, you know, the whole ambience of what we had, or what we were, was gone.'

There were other reasons, too, though, he admitted. 'What had really happened to me was nothing to do with Ronnie [Dio] or Oz.' The main thing was 'My addiction to drugs had become *foremost* in my life, the most important thing in my life on a daily basis, and I stopped functioning as a musician and as a person. So I came off the road and I went to bed – for a year. All I did was stay in my bedroom and get high – for a year.'

He said the final knockout blow came just a month later, when on the morning of 25 September he heard John Bonham had died – choking on his own vomit after another night of his own alcohol and drug hell. 'I know exactly where I was. I'd left the *Heaven And Hell* tour. Ozzy was no longer with the band and I was having a real struggle, because I was having a tough time fitting into Black Sabbath with the different line-up. I was having a tough time and I'd left the band. And what I did was, the dope dealer came around every morning with the allotted amount of stuff for the day. And one morning she came round and she was absolutely in bits, crying her eyes out, because she was a major Led Zeppelin fan, she absolutely fucking loved Led Zeppelin. I thought, oh, man, what's going on? She said, "Bonham's dead." The very first thought that I had was a selfish one, and it was: "I'll be next." Like, "I'm right behind you, Johnny. I'm right behind you."

'Because I was lying in bed like a skeleton, jacking up every day. I'm so gone I can't even live outside the house. At that point I was incapable of being anywhere out of the house because I couldn't function anywhere outside of the bedroom. And so that was my first thought: "I'm right behind ya."'

He paused, sighed, his voice suddenly shaky again. 'That could have been me, in a fucking heartbeat. It's a wonder it wasn't me. That could have been me on any given day. As a matter of fact, I was on a bender the night before except I lived through it. I was already junked out. You know, my dealer was coming round to fix it back up again, so I'm already crippled inside on that morning we got the news.'

Bill would remain that way for a long, long time to come.

EIGHT
TRAIN WRECK

'**N**inety thousand dollars I was given. And told to fuck off!' It was June 1979 and I had just been introduced to Ozzy Osbourne, back in London briefly after being booted out of Black Sabbath. We were at a stag party for former Rainbow bassist Jimmy Bain and anyone who was anyone on the rock scene was there that night, including members of Thin Lizzy, UFO, Iron Maiden and several other bands. Everyone was on an up, all save Ozzy who had been on a bender seemingly working his way through his 90 grand as quickly as he could. On closer inspection, he appeared to be drooling. 'Left to fucking die, I was,' he continued, staring right through me. 'I mean, what would you do?' But he wasn't waiting for an answer and staggered off, flanked by two Brum-accented minders who led him around the room like a prize exhibit. 'Ninety thousand dollars ... Told to fuck off ...' he blabbered in the direction of the next outstretched hand.

'I thought, that's it, my life's over,' Ozzy would reflect when I reminded him of the occasion some years later. 'I genuinely thought I was on my way to the fucking dole queue.' With Sabbath already on the comeback trail with Ronnie James Dio, Ozzy's plight looked all but hopeless. It was at this precarious juncture that two things occurred which would both transform the life and times of Ozzy Osbourne and eventually undermine any chance Black Sabbath had of maintaining their own high place in the rock god firmament beyond the novelty of their first 'comeback' album without him. The first was the decision by Don Arden's daughter, Sharon, to take Ozzy under her wing, both personally and professionally. Sharon had a point to prove to her father, whom she had so adored as a little girl, but now began to loathe, as his preposterous lifestyle, fuelled by his enormous earnings from ELO, had seen him forsake Sharon's mother in England for a new life in Hollywood, alongside a new American girlfriend, named Meredith Goodwin. Using Ozzy as a way of freeing herself from her father's clutches, Sharon was determined to make Ozzy a star again. For his part, Ozzy, always so low in his own estimation, always on the lookout for approval from on high, saw Sharon simply as his saviour.

'It was shit or bust for both of us, I knew that going in,' she told me. 'Ozzy, bless him, was just glad someone cared, I think. Whereas I knew that if I could get him back on his feet and prove I knew what I was doing people would have to take me seriously too. We both had a lot to gain – and a lot to lose if we fucked up and got it wrong.' 'I was always attracted to Sharon,' Ozzy said. 'And we just get on together. For a long time, people would think we were brother and sister, that we even looked alike. Then one time, she was taking Gary Moore and his girlfriend to San Francisco for the weekend and she says to me, "Do you wanna come, too?" I thought, "Fucking hell, it's on!" But then I got so fucked up I couldn't find her room. So the magical deed didn't happen for a long while. I think we were at [Ridge Farm] studios [in 1980] when it started to happen. But like a fucking idiot, I was married already and kept calling Sharon by my first wife's name, Thelma.'

Years later, Don would rant and rave about how it was he, not his daughter, who turned Ozzy into a star. Sitting with him in his Park Lane apartment, he would grumble about how he was the one who 'took him into my house, gave him somewhere to clean himself up and sort himself out. [Sharon] was just the day-to-day run around for him. By the time he started again he was on $5000 a night. By the end of it he was making $100,000 a night. Who did that for him? My daughter? Don't make me laugh. Oh, she did a good job in the years after that, I'll grant you that. But people forget he was already a star by then. And who made him that way? Me, that's who! Me!' I knew Sharon was equally capable of rewriting history too when it suited her. But there seemed little doubt that it was Sharon – not Don – who had summoned all the king's men when it came to putting Humpty Dumpty back together again. Not only that but having got him back sitting high on the wall, somehow she managed to keep him there for the next quarter-century. All that said, however, there was equally no doubt that both Sharon and Don – and Ozzy –benefited very early on from a huge stroke of luck that none of them could have manufactured on their own. And that was the discovery of the person who would actually write Ozzy a whole new soundtrack to live his life by, and build the foundations of a proper solo career. Not one built just on crazy antics or a controversial reputation – the very things, in fact, which had got him thrown out of Sabbath in the first place – but on old-fashioned concepts like making good music, recording groundbreaking albums and performing killer live shows. That person's name was Randy Rhoads.

The story of Randy Rhoads is the story of several different people. The first a slight figure, five and a half feet tall, weighing a little over seven stone. A sickly child, always getting fevers and colds, the baby of the family who liked playing with train sets and went on to become a teacher. Then there was the tough guy. The LA-wise street kid who walked out on his own band to find stardom with another, kept his head down as those around him were either fired or fucked over, then decided to walk out on that too, contemptuous of the close-mindedness of the so-called rock star life. Then there was a third person. The one whose best friend describes him now as having 'an angelic heart; he never wanted to hurt anyone'; an innocent, church-going soul whose shy, quietly spoken manner could charm and calm the most tumultuous personalities. And then there was another; the joker who as a teenager stole from rich people's houses, set fire to his own street and experimented with cocaine. The little guy who dreamed of becoming so big his week would always beat your year. Most of all, though, there was the amazing young man who wielded a polka-dot Flying V guitar and who, when he died, left behind an impossibly slender body of work that would nonetheless alter the sound of rock as we know it – for ever.

His name was Randall William Rhoads – Randy, to his friends – and everybody's memory of him is different. To the bereaved family and broken-hearted fiancée he left behind Randy was a kind and gentle soul whose destiny was ultimately to teach. To those that only knew the cocksure person who appeared onstage, in his platform boots and blue velvet suit, his bracelets and necklaces, his hair coiffed into a glam rock plume, he was 'a born star', as the man who would make him famous, Ozzy Osbourne, later told me. Randy himself never saw it that way. 'When I first got up and played [and] people started clapping it was a fluke. I was blown away.' It was that very insecurity, though, that fuelled his originality. 'I thought that everybody was better than I was. Therefore I couldn't copy licks. I just learned my own.'

The softly spoken boy also had a dark side: his favourite song that he wrote with Ozzy was 'Mr Crowley', named after the occultist once famously dubbed the most evil man in the world. 'You're gonna love this,' Randy told friends as the creepy *Clockwork Orange*-inspired intro swelled into the room. It was also Randy that provided the lyrical inspiration behind another of Ozzy's best songs, 'No Bone Movies' – after Randy's fondness for what he called 'bone flicks': porno films.

To the more than ten million fans that have since bought the two albums Randy and Ozzy made together, or were lucky

enough to see them live in the 18 months they performed together, however, he was simply the sound of the future. 'He was
the best guitarist I'd ever seen,' as his friend and fellow musician
Dana Strum says now. 'It was Randy's sound – along with Eddie
Van Halen's – that changed the whole way the next generation of
guitar players thought about music in the 1980s. The ones they
tried to emulate but never could. It was such a tragedy that he
wasn't able to stick around …'

Randy Rhoads was destined to play music. Born on 6 December 1956, in Burbank, a few miles north-east of Hollywood, he
was the youngest of three children. His mother, Delores, was
a 36-year-old, UCLA-educated music teacher who, along with
her husband, William, another music teacher, founded the now
famous Musonia music school – where all three of her children
would also become students. The eldest of the children, Douglas
Rhoads – known as Kelle (pronounced Kelly) – is now the 61-year-
old head of Musonia, as well as a professional musician in his
own right. His sister, Kathy, four years younger, runs the Santa
Rosa Winery in Sonoma County, owned by her husband, Richard
D'Argenzio, and his twin brother, Ray. They came together at
Kathy's Burbank home to speak about Randy.

They explain how their mother had studied under Herbert
Lincoln Clark – the cornettist and bandmaster who came up with
'The Stars And Stripes Forever' march – and Arnold Schoenberg,
whose innovations in atonality turned the classical world upside
down. Meanwhile, their father, William, had been a clarinet and
sax player in the army, while their maternal grandmother played
the piano and their grandfather was a doctor who played guitar: a
1918 Gibson model Army Navy Special. 'The gene pool was there,'
says Kathy. 'But Randy took it to a whole new level and even blew
my mom away because he was so gifted.' He was six when he
first picked up his grandfather's ancient guitar. 'He didn't even

know how to hold it,' says Kathy, 'he would just put it on the ground and play it.' Noting his aptitude, Dee arranged for Randy and Kathy – who were especially close – to start guitar lessons together at Musonia. When after just nine months his teacher told Dee that 'I can't teach him any more. He knows everything I do', she didn't believe him. It was too outlandish. But it was true. Folk, Hawaiian guitar, jazz, classical, blues and of course rock – Randy was a master of them before he'd reached his teens.

Yet home life was far from idyllic. His parents had divorced when he was two. 'It created quite a stigma,' says Kelle. 'Back in those days, that was like saying your mom was a drunk or something.' In fact, Dee was super-strict. When the kids got out of line they were beaten with a leather strap. 'Or anything else she could pick up,' says Kathy. 'She was not a warm fuzzy person.' Kathy recalls seeing Dee telling a 12-year-old Randy how gifted he was. 'He burst into tears, because she did not give out compliments.' The other main pivot to family life was the church and school they all attended, the First Lutheran, where Dee was also the choir teacher. 'Randy was actually kind of religious,' reveals Kelle. 'He was devout. He wasn't like running to a church every ten seconds. But he always wore a cross and I think he took it seriously.' Although the Rhoadses were one of the first families in the neighbourhood to get a colour TV, they didn't own a record player until Randy finally bought one with Green Stamps when he was 15. He and his brother had also begun attending live rock concerts. Kelle recalls taking Randy to an Alice Cooper show, in 1971. 'That influenced him very much. At that point I think he decided, "Maybe I could do this one day."'

Like most budding young guitarists in the Seventies, he admired Jimmy Page and Jeff Beck. He also liked Leslie West from Mountain. But what really turned Randy on was glam rock. He adored the instant-gratification flash of Cooper band guitarist Glenn Buxton; he admired the technical nous of Be-Bop Deluxe's

Bill Nelson. Above all else, he was in love with David Bowie guitarist Mick Ronson, whom he saw playing at Bowie's now famous
show at Santa Monica Civic Auditorium in October 1972. 'When
Mick Ronson held his finger on the guitar with one hand and
walked it around the stage during "Moonage Daydream", that
made a big impression on Randy,' Kelle recalls. 'It looks good,
sounds good, it makes really great theatre. Randy ended up getting a Les Paul very similar and a hairstyle very similar to Mick
Ronson.'

Randy also now began dressing in full glam regalia. He and
his best pal at Burbank High School, Kelly Garni, would spend
weekends rifling through thrift stores buying second-hand
threads. 'He'd come back with these outfits and dresses and
jewellery. I'd say, "What are you gonna do with those dresses
Randy?" He said, "I'm gonna fix them up, you'll see." He would
slash 'em up and make these great tops. He had quite a style.
He was very artistic. He used to draw a lot. He would have been
a fantastic clothes designer.' Kathy adds: 'He was nice-looking,
almost effeminate-looking, beautiful, for a guy.' Peacocked-out in
his new glam finery, however, Randy began to attract even more
attention – not always a good thing for an otherwise shy high
school kid. 'People really gave him a hard time. They used to want
to beat him up. It really upset me a lot and I would scream at
these people, because he just didn't fit in.'

A year younger than Randy, and inspired by his example,
Garni took up bass ('It had less strings than a guitar'). When the
two teenagers weren't out 'raising hell' they would practise together, something he now claims they did 'Every day for nine
years.' When Randy was ready to form his own band, Garni was
the natural choice as bass player. 'We had absolutely no academic
interest whatsoever,' says Garni. 'The more under-privileged kids
were the ones that gravitated towards us. The girls that were generally not as virginal.' As Garni suggests, shy and quietly spoken

Randy may have been, but that didn't mean he was a saint. 'He was by nature the angelic person that he's often described as. But he also had a sometimes dangerous sense of humour.' Outsiders at school, the pair would get their own back on what they saw as straight society by pulling off an increasingly hazardous number of 'pranks.' Like the night they poured gasoline across the road outside Randy's house then set alight to it when they saw a car coming – 'Hiding in the bushes laughing!' Sometimes the cops were called. 'Generally we were let go cos we were kids and the cops didn't want the hassle. We learned a few lessons. But it really was done with a sense of innocence too. Randy never wanted to hurt anyone. We were just young. We didn't understand we were causing anyone any distress.'

Inevitably, given the times, there were also experiments with drugs. 'Anything like mind-altering that were real psychedelic we were very afraid of,' explains Garni. 'We smoked weed quite a few times but decided it really wasn't for us. We did do some cocaine. Everybody was throwing it in our faces. We saw it as a very harmless drug, as something that allowed you to be able to stay up all night and drink and have fun. That's all it was to us. We didn't consider it getting high – at all.' Not then, but Randy would develop a more pragmatic understanding of how 'harmless' drugs really were by the time he came to work with Ozzy Osbourne, then at the height of his multiple addictions. He may have had the occasional 'bump' by then but Randy steered well clear of Ozzy's all-night binges, preferring to practise in his room or write letters home to Dee or his girlfriend, Jodi.

When they weren't running amok around the neighbourhood the two would make music. There was a high school band with Kelle on drums, and which the brothers named Violet Fox (Dee's middle name was Violet). Later Randy and Garni began backing a guy named Smokey at Rodney's English Disco. But it wasn't until they put together their own band, Little Women, that things began to get serious. They had been 'out partying all night' with a girlfriend named Hillary. When she started talking about a singer she knew, 'does this kind of Rod Stewart thing', they asked for an introduction. Enter: Kevin DuBrow, an 18-year-old Anglophile from nearby Van Nuys, then fronting what later became the LA punk band The Dickies. DuBrow was another English rock fan, though for him the goods were to be found in Humble Pie, not David Bowie. That was okay; most kids Randy knew didn't like Bowie either. DuBrow was also not the greatest singer. But what he lacked in obvious talent, DuBrow made up for with energy and enthusiasm. He could also write lyrics. Together he and Randy would eventually create a set of songs that sounded good onstage – loud, flash, anthemic – and occasionally even good on record. 'Slick Black Cadillac', one of their later numbers from 1977, was covered in other young LA bands' sets, notably Leather Charm, the band James Hetfield played in before Metallica. DuBrow described his main contribution to Quiet Riot as 'the motivator. I found managers and stuff like that. And you know these guys were just out of high school. They [were] a mess.' If that meant rubbing people up the wrong way sometimes – or even a lot of the time – DuBrow didn't care. He was on a mission.

Randy Rhoads would eventually spend five years trying to turn Quiet Riot into a success. But the closest they ever came to it was a second-rate Japanese-only record deal – from which came two decidedly so-so albums, Quiet Riot (1977) and Quiet Riot II (1978) – and regular, ever more soul-destroying appearances at sleazy LA nightspots like the Starwood. 'I would go to the Starwood just to see Randy play,' recalls Dana Strum. 'It was the first thing for me that wasn't good or bad – it was extraordinary – my jaw just dropped. I loved Queen and I saw Randy doing this acapella solo and it made me think of Brian May doing "Keep Yourself Alive". I thought, where's this person been: this guy in a polka-dotted outfit and frosted hair?'

The band got regular bookings, working four nights a week, sometimes two or three sets a night. But they weren't making money and Randy, still living at his mother's house on Amherst Drive, began giving lessons on the side to supplement his meagre income. Kelle Rhoads cites Kevin DuBrow as 'the biggest reason they didn't get signed.' Though Quiet Riot – still led by the irrepressibly thick-skinned DuBrow – would eventually find major success with their *Metal Health* album (a US No. 1 in 1983), as Kelle says, when Randy was in the band, 'People would come up and say to Randy, "I love your band, dude. When you gonna dump your singer?"' But while DuBrow's reputation seemed to diminish more each day, Randy's began to soar. Greg Leon, another young guitarist then fronting Suite 19 with future Motley Crüe star Tommy Lee on drums, recalls meeting Randy backstage at a Quiet Riot and Van Halen concert in 1976 at Glendale City College. 'I'm seventeen and I'm the hotshot guitar player in Glendale but I saw Randy and went, "Oh, man!" He just had that aura about him. He was wearing a blue velvet vest, blue velvet pants and platform shoes. He just loved platform shoes because he was so little. He walked out and he looked like a star. Then if you can imagine Van Halen is the next band on and that was it – my life was never the same after that one!'

The two would become such friends that when Randy eventually left Quiet Riot he recommended Leon as his replacement. The grateful younger guitarist would repay the favour by later helping Randy write what would become one of his signature riffs with Ozzy Osbourne – 'Crazy Train'. 'We were hanging out and I showed him the riff to Steve Miller's 'Swingtown'. I said, "Look what happens when you speed this riff up." And the next thing I know he took it to a whole other level and ended up writing the "Crazy Train" riff.'

The only thing missing was some words and someone to sing them.

*

They say when opportunity comes a-knocking it does so often from the least likely source. So it was with the story of Randy Rhoads. A local hero in the close-knit environs of Burbank and the Sunset Strip, he was used to receiving compliments at Quiet Riot shows from younger musical wannabes. One night towards the end of 1978, though, he was genuinely taken aback by the approach of a tall kid with long, waist-length hair. Dana Strum, then playing bass in his band Bad-Axe, now more famous as a founding member of melodic rock titans Slaughter and, more recently, musical director of Motley Crüe singer Vince Neil's solo group, had been watching Randy play for weeks before summoning up the courage to speak to him. 'I said, "I just gotta tell you, man, I think you're so good." He just looked at me like, "You do?" He was just extremely humble, soft-spoken, not a super outgoing personality person. I told him, "You know, man, there's gotta be something out there for you, man. You're just too good."' Six months later Strum finally stumbled upon what that 'something' might be.

It was early in 1979, and word was out in Hollywood that Ozzy Osbourne had been fired from Black Sabbath for being, as Tony Iommi put it with considerable understatement, 'too out of it – even for us'. Ozzy was left to moulder in a suite at the Le Parc hotel in West Hollywood. 'The coke dealer used to come by every day while I was just sat there in a pile of empty beer bottles and pizza boxes. For six months I never even opened the drapes ...' As he was still signed to Sabbath's label, the Don Arden-owned Jet Records, however, half-hearted attempts were made to get Ozzy at least thinking about putting a new band together. Encouraged by Sharon, rehearsal time had been booked for Ozzy to try out working with guitarist Gary Moore, recently of Thin Lizzy, and ex-Ian Gillan Band drummer Mark Nauseef. Moore was signed to Jet and would eventually record an album with Nauseef under the moniker G-Force. But Sharon wanted to get Ozzy out of his pity pot at Le Parc and at least get him thinking about working with other musicians. Lately, he had begun to ramble on about opening a wine bar back in Birmingham with Thelma. 'I remember someone from the office was staying at the hotel and they give me an envelope with six hundred dollars in it to pass on to Sharon. I did it on coke. She went fucking barmy at me!'

Still in need of a bass player though, when Ozzy was introduced to Strum at the Starwood one night an invitation was issued for the hotshot young bassist to audition for him. 'It wasn't like now where every young band pays homage to Black Sabbath,' Dana recalls, 'back then you either loved them or hated them. I was a huge fan so I was very excited to meet Ozzy. It was at Frank Zappa's rehearsal studio on Sunset. Gary Moore was there. I had no idea who he was [but] he was phenomenal, stunning. But when I started talking to Ozzy I ended up saying to him, "This guy [Moore] is not the guy for you." I was so into Black Sabbath and I thought Moore's more blues style was nothing to do with what Ozzy does. Then I said to Ozzy: "But I know the guy you need."'

Ozzy ignored that but did offer Dana the gig as his new bassist. The next day Dana found himself driving Ozzy around LA, checking out prospective guitar players. 'He had a list with names and addresses, and we would just show up. It was bizarre. And I'm saying to Ozzy, "Look, let's forget this. I *know* the guy" ...' He'd already phoned Randy all excited. 'I said, "You know I told you there had to be something out there for you? Well, you know the band Black Sabbath ...?" But before I could get another word out he said, "Yeah, man, I really don't like them." I was distraught. I'd never considered that possibility. But Randy really did not like Black Sabbath at all. I don't think he even knew the name of the singer. I'm like, "Look, just come down, see what happens." He's like, "Will I get gas money? Like, ten or fifteen bucks?" I'm like, "Yes. Please just come."'

As Kelly Garni confirms, growing up, he and Randy thought Black Sabbath 'was a ridiculous thing … a joke'. Nevertheless, Dana eventually talked Randy into coming down that evening to play for Ozzy at Dalton Records, the Santa Monica studio where Dana worked part-time. But by now Ozzy had begun knocking back Heinekens and keeping himself going with regular snorts of coke. 'I didn't do drugs at all. But I'd booked time at the studio and persuaded Randy to come down and play and there was no way I was going to let that slide now.' Dana, who does a good impersonation of a stoned Ozzy, recalls how by now Ozzy was taunting him: 'Okay, we'll see this Jesus of guitar players, this superstar that you just *know* is the guy! It's gonna be like the fucking Messiah.'

Years later, Ozzy would recall 'lying over the studio desk and Dana keeps throwing water and shit over me. I looked through the [studio] window and Randy says something like [softly spoken voice], "Whaddaya want me to play?" I says, "Do you got a solo?" He says, "Well, kinda …" I says, "Well, play anything."' Randy plugged in his tiny practice amp and began to play. I just went … *what!?!* I remember thinking, in my haze, this is not really happening, I'm asleep really. Cos this guy … I mean, you hadn't heard stuff like that before.' Dana: 'I'm starting to wish I'd never opened my mouth. Ozzy wants to go home. Randy says he doesn't like Sabbath … But I had the control room dimly lit, because I wanted Ozzy just to focus on the music. And Randy is sitting on a stool on the other side of the glass. We couldn't even see him. But I told him just to do the guitar solo he did at the Starwood, just to let Ozzy hear that.' Ozzy had now passed out and Dana had to virtually carry him into the control room. 'So I set the volume like super high by accident. But I thought, leave it, this will wake him up.'

As soon as he got his cue, Randy let rip. 'It was louder than hell, it sounded huge.' Less than a minute later, Ozzy tottered over to Dana and said, 'Tell that kid ... tell that kid ... he's got the job. And then take me home ...' Too embarrassed to stop Randy after just 60 seconds, Dana rushed Ozzy back to his hotel, with Randy still playing, then came back to tell him the news. 'He was like, "So what's gonna happen now? What's next?" I'm like, I don't know, dude, I really don't know ...' What happened next was exactly nothing. There had been a brief meeting at Ozzy's hotel the following afternoon during which Randy failed to endear himself to Ozzy by drinking Diet Coke and dressing so extravagantly that virtually the first thing Ozzy asked him was if he was gay. Randy's sense of humour won Ozzy over there. Randy replied, 'No, Church of England.' There followed a jam session a few days later at Pasha Music studios, where Ozzy, Dana and Randy were joined, at Randy's suggestion, by Quiet Riot drummer Frankie Banali. 'And that was it,' sighs Dana. 'I never heard any more, except that Ozzy was getting ready to go back to the UK ...'

Enter the man whose musical nous and clever way with words would become the yin to Randy's yang when it came to composing the songs that would, though they didn't know it then, resurrect Ozzy's shattered career: Bob Daisley. Now 63, the Australian-born bassist had first made his name in the UK in the early Seventies with innovative blues-rockers Chicken Shack, before forming Widowmaker with former Mott The Hoople guitarist Ariel Bender, another Jet Records act that never quite made it. When Daisley's next gig, as bassist in Rainbow, came to an end in 1979, Sharon's brother David – then running the London offices of Jet – approached him to work with Ozzy. 'They wanted to keep it a UK-based band,' Daisley now recalls from his home in Sydney. And so the search for a new guitarist began all over again. 'But really nobody in England wanted to know. Then Ozzy told me about this guitarist he'd seen in LA that was a teacher. I envisaged a bloke with a pipe and slippers and a cardigan. But Ozzy said he was a great guitarist so I said, well, let's get him over. David Arden didn't want to do it at first but eventually he said, and David's words were exactly this: "Against my better judgement I agree to fly this unknown kid over from LA."'

What nobody knew was how reluctant Randy was to make that leap into the unknown. According to Kathy Rhoads, 'My mom made him go. He was teaching at my mother's school and he *loved* teaching. But my mom said this is probably your break, your chance to be exposed. She knew he had the talent [and] she thought this would be his opportunity to finally be noticed. But he did not want to go. My mom said, "You're going." "Well, I don't have a jacket." "Well, we'll buy one."' When he got to London in September 1979 Randy would phone home and write postcards and letters every day complaining of how 'homesick' he was. Kathy: 'We had never been away from home, any of us. So to suddenly be thrust out into the world, especially with someone like Ozzy Osbourne, who was totally the polar opposite of Randy, must have been very difficult for him.' When Bob finally met the unknown kid at the London offices of Jet, 'I said to Ozzy, "Is he gay?" because he had perfect fingernails and this sort of coiffured hair and very fitted clothing and all that. But it became very obvious very quickly that, no, he wasn't gay.'

Randy and Bob would strike up a musical partnership that would both resurrect Ozzy's wrecked career and help change the direction of American rock in the 1980s. 'Ozzy was out of his mind, smoking pot and drinking all day. I used to get on his case about it and he started calling me Sid Serious. Randy had the chords and we would work them up into songs. Then we'd play the music and Ozzy would sing over it and come up with a vocal melody. Then I'd take a tape away of that vocal melody and write lyrics that would fit with his phrasing and melody.'

According to Daisley it was never meant to be an Ozzy solo album they were working on, but the debut album from a collective band named Blizzard Of Ozz. Certainly that was the impression ex-Uriah Heep drummer Lee Kerslake was given when he signed up in December 1979. And it was what Randy wanted to hear too – an impression reinforced when he asked Ozzy if he minded him laying down a 50-second classical guitar instrumental named after his mother Dee, to which Ozzy replied: 'It's your album too.' Or as Randy told one interviewer at the time: 'Ozzy's music is both of ours. A lot of times he'll have a melody, and I'll have a riff that fits in. He hums something and I go, "Hey, I have a chord progression that will go with that!" A lot of other times I'll be sitting practising, and he'll say, "I like that – remember it." Naturally, I never can. So we'll do it right there and build a song.' The idea of this being an entirely new band, however, lasted only as long as it took to make their first album. A message made even clearer when the first tour jackets went on sale – emblazoned with the words OZZY OSBOURNE. The concept of the Blizzard Of Ozz was kept as the title of Ozzy's first album, but it was launched as a solo project, however the members of the 'band' might have preferred to think of it.

Recording at Ridge Farm, a residential studio in Surrey, with first-time producer Max Norman at the controls, the result was a nine-track heavy metal masterpiece that remains among the best things Ozzy would ever release. Indeed, four of its tracks – the rousing opener 'I Don't Know'; the stirring anthem 'Crazy Train'; the ode to recently deceased AC/DC singer Bon Scott, 'Suicide Solution'; and the truly unsettling 'Mr Crowley' – would remain the cornerstones of Ozzy's live shows for the next 30 years. Released in the UK in September 1980, the album had an immediate Top 10 success that over-rode the ambivalence Randy was still feeling privately as he embarked on his first UK tour with Ozzy. 'Before I met Ozzy, I was very insecure onstage,' Randy reflected. 'If my amps acted up, or the sound system wasn't good, it really affected my playing. Being with Ozzy has given me a great deal of self-confidence. He pushed me into trying things and doing things I never would have done on my own.' Nevertheless, with only one album to draw from, the set ended each night with three cast-iron Sabbath classics: 'Iron Man', 'Children Of The Grave' and 'Paranoid'. All of which, Randy detested. 'He couldn't understand why they still had to play Black Sabbath songs,' says Kelle Rhoads.

Randy hoped that by the time the band recorded a second album it would no longer be necessary to carry on trading on Ozzy's past. When Sharon Arden – who'd recently returned to take over the day-to-day running of Ozzy's career – decided to rush them back into Ridge Farm to record another album before sending them out on their first US tour, Randy assumed that was the reason.

He was wrong.

The first thing Randy Rhoads did when he received his first sizeable royalty check was buy 'a very, very expensive' acoustic guitar, which he had made for him in Spain, in order for him to begin his classical guitar studies. The cost: $5000; a handsome sum in 1981. That, though, was his only extravagance. Speaking of his newfound success, Randy said: 'It still hasn't hit me yet. I've still got my past in me [and] I guess I'm trying to mature into it, but I don't have my feet on the ground at all. I don't even know who I am, or what I am. People say this will go to your head and make you egotistical. That's a load of shit. What it does is make you totally frightened and humble.'

Unlike their first visit to Ridge Farm a year before, there were few new songs written when the band went back into the studio at the start of 1981. Some were built on parts of songs from some of Bob's old bands: the bass riff from a song called 'Black Sally' that Bob had written for Mecca became the backbone of 'Little Dolls'. Another Bob bass riff from another band, Kahvas Jute, became the one they used on 'You Can't Kill Rock And Roll'. Randy dipped into his own glam past with Quiet Riot for the sleazy riff to 'Flying High Again'. A perfectionist unused to compromising his music in order to meet a record company deadline, Randy was not happy with the second Ozzy album. 'I really cringe about some of the songs,' he later confessed. 'We were so rushed for time in the studio because we had to get to America to start the tour.'

Nevertheless *Diary Of A Madman*, as it was called after one of Randy's most inspired moments, had its highlights. Not least the epic and genuinely chilling title track. Randy was particularly thrilled when Sharon later decided that his atmospheric intro to it would replace 'Carmina Burana' as the rousing opening overture at Ozzy's shows. What he was less thrilled with was the media shit-storm that was about to erupt in America when news broke of Ozzy biting off the heads of two live doves during a record convention meeting in LA. Nobody at CBS – Jet's distribution company in America – was taking Ozzy's budding solo career seriously, Sharon told me. So she decided Ozzy should 'make nice' by turning up at their annual convention and pressing corporate flesh. It was also arranged for him to give a short speech, lauding the efforts of the company workforce in the lead-up to the US release of *Blizzard Of Ozz*. The pièce de résistance was to have been Ozzy ending his speech by releasing three white doves into the gathered audience of CBS higher-ups and worker bees. The trouble was Ozzy had polished off a bottle of brandy in the car on his way to the convention. 'I just remember this PR woman going on and on at me,' Ozzy would tell me years later. 'In the end, I said, "Do you like animals?" Then pulled out one of these doves and bit its fucking head off. Just to shut her up. Then I did it again with the next dove, spitting the head out on the table, and she fell to the floor screaming. That's when they threw me out. They said I'd never work for CBS again ...'

And so it might have come to pass but for the resourcefulness of Sharon, who had learnt all the tricks of the music business trade at her father's knee. As soon as she got back to the Jet office that day she began working the phones. By the following morning, news of Ozzy's 'outrage' had made the front pages of every respectable newspaper in America. The story was all over the radio too. When Breakfast TV news also picked up on it the tide of publicity had turned into a media tsunami. 'The album began selling the same day,' said Sharon, propelling the *Blizzard Of Ozz* album up the US charts. It was the beginning of Ozzy's reinvention as the wild man of rock. Previously in Sabbath, he'd been seen, at best, as the mournful mouthpiece for an impossibly earnest band of sheet-metallists; at worst, as a clown. Now he became to a new generation of teenage metal dudes the very embodiment of party-hearty, Eighties-style 'Satanic' rock, and over the next year stories began to be told of fans bringing all manner of grisly gifts for him to the shows. There would, however, be a price to pay for such easy pickings. It may have provided Ozzy with some much-needed sales traction in the US – where initial sales had been so slow that Randy worried in letters home that 'maybe new wave and punk killed our music' – but Randy cringed at the way, in his view, the dove incident detracted from the music he was trying to make. 'He said at one show they brought a dead goat to present it to Ozzy,' Kelle Rhoads recalls. Randy told Kelle he didn't want to become part of 'a circus'.

Other changes, however, had proved less unsettling for the well-mannered guitarist with the surprisingly steely edge. When Daisley and Kerslake were fired just weeks before the US tour – for 'all this complaining and back-talk about money', as Ozzy put it, though Daisley now insists he was only given the boot because

The last New York show by the original line-up, Madison Square Garden, August 27 1978. Within months, Tony Iommi had announced he could no longer work with Ozzy.

London, August 1978. The band receive special 10th anniversary cakes at a reception at their record company, Phonogram.

The man with a plan. Ronnie James Dio in Paris, working on final mixes for Heaven And Hell, February 1980.

Dio onstage flashing the 'devil horns' with Sabbath at the Gaumont Theatre, Southampton, June 1980.

Randy Rhoads, the hotshot guitarist who saved Ozzy's
career, with trademark polka-dot Flying V, 1981.

Ozzy performing with Randy Rhoads, just weeks before
the plane crash that would kill the guitarist, January 1982.

'Without my wife I'd have been a hot dog salesman.'
Ozzy with manager – and soon to be wife –
Sharon Osbourne (née Arden), March 1982.

Born to die. Onstage with Ian Gillan (centre),
Long Beach Arena, LA, January 26 1984.

ALL AREA
ACCESS

Mob Rules tour pass, 1981.

he wouldn't agree to Kerslake being fired (partly on the grounds, Sharon later told me, of his scruffy-old-man image) – Randy was the only one who took the trouble to phone and wish them well. He was also the only one to immediately approach Sharon with suggestions for who to replace them with: his old pals from Quiet Riot, drummer Frankie Banali and bassist Rudy Sarzo. Sharon, however, had already lined up former Pat Travers and Black Oak Arkansas drummer Tommy Aldridge, so the only spot that still needed filling was on bass. Sarzo was duly approached – and with Quiet Riot now in temporary abeyance he instantly accepted. Speaking now, Dana Strum refuses to admit he felt put out by this development. 'Maybe my name had come up and [Randy] had been shut down.' Or maybe Randy simply preferred Rudy's playing. Either way, it shows that Ozzy and Sharon weren't the only ones prepared to look out for number one.

With the second Ozzy album already in the can, but unreleased until November 1981, the rest of the year was spent almost entirely on the road. Mainly in North America, but also on tour that autumn in Europe, where they opened for Saxon, and a fortnight of UK dates leading up to Christmas. Onstage Ozzy and Randy had developed quite a show, the singer playfully interacting with Randy in ways he would never have dreamed of with the stern-faced Tony Iommi, pulling at his hair, jostling him, laughing wildly as Randy ripped away at his solos. 'That first tour was fun,' Rudy Sarzo later recalled. According to Rudy, Randy even admitted to having a one-night stand with Sharon. Ozzy's wife, Thelma, had visited Ridge Farm during the making of *Diary*, leaving Sharon, who had begun a secret affair with Ozzy, with nowhere to sleep. Randy had offered to let her share his room. He told Sarzo: 'We started drinking and the next thing you know we were making out and ...'

'You guys did it, didn't you?' Sarzo yelled gleefully. Randy replied: 'Look, I respect Ozzy and Sharon and I don't want to be in the middle.' Besides, he added, he loved the girl he'd left behind in LA, his future fiancée, Jodi Raskin. For Sharon's part, it was also strictly a one-off. There was no way she was sacrificing her growing hold over Ozzy for Randy Rhoads, however talented and good-looking he was. In her memoir, written over a quarter of a century later, she even suggested that Ozzy had known about her and Randy's secret tryst and had taken it for what it was. 'Ozzy knows and has never wanted to discuss it,' she wrote. 'But don't read any dissatisfaction into it. Ozzy knows the one-time occurrence was loving, not lustful.' Actually, Ozzy didn't know anything at all until years after Randy's death.

During a short tour break that summer, back at the family home in Burbank, Randy regaled Delores, Kelle and Kathy with stories from his past nine months with Ozzy. He hung out with Jodi, and he played with his toy train set. On vacations when her children were kids, Delores had always taken the train not the plane – Randy's first time on a plane had been when he flew to the UK to join Ozzy. As a child, Randy had loved those long train journeys, gazing out of the window at the passing world and wondering. Now, as an adult, the co-author of 'Crazy Train' seemed to relive those times by building his own elaborate train set. Kathy: 'He had a track in his room. You could build the villages and he would work on those constantly when he was home.' Kelle: 'Everything that Randy drank should have had a little parasol in it. You know, a little bit of liquor and a lot of sugar. And he would make his little sugary drink and get his cigarettes and listen to classical music as he worked on his little model railroad. Boy, he loved that.'

Back on tour, though, the pressure was starting to tell. During off-time in Germany, Randy was delighted to discover the smallest-gauge toy trains he'd ever seen. But it was also in Europe that Ozzy truly went – like the song says – off the rails. His dalliance with Sharon had blossomed into a full-on affair – a fact his wife Thelma was still in the dark about – and Ozzy was starting to crack after months of living on the tour bus. Each night he would complain his back hurt, his voice had gone, he was sick, he couldn't go on. And each night Sharon – wise to his almost pathological stage fright – would push him out there. In the end, after another enormous drink and drugs bender, the dates were cancelled and the band returned to London, where they stayed until the start of their second UK tour, in November. As Ozzy later told me, 'The first two Sabbath albums were great fun and the first two Ozzy solo albums were great fun, when you've got fuck all to lose and everything to gain. Whereas, once you've got a couple of hits, you've got everything to lose and you've got to keep the momentum going.'

Rudy Sarzo recalls a visit with Randy to a high-class brothel in London, although the guitarist claimed to have run from the room when the 'lady' he'd been presented with began hitting him with her riding crop. 'All I wanted was someone to talk to,' he told Rudy. 'There are so many uncertainties surrounding this band. I'm just not sure about our future any more.' The pressure was only increased with the commencement of their next US tour in January 1982. With both *Blizzard* and *Diary* now platinum albums in America, Ozzy was ready to step up to arenas – something, on paper, his years of experience headlining major US venues with Sabbath should have allowed him to take in his stride. But that was then and this was now the Eighties: the dawn of huge production values and elaborate stage shows. Determined to keep Ozzy contemporary, Sharon had commissioned a new show for the tour, featuring a castle facade, replete with turrets, gantries and medieval costumes for the band to wear. And a dwarf – nicknamed Ronnie, after Ozzy's replacement in Sabbath, the diminutive Ronnie James Dio.

None of the band were happy with the new arrangement. Tommy Aldridge's drums were set so high among the castle's turrets that he complained he couldn't hear what the rest of the band were doing, while Randy's and Rudy's amps were hidden so far behind the castle's 'walls' they also had trouble relating to their own sound. Worst of all for Ozzy, he was required to stand on a giant mechanical hand for the encores, which would lift him above the front rows of the audience. 'If it's so fucking safe you do it!' Ozzy roared at Sharon before storming off. By now, though, Ozzy's fights with Sharon were such a regular occurrence the band accepted them as part of the touring landscape. '[Randy] fucking hated all the bollocks of them fighting and throwing things at each other and screaming and all that,' says Bob Daisley.

One thing for sure: Sharon was tough. Her brother David would tell people, 'Sharon is Don in a skirt' and they would think he was joking. But she proved it so time and again in the early years of Ozzy's post-Sabbath success. Facing down promoters who liked to try their luck by underpaying the band, or recalcitrant record company drones that simply weren't doing their jobs. Once, at an in-store signing, she leapt on a photographer she identified as a bootlegger – the kind who would take shots of an artist then sell prints outside their shows, making several thousand dollars in the process – and proceeded to punch his lights out. She may have been barely five feet tall but when one promoter tried to erroneously charge her for pre-concert advertising worth $6000, she began head-butting him and kicking him in the balls. As she later recalled, 'Apart from my father, I had no role model, so to a certain extent I had to make up the rules as I went along.' Word spread throughout the biz: you didn't tell Sharon Arden what to do. Or else.

By the start of 1982, despite being voted Best New Guitar Player by *Guitar Player* magazine in the US and Best Guitarist by *Sounds* in the UK, Randy was in bad shape. Rudy recalls Randy confiding in him: 'I don't feel like I'm myself any more.' He was uncomfortable even at home in LA, where suddenly 'everyone wants to hang out with me'. He talked of the night he got drunk 'and started throwing furniture out of the window with Ozzy. That's not really me. That's not the reason why I started playing the guitar.'

On 20 January came the incident in Des Moines where Ozzy bit the head off a bat onstage. He insisted he thought it was 'a fucking toy – until I put its head in my mouth and its wings started flapping'. But Randy was unimpressed. Then Ozzy began complaining about Randy's non-stop practice with a nylon-stringed classical guitar. The stars of the show were getting on each other's nerves. It was not a good sign and Randy began to withdraw from Ozzy's company, calling up local classical music teachers in each city the tour stopped in, taking lessons in musical theory and writing his own neo-classical compositions. The last straw for Randy came when he was told they'd be recording a show entirely of Sabbath covers for a double live album. He was told Jet wanted it. Sharon later told me it was part of her deal to get Ozzy off Jet – and away from her father. Whatever the truth, it caused a major rift between Ozzy and Randy. Randy tried to lead the band on strike against doing it. Ozzy threw a tantrum and fired the whole band. Sharon smoothed things over. The singer taunted Randy that both Frank Zappa and Gary Moore had agreed to play on the record if Randy didn't. Randy sighed and went back to his classical studies.

The growing differences between guitarist and singer were not just musical. When, in February 1982, Ozzy was arrested during a tour-stop in San Antonio, for urinating on the Alamo (while dressed as Sharon, who had stolen his clothes in an attempt to keep him from going out), Randy was aghast. This was not the sort of thing Mick Ronson would have had to put up with when he played with David Bowie. Alice Cooper was properly crazy and alcoholic too but even he'd never done anything as frankly disgusting as pissing on one of the country's most hallowed shrines. Once again, Ozzy latest 'adventure' made headlines around the world; ticket sales for his US tour also increased, as did sales of both the *Blizzard* and *Diary* albums, which would eventually total around seven million copies in America alone. They remain the biggest selling of Ozzy's career. The very next day, however, Randy dropped a bombshell. He would do the live album of Sabbath songs, he would record one more studio album with Ozzy, if they insisted, but that would be it, he would no longer subject himself to the humiliations and privations of an Ozzy Osbourne tour. He was quitting. Instead, his immediate future, he said, would entail going back to school to study classical music. Ozzy, still drunk from the night before, was furious and punched him in the face. Bob Daisley: 'I wasn't there but I've spoken to Tommy Aldridge and [keyboardist] Don Airey who both said when [Ozzy] heard Randy wanted out he punched him in the face and called him an ungrateful little shit. Tommy said it was a sucker punch too, one of those when he wasn't ready, wasn't even looking ...' The atmosphere on the bus after that was deadly, with neither man speaking to the other. Rudy recalls one night during a break back in LA, a stoned and drunken Ozzy telling him: 'You go tell your friend he'd better reconsider leaving the band. You tell him he's fucking up the best thing he's ever had. He's skating on thin ice.'

Eventually Ozzy would be more accepting of the situation. When I spoke to him about it years later, he talked about how he didn't think Randy would have continued playing rock music with anyone. How on that last tour he was already writing his own music, how it was all modal and very technical and that even Delores, a trained classical musician, couldn't work out what it was Randy was doing from the notes he left. And how when Randy said he was leaving Ozzy told him: 'Are you out of your fucking mind? Another few albums and you'll be able to buy your own university!'

As well as asking his mother to approach UCLA about him taking a Masters Degree in classical music, Randy had also spoken to John Stix, then editor of *Guitar World*, who'd offered to introduce him to New York scenesters like Steve Gadd, Jean-Luc Ponty and Earl Klugh. Randy had also been in touch with Richie Podolor, former Steppenwolf and Three Dog Night producer and a renowned classical guitarist who'd studied with Segovia, and who'd agreed to allow Randy to take part in classical sessions with him. Kathy says her mom 'knew Randy wasn't happy. But she knew what Ozzy did for my brother too. It's not that he got sick of Ozzy. He got sick of the road. It's not that he didn't like Ozzy. That's not true. He just didn't like that lifestyle. He wasn't raised that way.'

The first two shows of the resumed US tour were at the Omni Arena, Atlanta, on 17 March, and the following night at the Civic Coliseum in Knoxville. That night, on the 665-mile road trip to the next stop in Orlando, the whole band sat at the back of the bus watching the Second World War epic *Midway*. Rudy was first to retire to his bunk, 'After one too many kamikaze suicide crashes on the TV screen.' The driver of the tour bus was 36-year-old Andrew Aycock. Against Sharon's wishes he had picked up his wife, whom he was separated from, and allowed her to sit next to him for the drive to Orlando. Early the next morning the bus stopped over at a depot, the Red Baron Estates, near Leesburg. Aldridge recalls Aycock bragging about also being a pilot and promising the band 'a little joyride' on one of the small prop-engined planes also stationed at the depot. True to his word, Aycock offered the only other people awake – Don Airey and tour manager Jake Duncan – a quick spin in the air. The aircraft, a 27-year-old Beechcraft Bonanza F35, took a few passes over the tour bus then landed safely. At which point Aycock offered Randy and the band's seamstress, a fifty-year-old black woman named Rachel Youngblood, a quick trip in the air. Randy's fear of flying was well-known, as was Rachel's heart condition. Yet they both agreed to go up, persuaded by Aycock's promise 'that it would be just going up and down', as Rudy Sarzo recalls. 'Nothing fancy, nothing crazy ...'

Randy, who'd begun taking a camera everywhere with him, grabbed his case then stuck his head into Sarzo's bunk, inviting him to come along too but the bassist was half asleep and not interested. What happened next, once the plane was in the air, has since become a matter of lengthy, unresolved discussion. But for whatever reason the plane suddenly dipped and seemed to be heading straight for the tour bus. Don Airey, who'd been using a telephoto lens to snap the plane in flight, claimed he saw figures onboard struggling. Aycock's wife, Wanda, was standing in the doorway of the bus and many who were there believe the pilot, who'd been up all night driving and apparently arguing with her, had decided to kill her by ploughing the plane into the bus. Sarzo concluded that Randy had saved all their lives by forcing Aycock not to fly into the bus. Since then, however, rumours have circulated that Rachel, who was sitting in the front of the dual-control plane, had had a heart attack and as she slumped forward onto the controls had forced the plane into a dive – that the struggling figures Airey saw were in fact Randy, who was seated behind, trying to pull Rachel's inert form back as Aycock tried to force the plane out of its tailspin.

Whatever the truth, the result was that the left wing of the plane clipped the bus at about five feet off the ground, then flipped over and hit a large pine tree, severing the trunk, then ploughed straight into the garage of the Georgian-style mansion situated about 60 feet from the bus. The explosion killed all onboard instantly. The subsequent autopsy revealed that Aycock had traces of cocaine in his system at the time of the crash, while Randy's toxicology report revealed no illicit drugs. The National Transportation Safety Board's investigation also determined that Aycock's medical certificate had expired and that his biennial flight review required of all pilots was overdue. In other words, he shouldn't have been allowed anywhere near a tour bus, let alone an aeroplane. Rudy Sarzo recalls jumping out of his bunk on the bus and seeing Duncan down on his knees, sobbing, 'They're gone, they're gone ...' Meanwhile, Sharon was screaming at him, 'How could you let that baby get on that plane? How could you!'

Randy's funeral took place back home in Burbank on 24 March 1982. It was a dull grey day, LA struggling to wake beneath an overcast, gunmetal grey sky. It wasn't so cold but it wasn't so warm either and everyone pulled their coats just a little tighter as the memorial service began at the First Lutheran Church, which Randy had attended every Sunday with his mother and siblings, and where Delores Rhoads still teaches the choir to this day. Family friend Arlene Thomas played an acoustic guitar and sang gently in the background. She taught at Musonia at the same time Randy did and her presence was greatly appreciated by Delores. Nothing, though, could change the mood of sheer despair. This was not about saying farewell to someone who had lived their life. This was the final recognition of the unspeakable tragedy that had befallen the Rhoads family, and of how things would never be the same again.

Ozzy wept on Delores' shoulders throughout. A sobbing Jodi was comforted by Rudy. Ozzy, Tommy, Kevin DuBrow and Rudy were among the pallbearers, along with Randy's old friends Frank Santa Cruz and Kim McNair. Absent from the service was Kelly Garni. 'There's no way I wanted to see his coffin,' he explains. Kelle Rhoads had also been asked to be a pallbearer but couldn't bring himself to do so. 'I was in shock,' he says now. 'I didn't even believe it. I figured what it was, all right, it's a publicity stunt like the bat and pissing on the Alamo. All these years later, I've never gotten over it. I think about him every single day. It's almost like he dies every single day for me. I can go on with life but I really can't completely come to terms with it.'

Delores, whose fortitude throughout those last few, ghastly days had been otherworldly, made it her business to thank everyone for coming, comforting those she barely knew as warmly as she did her own grief-stricken family. Yet behind the kindly gestures lay an irretrievably broken heart. 'It was never the same for her again,' says Kathy Rhoads now. 'She never put up another tree at Christmas to this day. She's left his room exactly how Randy left it. It's like time stopped in her house. If you go there, it's like you're walking through that door in 1982. No one is allowed to go into his room. It's just the same as it was the last day that he was in there ...' Afterwards, a long motorcade wound from Burbank to San Bernardino, where Randy's remains were laid to rest at a mausoleum in Mountain View cemetery. 'It's a beautiful spot,' says Kelle, 'kinda like Lady Di's ...' Greg Leon recalls the funeral as 'being so sad. This was not supposed to happen to any of us. For Randy to go out that way, it was sickening. People were coming up trying to get autographs. There were some people across the street, kind of disrespectful in a way, because they were making noise: "Randy! Randy!" This was the guy's funeral, you know?'

Dana Strum had been driving in the same little white Triumph TR7 coupe he'd ferried Ozzy around town in two years before, when he heard the news on the car radio. He was so shocked he drove straight through a red light. 'It literally sucked the breath out of me and I just pulled over and started crying.' He says he was tormented with guilt for years. 'For forcing him to go, for talking him into it ...' His voice cracks at the memory. Years later, when his band Slaughter supported Ozzy on tour, he would sometimes look at Zakk Wylde, one of Randy's descendants as Ozzy's guitarist, and think: 'That really should have been Randy.'

Except of course Randy had already decided he was not going

to be part of Ozzy's long-term future. Ozzy later told me how from the moment he met Randy he knew 'he was only passing through'. He said he felt the same way when he saw Jimi Hendrix play at a Woburn Abbey music festival in 1967. Yet despite his genuine grief – 'I thought, that's it, it's over' – he was back on the road barely two weeks after Randy's death, with former Gillan guitarist Bernie Tormé in tow. Sharon made sure of it.

'After all the heartbreak of Randy's death, I just felt I couldn't face it any more,' said Ozzy. 'I told Sharon, "It's over, I'm finished."' Sharon, however, was determined not to let even this setback prevent Ozzy from making the most of his new solo stardom. She told him, 'You'd better not say anything like that to me again, Johnny Osbourne. Now get out on that stage and do your job!'

NINE
MOB RULE

By 1981, with the world at their feet again, Black Sabbath should have been set fair. Everything on paper finally added up. With Ozzy and Bill gone, they had removed their two weakest links. It had been something while it lasted but that line-up had reached its peak ten years before. It wasn't just the drugs – Tony Iommi was doing more coke than ever – it was their lack of self-control. The way they soiled themselves with their own emotions, the way they damaged everything they touched until it was as fucked up as them. Now they had replaced Ozzy and Bill with guys – Ronnie and Vinny – who were the exact opposite, who both liked to smoke a ton of weed, but were always reliable, and in the pocket when it came time to go onstage or in the studio, and who didn't need to be treated like recalcitrant children, forever having to be stopped from running under a bus or stealing candy from the store.

What nobody would realise until they began their second album together, in early 1981, was how unbalanced the band's creative ecosystem had now become. With Bill and Ozzy happy to leave the heavy lifting to Tony and Geezer, in terms of songwriting, coming into the studio only when they were called, even as their flair deserted them over the final, dismal Ozzy-era albums, at least everybody knew where they stood. Now, though, the creative chemistry had dramatically shifted. Never mind what the credits on the album sleeve said, everyone knew all the songs on *Heaven And Hell* had been written by Tony and Ronnie. Geezer and Bill had been so out of the loop, through choice, they could hardly complain. But when the album became such a success, it surely made sense for the next Sabbath album to follow suit – as closely as possible.

Not to Geezer, though, who now agitated behind the scenes to be reinstated as the band's lyricist, whispering in Tony's ear whenever he got the chance, decrying his lot at the same time as reminding the guitarist of how loyal he had remained throughout the band's prolonged identity crisis. Tony, who deplored confrontations, merely nodded his assent then left it to Ronnie and Geezer to sort it out between them. Ronnie, meanwhile, was not to be moved on this issue. Not at first anyway. His way of working was to allow the band to jam until they found a riff or a movement he could relate to, coming up with a vocal melody and lyrics almost instantly. What did he need a co-writer for? While Geezer's own modus operandi was entirely different: he preferred to sit alone, with a beer and a joint, as he composed his verses. In the end the compromise was reached whereby Ronnie would be solely credited for the lyrics, while Geezer would receive a co-writing credit for all the music. For now, then, as they laboured on new material in LA, they kept up the pretence of trying to work together, each man allowing the other the opportunity to participate in the other's thoughts and ideas. It couldn't last and resentment began to seep into their relationship like blood through a bandage.

Things had begun well enough with the track that became the album's demi-title track, 'The Mob Rules'. Written and recorded at John Lennon's old English pile Tittenhurst Park, near Ascot (the famous white house he recorded the *Imagine* album in), ostensibly as part of a soundtrack for a forthcoming animated movie, *Heavy Metal* – a self-consciously 'trippy' animated feature, starring John Candy, based on the comedic sci-fi magazine of the same name – that comprised musical relatives like Blue Öyster Cult, Journey, Cheap Trick and Grand Funk Railroad, it sounded like business as usual for the 'new' Sabbath. Fast-paced, punchy as hell, an impressive extension of the sound formulated since Dio had become involved. The movie would bomb but the track was a keeper. (By sad coincidence, Lennon was murdered just a few days before the band arrived at the studio. Not that the band let that dampen their mood. 'All the crew were nicking all the [gold] discs,' recalls Paul Clark. 'I had to make them put them back in the cupboard there. I took pictures of the bedroom and right by the side was [a small panel] with John and Yoko on, with two switches, so they could turn each other's lights out. In the toilet the dirty bastard had a video camera. I mean that was rare in them days! So they could watch them having a shit, I think, I don't know.')

The rest of *Mob Rules* would be written and recorded in LA, where they all now lived. Very much the companion piece to *Heaven And Hell*, the new songs followed the same formula, with showboating opener 'Turn Up The Night' a 'Neon Knights' part two. 'I told Tony it sounded like Thin Lizzy and he just gave me that look,' Paul Clark recalls. Similarly 'Voodoo', while trying to occupy the same space on *Mob Rules* as 'Children Of The Sea' did on its predecessor, comes across far more piecemeal. Good filler but no killer. For that we have to wait for the best track on the album, 'Sign Of The Southern Cross'. This was Sabbath at their most progressive metal best, from its tinkling acoustic intro, Ronnie in upper register, before the band rolls out the heavy artillery, like 'Children Of The Sea' and 'Heaven And Hell' rolled into one soul-deep crevice, Iommi's heart-drilling solo delivered at lightning speed, Ronnie's voice given all the space it needs to soar.

There were other highlights, like 'Falling Off The Edge Of The World', a proper ballad, huge, soulful, spine-tingling, its violin and treated-guitar intro, woven with choir and strings before the band bring the hammer down, a monstrous bell chiming in a monolithic ivory tower; the kind of epic journey-metal that Iron Maiden and Metallica would build their careers on later that decade; 'Country Girl', which begins like something off the first Sabbath album, all folksy psychedelia and enchanted darkness, before the lights come flashing on and the band start to conduct the stars; and 'Slipping Away', where Tony and Geezer finally get to live out their Led Zeppelin fantasies to the full, like something from *Physical Graffiti*, with Vinny more like Bonzo than Ward, Tony's elastic solo like vintage Page, with Geezer supplying a more than passable funk bass and Ronnie's multi-tracked vocals adding a distinctly Plant-esque veneer.

There were also some less inspired moments. Not least the self-consciously creepy 'E5150' – 'EVIL', in Roman numerals, geddit? – a radio-signal-from-space instrumental from Geezer that is eminently skippable in this context but which would provide a suitably tremble-tremble intro tape to all their forthcoming shows. And the overwrought closer, 'Over And Over', which tries so hard to end the album on a towering note it all but suffocates itself in a distorted kaleidoscope of sound.

Downtime in the studio found the band in good spirits too. When Thin Lizzy guitarist Scott Gorham dropped by, Tony told Paul to give him a spin in his Rolls-Royce. Then winked at Paul as he walked out the door. The tour manager got the message and 'drove like a madman doing fucking ninety-five, going round corners with the tyres squealing. And Scott's in the back going, "Oh God!"'

Tony also took to winding up Martin Birch, 'to a point where he almost killed hisself' after the producer, used to working with Ritchie Blackmore, who sometimes conducted séances in his hotel room, kept asking him if he was involved in occult practices. The pair would work late into the night, blasted out of their brains, until Birch began drilling Iommi. 'He used to keep asking these questions, "Are you doing black magic or what?" And I carried this little black briefcase, and I got fed up with him keeping asking so what I done, I bought this piece of wood and I carved it out and made a doll and put some hair on it and all the rest of this stuff and I wrapped it in this black cloth and put it in my briefcase. Then I went to the studio and I opened my case just enough so he could see this doll. And I opened the wrapper like and he went, "WHAT'S THAT?" I put it back in the briefcase and closed it and went, "What?" He went, "That's me, isn't it? That's me! I know that's me!" I was dying to burst out laughing but I just kept a straight face. "What you talking about?" "Open your case!" "No, why?" "That's me in there, I know it! I know it!" And he freaked out, absolutely freaked out. I had him on this for so long. He'd say things like, "I had a headache last night. It's you, isn't it? You've given me a headache." And I'd be like, "I don't know what you're on about." Then he'd cool off a bit after a while and I'd go, "Have you had any problems lately, Martin?" "WHY? WHAT HAVE YOU DONE?"' He chuckled malevolently.

Mob Rules was released in November 1981 and immediately replicated the success of its predecessor, hitting No. 12 in Britain and again making the Top 30 in America. Reviews were largely kind, too. Allowing that Sabbath had reinvented themselves just in the nick of time to take a place in the new wave of heavy rock goliaths that ruled Eighties rock, such as Judas Priest, Whitesnake, AC/DC – and Ozzy Osbourne, whose second solo album, *Diary Of A Madman*, was released the same month, and to greater acclaim.

It pained Tony, Geezer and, most especially, Ronnie to see Ozzy's album doing so much better than theirs. Musically, there actually wasn't much overlap, with Sabbath essentially holding true to their Seventies principles, while Ozzy wholeheartedly embraced the Eighties, relying on his hotshot young guitarist, Randy

Rhoads, to provide the musical thrills and spills. On tour only six of the 13 songs in Sabbath's 1982 set, including the encores of 'Paranoid' and 'Children Of The Grave', came from the Ozzy days. For the fans, it didn't appear to be an issue, happy to support both sides. But for Tony and Ronnie, it stuck in their throats like old chicken bones they could never quite cough up and spit out.

'We're a very different band to the one Ozzy was in,' Ronnie maintained. 'The only similarity is the name.' While for Ozzy, 'I couldn't give a fuck what they do. I'm out of there and very happy about that thank you very fucking much.' It was an outward non-chalance belied, he later confessed, by a very real feeling of anger towards the band that, as he saw it, left him behind to die. 'It was like a whole war,' Ozzy told me. 'I mean, I don't buy all this shit about, you know, I'll get fired but we'll still be friends. If you're still friends why get fired in the first fucking place?'

What Ozzy didn't know was that Ronnie was also becoming increasingly unhappy in Sabbath. The singer may have felt a certain affinity with the Brits – even a kinship: Wendy, after all, had been born in Epping, only moving to the US in 1973 – but he was feeling increasingly alienated from Tony and Geezer. The latter he didn't mind so much: he was quietly spoken, a solid bass player, and now he was with his new American girlfriend, Gloria, on tour he tended to keep to himself. As long as he understood that Ronnie was now the principal lyricist in the band things would be cool. The only thing Ronnie wasn't really sure about was whether Geezer actually liked him. He would catch those deep brown eyes looking at him sometimes and wonder what they were really thinking. Mainly, Geezer stuck by Tony: if Tony was okay with it, so was Geezer.

According to Paul Clark, whose increasing alienation from his 'brother' Iommi, who still hadn't forgiven his faithful retainer for warning him off his new American wife, Melinda, drew him closer to Dio, 'It was Ronnie who called the shots now.' He goes on: 'It's no coincidence that the band with Ronnie got really big again, even though we had no manager. Without Ronnie that band wouldn't have made it again without Ozzy, simple as. Ronnie and me worked on everything together. Ronnie taught me such a lot. Oh fuck, yeah. He was a great guy. He was a really lovely guy. But he got fucked over in the end.'

The trouble was, Ronnie was no longer sure how okay Tony was about anything. The guitarist had lately begun freebasing cocaine – a complicated procedure involving water, ammonia and much filtering, in order to end up with rock-hard pure 100 per cent unadulterated cocaine, and then smoking it. 'He'd be out of his fucking mind,' remembers Paul Clark. When they were staying at the Sunset Marquis in LA, 'We used to get a cab driver, Tip his name was, and he's the one that used to get it somehow. Him and that silly bastard keyboard player, Geoff Nicholls. Tony was so into it he was that bad that he couldn't do fucking interviews. I used to have to do the phone interviews for him, cos I've got the same accent.'

Ronnie liked to smoke pot and drink beer but he didn't do coke, was not fond of Quaaludes or Mandrax, and didn't go in for groupies. He and Tony may have hit it off when they were jamming or writing together, but socially they had grown remote, Tony repairing to his dimly lit hotel cavern after each gig, while Ronnie liked to go out and see what was going on. Liked to read and talk and think and talk some more. Tony hardly said a word some days. Was this it then, Ronnie wondered? How it would always be. Had they already peaked, this band that enjoyed so much success first time around, while Ronnie still had enough unfulfilled dreams to fill a magic castle?

Sandy Pearlman, whose laidback style of management none of them were impressed by, had been fired halfway through the last US tour. He seemed phlegmatic about it, when we met years later, claiming he was still a Sabbath fan, and always had been, but that perhaps the maxim about never meeting your heroes was a correct one. Pearlman remains an enigmatic figure, his brief sojourn with Sabbath seemingly airbrushed from his official history. With the band back to managing itself, Ronnie, a born leader, inevitably took the lead whenever the occasion demanded it, which was often, that space having been evacuated more times than not by Iommi, as he lost himself for days on end to the crystal illusions of coke and downers.

Ronnie was also becoming concerned with other aspects of Tony's ownership of the band, after Paul alerted him to the exact nature of keyboardist Geoff Nicholls' contributions onstage each night. Paul plays me the same cassette recording of a Sabbath show from the tour that he made Ronnie and Geezer listen to back then. We happen to stop at 'Heaven And Hell', which features Geoff on organ. He sounds like a child playing occasional block chords on a cheap catalogue-bought keyboard. There is a bit of vocal woo-wooing as well.

Paul sighs. 'Geezer said to me one night, "What's that fucking noise?" I said, "It's Geoff." He said, "You what? Get rid of him! Don't put him in the fucking mix!" I thought if I told anyone this they wouldn't believe me! If I told 'em the biggest band in the world has got a fucking dick on keyboards . . .' He shakes his head in disbelief. 'When I played it to Ronnie he said, "You've got to tell Tony." I said, "I ain't telling him. You tell him."' Instead, Geezer said he would tell Tony, 'But his bottle went and so we carried on for another fucking two years with Geoff Nicholls on keyboards.' Paul says the road crew became even more disgusted when they would have to clean Geoff's thinning hair from the keyboards every night. 'From where it was falling out and sweaty when he shook his head.'

Things finally came to a head in July 1982 when mixing began on what would be the next Black Sabbath album – a live double entitled *Live Evil*.

*

They would argue about it in public for years to come. How Dio and Appice snuck into the studio at night, after Iommi and Butler had gone home, and began fiddling with the mix, bringing Ronnie's vocals and Vinny's drums further up into the mix and pushing Tony's guitar and Geezer's bass down. How it led to a final falling out which then caused Ronnie and Vinny to walk out. Or the other one: how Tony fired Ronnie for trying to take over the band. How he'd always wanted Vinny to stay but that Ronnie had worked his spell on the younger man, forcing him to follow the singer back out onto the street. Yet none of it was true – or very little. And even the parts that were – arguments over the mix of the *Live Evil* album – were really just the last skirmishes in a growing war that was about to split Black Sabbath into atoms anyway.

Geezer was already bent out of shape over Ronnie's increasing influence in the band's affairs. Not just that he'd been supplanted as the band's lyricist but how Ronnie appeared to be running the offstage business of Black Sabbath as well – which, in the absence of a manager or any other strong figure in the band taking a keen interest, was of course true. 'We just saw it as he was trying to take over the band,' said Geezer more than a quarter of a century later, 'and we didn't like that.'

Speaking now, Vinny Appice recalls how 'the relationships between Tony and Ronnie, and Geezer and Ronnie, were starting to go downhill' long before they got into the studio to mix the live tapes. 'Tony and Geezer had no problems with me. It was just with Ronnie.' What he describes as 'the clash of a lot of egos'. By the end of the *Mob Rules* world tour, there had been 'fights backstage with Tony and Ronnie screaming at each other'. He adds: 'By the end of the tour you could feel the vibe between them – Tony and Geezer would get in one car and Ronnie would get in the other. I tried to keep it going by getting in all the different cars ...'

As for Tony's later accusation that Ronnie was sneaking into the studio behind his back to alter the mix on the live album, something he says he discovered after the engineer, Lee Di Carlo, eventually broke down and told him ('He said, "I can't stand it any more. You guys are going home after doing a mix and then Ronnie is wanting to come in and do his own mix. I don't know what to do".'), it runs counter to the fact that Ronnie was very much a daytime person, and would have found it all but impossible to wait for Tony and Geezer to go home before 'sneaking' into the studio, as the others rarely finished before dawn.

In fact, as Vinny Appice explains, 'What happened was, they booked the studio for two o'clock. But [Tony and Geezer] wouldn't get there until four or five o'clock, and this was an expensive studio. Me and Ronnie would be there at two. I had no say in this, I just came in when they wanted me in. But Ronnie wanted to do some work, so he would start doing whatever needed to be done, and they took that as Ronnie sneaking in the studio and doing stuff behind their back.' Other times, he suggests, 'they might have left and went to the pub, or went early. Well, Ronnie's there, he's a workaholic ...'

Whatever the truth, Tony felt he was being placed in an impossible position. On the one hand, here was his singer, steaming ahead on the job at hand without consulting him. It had been more than a decade since Iommi had allowed anyone to work without his knowledge and consent so freely on a Sabbath album. On the other hand, he'd got his bass player whispering in his ear, telling him to stand up for himself, that this was all wrong, that this wasn't how Sabbath did things. In an effort to simply shut their voices up, Tony, mentally tied up in his cocaine psychosis, tried to impose a ban on Ronnie even entering the studio. By then, he says, somewhat unnecessarily, 'It had got pretty bad.' He got Geezer to give him the news.

Ronnie had already decided the whole situation had become

'an absolute nonsense' by the time Geezer spoke to him. 'Something had come to a head and it was that whole avoiding confrontation thing, which Geezer and Tony specialise in. Eventually Geezer phones me and says, "I don't think this is working out. We really want Tony to produce the album on his own." Now I know this kind of cryptic talk, so I say, "So if you don't want me involved with this album are you saying it's over then?" And Geezer says, "Well, er … yeah, I suppose so." They could never just tell you straight. It was all a device to force me out.' Their parting shot: knowing he got hung up whenever his name was shortened for convenience in reviews, Tony and Geezer deliberately credited him on the *Live Evil* sleeve as simply: Ronnie Dio.

Lost somewhere in all this was the music. In the end *Live Evil* was a good enough album, despite being later dismissed by Ronnie as 'a piece of shit', throwing further fuel on the fire by claiming that most of the supposedly live album was full of studio overdubs. 'Not the vocals, though,' he insisted. 'Just everything else.' What he was ignoring was that most top-drawer live albums, then as now, were essentially studio constructs. Speaking of the Thin Lizzy live double, *Live And Dangerous*, released four years before *Live Evil* and subsequently regarded as one of the best 'live' albums of the genre, producer Tony Visconti had no qualms in admitting that 'Seventy-five per cent of it was done in the studio.' While Judas Priest's best-selling *Unleashed In The East*, from 1979, was jokingly referred to by those in the know as *Unleashed In The Studio*. More importantly, the most significant aspect of *Live Evil* was the one thing Dio insisted had not been overdubbed – his magnificent voice. Ironically, this comes to the fore most especially on Ozzy-era tracks like 'War Pigs, 'Children Of The Grave' and, most spectacularly, on 'Black Sabbath', where he doesn't just add his own colours to the musical canvas; he actually reconfigures the original, making it more distraught, more spellbinding and even more believable.

All of which got buried beneath the tide of bad publicity that followed in the wake of news of Dio's departure. Sabbath would say hello and wave goodbye to a great many more vocalists over the coming years, but none that ever touched their fans' hearts like Dio. There would remain a great nostalgia for the vintage Ozzy-era recordings, and rightly so, but for the generation of rock fans that grew up in the Eighties, there would remain only one Sabbath vocalist supreme, only one heavy metal singer par excellence, and that would be Ronnie James Dio.

The fans were not happy. The difference was that the Seventies era of the band was already good as dead, musically, when Ozzy was shot from the cannon. Bill Ward then leaving was tolerated because the new, Dio-led Eighties era of the band was otherwise on an upswing. They could always get another good drummer and they did. Ronnie leaving the band when he did, however, cut that version of Sabbath off in its prime. From a fan's point of view, nothing short of a reunion with Ozzy could salve such a wound. And that was never going to happen, now that Ozzy's own career had taken off like a rocket. Tony Iommi and Geezer Butler might have thought they were standing up against the threat of a Dio-sized Sabbath takeover when they ousted the singer, a situation they could argue was largely out of their hands, but they now found themselves in an even more invidious position: no longer seen as keepers of the Sabbath flame, but little more than imposters, flogging a dead horse. The stench of which would follow them around wherever they went for decades to come.

Ronnie James Dio, meanwhile, would be back on his feet, career-wise, almost immediately. He later described being 'filled with both optimism for my new band and sadness for what had just happened. I wasn't happy with the way everything ended, but I could feel proud of what I had achieved ... I gave as much to Sabbath as Sabbath gave to me, probably more so.'

When, the day after his phone call from Geezer, Ronnie took Vinny for dinner at the Rainbow and told him of his plans to start his own band and did Vinny want in, the young drummer nearly bit his arm off. 'I said, "Yeah. Fuck, yeah! Let's do it!" I was just a young kid but Ronnie was such a great person and a great leader, and he was already known and huge and it was just so many positives to working with Ronnie. I looked at him as a brother, you know? I loved Tony and Geezer too. They asked me to stay but it would have meant going to England and spending a lot of time there. It was a different atmosphere and a different mood. It was just a lot easier to go with Ronnie and start something new.' And if it turned out to be the wrong decision, 'I was young. It didn't matter.'

Within weeks Ronnie had completed the line-up of his new band – named simply Dio, leaving no one in any doubt this time about who was in charge – with the addition of former Rainbow band mate and well-known Scots reveller Jimmy Bain on bass, and a new, 20-year-old wunderkind guitarist from Northern Ireland named Vivian Campbell. (In yet another weird criss-cross, Ronnie had earlier rejected a young, LA-based guitarist named Jake E. Lee, who would then join Ozzy's band as the full-time replacement for Randy Rhoads. While Ronnie's first choice as bassist, another ex-Rainbow pal named Bob Daisley, turned down the chance as Ozzy had just signed him up too.)

The first Dio album, *Holy Diver*, released in the early summer heatwave of 1983, would be acclaimed as one of three all-time classic albums the singer would helm. But where the first two – Rainbow's *Rising* and Sabbath's *Heaven And Hell* – had made Ronnie the most celebrated career-rejuvenator in rock, *Holy Diver* proved he was a frontman on every level. Indeed, in a year when both Rainbow (with their final album, the abysmal *Bent Out Of Shape*) and Sabbath, now struggling to find a credible new singer, appeared to be on their last legs, *Holy Diver* looked down with contempt from a very great height indeed. By the end of the year it had gone platinum and turned Dio into an arena-headlining act worth millions.

'The elation was amazing,' says Wendy Dio now. 'After all the things we'd gone through, the trials and tribulations, having no money, having nothing, and then all of a sudden it was all happening. It was fantastic! Not "I told you so" because I never ever thought it was gonna get like that. More, "I showed you!" It really was *great* for Ronnie. It was unbelievable.' An achievement Ronnie would cherish for the rest of his career. 'I feel like I've been given a new lease of life,' he told me. 'Only this time I'm in charge of my own destiny. After Rainbow and Black Sabbath, I feel like I've earned the right.'

For Black Sabbath – what was left of them – fortune was no longer smiling. Having fired two singers and lost two drummers in little more than two years, though Tony Iommi remained steadfast in his coke-fuelled belief that they had done the right thing in cutting Dio loose, Black Sabbath were now facing the very real prospect of extinction. Indeed, Geezer was already talking of giving a new name entirely to whatever musical journey the two surviving original members next lit out on. Geoff Nicholls was still on board, of course, but though Geoff had his uses, he was still only a salaried member of the team. Nobody outside Sabbath's increasingly bedraggled inner circle knew his face. Only those fans that took magnifying glasses to their record sleeves recognised the name. Worse still was the sudden dawning that without Ronnie the band no longer had any kind of effective decision-making mechanism. Not only did they need a new singer and drummer, they needed a new name, a new manager, and a new and better sense of what the hell they thought it was they were actually supposed to be doing.

They needed someone strong, who could pick up their baton

and really run with it. A new leader, unafraid to show them where to go, and how to get there, and how not to be afraid because he would fix everything, baby, you just leave it to me. They found him, after a chance meeting at Detroit airport one morning, when Tony Iommi bumped into Don Arden once again.

Talking to Don about it nearly 20 years later, his sense of told-you-so was high as Tony recounted the way the band had fallen apart after Don left them to get on with it with Dio. Tony now coming to him, cap in hand, as he saw it, repenting his sins and begging for help, also appealed greatly to the old rogue's vanity. None of which figured hugely in his evaluation of the situation from a financial point of view. What persuaded him, in the end, to take another punt on rebuilding Black Sabbath were two things. The first, that in Tony and Geezer at least Sabbath were left 'with the creative half of the original four, so there was still hope for them yet'. The second, equally significant reason was more personal. On 4 July 1982, on the Hawaiian island of Maui, Sharon and Ozzy had married. Although Don claims to have given Sharon Ozzy's management contract as a wedding present, when she then tried to steer Ozzy away from his deal with Don's label, Jet, and on to a new deal with its distribution company, CBS, he became so furious 'It started a war between us that would last for years.' When, in 1983, he had the chance to again manage Sabbath, Don saw it as his golden opportunity to go head to head with his estranged daughter and prove who the dominant force in the family still was.

Father and daughter had fallen out to a catastrophic degree when Don began what would prove to be a lifelong affair with the attractive, much younger Meredith Goodwin. As far as Don was concerned, this was a situation his much older wife back in England, Paddles, had no problem with. They did not divorce and Don continued to provide for her in the well-appointed house they had bought together years before. But Sharon had taken against

Meredith from the word go, he maintained, seeing her arrival into the Arden Hollywood household as at best offensive to her mother, and at worst as the premeditated move of an old-fashioned gold-digger. Don, though, was oblivious to his daughter's anxieties. He was, by his own admission, 'completely obsessed' with Goodwin. The truth of which only cut Sharon even deeper. Always a daddy's girl, she now mimicked her father's notorious temper by swearing vengeance on him. Over the course of 1981, she went from tour-managing Ozzy to marrying him and taking over from her father as his full-time manager. Don had reacted well to this initially, but when Sharon made it clear she intended to take Ozzy's recording contract with her father's label, Jet, as well – re-signing Ozzy to CBS in a deal worth many millions in the wake of the overwhelming success of his first two multi-platinum solo albums – it signalled the bust up between them that would disfigure the Black Sabbath story from hereon in.

Sharon, never one to back down from a fight, was determined to thwart her father at every turn. Spotting Meredith having lunch in an LA restaurant one day, she went over and calmly poured a bowl of soup over her. Don was outraged and began making threatening phone calls to his daughter. This was now something more than just a daddy–daughter dispute, this was business, and Don's way of dealing with his business adversaries was well established. A close of friend of Sharon's recalls finding her one evening 'huddled in a corner crying and trembling with fear' after one such call from her father.

What Sharon had going for her, and that held her in good stead in her early battles with Don, was the fast-rising success of Ozzy's solo career: by 1982 *Blizzard Of Ozz* and *Diary Of A Madman* had sold a total of over five million copies in the US. The other thing she had on her side was the endless goodwill of those many music industry figures that would privately like nothing more than to see the fire-breathing dragon that was Don Arden in the early Eighties finally slain. Everyone, it seemed, was willing Sharon and Ozzy on in their combined fight to free themselves of their joint pasts. When, as part of their settlement, Ozzy was forced to record two more albums for Jet, Sharon devised what she saw as a double-whammy: a live double Ozzy album, released at the same time as *Live Evil*, and comprised entirely of Ozzy-era Sabbath songs. Something that would not only go in direct competition with Tony Iommi's Dio-Sabbath, but would dilute the market for such an album significantly. She didn't care how well Ozzy's album sold, as it would be on her father's label and she felt sure 'We'd never see a penny from it anyway.' If it helped scupper Iommi's Sabbath too, that was just icing on the cake. As she later told me, 'We had to give the old man two albums, well, a live double album counted as two. I knew he'd go for it because it wouldn't cost anything to make and it could be done quickly, while Ozzy was still hot. But Don was expecting something with Randy [Rhoads] on it and I thought fuck that. I'm not giving him that. He can have something with a load of old Sabbath shit on it.' The fact that the eventual album, *Talk Of The Devil* (*Speak Of The Devil* in the US) sold more than three times what *Live Evil* eventually managed was seen as yet another nail in the Sabbath career coffin.

When Tony Iommi inadvertently walked into the middle of this entrenched dispute between father and daughter, he didn't know it yet but he was sealing his fate – and that of Black Sabbath's – for ever. Yes, Don, would take the band on again and help the guitarist rebuild his rapidly becoming more ridiculous career. But it would come at a price, both in the immediate sense and in a more far-reaching one that continues to this day.

Reinstalled as Sabbath's manager, Don was more determined than ever to 'get one over my bitch of a daughter', as he put it. He would do whatever it took to put them back at the top – or, at the very least, somewhere ahead of Ozzy. Tony, though, would have to do exactly as Don told him. Tony, who'd already sold his soul to the devil so many times he was ready to try anything, didn't argue. Not even when Don suggested an idea so outlandish Tony laughed out loud the first time he heard it: bringing in former Deep Purple vocalist Ian Gillan as the new singer in Black Sabbath. Don had another previously unthought of idea up his sleeve too. In order to re-establish the credibility of the Sabbath brand, they would also bring Bill Ward back into the line-up. 'I thought he was joking,' Tony said. 'He had to be, surely?' But Don wasn't smiling when he said it. He had dollar signs in his eyes. Soon, Tony would too.

They had already tried out a number of different singers before Gillan's name came into the frame. Opening the doors to all comers, they began by giving out tapes of Sabbath backing tracks, which any potential recruits could record their own vocals to. That way, they could filter out 'the nutters', as Paul Clark puts it, before inviting those with a real chance in for an audition. Ultimately, this comprised a small handful, none of which ticked all the boxes. Top of the list was Samson singer Nicky Moore, whom Geoff Nicholls recalled having 'a phenomenal voice, absolutely brilliant'. But Moore was short and rotund, 'just didn't look the part'. John Sloman was also given an audition but his clean-cut image and cutesy voice were considered too lightweight to carry a Sabbath tune. A young Michael Bolton, then pursuing a career as a longhaired rock singer, was also briefly considered. But while he had a tremendous voice, as evidenced by his later ascension to superstar status as a crooner of pop ballads, Bolton again lacked the heavyweight presence. Besides, the band had had enough of American singers, they'd decided.

Next up, in a strange precursor to eventually working with Ian Gillan, Tony invited Gillan's successor in Deep Purple, David Coverdale, now fronting his own band, Whitesnake, to join Black

Sabbath. Geoff Nicholls recalls going with Tony to a meeting with Coverdale at the Rainbow in LA to discuss the idea. To make the possibility of an alliance even more attractive, Coverdale brought Whitesnake drummer Cozy Powell too. 'We had a good chat and we kind of agreed in principle that it could work,' recalled Nicholls. 'Tony had always been keen on working with David. Anyway, we left it a while and the next thing we hear is that they had gone off camping on Dartmoor and were getting Whitesnake back together.'

It was now that Don stepped in and urged Tony to get in touch with Ian Gillan, whose own post-Purple career with his eponymously named band had enjoyed success in Britain and Europe, but had singularly failed to take off in America. When the final Gillan album, *Magic*, released at the end of 1982, barely made the UK Top 20, Gillan called time on the band and readied himself for an eventual reunion with Deep Purple, then one of the worst-kept secrets in the industry. The only snag was Ritchie Blackmore's contractual obligation to make one more Rainbow album, which would be released in 1983, and feature Purple bassist Roger Glover. Keyboardist Jon Lord was also staying on for one more Whitesnake album, *Slide It In*, released the same year. Drummer Ian Paice filled in the time making Gary Moore's 1983 album, *Victims Of The Future*.

The only member of Deep Purple left kicking his heels before their planned reunion in 1984 was Ian Gillan. When, in the early spring of 1983, he received the phone call from Tony Iommi, inquiring whether he'd like to discuss working together, at first Gillan couldn't see it at all. As he later admitted, 'I never really liked their image.' In fact, he had always tended to look down on Black Sabbath. Gillan was not a heavy metal guy. He saw himself as coming from a 'more pure blues tradition'. The boys from Brum simply did not belong in the same league as the more free-thinking, musically open-minded Deep Purple.

But Tony Iommi was not the only one with a more strategically thinking manager. It was Phil Banfield, Gillan's long-time manager, that persuaded the singer to at least meet with Iommi. What else was Ian going to be doing with his free time until the Purple reunion kicked in?

They agreed to meet halfway between where Tony and Geezer were then staying, in Birmingham, and where Ian lived in Reading – at a pub called The Bear in Woodstock, Oxfordshire. Paul drove Tony and Geezer down in one of Tony's Rolls-Royces, 'Cos they thought it would impress Gillan turning up like that.' Gillan drove himself – and crashed his car en route. 'Some bugger rammed me up the arse, so I arrived in an L-shaped car and not in the best of moods,' he later recalled. He says that Tony's first words to him were: 'Cor, you're a big bugger, aren't you?'

'Of course, we all got pissed,' said Tony. 'I don't remember even really talking about Black Sabbath much, just talking to Ian about working together, perhaps. We all had such a laugh though, that was it, I suppose. Next thing we knew it was all happening.' A badly hungover Ian Gillan awoke the next day to a phone call from Phil Banfield telling him: 'If you're going to make career decisions, do you think we could consult on them first?' The singer struggled to remember how he had got home. Banfield jogged his memory with the words: 'Apparently yesterday you agreed to become the new singer for Black Sabbath!'

When news broke that Ian Gillan was the new singer in Black Sabbath reaction from critics and fans was mixed, to say the least. It was one thing to cross the Sabbath–Purple bloodlines with Ronnie James Dio – he may have worked with founding guitarist Ritchie Blackmore but he'd never actually been in Deep Purple. Ian Gillan, though, had been at the helm of the Purple line-up that had become one of the unholy trinity of British hard rock giants in the seventies: Led Zeppelin, Deep Purple and Black Sabbath. For him of all people to be named as Sabbath's new singer jarred. Like, in an earlier age, Mick Jagger joining The Beatles, or, in more recent times, Damon Albarn replacing Liam Gallagher in Oasis. Some things just weren't meant to be. How would Gillan, with his bluesy, soul-deep wail manage on strident tracks like 'Iron Man' and 'Children Of The Grave'? Actually, he wouldn't do badly at all – when he could remember the lyrics. Would he dress in black and wear a cross? The answer from the singer on both counts was a definite no, though he did secretly try on some of Tony's stage wear, but thought better of it.

Even Ronnie James Dio expressed bafflement. 'I was expecting them to try and patch things up with Ozzy or go for a certain type of singer, but never in a million years would I have guessed Ian Gillan. Everyone knew there was no way in hell it could last.'

For Don Arden, though, it was simple. As he later told me, 'It put them back in the headlines again. This was a great package! Something I could sell in America.' For Geezer Butler and, to a lesser extent, Tony Iommi, it was, on paper at least, a dubious prospect. 'We'd finished with the Ronnie version of the band,' recalled Geezer, 'and I said to Tony, "It's getting to be a bit of a joke calling it Sabbath, ain't it?" And he totally agreed. I think [Don Arden] suggested getting Ian and calling it a Gillan/Iommi/Butler/Ward album, not a Black Sabbath album, which was the way we and Gillan felt. We just thought it would be an interesting thing to do as a one-off.'

Not for the last time, however, Tony was soon persuaded by Don to play it safe and keep the Black Sabbath imprimatur. 'I told them they could virtually add another zero to the record advance if they did,' said Don. 'Anything else wouldn't have made sense.' Geezer was deeply unhappy about the decision; his objections eventually offset by the windfall in record company merchandising and promoters' advances it guaranteed the 'new' Sabbath. 'That album with Ian Gillan ... wasn't supposed to be Black Sabbath. That was the manager and the record company insisting we use the name and I was opposed to it, but they are the ones who can turn the tap off when it comes to paying for everything, so it became a Black Sabbath album. It wouldn't be the last time that happened either.'

According to Gillan, however, there had never been any other thought than to call the band Black Sabbath. 'I have no idea where this "Supergroup" idea came from,' he insisted. 'From our first conversations we were very clear about discussing myself joining Black Sabbath.' Indeed, though it was never overtly made clear at the time, as far as Gillan was concerned this was to be strictly a temporary alliance. Something he and his manager, Phil Banfield, reasoned would raise his profile again in America, ready to be taken full advantage of come the Deep Purple reunion the following year.

More remarkable still, however, was the trick Don pulled off of getting Bill Ward back into the band. His friend John Bonham's death nearly three years before had shaken Bill to his bones. It hadn't stopped him using, but 'indirectly, a seed had been planted in me, which was one of: there's a possibility you don't have to die. [Unlike Bonham] you may have a way out here. Because his death shook me to the ground, I was just absolutely dumbfounded. Obviously upset and, you know, just really, really sad … Indirectly, though, one of the things that helped push me into sobriety was his death.'

It wasn't easy, and so far every time he'd tried to get his act together, within weeks the pressure had proved too great and he'd relapsed. 'I was dying, but even though I knew I was dying that was overshadowed by: who gives a shit if I die? In other words, self-pity. Self-pity didn't care if I was gonna die or not, you know? But I thought about John a *lot*.' At the time he got the phone call from Don Arden's office, inquiring into his health, Bill was on his longest stretch sober since his teens. He saw the offer of a chance to return to Sabbath – to start a new life again – as 'some kind of karmic reward' for his efforts in recent times to get clean and stay clean. It was typically muddled post-addiction thinking – the only ones Black Sabbath were looking to reward were themselves: though he was unable to see it yet, Bill was just another pawn on the chessboard – but everyone was relieved when he said yes.

Within weeks contracts had been signed and the band had begun working up material in a small rehearsal room in Birmingham. Bill wasn't there for these initial sessions, his spot being taken for the time being by Malcolm Cope, the drummer of Geoff Nicholls' old band Quartz. A great deal of the material eventually used on the subsequent album – which they had already decided to call, pun fully intended, *Born Again* – had been written by the time Gillan joined them. 'I can remember him writing up lyrics in the studio,' recalls Cope. 'I just kept all of the drums really simple because I knew Billy was coming in to do the actual recording.' By the time Bill arrived back in England, all the songs had been written and demoed. All he had to do was join the dots and add any splashes of his own. Just in case it all went horribly wrong, Cope was retained in the background, officially to 'help Bill out'. In reality, to step in at a moment's notice should it be required. 'He had some emotional problems at the time I remember,' said Cope tactfully.

With both Gillan and Ward in tow, in April 1983 Black Sabbath began recording their eleventh studio album, at the Richard Branson-owned Manor in Oxfordshire, a residential studio in spacious grounds, resplendent with nearby river canal, custom-built go-kart track and floodlit swimming pool. In an early indication that their new singer still saw himself as not entirely at one with the band as a whole, Gillan insisted on having his own luxurious marquee tent erected in the grounds, on the basis that he preferred sleeping outdoors. 'Everybody thought it was stupid,' says Paul Clark, 'Especially after me and Tony used to see him creeping back into the house to sleep when he thought we were all in bed.'

Paul's main concern was looking after Bill, who was back and playing well again, but clearly still extremely fragile. 'Bill was reborn, that's how I looked at it,' he says now. When Paul was charged with buying the band members a car each for the forthcoming British tour – functional Ford Granadas they would sell on after the tour – he told Bill, who had never passed a driving test, 'We can go round the go-kart track and you can learn to drive properly.' His thinking was simple: 'That would occupy his mind, from the booze.' The cars duly arrived. When Paul went home for the day though, to Birmingham, he came back the next day to find written on the blackboard, used as a communal message board: 'Paul, the keys to Bill's Granada are down by the swimming pool.' He thought to himself: 'The fuckers are up to something.' But he walked down to the pool, where he found the car: in the pool. He went looking for the band and was told Ian Gillan had driven it there the night before. 'I thought, you fucking arsehole, because I was trying to get Bill on his feet, you know what I mean? You fucking bastard, that was wicked!'

Paul, furious, went looking for Ian but couldn't find him. The tent was empty and he was nowhere to be seen in the studio. He got his own back though when he spotted the singer's rubber dinghy with outboard engine, which was moored on the banks of the canal. 'I thought, right, you fucker. I got the boat, got some petrol, poured it all over the boat, got his T-shirt, which was in there, lit it and threw it into the boat. Then kicked it up the canal. And that was it. He never saw his boat again. I gave it a Viking funeral.'

Gillan was getting on everyone's nerves. Poles apart from the serious-minded Dio, but not as sneaky with his pranks as Tony, or as likely to be the butt of them as Ozzy or Bill, Ian liked to drink and raise hell. Racing Bill's car around the go-kart track in the middle of the night, 'completely out of control and rolling upside down', was just the latest in a long line of misdemeanours the singer would be responsible for. Another night, drunk again, he and Richard Branson ran around the entire mansion, throwing stones through the windows. Bill, meanwhile, recently dry and forlorn at his prospects of staying so while he was stranded among the riotous antics of his old band mates, looked on despairingly. He would do his drum parts and that would be that, he decided.

Born Again was destined to become the either-or album of the Sabbath canon. You either loved it for its outré preoccupation with darkness and unreality, or you hated it for its bullying insistence on being taken seriously, in spite of the plainly contrived line-up forced together to create it. Ironically, Dio – reputed writer of gothic rock epics – had appeared to be leading Sabbath in a much more melodic, mainstream direction on his final recordings with the band, while Gillan – fabled ambassador of the hip-shaking bad-woman blues – now took them right back to their twisted horror-fantasy roots. From the cathedral-like organ that oozes like fog over the intro to the album opener, the furiously paced 'Trashed' – featuring an autobiographical lyric based on the night the singer trashed Bill's car – to the self-consciously spooky two-minute instrumental that follows titled 'Stonehenge' (written, uncredited, by Geoff Nicholls after he visited the hallowed site during a break in recording), on to the blustering 'Disturbing The Priest', replete with cringe-making cackling from Gillan, and again based on a real-life incident that took place at the Manor, when the local priest knocked on their door one morning, complaining about the noise emanating from the place night and day, this was Sabbath at their most determinedly obnoxious. Where it worked well – on the brief house-of-horrors sound effects of the Geezer-contrived instrumental 'The Dark', which spirals into the brutal 'Zero The Hero', a bitter diatribe about a 'zero' whose 'head is firmly nailed to your TV channel' but with 'someone else's finger's on the control panel' and who deserves not a jot of sympathy, apparently – it left a convincing trail of blood. Where it worked less well, as on the next track, 'Digital Bitch', about 'the richest bitch in town' whose 'big fat daddy is a money machine', with its faux punk shouted chorus and rolling-shoulder rhythm, it's hard not to feel we are back in 'Dirty Women' territory. Big, bad and utterly indifferent. Certainly Gillan's famous lyrical humour seems to have deserted him. When the rumour later went around that the song was about Sharon Osbourne, they all denied it of course. Whoever it was about, though, the feeling of resentment comes across as disturbingly real.

By far the best track on the album – and a fascinating glimpse into where they might have taken this line-up if everyone had seen it as more than just a one-off – is the superb title track: a gloriously studied piece, its processional rhythm lifted to even greater emotional heights by Gillan's truly staggering vocal, employing all his Deep Purple tricks, from the weirdly mellifluous screams to the strangled asides, but here with something else, something different he'd never pulled off before, an almost too real sense of genuine despair and dying passions suddenly rekindled, the fire in the grate blown suddenly back into life for one last, gloriously brief moment before dying again. Its message, sent to those who 'use us for fortune and fame', sounding like it really was written in something more heart-stopping than the fake blood that smothers the rest of the album.

The final brace of tracks – the rock-by-numbers 'Hot Line' and the slow-stepping ballad 'Keep It Warm' (the latter dedicated to Gillan's then girlfriend, and later wife, Bron) – sound like what they are: cheesy attempts to marry the Gillan sound – warm, reaching, all-inclusive – with the irradiated Sabbath mien

– limb-dragging, heads-down, heavy metal – and coming up with the mongrel offspring no one really wants.

None of which, ultimately, mattered. By the time *Born Again* was released in August 1983, Black Sabbath were in disarray again. The album may have returned the band to the UK Top 5, but it failed to match the sales of either of the Dio albums. Bill Ward had gone by then too, the victim, as he later put it, of a lot of 'anticipatory fear' which he didn't 'share'. The truth was he couldn't stand to be around the others. Not while Tony was still utterly immersed in cocaine and Gillan was running wild on alcohol fumes. The others were outwardly understanding – 'Bill was very ill,' said Gillan – but privately Iommi and Butler rolled their eyes and thought: 'Here we go again.' For Bill, though, there was simply no other choice, given the circumstances. His triumph was that he'd recorded the album clean and sober. 'The first time in my life I'd ever done that.' Whereas in 1980 'I left in shame and guilt. When I left in 1983, I left making a good decision. I walked away knowing that I had to now seek a new life, basically, wherever it might take me.' He was home in America barely three weeks before he started drinking again.

The band fared not much better without him. When it was announced that Bill's replacement in Sabbath was to be ELO drummer Bev Bevan, the last vestiges of whatever reserves of credibility the band still had with the hardcore rock audience were finally used up. Bevan was a good drummer and ELO had ended the Seventies as one of the biggest bands in the world. He was also another old mate from Brum and, on paper at least, ticked all the boxes. But there was a cultural divide in the mind of rock fans – and critics – between bands like Black Sabbath and ELO. One that Tony Iommi and Geezer Butler would have also recognised. But, as with Gillan's appointment, and Ward's return, albeit temporarily, to the fold, the thinking behind the drummer's recruitment as 'a marquee name', as he put it, was all

Don Arden's. 'Bev was a fucking great guy,' Don insisted. 'They were lucky to have him.' The music press wasn't having any of it though. First the threat of Deep Sabbath, now a suggestion of Electric Black Purple?

Adding to the general feeling of untogetherness came whispers of the first serious rift between the band and its 'new' singer. Once again, there were heated arguments about the final mix of the album. 'It's crap,' said Gillan bitterly. 'There is no other word to describe it.' Gillan claimed to have stood behind the studio desk at the Manor and given his resounding approval to all the tracks, before leaving for a short vacation while the album was being mixed. Then when he returned he was 'frankly appalled' by what he heard, laying all the blame 'in Geezer's lap', who, he suggested, 'said he couldn't hear his bass'. But as Geoff Nicholls pointed out, 'Tony Iommi was in charge [for the mix] just as he always has been.' It didn't alter the fact that the final sound on *Born Again* was sub-par, to put it kindly. According to Nicholls, Tony's mix had been tailored towards American radio, which at that time 'had this nasty habit of compressing the hell out of everything, so you needed to present the sound of the album in a certain way to cope with this. If you didn't do it there was a great danger of the thing sounding shit on US radio.' Here, though, one suspects the keyboardist doth protest too much. Nothing on US radio in 1983 sounded anything remotely like the buried-under-six-feet-of-earth sound of *Born Again*.

The rows were still simmering about the mix when all hell broke loose about the album cover. Keeping with the 'born again' theme, sleeve designer Steve 'Krusher' Joule – then working for *Kerrang!* magazine, and who had also just designed sleeves for Ozzy Osbourne – had come up with what he thought was a suitably 'Satanic' image: that of a newborn baby, sprouting devil horns and claws. Tony Iommi liked the cover enough to approve it. But when Ian Gillan first clapped eyes on it, as he famously later recalled, 'I saw the cover then puked.' Before adding: 'Then I heard the record then puked.' It was faintly comical, if also faintly distasteful. But nowhere near as offensive as the fact that Tony began referring to the baby on the sleeve as Aimee – the name of Ozzy and Sharon's daughter, born a few weeks after *Born Again* was released.

When Sharon found out she went insane. She later told me how she eventually paid Iommi back by getting a friend of hers – a *Vogue* cover model – to arrange a date with the guitarist at one of LA's most chi-chi restaurants, Le Dome. When the guitarist turned up 'dressed in all his fucking crosses' there was a gift box waiting for him. Assuming it must be from his date, Iommi untied the pink ribbons and lifted the lid expecting to find some sort of gift. He did. 'Two big turds – one each from me and Ozzy!' she cackled. You had to admire her chutzpah. Her father would have been proud – if he hadn't been so intent on wiping her off the face of the earth at the time, and she him.

According to Krusher Joule, speaking now, however, the back-story to the *Born Again* sleeve was itself rooted in the burgeoning war between Sharon and her ruthless father. According to the designer, Don had 'decided that he would wreak his revenge' on his daughter 'by making Black Sabbath the best heavy metal band in the world', which as well as bringing Gillan and Ward in included 'stealing as many of Sharon and Ozzy's team as possible, and as I was designing Ozzy's sleeves at the time I of course got asked to submit some rough designs. As I didn't want to lose my gig with the Osbournes I thought the best thing to do would be to put some ridiculous and obvious designs down on paper, submit them and then get the beers in with the rejection fee.'

In all he submitted 'four rough ideas', one of which was the devil baby. Taking the image from the front cover of a 1968 magazine called *Mind Alive* (credited to 'Rizzoli Press'). 'I then took some black-and-white photocopies of the image that I over-exposed, stuck the horns, nails, fangs into the equation, used the most outrageous colour combination that acid could buy, bastardised a bit of the Old English typeface and sat back, shook my head and chuckled.' The story he was later told was that at the meeting Tony Iommi and Geezer Butler were present but not Ian Gillan or Bill Ward. Apparently, 'Tony loved it and Geezer, so I'm reliably informed, looked at it and said, "It's shit. But it's fucking great!" So suddenly I find myself having to do the bloody thing. I was also offered a ridiculous amount of money (about twice as much as I was being paid for an Ozzy sleeve design) if I could deliver finished artwork for front, back and inner sleeve by a certain date.' Working with a friend, he stayed up all night, speeding and drinking beer, as he finished the artwork in time for the deadline.

As for Gillan's famous 'I puked' comment, as Krusher wryly observes, 'Over the years I've said the same thing about most of Gillan's album sleeves.' He goes on to relate how he was told the singer apparently threw a box of twenty-five copies of the album out of a hotel window. In an extraordinary final touch, he recounts a story he was told years later about the fondness Nirvana singer Kurt Cobain, a self-proclaimed Sabbath fan, had for the sleeve. 'An amazing story that I've never verified, but on Kurt Cobain's sixteenth birthday his mum took him to Walmart and told him he could have any album he wanted. He picked *Born Again* [but] his mother took one look at the sleeve and told him that there was no place in the Cobain home for such a monstrosity! I've always wondered if it played any part in there being a baby on the *Nevermind* cover.'

The feeling that the Black Sabbath story was beginning to become a shambles was only compounded by the band's headline Saturday night show at the Reading Festival that summer. When it quickly became apparent that Gillan – who would later joke that he couldn't even remember his own lyrics half the time – simply could not remember any of the Black Sabbath song words, the press began to sharpen their pens. When Gillan thought he'd created a failsafe for himself by scrawling the lyrics onto giant-sized scrapbook pages which he'd concealed behind his vocal monitors, only to be undone when the dry ice made it impossible for him to read without literally getting on his knees and squinting through the fog, the crowd made their own feelings felt when one yelled out, 'It's Dio, they got Ronnie James Dio back!' When the band then encored with the old Deep Purple chestnut, 'Smoke On The Water', the sense of unreality – of absurdity, of shamelessness – was complete. Their first major British show together, it was, as Paul Clark jokes now, 'two shows in one for the Gillan line-up: their first and last.' (It later emerged that they had also toyed with the idea of performing Purple's 'Black Night', jamming on it at soundchecks but never quite finding the nerve to play it. More astonishingly, with Bev Bevan now in the band it was also suggested – by Tony but at Bev's quiet urging – that they also have a crack at ELO's 'Evil Woman'. But every time Tony began the chord sequence, said Nicholls, 'it would make us all fall about laughing!'

Nobody else was laughing though and with the *Born Again* world tour eventually stretching woefully over seven excruciating months, it became one of those tours that would remain talked about for years, but for all the wrong reasons. A week before Reading, they had all nearly been arrested when Geezer threw a Molotov cocktail from his hotel room window, destroying another guest's Cortina. 'I went to his room, which was the only one with the curtains open, and there were all the matchsticks on the window ledge,' says Paul Clark. When, however, the hotel staff decided Paul was the culprit, Geezer did nothing to dissuade them.

Less than three weeks after the embarrassing Reading Festival show, the band sank to even greater depths when Geezer and Paul were arrested after a Gillan-induced fight at a club in Barcelona.

'We were sitting at a table in this disco shithole with the pro-moter. Gillan's had a few too many and he's got my lighter, starts burning this waiter's arse with the lighter. I said, "Don't be a cunt. You're gonna cause trouble there. This ain't our town, leave it." But he carried on, did it again. So this Spaniard's gone back upset and he's telling everybody at the bar and the other barmen are telling these other people, who are all regulars there. It was like causing trouble in the Rum Runner. You wouldn't stand for it. So it went on like that.'

Paul could see it was about to go off so he told the band to walk slowly and follow him up the stairs to the exit. Too late. 'As we got to the top of the stairs the doormen shoved me out the door – and locked it. And I can hear all the screaming and goings on.' Kicking the door down, Paul was hit by the doorman with a truncheon. 'I took it off him and whacked him with it. I go to the band, "Run now! Get in the cars!"' Again, though, it was too late and a bloody melee ensued on the street outside the club, during which Geezer and Paul were arrested after jumping into the back of a police car, mistaking it for a taxi.

'By the time we got to the cop station, Geezer was crying, "We're gonna die, we're gonna die!" It was fucking embarrassing. I said, "Don't worry about it. We'll get through this." I was scared too, but I just smiled at the fuckers.' Across the room another member of the band crew, Harry Mohan, was being savagely beaten by three policemen. When another cop punched Paul in the eye, he fought back, 'nutting him. Then the coppers started hitting me with their truncheons. And all the while Geezer's wail-ing and weeping. Soft as shit ...'

After a night in the cells, during which a phone call to the local British consulate brought the response: 'I hope you rot', they were driven to a courthouse where dozens of people from the night before were also in attendance. 'All in bandages and splints and everything, all gabbling in Spanish and pointing at me and

Geezer.' Paul took his shirt off and bared his newly scarred back, all cuts and bruises where he'd been beaten. He began pointing at the crowd. 'Him, him, him! They did this. Just two of us.' The next thing they knew they were back on the street. 'To this day I don't know what happened. We didn't know if we were on bail or fuck all.'

Back at the hotel, they discovered the rest of the band all cowered together in Geoff Nicholls' room. 'He refused to open the door. Like, "Who is it?" Geezer said, "It's Geezer, you prat, open the fucking door!" He finally does do. He had put the bed behind the door and the wardrobe. Him, Gillan and Tony were in the room, shitting themselves. Never bothered, never sent nobody out to rescue us, or nothing. Just worried they might be next ...'

The most eye-wateringly embarrassing aspect of the Black Sabbath *Born Again* tour, though, was the new stage set. The 1980s had seen rock tours undergo a revolution in terms of stage production. No longer was it considered enough for a band headlining major arenas to simply turn up and play. It was now deemed necessary to evoke a full-on musical production more akin to a West End or Broadway show than an old-fashioned, spit-and-sawdust rock concert. Ronnie James Dio would soon be seen onstage battling a giant animatronic dragon; while newly arrived challengers to Sabbath's heavy metal throne Iron Maiden had a recurring nightmare figure called Eddie, who not only emblazoned all their record sleeves and T-shirts but appeared as an ever larger monster figure at their shows.

Never slow to spot a trend, Don decreed that the new improved Sabbath should have something similar for their 1983 world tour. What that should be remained open for debate for all of five seconds before Geezer uttered the immortal phrase: 'Stonehenge.' He was thinking of the instrumental track on *Born Again* as the jumping-off point. Nowadays we instantly think of Spinal Tap.

Rightly so, in fact, as the producers of the movie – or 'rockumen-tary, if you will', as the Rob Reiner character cringe-inducingly describes it – later confessed that is where they got the idea for the now famous part in the movie where the fictional band also adopt Stonehenge as the theme for their new stage show, only to discover the models have been built so small that a dwarf can tower over them.

In reality, Sabbath experienced the exact opposite problem: that their models of Stonehenge were so huge – built to scale, as Geezer had suggested – that they couldn't actually fit them into more than a handful of the arenas they were booked into in America. 'The bloody things were forty feet high,' Gillan recalled. As if that weren't enough, Don's final touch – the addition of a dwarf dressed as the red, devil-baby on the *Born Again* sleeve – ensured no one who witnessed the early performances on Sab-bath's 1983 tour would ever forget them – or remember them without squirming.

Rehearsals for the first show – at the Maple Leaf Gardens arena, in Toronto – began with a tape of the strangled cries of a newborn baby played over the PA, 'distorted and flanged to sound utterly horrible'. The dwarf-dressed-as-devil-baby then appeared crawling atop the Stonehenge pillars, before falling backwards with a scream onto – unseen – a pile of safety mattresses. The screaming then stopped and a bell began to toll and a parade of roadies dressed as monks crossed the stage, as if in prayer. When the show began that night, however, Gillan recalled, 'When the dwarf-baby fell backwards his screams didn't stop, they just got worse. Someone had forgotten to put the mattresses out! I was looking out from the side of the stage and you could see people turning to each and going, "What the fuck?"'

It was downhill all the way from there. When Gillan an-nounced before Christmas that he would be leaving sometime in the New Year to rejoin the re-formed Deep Purple, the band felt let down and betrayed. Gillan feigned astonishment. 'Myself, Tony and Geezer all knew that once the world tour was over I would be teaming up with Deep Purple ... The Purple thing was always there from day one and pretty much on schedule for when I came out of Sabbath. It all slotted in very nicely as it happens.' He added: 'We all parted on amicable terms.'

Not quite. Geezer, who would continue to insist that it was never part of the deal to call the alliance with Ian Gillan 'Black Sabbath', now railed against the singer's decision to split, claiming the subject of Gillan staying just long enough before returning to Deep Purple had never been discussed. Not with him present, anyway. He was so dejected he now threw in the towel and announced he, too, would be leaving the band as soon as their touring commitments were complete.

Paul Clark had also quit by then, leaving after their show in Chicago, in November, disillusioned by the way he was treated, first by his once true friend Tony, but also by Bill's departure, and then, finally, Don's ham-fisted way of making things worse. He held a big farewell party for himself and the crew back at the hotel after the show, then signed the $10,000 bar bill to Don Arden's room number. 'But I signed it Don Ard-On. I said, "Fuck him, I don't care any more."'

With Gillan and Geezer and Bill and Paul, and Ozzy and Ronnie and Vinny before them – and the stupid dwarf idea and the rotten Stonehenge set-up – went what remained of Black Sabbath's reputation as a serious rock band. Something they would never quite claw back again. Until decades of missteps and bad breaks later, Ozzy – and, more crucially, Sharon – gifted it to them. Another box of poo, perhaps, but this time one lined with silver and gold. Hey, if they were good boys and did what they were told, maybe even platinum ...

TEN
UPSIDE DOWN CROSSES

13 July 1985. The JFK Stadium in Philadelphia. It was the morning of Live Aid, the defining event in popular music of the 1980s, and the four original members of Black Sabbath were about to take to the stage and perform three songs to more than 90,000 people. Broadcast on TV to many millions around the world, this was meant be a huge, celebratory event – globally, for the peoples of Chad, the Sudan and all the other desperately impoverished African countries the event was raising money for, and on a personal level for the band: here doing the thing all four members had said would never happen. Now suddenly here they were, back together again. Yet, for all the build-up, it was a desultory affair. Full of confusion, bitterness and an overall weariness brought on seemingly by just being in the same room together again. The band were due onstage at 10.00 a.m. and before they had even struck a note, everyone was in a hurry for the whole thing to be over so they could split up and go their own separate ways again.

While I no longer worked for the band as their PR, I had recently begun working on Ozzy's memoir, *Diary Of A Madman*, and was there in that capacity, as well as filing magazine stories about the event. I was travelling with the band from the hotel to the gig in the back of a white Transit van. Just as we were about to close the doors, a middle-aged man with fair hair and long Elvis Presley sideburns came lumbering breathlessly up and asked if he could squeeze in with us. We all moved up one and the van drove off.

'I'm Martin Chambers, by the way,' he announced.

'Oh, aye,' said Bill dolefully.

'You know? From The Pretenders?'

'Oh, aye. What do *you* do?'

'I'm the drummer.'

'Oh, aye.'

The van lapsed into silence. It was still early. There wasn't anything to say yet.

Martin leaned across the seat. 'You're Ozzy Osbourne, aren't you?' he asked.

'That's right, mate.'

'So the rest of you must be Black Sabbath,' he said. 'I've always loved that song you did … "Paranoid", is it?'

Nobody spoke.

He had another go. 'So what are you doing, just three numbers like the rest of us?'

'That's right,' said Ozzy with a straight face. 'But we've got a special surprise worked out for them. For an encore we're gonna come on and do "Food Glorious Food".'

The rest of the van began to titter. Martin looked vaguely disturbed. Then Ozzy broke into song: 'FOOD GLORIOUS FOOD! HOT SAUSAGE TOMATO!'

Martin smiled but was clearly uncomfortable. Martin was like most people. They never really knew if Ozzy was joking or not. They never really would.

'I know it's for a good cause, but to be honest, I don't really care,' Ozzy had told me the night before. We had been in the bar, where he had been sipping Diet Coke. Ozzy had been officially on the waggon since checking out of the Betty Ford Clinic some months before. 'It's like my father used to say: in the war, everyone was friendly and helped each other, but as soon as the war ended they were back to being pricks again. And I bet there'll be people there tomorrow who'll be telling each other to go fuck themselves again the next day.'

Did it matter though, as long as the money was raised? Yes and no. 'The thing is,' he said, 'they'll get the money, and food will be taken over and they'll feed them and they'll *still* fucking starve again! Because the food, no matter how much is raised today, won't last for ever. I think that not only rock'n'roll groups should do this, but industry, too – the IBMs and GECs. They should say, "All right, one week a year our output will go to charity", whatever that might be. I mean, they spend hundreds of millions on nuclear defence, but would they ever say, "Okay, let's save a hundred million today and feed these fuckers"? That's nothing to the government; it's not a piss in the ocean! It's like giving a tramp a dime. But no, they'd rather burn leftover supplies of wheat than stop people dying. They crush billions and billions of apples back into the ground because of surplus stocks ... I mean, I know it's only apples and they'd probably be bored stiff sitting back in the old desert eating a ton of fucking apples, but it's better than a fucking pile of dirt, ain't it?'

Ozzy was bored and distracted. It was one thing being sober again after all these years, quite another to test those limits by getting back together with Black Sabbath. It was a fraught time for them all. Geezer hadn't played live with Tony since the end of the ill-fated *Born Again* tour eighteen months before; Bill Ward hadn't played live with the band since making his midnight flit five years before; and Ozzy hadn't been on a stage anywhere near any of them for nearly seven years. You wondered what was in it for them? Fame, certainly. A place in the history books, of course. But it would be little more than a footnote, surely, in terms of Live Aid. That day would belong to true household names like Queen and Elton John, Bowie and Bob Geldof. Even Status Quo would be associated with Live Aid more than Sabbath's 'blink and they're gone' 10.00 a.m. appearance in Philadelphia.

In fact, the idea, as with all Ozzy's big ideas now, had come from Sharon. Foiled in her attempt to finagle Ozzy onto the bill as a solo artist, she had been tipped the wink, however, that a re-formed Black Sabbath might be just the job. And so it proved, on paper at least. Sabbath's actual performance, though, was incongruous, to say the least. While 'Children Of The Grave' bore some passing resemblance to the subject matter that day, it was hard to see what 'Iron Man' or 'Paranoid' had to say about the plight of starving Africans, even in the most metaphorical sense. In truth, the band looked old, out of synch. They looked like what they were: a dusty relic from a bygone age. Ozzy, who hadn't sung live for several months, looked breathless and overweight, his dull imprecations to 'Go fucking crazy!' again hardly reflecting the desired aims of the rest of the show. His double chins were starting to take over. Never mind. Sharon would soon fix that. (Years later he would moan to me about how 'very ugly and grossly overweight' he was that day. 'I looked like Mama Cass on a weekend at a gay party.') The rest hardly seemed to matter. It was just enough that *they were there*. Then, suddenly, it was over. The band were led off the stage and whisked back to the dressing room area. It wasn't even 10.30 in the morning yet. Now we had the rest of the day to get through.

Back at the Four Seasons hotel that afternoon, I asked Ozzy what this was really about, given his cynicism about the event? Were Sabbath preparing to get back together, perhaps, à la Deep Purple? He looked suitably appalled. 'No fucking way, mate!' But why not? He went around the houses for a bit, swilling his Diet Coke around his mouth thoughtfully before he finally said it. 'At the end of the day, I have to ask myself, if Black Sabbath had done as well as I'm doing now and kept hold of Ronnie Dio in the group or whatever, and I was where they left me, down and out in a fucking LA bar, would they give everything up just to bring me back into the group?' He looked at me. 'Christ,' he said, 'do you know how many years it took me to get *out* of that fucking mess with Sabbath? And all these cunts who *do* get back together, don't ever believe that it's for any reason other than the fucking money. If there *was* another reason, they'd never have called each other cunts and split up in the first place. No, bollocks to all that. I've got enough to worry about trying to kick this drink thing, you know?'

The other major obstacle to any possible Black Sabbath reunion, though Ozzy didn't say so, was the fact that his father-in-law was still managing the band – or rather, Tony Iommi, the only active member left in it. And that neither Sharon nor Don was in any mood for reconciliation. Something that had been made abundantly clear when, halfway through a live televised news interview two days before the Live Aid performance, Ozzy had been served a writ, issued by Don's lawyer's office, forbidding him to perform with Sabbath. Of course, the whole band ignored it and carried on with the show. But it was a typically low blow from the old man, designed to rankle – which it did. 'That was the last straw for Sharon,' a close friend told me. 'Any tiny chance whatsoever of Ozzy getting back together with Tony was gone after that.'

Iommi was hardly any more pleased. 'I thought it was great for us to be able to get back together and play and do it,' he later told me. 'We were supposed to have been rehearsing and there we were talking about old times. I'll never forget, Madonna was after us and she's trying to get in, and she kept walking in and walking out and we were still there talking about old times. There was a lot to catch up on, and it was just great to see everybody and great to go out there and play. But of course ... Ozzy got a writ from Don ... and it made a bit of a bad taste in everybody's mouths, you know?'

If Don hadn't stuck his oar in, would the re-formation have been possible after Live Aid, as the rumour mill suggested at the time? 'I'm not sure at that time if it would have been.' He puffed out his cheeks, smiled wearily. 'There was things that had gone on … particularly because I was with Don and Ozzy was with Sharon. And it became a very sort of … a war against everybody, you know? And I was stuck in the middle of it. So it did become very awkward for us, personally. Although, when we'd sit and talk together, me and Ozzy, it was just as if nothing had happened. It was more the things behind the scenes that caused a lot of the problems.'

Sharon had been monitoring the Sabbath situation carefully. Even as Don had been trying to steal away the best of Ozzy's staff and crew, Sharon had been in regular touch with Paul Clark while he worked with them. 'Sharon used to phone me up every day while I was on [the *Born Again*] tour and ask me to go and work for Ozzy. Every fucking day. I'd say, "Look, Tony's me mate and I can't, Sharon." That went on for ages. Then she invited me to Ozzy's birthday in the South of France somewhere. She said, "I've got you a ticket already" and that I'd be home on such and such a date [of the Sabbath tour]. I'd be like, where the fuck is she getting all this info? I don't even know where we'll be on that date yet. She'd say, "I've got you a ticket, it's first class, you must come. Ozzy would love to see you." So I gets on the plane. I told the band I was going. They were okay, they didn't give a fuck. I think they thought I was gonna spy for them. Cos they were always interested in what they were doing. But I never told them that Sharon rang me most days.'

Sharon had bigger fish to fry now, though. Ozzy was about to record an album, *The Ultimate Sin*, that would sell more copies in America than any Black Sabbath album, past or present. Sabbath, meanwhile, no longer existed, officially. With only Tony left to man the fort, even he was on the point now of giving up, and recording his first solo album. Why should Sharon and Ozzy reach down to help the very people that had left them both for dead? As

Sharon saw it, her job now was to feather her and Ozzy's nest as best they could, making hay while the sun still shone. With Sabbath down and almost out, and Ozzy's career beginning to soar again, what did she need the hassle of bringing those fools back from the grave for?

Ozzy donned that far away look, so familiar now. 'Sharon keeps saying to me, "Do you want to be singing when you're forty?" But I don't know. I keep saying to myself, I'll give it another two years. I'll give it another three years. But until there comes a day when the kids stop having fun, until *I* stop having fun, I'll probably keep going. It's too fucking late to stop now anyway, ain't it? And I've got a lot of respect for the kids. They get on your fucking nerves sometimes, but if it wasn't for them there wouldn't be an Ozzy Osbourne, there wouldn't be a Queen, there wouldn't be *any* of us poncing around like pricks! As long as my band don't look like a darts team onstage, that's all I worry about, do you know what I mean?' He peered dolefully into the bottom of his Diet Coke glass, and added: 'It's the easiest thing in the world to be a cunt all your life. It's somebody else's turn now to be a cunt. I don't wanna be a fucking douche-bag that goes up there every night, a fat, boring old fart ...'

It was Sharon, of course, who had forced Ozzy to enter the Betty Ford Clinic. She was damned if she was going to see him end up like Bill. After leaving Sabbath for the second time two years before, Bill had 'tried to be sober on and off on ten or eleven different occasions, and I failed every time'. The first time he'd stopped, the night-sweats lasted 'about fifteen months'. He got to the point where he found himself begging on the sidewalks of Huntington Beach, not far from where he lived. 'I was panhandling for nickels and dimes. Just to get what we call a short dog. A short dog is a strong, small drink, so it could be a small bottle or shot of something. I was doing that in 1983 after I'd done *Born*

Again ... There was no money. I had no money. I blew whatever earnings I got. Whatever earnings I got were just ... I drank it all. I drank my farm. I put that up my nose with cocaine. My Rolls-Royce, I put that up my nose. My Bentley, I put that up my nose. Just sold everything which I thought I coveted. It was a joke, I just gradually sold it all off, man. I needed to be high.' He still hadn't quite reached rock bottom. 'I just couldn't stand how I felt when I got sober. So I was hoping to die. I just, basically, wanted to drink and die. It's possible to get to a place like that. Not because of anything bad was going on. Just that the booze meant more to me at the time than my children, my wife, it meant more to me than Black Sabbath. A bottle of booze meant more to me than anything else on Earth. Because it took away the pain, it took away the pain cos that's what it does, and gives a feeling of euphoria for about thirty minutes.'

Still, Tony Iommi, stone-faced and coked out more than ever, had been prepared to embrace a new era in Sabbath, as readily as he had let go of the old. The months leading up to the Live Aid appearance had been farcical though. With Bill still in the early newborn foal stage of rehab, but in urgent need of money, Tony once again talked him into joining a new line-up of Sabbath. Geezer, too, though still stinging from the Gillan debacle, was willing to hang around long enough to see what might happen next. While Geoff Nicholls – Iommi's staunch ally in both the creation of new music and the inhaling of mountainous quantities of cocaine, stood by him, awaiting fresh orders. All they needed – as ever – was a singer.

Tony was now living in a penthouse apartment on Sunset Boulevard with his new girlfriend, the former Runaways guitarist, now turned solo artist, Lita Ford. They had begun an affair when Ford supported Sabbath on some of the *Born Again* dates, and had moved in together in 1984. Despite the guitarist still being married to Melinda, with whom he'd had a daughter, Toni,

in 1983, he had split from her soon after, and so now proposed
to Ford, who accepted and began making plans for a wedding in
which the bride would be resplendent in a black wedding dress.
She even made an album, with Iommi producing, tentatively
titled *The Bride Wore Black*, which would never be released. They
would also appear together on a 1986 edition of *MTV Guitar
Heroes*. Lita, though, did not do coke and Tony's spiralling use ultimately cost them their relationship. Iommi knew he'd gone too
far, he recalls in his memoir, when he and Geoff Nicholls were
working in the penthouse one day when they decided they should
chain the front door and place furniture up against it, 'because
you get paranoid when you do a lot of coke. We were working on
this song when we heard a loud bang. It was Lita.' He added: 'It
was a shame, because I messed up the relationship by being constantly out of it.' When Tony then invited Lita's regular drummer,
Eric Singer, to join Sabbath, it was the last straw. They split and
within a year Sharon Osbourne took over her management and
teamed Lita up with Ozzy for what would be the biggest single
hit either of them would ever have, the Mike Chapman-produced
rock duet 'Close My Eyes Forever'.

Tony, meanwhile, could only look on and rue his latest mistake. Indeed, the missteps and wrong turns were mounting up
to such an extent the name Black Sabbath was becoming a joke
within the music industry. A very bad joke. In their search for a
new singer, they again invited hopefuls to send in tapes, which
Tony and Geezer would then listen to at Don Arden's office,
inviting any that really stood out to come along for an audition.
This led to the farcical situation of one singer, 'who we thought
was amazing', being invited down on the strength of a tape that
didn't actually feature his singing. 'It wasn't until we were in the
rehearsal room, me and Geezer are looking at each other going,
what's this? This guy can't sing! But he sounded so good on the
tape.' It wasn't until later, when they played him the tape, that

their prospective new singer admitted it wasn't actually his voice on the tape, and that they had been listening to the wrong side of the cassette.

Then, in May 1984, they thought they'd found The One when a former male model named David Donato walked through the door. Tall, toned, LA tan, with long ringlets of hair running down his back, if he sounded as good as he looked he was in, Tony decided. Unfortunately, he didn't, his voice lost somewhere between a downscale Dio and an asthmatic Ian Gillan. He looked better than either of them, though, and was significantly younger, and Tony felt confident enough to schedule a full-scale announcement of his appointment as Sabbath's new singer, via a soon to be notorious interview with *Kerrang!*, featuring a spread of colourful 'glamour' shots of a pouting, hair-sprayed Donato, who told the writer: 'It all seems to be going very smoothly. I always had a picture of what the right singer in Sabbath should be – and it was me!' Geezer also got his shots in, with: 'We're trying to get back to the old sort of lyrical ideas, because before, when Ozzy was with us, I used to write all the lyrics for him, and a few of our fans have criticised our lyrics since Ronnie and Ian came on the scene.'

A month later, news broke that Donato was out of the band. Tony Iommi would later go as far as to suggest he'd never really been in it. 'David was there but nothing was really set in stone ... the Donato thing was done in haste, it never should have gone that far. We went public before we were sure about it.' Adding how by that point in Sabbath 'everything turned into chaos'. The truth was, Donato had done a good enough job mimicking Dio and Gillan on the older material, but when it came to putting an interpretation onto the new material the band wanted to write, it became plain he didn't have what it took.

That chaos escalated still further when it was then announced on MTV that another American singer, 24-year-old singer-guitarist Ron Keel, was the new singer in Black Sabbath. Another passing whim – this time of prospective Sabbath producer Spencer Proffer, hot off the back of the multimillion-selling Quiet Riot album *Metal Health*, who had heard some demos of Keel's own eponymously named band – that resulted in a brief foray in the rehearsal room with Tony and Geezer before again coming to nought. According to Keel, 'I demoed some of the material that Spencer wanted them to record and we hung out for a few days plotting the future', which, he added, essentially involved 'Tony and Geezer wishing they could get Ozzy back.' When, however, 'something went sour in their deal with Spencer Proffer', Keel was out of the picture again. 'They went through a bunch of other singers, but all they really wanted was Ozzy. I know for a fact that no singer, including me, was ever "in" Black Sabbath except Ozzy Osbourne.'

Things really fell apart, though, when Bill – yet again – couldn't stand it any more and walked out, vowing that this time it was for good. Or until the day when Ozzy came back. 'I had the same feelings that I'd had when Ronnie and Ian were in the band,' he later told Joel McIver. 'Which was basically that it didn't feel the same as it had with Ozzy. I would have loved to have continued but it felt that I was being dishonest with myself. So I said my goodbyes. After that I basically knew that there was no way back. And it was at that time that I decided – by my own truths – that I couldn't do Sabbath without Ozz.'

When Geezer, exasperated finally by both the shambles the whole deal had become, and by Tony's inability to get to grips with anything outside his coke habit, followed Bill out the door soon after, it seemed like that was it. 'Geezer had been writing stuff that didn't sound like Sabbath at all and he was just fed up and wanted to try that stuff out somewhere else,' said Tony desperately trying to paper over the cracks. It was true, when the bassist formed his own outfit, the modestly named Geezer Butler Band, it was as 'a fun group that played around in England with a bunch of songs I'd had in my pocket for fourteen years'. He underplayed it but on the demo that briefly did the rounds of the major labels in LA and London, it was notable that David Donato was the vocalist, offering up the prospect, had they been signed to a deal, of yet another Sabbath offshoot outfit. According to Geezer later though, in a face-saving exercise, being out of Sabbath and having nothing else going on professionally 'was great because I hadn't seen much of my kids. My second one was born in 1984 and he had a lot of problems. I wanted to stay with him and take time out.'

Even Tony Iommi now began to falter. No matter what Geoff Nicholls might have told him as they sat there at the apartment doing coke all day and night and writing songs for a Sabbath album, the guitarist now knew in his bones it was not going to happen. Don Arden was adamant, however: as long as Tony had the Black Sabbath name he should use it. So next up he worked on new material for a short period with 34-year-old American singer Jeff Fenholt, whose then claim to fame was that he'd starred in the title role of the original Broadway production of *Jesus Christ Superstar*. With Geezer and Bill gone, these were songs largely written by Tony and Geoff, some of which would later surface as finished Sabbath tracks – but with Fenholt's lyrics excavated from the finished songs. It was later claimed that Fenholt, who soon after leaving Sabbath 'found God' and became a TV evangelist, was forced to retire from the project after coming into conflict with the band's supposedly 'satanic' image. In fact, Fenholt countered those claims by suggesting it was a row with Don Arden that almost led to the pair brawling which spurred him to drop out. Again, however, Iommi would attempt to cover his tracks by insisting Fenholt was never a fully fledged member.

By now it hardly mattered. Nobody could keep up with the story and, after a final blaze of press noise over the Live Aid 're-union', the Sabbath camp fell, at last, mercifully, into silence.

*

Black Sabbath were now officially over, as far as Tony Iommi and the other original members were concerned anyway. They had simply come back from the dead too many times for it to work any longer. They had braved the decline in both sales and quality of the later Ozzy years, and somehow, miraculously, turned it around by bringing in a plausible replacement in Dio. But Dio had worked hard to win the fans over, and had helped them deliver one of their best albums, with or without Ozzy, in *Heaven And Hell.* When they turfed him out, too, they thought they would simply repeat the trick by bringing in an even bigger name in Ian Gillan. But Sabbath were not in decline when Dio left, his departure made less forgivable by the shambles that surrounded the already dubious appointment of the Deep Purple singer. Even then, they had tried to continue, bringing Bill back and virtually twisting Geezer's arm to stay, but that had led to the even more demoralising fiasco of first Donato's appointment, then the leaked Ron Keel deal, and the unseemly haste with which everyone bailed out after Live Aid.

Tony Iommi had made up his mind. He was going to make a solo album. Ozzy and Dio had made a decent fist of it, why shouldn't he? He envisaged bringing in a variety of guest musicians and singers. But Iommi's hopes of getting vocalists of the calibre of Robert Plant and David Coverdale involved had been met with astonished horror, in the case of the former, and a polite swerve by the latter. When feelers put out to Rob Halford of Judas Priest and even Ronnie Dio were also rejected – both of whose careers were then in the ascendancy, and who therefore saw no leverage in tethering their own rapidly rising stars to the sinking battleship that was Black Sabbath and by implication Tony Iommi.

By then work had already begun at Cherokee Studios in West Hollywood, getting down the basic instrumental tracks, with

Geoff on keyboards, and drummer Eric Singer and bassist Dave Spitz from Lita Ford's band. With still no name vocalists lined up, the guitarist began to scale down his ambitions. When someone suggested bringing in Glenn Hughes to sing on a couple of tracks, Tony leapt at the idea like a drowning man reaching for driftwood.

Hughes was yet another former Deep Purple singer, but, unlike Gillan, his reputation both preceded and superseded his involvement with that band. Another product of the same over-fertile mid-Sixties Midlands scene that birthed Sabbath, Hughes was a founding member of funk rock pioneers Trapeze, where his gritty, soulful voice and extremely rhythmic bass helped propel the band to arena-headline status in America, briefly, in the early Seventies. Hughes became a world-acclaimed performer, though, when he became part of the two-man vocal team – along with the previously unknown David Coverdale – that replaced Ian Gillan in Deep Purple in 1973. The three Purple albums that Hughes appeared on before the band's eventual dissolution in 1976, had seen the band moving into the same funk rock terrain that Trapeze had been among the first to explore. Sales eventually suffered, as did their standing in the more conservative rock-buying community. Yet they remain some of the most enduring recordings Deep Purple would make. By the time the singer-bassist left, his own reputation was at its peak. David Bowie offered to produce his first solo album; Jeff Beck talked of them making an album together; Ozzy Osbourne talked of leaving Sabbath and forming a band with him.

By 1986, however, Hughes' career had taken a downward turn. His solo album, while justly acclaimed, had sunk without trace. His next project, teaming up for an album in 1982 with guitarist extraordinaire Pat Thrall, then hot from the Pat Travers Band, resulted in another critics' favourite that failed to persuade the fans. Since then there had been various 'projects' mooted

– including, at one point, a band with former Thin Lizzy guitarist Gary Moore, then on Arden's label, Jet, which dwindled down to guest appearances on a handful of tracks on Moore's 1985 album, *Run For Cover*. At least the latter had been a Top 20 hit. All hopes of Hughes ever getting back to his best, though, were stymied by, in his own words, 'multiple addictions – the most destructive of which of course was to cocaine'.

Clean and sober now for many years, and with a career back on track with UK chart albums in recent times with Black Country Communion – the supergroup vehicle also featuring guitarist Joe Bonamassa and drummer Jason Bonham – and, most recently, his current project with former members of Stone Temple Pilots, guitarist Don DeLeo and his brother, bassist Robert DeLeo, Glenn Hughes is, as he says, 'in better shape now than I've probably been in my life'. The very opposite, in fact, of what he was like in 1986, when Tony Iommi invited him down to sing on a track on Tony's solo album.

Hughes says: 'I'd known Tony from when Trapeze supported Sabbath at an all-nighter in Birmingham, just after 'Paranoid' came out and they'd been on *Top Of The Pops*. I considered them to be the heaviest band I'd ever heard.' They had met up again when Sabbath and Purple shared the bill at the 1974 California Jam. 'So we'd hung out, we knew each other.' The main difference in the Eighties, says Hughes, is that 'Back in the Seventies, we were told cocaine was non-addictive and you could stop any time you wanted to. And when you're young you're able to pack as much shit up your nose as you could. We were going on six-, seven-day benders. Nevertheless, back in the Seventies I'd been in semi-control of my situation, and I'm sure Tony had felt the same way. But by the Eighties I was completely out of control.'

As seemingly addicted to candy bars and fast food as he was to coke and alcohol, Hughes was also grossly overweight – 'about 210 pounds' by his own estimate, 'and feeling utterly lousy about myself. Self-esteem at an all-time low.' Once a wealthy man in Deep Purple, he had seen his bank balance dwindle to almost nothing in the intervening years as the coke took away his money, then his life. The only thing he had left was his voice – by common consent, one of the most soulful and mellifluous in rock. It was this latter quality that so impressed Tony Iommi when he met Glenn again at Cherokee.

'Tony had never seen me work before. But even when I was loaded I could sing – not onstage but in the studio. I couldn't speak but I could always sing.' The first song Glenn 'scribbled some lines for' was a moody ballad they called 'No Stranger To Love', a melodic power ballad in the quintessential Eighties mould. You could almost feel the dry ice blowing through you as Iommi laid down his aching guitar and Hughes extrapolated on the grand scale. It went so well, Tony invited Glenn to come back the following night and try his hand at another piece he'd laid down parts for, conceived during the Fenholt sessions and called 'Danger Zone'. Again Hughes wrote some scattershot lyrics and they had the track recorded within a couple of hours.

At which point, recalls Hughes, 'Tony must have called Don Arden up cos that's when I got asked if I could do the whole album. And I was into it, because I like Tony. He wasn't giving me booze. He wasn't giving me drugs. I found my own thing. But we spoke the same. It was okay, I liked where we were going with that record. It was fun. Tony definitely wasn't looking at it as a Black Sabbath album.'

The album that was to be called *Seventh Star* certainly was not a Black Sabbath album, the only DNA from the original group found occasionally in Tony Iommi's signature slabs of abrasive sheet metal. He was never a soloist in the same category as a Ritchie Blackmore or Jimmy Page and this left most of the material on the album sounding like generic mid-Eighties melodic rock. Even the by now obligatory mini-instrumental, 'Sphinx

(The Guardian)', complete with sounds of the wind blowing and melancholy synthesiser, which segues into the portentously plodding title track, is still closer to the poodle-haired Bon Jovi than woolly-mammoth Black Sabbath. But then it was never meant to be Black Sabbath. In this new context then, tracks like the self-consciously melodramatic album finale, 'In Memory', a breathy mix of light acoustic and shady electric guitars, fitted right in with the rock music that was then pulling in the crowds on American radio: somewhere between the faux heaviness of the Scorpions and the equally formulaic Whitesnake. While something like 'Angry Heart' sounds like Foreigner or any number of other palsied AOR mid-Eighties Goliaths.

As a Tony Iommi solo album featuring Glenn Hughes on vocals, *Seventh Star* does the job it set out to do: good not great. A stopgap, perhaps, until the real Black Sabbath could get itself sorted out again. Alas, it wasn't to be and everything 'stopped being fun' when Tony informed Glenn it *was* now a Black Sabbath album. Iommi recalled later how it had been a meeting that Don had taken him to at the offices of Mike Ostin, son of Warner Bros. label president Mo Ostin, that forced the decision. It was Ostin Jr, said Iommi, 'who suggested we should still carry on as Black Sabbath, and use this album as a Black Sabbath [one]'. Who was this 'we' Iommi was referring to? He and Don Arden, certainly. Other than that, the decision was entirely Tony's. Not for the last time, he would take the easy way out and allow the Black Sabbath name to be used and abused at will, in exchange for money and the chance to avoid the inevitable and admit, finally, that Sabbath were over.

Ostin's reasoning was clear: a Black Sabbath album could expect a much higher level of financial advance and promotional support than a Tony Iommi solo album. It could also expect far better sales. As for touring, the choice was simple: continued big paydays by headlining arenas as Black Sabbath, or starting over from the ground up in clubs and theatres as a solo artist. For Tony Iommi, sitting in his penthouse apartment doing lines with ever-faithful Geoff Nicholls, it was a no-brainer. For Glenn Hughes, sitting across town, also doing lines, it was the cause of 'total fear and fucking pain'. You can still hear it in his voice today. 'This was where it got fucking freaky with me. I thought it was a great idea to go out and play a Tony Iommi solo tour. When Tony phoned me to tell me it had been changed to a Sabbath album and tour, I went, oh fuck! It was one thing to go out and sing with Tony. But to be the new singer in Black Sabbath … Dio's just had a successful go with his dungeons and dragons thing. Then Gillan, who had his whole thing going on. Now here I am. I've got a fucking monkey on my back. I weigh about 210 pounds. I've got a beard. I've got a tooth missing. I'm having to put the bass down and just front it as a singer. I'm in so much fucking fear before we've even started rehearsing, that I've got to face fifteen-fucking-thousand angry young men, mostly young blokes with black leather jackets on, and I'm gonna have to sing "War Pigs"! No disrespect to the writers and performers of that song but when I look back on it, it was like James Brown fronting Metallica.'

Most people agreed. When *Seventh Star* was released in Britain as an album by Black Sabbath *featuring Tony Iommi*, it only added to the confusion. Was this Black Sabbath or not? Was this an Iommi solo album or not? The answer seemed to be it was both of those – and neither one. Barely scraping into the UK Top 30, in America it became the lowest-charting Sabbath album since *Never Say Die*, and sold barely half the amount of copies. It was as if the rock gods who had looked favourably upon Black Sabbath for so long now turned their backs on them. The accompanying American tour was an unmitigated disaster. The line-up with Glenn Hughes managed just five performances before the singer was unceremoniously dumped and replaced by a previously

July 13 1985. JFK Stadium, Philadelphia. The temporarily reunited Sabbath line-up about to go onstage at Live Aid. 'We're gonna do "Food Glorious Food",' Ozzy told reporters.

Killing yourself to live. In every hotel, Tony would have blankets draped across the windows. Black candles would be burning and gallons of iced-orange would be in the refrigerator, next to metal boxes filled with pharmaceutical cocaine.

The short-lived touring line-up for the *Seventh Star* album. Glenn Hughes, standing to the far right, slightly apart from the others, would be fired after just five shows.

Cozy Powell, briefly, in the early 1990s, he was more than just Sabbath's drummer, he was Iommi's closest collaborator. Later sacked after falling off his horse.

Forgotten man. Tony Martin sang on more Sabbath albums than anybody bar Ozzy. Yet his role has now been written out of their official history.

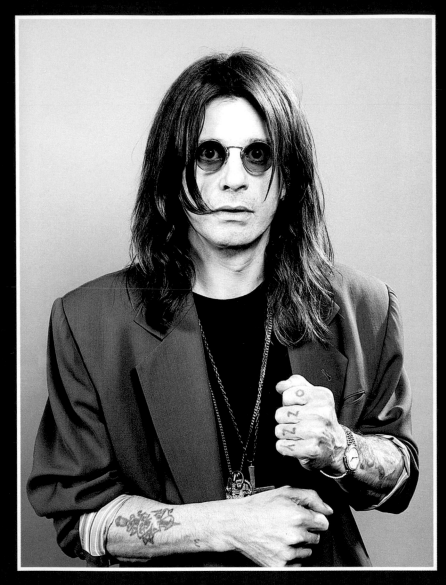

Ozzy in November 1992, just days after his 'farewell' shows at Costa Mesa in California, which saw the first of his many 'reunions' with Sabbath.

Ozzy onstage with Sabbath again at the 2001 Ozzfest, in America. By now an almost annual occurrence.

High Voltage Festival, London, July 24 2010, just two months after the death of Ronnie James Dio. Wife Wendy Dio is comforted by Glenn Hughes (centre) and Jorn Lande, during a tribute show by Heaven And Hell.

February 10 2013. Sharon and Ozzy Osbourne, at the Grammy Awards after show party, in Brentwood, California.

unknown kid from New Jersey named Ray Gillen. Something Hughes claims he hasn't recovered from to this day. 'The worst thing that ever happened to me as a human being was when I let Tony down,' he says. 'I was in my cups. I wasn't the man I am today and I was trying too hard to be good around Tony.' But he just 'wasn't sober enough' to figure out how to do it convincingly. 'When you're high like I was, you have no self-esteem and so much fucking fear, it was just impossible.'

The trigger had been a punch-up on the eve of the first date between Hughes and stage manager John Downey. The two had been carousing at the Cat & Fiddle English pub. Later, back at their Hollywood hotel, Glenn had run out of coke but knew John had some on him and had been caging lines. 'I got a bit belligerent because he wouldn't give me any more coke.' Downey decided he could take no more and punched Hughes smack on the nose, 'He hit me so fucking hard I went down like a sack of spuds. Did I deserve it? Yeah, but not on the fuck-ing nose.' The next day as the band completed dress rehearsals for the tour, the already ill-at-ease Hughes had 'a black eye that covered half my face, and a cut above my eye'. He tried covering it all up with make-up but no dice. 'You could have hit him in the stomach!' Arden complained to Downey. Tony, meanwhile, according to Glenn, wouldn't even talk to him about it. 'Just, "Oh, here we fucking go", like that.'

It wasn't until the first couple of shows, though, that the real problem with Glenn surfaced. 'I couldn't sing! My voice just got worse each show.' By the time they arrived in Worcester, Massa-chusetts, for a show at the Spectrum arena, 'it had completely gone. I couldn't breathe, couldn't sing through my chest, just through my nose.' Nobody stopped to wonder why. They merely assumed Glenn was doing so much coke it was finally fucking up his voice. As a final desperate measure to try and get him back on track Don Arden hired a personal minder named Doug

Goldstein to come and watch over him. Goldstein, who would go on the next year to work for Guns N' Roses, doing a similar job on recalcitrant GN'R drug users like Slash and drummer Steven Adler, was as dedicated to his job as a drill sergeant. 'He was a minder and a fucking good one,' says Hughes. 'He would shadow me, wait outside the bathroom. He would stick a thread around his toe that would go to my door. If my door opened he would fucking wake up. From the moment this guy came on the scene I never did any cocaine. I tried to but Tony had told everybody in the crew: "Do not give Glenn coke. If you do you'll be fired."'

But with his voice growing progressively worse with every gig they did, it wasn't enough to save Glenn from the chop. By show two, they had already got Ray Gillen on the phone. By show three, at the Meadowlands in New Jersey, Gillen was a member of the touring party. When Hughes was no longer invited to the sound check, he knew something was up, but hadn't realised it was because they were using the time to rehearse his replacement. When, after struggling through the Spectrum show, barely able to sing, Glenn was told he was fired, he went berserk, running to Tony's dressing room door furiously demanding to be let in. but the door was locked and though he stood there for half an hour screaming and banging on the door, it remained so until, finally, Goldstein led a tearful Hughes away, still raging at the injustice of it all. '[Tony] wouldn't let me in. I'm banging on it yelling, "What the fuck's going on!" I'm glad he didn't come out because he probably would have popped me one. But Doug Goldstein collected me and very calmly put me in my room and gave me a plane ticket home and said, "Glenn, we're really sorry. We can't cancel any shows. We've got to move on with a replacement. Maybe we can get this together later." That's when it hit me like a ton of bricks: I'd let Tony down.'

Pressed on the subject years later, all Iommi would say was that Glenn Hughes was 'a great singer, but he's not a Black Sabbath singer, as those few gigs we did with him proved. It also didn't help that Glenn was in a very bad place personally at that time. He was heavily into drugs and alcohol and he was constantly surrounded by drug dealers and all sorts of shady characters.' Quite a statement considering Iommi was still heavily immersed in his own self-destructive drug trip at the time. To add insult to injury, the following morning, before leaving for the airport, Doug drove Glenn to an ear, nose and throat specialist, who x-rayed him and discovered he'd suffered a broken bone in his eye socket, on the side Downey had punched him so ferociously. It had splintered into the top of his nose causing drainage of mucus and blood to gather in his vocal cords and in his throat, hence the closing off of notes, timbre, eventually everything. 'It was sitting on my cords. The doctor told me that what had happened when Downey hit me, it had done some serious fucking damage. But I didn't find out until it was too late ...'

But if Glenn Hughes felt hard done by, skewed by what was beginning to seem like the curse of Black Sabbath, Tony Iommi was arguably in for an even rougher ride, as he and his band's standing plummeted throughout the Eighties, until by the end of the decade Sabbath had become little more than a joke, as far removed from the centre of things in the rock world as a bunch of old farts too dim to know when to quit could be.

The US tour staggered on for another dozen shows then was cancelled. Nobody seemed too bothered. Ray Gillen was proving himself an exceptional singer and, in many ways, the ideal young frontman they had sought when Geezer and Bill were still in the frame. But the Black Sabbath franchise was looking increasingly threadbare. A 12-date British tour in May added some skin to the bones – the new Gillen-fronted line-up warmly welcomed by fans and grudgingly by critics, who now cast a jaundiced eye over all Iommi's doings. With his long straight hair, his tall statuesque figure and his very un-American sense of humour, Ray Gillen appeared to be making new friends everywhere the band went. At 27, the closest he'd previously come to anything at this level of the game had been singing, briefly, with former Rainbow drummer Bobby Rondinelli's solo band. He'd got the gig with Sabbath primarily on the recommendation of Dave Spitz, and because he was available at a moment's notice. 'I didn't have time [to worry],' said Gillen. Even though he'd needed cue cards for the earliest shows, by the time the band reached Britain, he was prancing around the stage as though he'd been born to do it.

Maybe he had. Self-confidence certainly didn't appear to be an issue. 'I came in during the height of the response to *Seventh Star*. Everything was all Glenn, Glenn, Glenn … A few times I had people coming up to me saying, "Glenn, what's up?" They didn't know. All they did was hear Glenn Hughes and they saw me instead. Nobody knew who the hell I was! The shows I did helped spread the word about me. The band started to regain some lost confidence [and] I wasn't intimidated by the Sabbath name or crowd.' On the contrary, 'I sang like I've been a part of that band all my life. That's the kind of attitude I had to take and I had to show them that it's the way I'm going to be. I'm going to deliver the goods whether you like it or not. Singing all of the Ozzy and Ronnie songs are fun, but I can't wait to get my own stuff out there.'

Nor could Tony Iommi. Reconciled to continuing with the Black Sabbath name, by the time sessions had begun on a new Sabbath album with Gillen installed now as vocalist, Tony, who still harboured hopes of enticing Geezer back into the band one day, turned instead, ironically, to Bob Daisley, Ozzy's original *Blizzard Of Ozz* bassist and lyricist. Thus, even though Dave Spitz would be credited on the subsequent album, it was the Iommi–Nicholls–Singer–Gillen–Daisley line-up of Black Sabbath that flew into Air Studios in Montserrat, in October 1986, for pre-production sessions with veteran American producer Jeff Glixman. Without Geezer there to provide the kind of lyrics Tony knew he could work with, and with Gillen still an unknown quantity when it came to lyrics – his early attempts more like the kind of wine-women-and-song stuff Whitesnake would come up with than what Iommi envisaged Sabbath re-establishing its reputation with. Not only was Daisley a solid, reliable bassist, he was also a crack lyricist who had penned all Ozzy's finest songs since leaving Sabbath. Tony banked on Bob doing the same for him, not least as Daisley was then in a contretemps with the Osbournes, who had recently fired him from Ozzy's touring band – for the second time in three years – for not being young and good-looking enough.

The only person allowed to speak to the press about any of this, however, was the aw-shucks Gillen, who spouted some predictable guff about Spitz having 'personal problems' he needed to deal with, and how much they were all looking forward to his return – after the bass parts and lyrics for the new album were completed, he pointedly did not add. Asked instead about how he was finding recording in his first big band, Gillen shook his long mane agreeably and said: 'When [Tony]'s ready to go into the studio, you have to have your homework done. He doesn't tell me how to sing. He just lets me know whether it's good or bad … He's got that look to him that is very domineering and intense … He can give you a look that will put you in your seat. I feed off of Tony. Everybody sort of lugs into his energy and we all fire up … When he sits down next to you and tells you something, you know he's been through it.'

What Ray Gillen didn't talk about was how he and drummer Eric Singer were secretly planning their own exit from the band. Happy to get paid – and paid well – for recording an album with Tony Iommi, they didn't see their long-term future in a band that now sounded as old as yesterday's news. Hard rock and heavy metal had never been so hot as it was in the mid-Eighties. Just as Sabbath had entered the mainstream with their weakest album yet, *Seventh Star*, the biggest band in the world was suddenly Bon Jovi, whose breakthrough 1986 album *Slippery When Wet* was to the mainstream rock album what movies like *Top Gun*, also released that year, were to the film industry: a high-concept, ultra-flash, two-dimensional commercial lollipop that packed a punch far beyond the inscrutable ponderings of a Black Sabbath featuring Tony Iommi album, thank you. At the same time, newer British metal bands like Iron Maiden were also hitting their commercial peak, their *Somewhere In Time* album becoming their biggest US chart hit that summer. Meanwhile, again, just as Sabbath were exposing their soft white underbelly, the heavy metal world was being turned upside down by a gang of truly anarchic musical misfits from San Francisco called Metallica, whose own 1986 album, *Master Of Puppets*, would come to be regarded as up there with anything Sabbath had done, even in their heyday, now seen as almost a bygone age in the new, increasingly MTV-driven 1980s.

Gillen and Singer were both a decade younger than Tony Iommi and Black Sabbath, and a generation smarter they felt sure, too. When – in yet another bizarre turn of events – Ozzy's 28-year-old-guitarist Jake E. Lee phoned Ray, whom he knew through his wife, Jade, at the end of 1986 to tell him he'd just been fired from Ozzy's band, the next move seemed obvious – at least to Ray and Jake and Eric.

By then work had been completed on what would become the thirteenth Sabbath album, to be titled *The Eternal Idol* (filched from the famous Rodin sculpture of the same name, and from which they took the cover art, using male and female life models spray-painted bronze to replicate the original study). Maybe Ray and Eric thought they'd be doing Tony a favour by waiting until the album was finished before giving him the news. Maybe they just wanted to pick up their money first before bailing. Or maybe they simply felt they had no choice. Singer was first out the door, taking a lucrative gig on a six-month Gary Moore world tour. Gillen followed soon after, but he flew straight to Los Angeles, where he also picked up a handy pay cheque recording demos for John Sykes' new solo outfit, Blue Murder. By the following summer, though, both Ray and Eric had locked into their own new project with Jake E. Lee, to be called Badlands.

In one of his first interviews after Badlands formed, Gillen said: 'The last guitar player I worked with [Iommi] was a little weird, the band [Sabbath] wasn't weird, but they had their own thing about how they wanted to work and they didn't open up to new things, ideas.' He added: 'With Sabbath and Ozzy, Jake and I had to fill certain shoes and you can't really project your inner feelings of what you want to do, you go by the guidelines of the band. Now it's more coming off singing my own melodies and writing my own lyrics and doing what I want to do. It's not that I want it to go this way or that way. The style of the band is like that.'

He was trying to be polite. Whatever the reasons, when news leaked in March 1987 that Black Sabbath had lost yet another singer and drummer, the press could only crow in disbelief. For Tony Iommi it was another crushing blow. But, as ever, it was too late to stop now. The album was recorded, there were already release dates and tour schedules being finalised. He was damned, though, if he was going to release a Sabbath album on which the singer had already left. Instead, he looked for another quick fix: someone who could come in and reproduce Gillen's vocal tracks almost to the letter. The question was: where would he find someone with those kinds of musical chops, but whose own career was so far off the commercial map he'd be prepared to subsume his own creative input just for the chance to join Black Sabbath.

As so often before, he found what he was looking for on his own doorstep in Birmingham. His name was Anthony Martin Harford, and though he was nearly 30 the closest he'd ever come to rock stardom before had been a session with his band, The Alliance, on the Tommy Vance *Friday Rock Show* on Radio One two years before. Tony Martin, as he billed himself, was a good singer. Not quite in the Dio mould, his voice not quite powerful enough to scale those stratospheric heights, yet not quite characterful enough to compare with Glenn Hughes' rich melodic tones. Yet sing he could. Best of all, he was local and he was available. With a manager, Albert Chapman, who had been a major figure on the Sabbath crew, working alongside Paul Clark, in the band's glory days, Tony seemed like a shoo-in, and though he tried to play hard to get, he was never going to turn down the chance to finally turn pro after a lifetime of getting nowhere on his own.

Speaking in 2012, Martin recalled how Chapman had phoned him out of the blue one day. 'He called me up and said, "Listen, kid. I want you to meet me somewhere", and I went, "Okay, what have you got?" So he got me in the car, drove me off to this big house, rang the bell and Iommi answered the door! I was like, "Fuck, you could've warned me!" So anyway, we went through some songs, I played him some stuff and he went, "Okay, come down to London, we'll do an audition." I did "The Shining" and that was it; I got the job. And it was just excellent.' Nevertheless, Martin was also painfully aware of the position Black Sabbath found themselves in, in the spring of 1987, when he walked into the recording studio the first time with Iommi and the rest of the band. 'They were really in a difficult time when I joined,' he later recalled. 'Because they had gone through a number of vocalists already and it was beginning to become a joke here and in a few other places.' After years of struggling to get nowhere, he wasn't going to let that stand in the way of him joining a world-famous band though.

Unfortunately, for both Tonys – Martin and Iommi – Sabbath were about to become an even more toxic joke when it was announced that they'd agreed to perform six shows at the 6000-seater Superbowl Arena, in Sun City, South Africa. That, in fact, Tony Martin would be making his live debut with Black Sabbath in Sun City. As an introduction to life in Black Sabbath it was about as deep-end as it was possible to imagine in those days of strict apartheid, when most showbiz and sports superstars would not have been seen dead appearing there, lest they be accused of endorsing the brutally authoritarian regime that had prevailed for over 30 years, bringing misery to millions and the condemnation of the world.

Nevertheless, the internationally notorious luxury casino resort in the Northwest Province of South Africa, about two hours' drive from Johannesburg, had successfully tempted many British and American rock stars to its whites-only venue simply by dint of offering fees way beyond the numbers they could expect to make for a week's work anywhere else in the world, short of a high-profile residency in Las Vegas – a concept which would also find its time but not for some years. Queen had done it; Rod Stewart, Elton John, and Status Quo had done it; even Cliff Richard would do it. And, as Iommi privately admitted to friends, they had given him a brand-new Rolls-Royce just to sign the contract. How could he refuse?

Perhaps the most damning aspect of the ill-judged enterprise was that it shocked so very few back home. A year before, Bruce Springsteen's guitarist Steve Van Zandt had made headlines around the world with his *Sun City* protest album, featuring such rock luminaries as Bono, Peter Gabriel and Keith Richards. The message seemed to be clear: we ain't gonna play Sun City. Not those of us in the rock community with a shred of decency or political conscience anyway. Clearly, Tony Iommi saw neither himself nor those who would fly now or in the future under his increasingly black Sabbath flag in the same category. But then, as their not so wide-eyed new singer said, by 1986 both Iommi and the band he had once been so proud of 'were beginning to become a joke'. When Ozzy Osbourne heard about it, he said, 'I thought, fucking hell, they've really fucked it this time! I asked myself, what would I do, if they offered me a ton of money to play there?' he told me. 'And I thought, well, if it was the end of my career, I'd probably say yes too. But not if I wanted my career to carry on.'

Quite so. Nevertheless, reaction back home was muted. The grim fact was that Black Sabbath now registered so low on the mainstream media's radar there was nothing like the sense of public outrage later stirred up when Queen and Rod Stewart played there. With Dave Spitz back on bass but Eric Singer having departed with Gillen to work with Jake E. Lee in Badlands, Tony had asked Bev Bevan if he fancied some easy money. But the ELO drummer refused outright. There was no way he was fucking his career for a bag full of cash. So again Tony allowed expediency to rule and hired the first half-decent drummer that made himself available: Terry Chimes, formerly of The Clash, and a regular fixture at various gigs and sessions for Johnny Thunders & The Heartbreakers and Hanoi Rocks, to name the most well-known.

Called on it in the very next interview Iommi gave, to *Kerrang!* in November 1986, the guitarist offered the flimsiest of excuses: 'Lots of artists have played [Sun City] so I didn't think it would be a problem if we did, but I was wrong. Personally, I don't think that politics and music belong together at all. We have fans in South Africa as well and we played for them and not for the politicians or anybody's politics.'

Not forgetting, either, that nice new Rolls-Royce. What had Tony Martin got himself into, he wondered. He already feared the worst. How would it all end? He would find out soon enough.

ELEVEN
DEHUMANISED

No one knew who Black Sabbath were any more. Not even Tony Iommi. Certainly not Tony Martin. It was humiliating. As the 1980s reached their conclusion, rock and metal reigned supreme, their best-known proponents selling more records and concert tickets, and more millions of dollars' worth of merchandise off the back of them, than at any time previously in music business history. Guns N' Roses were now the most successful and admired rock band in the world, Metallica the most influential. But while rock fans paid lip service to Ozzy Osbourne and the impact his music had had on that decade, and offered unfailing respect for the hit albums Ronnie James Dio had enjoyed with his own solo band, Black Sabbath had slipped so far from the minds of most fans, especially in America, they had all but ceased to be.

When the first album with Tony Martin officially installed as vocalist, *The Eternal Idol*, was released in November 1987, it became the worst-selling record in the band's history, scraping to No. 66 in the UK, where it stayed for a single week, barely making the Top 200 in America. For the first time since they'd been releasing albums, Sabbath failed to tour America, where demand for them was so low promoters would not risk putting them on – unless they agreed to forgo arenas for clubs and theatres, something Iommi's planet-sized ego would not yet countenance, consoling himself with the thought that the new Tony

Martin-fronted line-up needed 'to bed in' first with their fans there. Within weeks of the first Martin album's release, however, both Warner Bros. in America and Phonogram in Britain (and the rest of the world) had dropped Black Sabbath.

It wasn't that the album was so bad – tracks like the pleasingly anthemic 'The Shining' or the doom-laden title track re-called the best of the Dio years; while the more generic-sounding melodic rock of tracks like 'Hard Life To Love' and 'Glory Road' were closer to what Glenn Hughes brought to the party on *Seventh Star*; there was also another convincing stab at a radio-friendly power ballad in 'Nightmare' – just that no one could get excited about it as a Black Sabbath album. When Tony Iommi, Geezer Butler, Bill Ward and Ozzy Osbourne had recorded stone-cold Sabbath classics like 'War Pigs', 'Paranoid' and 'Iron Man' they had not concerned themselves with how they might – or might not – fit onto the radio. Nor what the critics might make of it all. Nor indeed what anyone thought about what they were doing, except themselves and their rapidly growing legion of fans. The reason they became so colossal so quickly was because they sounded, simply, like nothing else out there. They sounded like they truly, truly did not give a fuck, and invited you to revel in that fact. Nearly 20 years later, the sound on *The Eternal Idol* was that of a collection of hired hands – one set of musicians and singers at the start, another by its end – desperately trying to fit in with whatever current trends in rock demanded. Unable to deliver the kind of hard-nosed metal of new young outcasts like Metal-lica, Anthrax and Slayer – all of whom made Sabbath sound as safe as mother's milk – they opted for poise and melodrama. Or what passed for it in Tony Iommi's fevered, drug-fuelled brain. Unable, however, to improve significantly on what old hands at that game like Whitesnake, the Scorpions and Van Halen were able to offer, Sabbath fell by the wayside as also-rans, has-beens. Not even in the same commercial race as new dicks on the MTV block like Poison, Def Leppard and Motley Crüe. In short, they were nowhere, baby.

To make matters worse, their management situation had reverted to one of chaos. By 1986, the chickens had all come home to roost for Don Arden. Sued by ELO for years of unpaid royalties and commissions, losing in his war with his daughter Sharon, whose guile and wit had helped turn Ozzy into a bigger star than he ever was in Black Sabbath, the final straw for the Arden empire came when he was arrested on charges of kidnapping, blackmail, torture and assault of a former accountant named Harshad Batyu Patel. When Don discovered that Patel had been siphoning off money from various Jet Records accounts into his own secret account, instead of tackling the problem through the courts, as most people would, Don's deep-set roots as a street fighter came to the fore and he had the hapless accountant abducted and brought to his Los Angeles home, where he set about brutalising him. 'I gave him a whack across the nose with the butt of my gun,' Don told me. At a second meeting, this time in London, where the terrified Patel had fled to, Don again ordered his thugs to pick Patel up and bring him back to Arden's home, where he tortured him further. Reaching for a toolbox: 'I wanted to make sure he never had a child.' When he was done he locked the beaten and bloody Patel in a room.

When Don's son, David, arrived at the house and saw what was going on, he forced his father to free Patel. The police were brought in and the resulting court case made newspaper headlines in Britain and America. The trial reached the Old Bailey a year later and both Don and David were found guilty on several charges. Don, however, had spent a fortune on hiring the smartest, most expensive legal representation and managed to walk away from the courts a free, if much poorer man. David was not so lucky and was sentenced to two years in prison with a year's suspended sentence. He eventually served seven months in an open prison, but by the time he got out Don was a broken man. 'After the trial, I went away for a long holiday,' he told me. 'I'd had enough excitement for a while.' Don was now in his early sixties; he relinquished his control of Black Sabbath and most of his other business interests. He hadn't quite retired – people like Don Arden don't know what real retirement means – and would return to the fray in the early Nineties with yet more high-stakes music biz adventures, but his days of trying to keep Tony Iommi happy were over.

Panicked, fearful and, in his own words, 'back into doing a lot of coke again', Tony Iommi did 'a stupid thing' and brought Patrick Meehan Junior back in to manage his affairs. 'It went pear-shaped immediately,' he later admitted. But not before Meehan had arranged for Sabbath to play in South Africa, oversee the worst-selling album in their history and watch them lose their record deals. 'Everybody just left,' Iommi would later write in his memoir. 'But I couldn't leave. I had to hold the fort and put it all together again.' By the start of 1988, Patrick Meehan had also once more slipped from the picture, leaving Tony Iommi where he had found him, scrabbling around in the dirt looking for a way out of his troubles. It felt, he said, 'Like we'd gone so far down there was only one way left to go. Thankfully, that's how it worked out.'

His luck changed when he at last hooked up with a manager that he could trust: Ralph Baker, a music biz veteran then working in partnership with Jeff Beck's manager, Ernest Chapman. When the first question Chapman asked Iommi was whether he took drugs, as he never did business with anyone involved with drugs, the guitarist told Chapman he did not. 'Lying through my teeth.' Taking the guitarist at his word, Chapman introduced him to Baker and the new team set about trying to get Iommi and Sabbath back on their financial feet again – starting with cutting a deal with the British Inland Revenue office, who were leaning on Iommi to sell his house in order to pay off years' worth of back taxes. In the meanwhile, they had moved to freeze his assets, making him effectively insolvent. Chapman worked his magic but remained unimpressed. 'These are not your accountant's problems, these are *your* problems,' he told him. 'I still had a huge bill to pay,' said Tony but Chapman had got the taxman off his back while he and Baker attempted to rebuild Black Sabbath.

As before, Tony knew the key to repairing Sabbath's damaged reputation lay in enticing at least some of its original members back. With Ozzy now out of sight – the five solo albums he'd released since Tony had fired him from Sabbath having all gone platinum in America and sold millions more in Britain and the rest of the world, and Bill unwilling to risk his hard-fought sobriety for anything less than a full-blown Ozzy-led reunion – Tony again turned to Geezer Butler to parachute in and save his skin. He began phoning and telling Geezer how great the new singer was, how together the new management situation was, but oh how so much better it would all be if Geezer could just turn back the clock and agree to rejoin. But Geezer had other plans. 'It got so bad,' he told me at the time, 'that Tony started turning up outside my house, just sitting there in his car, like he was waiting for me to run off with him or something.'

When it was announced in the summer of 1988 that Geezer – in the most convoluted twist yet to the seemingly never-ending Ozzy–Sabbath saga – would not be returning to Black Sabbath but would instead be joining Ozzy's solo band, Tony's nightmare was complete. The final nail in the coffin appeared to be when rumours then began circulating that even Tony Martin had now left, his head turned by an offer to join former Whitesnake and Thin Lizzy guitarist John Sykes' new band, Blue Murder – originally, to replace Ray Gillen, who had gone on to Badlands. Gallingly, Iommi found himself having to cover this up as best he could by issuing a statement saying: 'He was offered a job by John Sykes and was all ready to take it, but he was talked into staying with us and, contrary to other reports, never officially left Sabbath.'

As ever, it was all down to money. Without a record deal, and with Iommi facing his own insolvency issues, Martin had weighed up the options of staying with a notional band named Black Sabbath – minus drummer and bassist – that couldn't actually afford to pay him any wages, at that point, or leave for a frankly far more promising situation with a group that had the whole-hearted backing of Geffen Records – home of Guns N' Roses and Whitesnake – behind it. Martin went as far as co-writing a song with Sykes called 'Valley Of The Kings', which did eventually end up on the debut Blue Murder album a year later. What eventually convinced him to stay with Iommi was the offer of a new record deal for Sabbath that Ralph Baker had managed to engineer with the happening American independent label, IRS – then home of R.E.M. Equally significant was the arrival, in the summer of 1988, of Cozy Powell, then one of the world's best-known and most highly regarded rock drummers. A year older than Iommi and a veteran of several star groups, from the Jeff Beck Group, to Rainbow, Whitesnake and even an Eighties-style reconfigura-tion of Emerson, Lake and Palmer renamed Emerson, Lake and Powell, Cozy (real name: Colin Flooks) was a Cotswolds' boy made good who was fond of fast cars and faster women but was currently without a gig. (He, too, had recently passed through the ranks of Blue Murder.)

As well as having amazing technique and speed, Cozy was an outspoken character who had already talked himself out of other-wise successful musical relationships with other headstrong personalities like Ritchie Blackmore and David Coverdale. He wasn't about to simply be the 'new' drummer in Black Sabbath. His appointment would have to come with real status and respect from Tony Iommi. To the extent that for the next two Sabbath albums, Powell would effectively operate in the right-hand-man capacity only previously occupied by Ronnie James Dio – a situation Iommi would never previously have considered an option, but beggars can't be choosers and he grabbed with both hands at whatever credibility Cozy's alliance might offer now. With Cozy also came the possibility of solving the bassist problem, when he suggested his fellow former Whitesnake member Neil Murray. But Murray – another Brit-rock vet who had made his name in Whitesnake, Gary Moore's band and, latterly, as the unlikely bassist in Japanese metallists Vow Wow – turned them down.

As he says now, 'Following Cozy joining Sabbath, I was asked if I was interested in joining, but I wasn't very excited by *The Eternal Idol*, and was fairly committed to Vow Wow at that point. Sabbath tried out many bassists then, and couldn't really find the right person, so they used jazz/session bassist Laurence Cottle, who Cozy had worked with on Ray Fenwick's Forcefield project.'

Cottle was retained for the recording of the next Sabbath album, *Headless Cross*. The first to reflect Tony Martin's songwriting skills, as well as feature Cozy Powell in a strong co-writer's role and as an overall voice in Iommi's ear, *Headless Cross*, released in April 1989, was a fearfully underwhelming achievement. In an apparent attempt to return the band to its heyday image as would-be musical occultists and lyrical merchants of doom, there is a loosely conceptual strand to the album. But not one that engages on anything like the level of their classic Ozzy- or Dio-era work. All the misfires and wrong turns are there to be seen in the first single and video from the album, the title track 'Headless Cross'. With the camera focusing for the first minute almost entirely on Powell – as gym-trim as the horrible compressed drum sound the stereotypical Eighties production demands – and Iommi – standing, as he had for two decades, stage right, stone-faced, dressed in black, crosses dangling, older now, though, less sure – Martin, the supposed frontman, is first half glimpsed through a sea of dry ice. When he does finally come into focus it is not worth the wait. His handwringing and vibrato-drenched vocals; his 'shapes' borrowed almost entirely from the rock encyclopedia – all are delivered to the point of generic rock cliché.

By this stage, the rock press had jokingly taken to calling Martin by his supposed nickname, The Cat. In fact, he'd first been called just Cat in his earlier band, The Alliance, due to his likeness to the early-Seventies children's TV character Catweazle – an unwashed, hairy rake and failed alchemist accidentally transported from medieval England to the twentieth century. It was a horribly apt description for the heavily postured, ultimately meaningless 'theatre' Martin's histrionic vocals and cringe-inducing stage presence conjured up. The rest of the album was hardly better. Opening with a ponderous, not in the least forbidding one-minute instrumental titled 'The Gates Of Hell', and ending barely 40 minutes later with another dry-ice and video-lightning ballad titled 'Nightwing', it was the sort of rock-by-numbers fare the Scorpions had already taken to a higher level, but which worked well enough to satisfy audiences in Europe, where English is not a first language and where, unsurprisingly, the album sold respectably. It also did better in Britain, where it tiptoed to No. 31. But not so in America, where it belly-crawled to No. 115.

Although Cottle appeared in the 'Headless Cross' video, by the time both single and album were released Sabbath were back on tour – but with Neil Murray now safely ensconced in the revamped line-up. He agrees it was a strange time to be in Black Sabbath. 'Playing Sun City etc. left the band in a bad way, whose music and reputation needed repairing badly.' Although Tony now relied on Cozy to shoulder much of the burden, in the public mind it was always going to be down to Tony Martin to somehow re-establish the Sabbath identity as a band to take seriously again.

It was always going to be an uphill task for an unknown,

inexperienced singer such as Martin. As Murray says, 'To find someone who can be as individual and charismatic as Ozzy is virtually impossible; to find someone who can sing as well as Ronnie James Dio – plus his stage presence and songwriting talent – is virtually impossible. There are incredibly few good rock singers in the UK, so to find a singer who could make a reasonable fist of the job in Tony Martin is just about the best that Sabbath were ever going to be able to do. Unfortunately he lacks charisma and believability as a frontman for Sabbath, which all the vocal ability in the world doesn't make up for. Still, compared to just about any of the alternatives, he was okay.'

A point that was painfully emphasised by the disastrous early end to the Martin line-up's one and only US tour. Originally scheduled for 36 dates, from May to July 1989, ticket sales were so poor the tour had to be cancelled after just eight shows. According to Neil Murray: 'How true it is I don't know but there was much talk at the time that the Osbournes did all they could to scupper the tour, getting people to paste 'Cancelled' stickers on gig posters etc. But I think the major problem was the lack of clout that IRS Records had in the US – there was a serious lack of promotion.' As always, it was somebody's else's fault. In Iommi's words: 'Cozy and myself went into record stores in Toronto, Canada, where we are pretty big – nobody could get the record, it wasn't in the shops, nobody could get it – unbelievable. We had such a fight with the local rep – I really came close to chinning him! It really was that bad. At the end of the day it's us that suffer: they say, "Oh, it didn't sell." How can it sell if you haven't got the record in the shops?'

Tony Martin may have claimed at the time that *Headless Cross* was 'the most important record that Black Sabbath has released since *Heaven And Hell*', but very few Sabbath fans agreed with him. The main complaints from Sabbath diehards at the time centred around a shared perception that the recruitment of musicians like Martin, Powell and Murray took Sabbath into a far more melodic direction than the band's history could comfortably stand – almost as if against Iommi's will. An idea Murray scoffs at. 'In fact it was Tony Iommi's musical choice to go in a more melodic direction. He came up with almost all of the musical ideas, then Tony Martin would add vocal melodies and lyrics to the riffs and song structures. It's not possible to get Tony Iommi to do something he's not happy with.' He adds that 'Although technically a very good singer, Tony Martin had rather an AOR tone to his voice, so it was hard for the songs, no matter how heavy, to sound like the Sabbath of old.'

When the band tried to redress the balance with their next album, *Tyr*, in 1990, where several tracks appear to be drawn from Norse mythology, notably a three-track suite on side two beginning with 'The Battle Of Tyr' (the latter named after the son of Odin), leading into 'Odin's Court' and 'Valhalla' – eight and a half minutes of progressive rock on the grand scale, replete with soundtrack synthesisers, silver sunset acoustic and electric guitars, mountains-of-fire drums and down on one knee misty-morning vocals – it seemed like they might actually have broken through to a genuinely new era for the band. 'During the 1988–90 period of the band,' says Neil Murray, 'it was very much a co-partnership between Tony Iommi and Cozy as leaders of the band. Cozy would go to Tony's house and they'd sift through the huge numbers of riffs that Tony has on tape. Geoff Nicholls would sometimes come up with song ideas, and he was very much Tony's shadow, hanging out with him all the time, especially on tour, and generally being the loyal sidekick.'

The *Tyr* album was not a major hit, but it received sympathetic notices in the British and European rock press and led to their highest-charting album in Britain, at least, for five years, when it got to No. 22. In London, in September 1989, they had been able to headline two shows at the Hammersmith Odeon, something they had not been able to do for years. The same year they completed a run of 13 sold-out shows at the Olympski Hall in Moscow, followed by 12 in Leningrad at the EKS Hall, to a total of over 230,000 people. The British and European *Headless Cross* tour dates the following year were of a similar scale. Suitably encouraged, Tony Iommi talked up the band's imminent return to America, but in reality the Tony Martin line-up had utterly failed to capture the imagination in a market now saturated with rock and metal bands of real imaginative power, not just treading the boards and relying on former glories but actually breaking new ground. At the same time as *Headless Cross* failed even to reach the Top 200, albums by Megadeth, Slayer, Anthrax, Judas Priest, Iron Maiden and, most gallingly, Ozzy Osbourne all leapt into the US Top 30.

The result was no Sabbath American tour to support *Tyr*, the entire 'world tour' lasting just three months, focused on the only territories left in the world in a hurry to buy Black Sabbath tickets: Britain, Italy, Switzerland, Germany, Sweden, Denmark, Norway, Holland and France.

Back home for Christmas 1990, Tony Iommi looked ahead to the New Year with a jaundiced eye. Increasingly 'frustrated by the lack of success and income compared to the Seventies era', says Murray, the guitarist 'laid a lot of blame at IRS Records' door, although they were always enthusiastic supporters. The feeling was that Miles Copeland, who owned IRS, didn't understand heavy rock, and that the band would never get back to the position they had been in ten years previously with that label.'

Iommi was on the warpath. He had knuckled down, put together the best, most stable and productive Sabbath line-up since the Dio years, yet after four years of trying, trying, they were – commercially speaking – worse off than they had ever been. Something would have to be done. Ralph Baker agreed.

Fortunately for them, so did Ronnie James Dio.

*

The early 1980s had belonged to Ronnie James Dio. Now, though, in the early Nineties bad karma had caught up with him. After the first two Dio albums – *Holy Diver* (1983) and *The Last In Line* (1984) – both went platinum in the United States, he seemed set fair for a post-Sabbath career at least as big as Ozzy Osbourne's. Indeed, there were many fascinating parallels between the two singers' careers. Both had lost their gigs in Sabbath to a guitarist so pumped up on ego and drugs he was convinced he could do better; both were now managed by wives who held a shared sense of protecting menfolk who they felt strongly had been deceived and trodden on; and both had set out, ostensibly, by forming their own bands only to quickly shed that notion as success and acclaim almost instantly overtook them.

But where Sharon Osbourne had overcome all obstacles to keep Ozzy at the top of his career ladder throughout the 1980s, constantly upgrading his band, his image, even his sound, Wendy Dio had battened down the hatches to ensure nothing got in Ronnie's way or altered his musical course, not even the people who had helped him write his most successful songs: two different strategies that had resulted, by the start of the 1990s, in two very different outcomes. Where Ozzy still seemed relevant, ensuring credibility by association over the years by always touring with whoever happened to be the hot new band of the moment as his support – Motley Crue in 1984; Metallica in 1986; Anthrax in 1988 – Dio's audience had steadily decreased, his niche narrowing the more he ploughed it to the point where his 1990 album, *Lock Up The Wolves*, was an unmitigated disaster, bouncing off the UK Top 30, and levelling off early in the US at No. 61. All three original members of Dio – bassist Jimmy Bain, guitarist Vivian Campbell and, most notably, drummer Vinny Appice – had eventually walked out, disillusioned that the band they had ambitions to turn into what Bain now calls 'a Zeppelin for the Eighties' had dissipated instead into a second-string outfit now reliant wholly on the past.

'He was so stuck in the past,' says Campbell now. 'It kind of was like being in a band with your dad. Except your dad happens to be this rock star guy you don't have a relationship with.' He recalls staying with Ronnie at his house in LA in the mid-Eighties. 'It was especially apparent to me in those months when I did live in his house. Like when I'd go out at night. "Where you going?" I'm going to the Rainbow. "What time you coming back?" I don't know! I remember sitting there watching MTV and Def Leppard videos coming on. He'd be like, "What do you think of this band? What do you think of this sound they've got?" And I kinda liked it, you know? He'd be, "It's shit!" He was so old school and half jealous kind of thing. He'd sit there and roll joints and critique all the videos of all the bands that would come on. And I'd sit there and say very little because my opinions were in stark contrast most of the time, you know? It was kind of awkward.'

Campbell left in 1985, just after the release of the third Dio album – and the last to sell a million – *Sacred Heart*. There were bitter disagreements over money, disputes over songwriting credits, all three band members now insisting everything was weighted in Ronnie's favour, which Wendy Dio does not dispute, merely pointing out how she and Ronnie had mortgaged their house to fund the band in its initial stages, that the band were always on retainers, and always earned money from the songs they co-wrote with her husband. 'Let's put it this way,' she says, 'the band was called Dio.' Before Ronnie handpicked the musicians he wanted to join him on his post-Sabbath career, 'All these other people were unknown.'

But these sorts of squabbles are staples of the music business. What finally derailed first Campbell, then Bain and Appice, they say now, was the shared sense of a golden opportunity squandered by Ronnie's short-sighted determination to have it all his way now that he no longer had ogres like Ritchie Blackmore or Tony Iommi to answer to, and Wendy's tunnel-vision about how to manage his career. 'She was always telling Ronnie it didn't matter who he had in the band,' says Bain, 'that it was his name, his band, and he could do whatever he wanted.'

Whatever the rights and wrongs, nobody could dispute the fact that by the start of 1991, when Ralph Baker began making discreet overtures to first Gloria Butler – also now managing her husband's career – and Wendy Dio about a possible Black Sabbath reunion, all of them were ready to listen. Within weeks, an announcement had been made in the UK and US music press: Dio, Iommi, Butler and Appice (and Nicholls, though no longer as an official member of the band but back to his metaphorical behind-the-curtains role) were back together and getting to record their first album together since *Mob Rules* exactly ten years before.

For Tony and Geezer, it was, 'a life-saver', as the bassist put it. For Dio it was no less than 'a new beginning for the best band on the face of the Earth. I thought we'd all probably end up finishing our careers with this band.'

The first Tony Martin heard of it was one morning as he was getting ready to leave to meet the band. 'I was actually walking out the door to go to rehearsals. They'd given me all the rehearsal times and dates and everything. Literally, on the way out the door and the phone rang and it's my manager. He said, "You better sit down."' Martin was devastated, baffled, hurt. When he recovered his equilibrium long enough to consider where it left him, to his credit he secured a modest solo deal. But the scars would never really heal. Speaking in 2012, still dressed in head-to-toe black leather, his head now shaved, he recalled how Tony never called him directly. 'It always goes through somebody else. It's all very bizarre and the only thing I can think of is that they, as people, are just not used to dealing with other people face-to-face. They've lived in a bubble, in this big space, for a long time, and they have "people" around them and I'm not like that. I'm face-to-face, me. I like to sort my problems out.'

The first Neil Murray heard of it was when … he heard nothing. 'After the European dates in the autumn of 1990, things went mysteriously quiet,' he says. 'Eventually I called the management to find out what was going on. They admitted that Geezer was returning to the band, along with Ronnie Dio.' Murray, who had seen this movie before when he was ousted from Whitesnake shortly after recording what would become one of the biggest-selling rock albums of the decade, *Whitesnake 1987*, was nonplussed but hardly shocked. 'This is a good example of Tony Iommi disliking face-to-face confrontation, though one has to be sensitive to his mood – if you start to aggravate him, and don't notice the signs of him getting agitated, suddenly he'll explode in anger and pin you up against the wall, which I saw happen a couple of times. He is also rather inarticulate, though very intelligent, funny and creative, so one has to tune in to his mood rather than expect to be told things straight out.'

Cozy Powell, who was less sensitive to others' moods, saw it simply as 'a stitch-up.' He had been more than just the drummer who had saved Tony's neck. He had been a collaborator, co-conspirator and confidant in the Tony Martin line-up. Iommi's original plan, in fact, had been to keep Cozy. But when the luckless drummer broke his pelvis in a horse-riding accident – the horse he was riding having a heart attack and falling on him – meaning he would be unable to play for several months, Ronnie, who had been apprehensive about dealing with the opinionated drummer whom he had previously bumped heads with in Rainbow and who had grown used to in recent years seeing Sabbath as partly his possession, moved quickly to suggest bringing Vinny Appice back in. Desperate not to delay the project, lest Dio and

Butler have a change of heart, Tony sanctioned the move. Cozy was apoplectic with rage.

'I was kicked out of the band because a horse fell on top of me and I couldn't play for six months,' he fumed. 'Also a few dirty tricks were played and Tony suddenly ran off with an American version of Black Sabbath. Ronnie James Dio was hired as a singer, and he demanded that Vinny Appice was hired as drummer. I didn't agree with Dio's choice because I already worked with him in Rainbow. I was disappointed in Tony's choices and especially because he didn't want to wait for me to recover. Whether I wanted to play with Dio remains to be seen, but I thought Tony was my friend. I was too naive, of course, I ought to know better in this business.'

But Tony played it down, told him the 'Dio thing' was merely a one-off, to re-establish the brand. That Cozy would be back at the first available opportunity. None of which was true, though that would be exactly what happened in the end, give or take several more broken promises and dashed hopes.

To begin with, it was just like old times. Ronnie and Vinny were installed in a house together in Stafford, where Tony and Geezer would join them most days, 'to jam and see what we came up with,' recalls Vinny, with their gear set up in the living room, 'with little amps, it was pretty funny!', and the drummer in charge of taping the various jams on cassette, then playing them back the highlights before they began work each day. 'By the time I got there they had three or four songs already written,' he recalled. 'We did the rest of the writing in about two weeks, everything was smooth again. We demoed it at Monnow Valley, came back home for a couple of weeks and then went back and recorded it at Rockfield. So it took two groups of six weeks to record.'

The completed album, titled *Dehumanizer*, was a marked improvement on anything they'd done in recent years; their best, certainly, since *Heaven And Hell*. What it lacked in the warmth and sheer exuberance of the latter, it made up for by being simply the most convincing Black Sabbath album since then. Stripped of the melodic pretentions of the Hughes and Martin albums, injected with the kind of bloody vigour unheard since the long-ago days of genuinely monstrous statements like 'Symptom Of The Universe' and 'Snowblind', it was raw and unapologetic. The best work Dio or Iommi had recorded for too long. As Geezer said, 'Musically, it's back to the original sound of Sabbath; that's what we all wanted. Lyrically, I think Ronnie has advanced. So it's a bit of both. Going back to the roots, yet moving forward.'

For once, their timing was also good. By the time *Dehumanizer* was released in June 1992, the rock world had undergone a revolution. Hair metal was history; replaced by a new phenomenon the critics had dubbed 'grunge'. The band that singlehandedly changed everything was called Nirvana, whom their singer, guitarist and principal songwriter, a woe-faced streak of anger and easily hurt feelings named Kurt Cobain, liked to describe as 'a cross between The Beatles and Black Sabbath'. Cobain wasn't talking about the Dio line-up, of course, but that didn't dilute the endorsement he now appeared to give to those old warhorses – whoever might now be in the line-up – of Black Sabbath.

In Nirvana's wake now came a generation landslide of acts like Pearl Jam, Soundgarden, Stone Temple Pilots, Mudhoney and Alice In Chains. Image and artifice were dead. Earnest, soul-searching vocals and emotionally spent, down-tuned guitars were in, along with thunderous drums and stormy weather productions. Suddenly, the new Sabbath album, with its songs about 'real things' like 'TV Crimes' (the brain damage of slush TV), 'Computer God' (the new master and slave eruption of technology) and 'Sins Of The Father' (childhood demons that grow ever greater as the years pass and so-called adulthood congeals around the mind like dry blood), put the band back right where they needed to be. 'I am the crazy man who lives inside your head,' warns Dio, and you momentarily believe him.

'It's really good,' enthused Geezer, 'Ronnie and myself sat down to discuss lyrical directions, and he didn't want to do all the dungeons and dragons and rainbow stuff, and neither did I. So we said, "Let's deal with what's going in the world now." There was loads of material to delve into and write about.' Musically, too, the band had finally shaken off the inertia of the Hughes and Martin years and rediscovered its edge. 'What we have learned is that if you keep polishing the work, you lose the soul of the band. Plus, we knew that we weren't going to be played on radio, so we didn't have to try to be commercial.'

And, in not trying, they finally succeeded in selling significant quantities of records again. They were still some way from their platinum heyday, but *Dehumanizer* was Sabbath's biggest album for a decade, making the UK Top 30 and, more ecstatically from the band's point of view, tipping into the US Top 40 for the first time since Dio last fronted the band. Even the sleeve seemed to consciously burn off the unwanted layers of so-called class that had built up like calcium on their brains: a grizzly cartoon image of Death as Robotic Terminator, 'dehumanising' a would-be Sabbath fan by aiming thunderous bolts of lightning direct into his heart; in the background a computer god atop an irradiated altar. Not the sort of thing a fan of 'mature' rock might wish to be seen carrying home with him but something more bold and delightfully tasteless. The sort of thing parents of a new generation of Black Sabbath fans definitely would not like, nor care to consider. Even weaker moments like 'Time Machine', originally written and recorded for the *Wayne's World* movie – and later featured on the official soundtrack album, which hit No. 1 in the US – are delivered at such pace they take on a special light of their own. It's the really heavyweight tracks, though, that ultimately stay with you; most especially, the penultimate track, 'I', as great and as epic a track as anything the band had achieved with either Ozzy or Dio. There is even an impressively knowing nod to Nineties-style rock modes with closing track 'Buried Alive', its swaggering, staccato riff and evil-twin guitar and bass down-strokes straight from the hip pockets of contemporary new giant-killers like Pantera. Like Sabbath channelling Metallica channelling Sabbath channelling something very close indeed to pure painful pleasure.

'That's right up there for me,' says Vinny now. 'The sound is so loud and aggressive. It really brings it. I remember me and Ronnie listening to it together, smoking a joint or something, we were like holy shit, man! Listen to this!' Dio positively revelled in the album's sinister strength, later telling Joel McIver: 'I'm sure the media were thinking, now we're gonna get another *Heaven And Hell*. [But] that's not what we wanted to do. In going so dark, we alienated ourselves right away just a little bit to the people who were expecting that. It was probably way, way too heavy for its time.' But he didn't care. For Dio, 'This was just the start of what we could now do.'

Nevertheless, the making of *Dehumanizer* had not been plain sailing. According to Tony Martin: 'As soon as they'd started, within weeks, they called me up and said, "This is weird, this is not going well. Can you come back and have a chat?" So I went down to see Tony but I couldn't do anything because I'd already started my solo album.' They toughed it out, as they always had, as they always would. 'We didn't have a problem,' explained Dio, speaking just a short time later. 'We ended up creating our own [and] we created a lot. This album took about a year and a half to do, from beginning to end. An album shouldn't take that long. But everything got real political. By the end of the album, nobody was talking … Or rather, they had simply gone back to their old ways: Ronnie and Vinny were talking; Tony and Geezer were talking. Just not to each other.

The tour began the day after *Dehumanizer* was released with eight dates in Brazil and Argentina. Tony was in his element, able to get his hands on some of the strongest – and cheapest – cocaine in the world. Geezer was drinking heavily. So much so, 'I was trying to pick a fight with everybody. In the end I nutted this statue! I completely split my eye open, and I was so drunk I didn't even know. I went to bed and I woke up the next day and my head was stuck to the pillow. I couldn't figure out what was going on, I was covered in blood.'

As on so many occasions before, Dio watched all this with varying degrees of dismay and contempt. As he told me years later, 'I really thought getting back together with those guys, it would be totally different this time. I thought, you know, it's been ten years, we've all moved on, this could be really something good. I'd gone on and had some pretty big albums without them, and they'd gone on and did what they did. We were more equals this time, I thought. And I was very proud indeed of the album we made together, though if I'm really honest, by the time it was finished I couldn't wait for it to end, so I could get back home. It was as if Tony hadn't really changed that much at all. Or maybe it was just me. But then we got out on tour and that's when I knew. Something was wrong. It was either gonna really come together and we were going to get back to being a great band again, one of the greatest bands ever, I thought anyway. Or something else was gonna happen. I just didn't know what yet ...'

In the summer of 1992, just as the *Dehumanizer* album was doing a good job of putting Black Sabbath on the map, Ozzy Osbourne received some genuinely bad news. He'd been diagnosed with multiple sclerosis. 'That's what some fucking asshole doctor in LA told us,' Sharon told me later. 'And of course we believed him! Ozzy had had the shakes for years, you know that, but suddenly he developed a limp and so I sent him for a check-up, the next thing they're doing blood tests and brain scans and they're telling us he's in the early stages of MS. I nearly fucking died when they told us!' It was months before a second and third opinion contradicted the first and Ozzy was given the all-clear. In the meantime, he had discussed his will and co-written a new song called 'See You On The Other Side' (which later appeared on his 1995 album, *Ozzmosis*). 'That's what that song is about,' said Sharon. 'We really thought he only had a few years left to live. So what with trying to keep him off the booze and drugs as well we decided he shouldn't tour any more. Hence, the whole retirement thing.'

'I thought that was it, old bean,' Ozzy would tell me. 'I told Sharon, "I'll see you on the other side …"' It turned out to be a misdiagnosis. But neither Ozzy nor Sharon found that out until much later. At the time it seemed all too believable. Ozzy had been shaky – literally, suffering from tremors and slurring speech – for years. Everyone that knew him put it down to the lasting side-effects of decades of drink and drugs. A decade of going in and out of rehab had not appeared to help, either. As he liked to joke, 'I've fallen off the waggon so many times I feel like a fucking Red Indian in a John Wayne movie!'

When, in the autumn of 1989, he was arrested in England on charges of attempted murder – the result of an utterly deranged fight he'd had late one drunken night at his Buckinghamshire mansion with Sharon – again, it seemed almost par for the course. I had run into him and Sharon just a few days before in London. As soon as he started speaking, it was obvious he was out of it. Another legacy of Ozzy's periodic 'clean-ups' had been his transformation into a walking pharmacist. Along with the bundles of high-denomination notes he also habitually carried around with him – a hangover from his poverty-stricken past, he explained – he now carried enough bottles of pills to make him rattle. This was definitely something different, though. He just didn't seem all there. Not in his usual semi-befuddled way. He seemed genuinely to have vanished inside himself somewhere. I noticed he was perspiring heavily too. He looked like a ghost in chains. One of those ghosts that carries its head around under its arm.

Sharon hid whatever she was really feeling behind the smile and the charm as she always did when Ozzy was having one of his 'bad days'. They were off to Hamley's, in Piccadilly, she said, to buy their daughter Aimee a birthday present. 'My precious baby is going to be six,' Sharon grinned, holding tight to Ozzy's arm. They were having a little party for her that Saturday night.

That Sunday night I was at home watching *News at Ten* on the telly when an item came on that it took me a few moments to take in. 'Rock star Ozzy Osbourne has been arrested ...' I assumed it would be something to do with drugs. It wasn't. Instead: 'Osbourne, forty-one, was arrested in the early hours of Sunday morning after allegedly trying to strangle his wife and manager, Sharon Osbourne ...'

The next couple of days the papers were full of it. '"DEATH THREAT" OZZY SENT TO BOOZE CLINIC!' screamed the headline in the *Sun*. 'BAN ON SEEING WIFE!' cried the *Mirror*. 'HELL OF DRYING OUT!' wailed the *Star*. According to the reports, the police had arrived at the house in the early hours of Sunday morning and subsequently arrested Ozzy for trying to strangle Sharon, or 'intending her to fear that the threat would be carried out' as the official police report put it. They also trotted out a slew of unsubstantiated rumours which may or may not have had anything to do with anything: Ozzy was clinically insane; Sharon had been having an affair; Don had got to Ozzy and persuaded him to get rid of Sharon. Typical tabloid fare but damaging enough.

When I spoke to Sharon a few days later, she explained it had all started with a case of Russian vodka the organisers of some shows Ozzy had just played in Moscow had given him (the Moscow Music Peace Festival, a two-day event that Ozzy had appeared at just weeks before). Ozzy had been steadily working his way through a bottle over dinner that night when a niggling argument escalated into something 'completely out of control'. She sighed. 'We've had lots of fights before,' said Sharon, 'you know what we're like, but nothing like this. I knew I was in serious shit when he started talking as "we". As in, "We've decided you've got to go ..." It wasn't Ozzy and that's what terrified me. Ozzy would never ever have done that to me, because he's just not capable of it. But when Ozzy gets loaded, Ozzy disappears and someone else takes over ...'

Following his arrest, Ozzy had been bailed on condition he check straight into Huntercombe Manor: a private, £250-a-day rehab centre in Buckinghamshire already familiar to the singer, who had been admitted there briefly for treatment twice already in the past year. Sharon had dropped the attempted-murder charge as soon as Ozzy had agreed to go into rehab. 'Alcohol is destroying his life. To be an alcoholic means you have a disease. If Ozzy had cancer people would feel sorry for him. But because he's an alcoholic people don't understand. He just needs to get help.'

She invited me to visit him at the Manor. 'He's got a lot he wants to get off his chest.' A few days later, on a darkening Sunday evening, almost two weeks to the day since Ozzy's arrest, I presented myself there at reception. The lobby was part plush hotel reception, part gleaming dentist's waiting room. Sunday was one of the two days a week the patients were allowed visitors and various people milled about while I waited for Ozzy in the communal TV room. It was easy to separate the 'guests' from the 'visitors': the former were the ones sitting around looking relatively relaxed; the latter the ones shuffling self-consciously and snatching furtive glances at their watches.

Suddenly there he was, 'feeling nervous', he said, and 'in need of a ciggy'. He had just finished another session with his therapist and 'me fucking head is still going'. Ozzy's living quarters comprised one large bedroom-cum-living room, with en suite bathroom and toilet, plus another smaller sitting room. Well furnished but bland. I noticed there was also a phone and fax machine in the main room. No TV, though. 'They don't want you sat on your own in your room for too long,' he explained.

'It's a bit like a hotel,' I remarked, trying to lighten the mood.

'Yeah, except you can't go downstairs to the bar ...'

We spoke for several hours, and Ozzy talked about how he'd become 'a blackout drinker about a year ago'. He had been in jail before, of course, but the two nights Ozzy spent at Amersham police station were 'the worst of my life. I just couldn't believe what they said I'd done.' Fortunately, the police had treated him kindly. 'I was in a cell on my own and they gave me cigarettes and chatted to me once in a while. Conditions were disgusting, though. I know they're not meant to be like Butlin's but they were terrible. Not fit for a rat ...'

What really bothered him, he said, was the way the whole story had been played out in the press; from unsubstantiated rumours that Sharon had been having an affair and it was this that the couple had been arguing over that night, to rumours that Ozzy was intending to fire Sharon as his manager and go back to her father, Don Arden, thereby sparking a full-on Sabbath reformation. He shook his head wearily. 'They've built the whole thing way out of proportion. I'm *not* divorcing Sharon. I'm *not* rejoining Black Sabbath. I'm *not* going back to Don. I just wish everybody would back off and leave my family alone, you know? Leave us alone!'

I asked what sort of medication he was on. 'Anti-depressants, mostly. Because the side-effects of the cortisone make you very depressed, you think the whole world's coming down on your shoulders. And I'm on various anti-fit pills because I became a fit-drinker, a spasm drinker.' He explained how when withdrawing from alcohol once before he had gone into a spasm because he 'didn't have a medical detox'. He went on: 'This was about six months ago. It's not as bad as it sounds, but if you've got a record of having these seizures they keep you on this medication. I'm on all kinds of different medication.'

His 'number one priority right now', said Ozzy, was 'to get sober and stay sober. I know I've got to go to constant therapy classes for the rest of my life. I've got to go to [AA] meetings ... I've got to meet up with other recovering alcoholics. Two recovering alcoholics can do more for each other than any psychiatrist or therapy. Ultimately, I've got two choices: either get it right this time or screw up again. And if I don't get it right I'll either die or go insane ...'

I asked him if there was any truth whatsoever in the newspaper stories that Don had been in touch with him again and to my surprise he said that both Don and Sharon's brother David had tried to get in contact with him, even going so far as to send him faxes to his room at Huntercombe. He got up and showed me one in which Don referred to Sharon as 'that witch' and basically offered to take over things for him in the event that Sharon decided to make good on her threat to divorce him or proceed with her court action. 'They even tried to call me in the jail,' Ozzy said. 'I got telegrams and all that. I mean, I appreciate the thought, but I think they need to take care of their own business and leave me alone. Me and my family are doing okay as we are. I don't need their help. I'm a big boy now. I'm not the vegetable that they used to call me any more.'

He went on: 'I've always been a paranoid person. Always. Ultra-paranoid. I'm very nervous and shy, too. When I'm performing, that's a different person again. The performing Ozzy is nothing like the person you see now. At least, I fucking hope not ...'

Before we turned the tape off he mentioned that Tony Iommi had also phoned him while he'd been in rehab. 'I wouldn't pick up his call, though. I haven't spoken to the fucking dickhead since Live Aid and even then he didn't say goodbye. So what's he suddenly become my old pal for? I mean, I'm not that much of a dickhead that I can't see that. I'm stoned, I'm not fucking brain-dead! Not yet, anyway, old bean. Not yet ...'

The next time I saw Ozzy was about 18 months later. He was in LA making a new album, to be called *No More Tears*, and from the demos he played me it sounded like the best thing he'd done since losing Randy Rhoads all those years ago. He was also drinking again, smoking weed from a brand-new bong he'd just bought and snorting coke from a huge polythene bag. He was high on everything: the booze, the drugs and the quality of his new album. Sure enough, when *No More Tears* was released later that year it became his biggest hit since *Blizzard Of Ozz* ten years before, going to No. 7 in America and selling nearly five million copies. The US tour he embarked on in November 1991 to pro-mote his latest multi-platinum hit – supported by latest flavours of the month, Ugly Kid Joe and, further into the tour, Alice In Chains, would last for a solid 12 months, including 16 dates in Britain and Europe the following spring. The biggest tour of Ozzy's life.

He was halfway through the tour, at home during its only break, in May 1992, when he received the news that he was dying. A pro to the end, when it turned out that Ozzy had, in fact been misdiagnosed with MS, and would live to fight for many more days to come, Sharon still went ahead and resold the tour as Ozzy's farewell tour. Ozzy might not actually be on the way out just yet, but she shrewdly seized the opportunity to make damn sure this would be one of Ozzy's more memorable – and success-ful – tours. Ozzy would never be forgotten, by anyone. Including Black Sabbath. Something that, paradoxically, would spell the end of the Dio line-up of Black Sabbath – for ever. A bonus, from Sha-ron's point of view, and one she would later exploit to its fullest potential. You could be absolutely sure of that.

TWELVE
SAVIOUR

By the summer of 1992 it was official. Ozzy Osbourne would continue to make albums, the press release said, but he would be retiring from touring. Billed as the No More Tours tour, Ozzy's farewell tour would comprise 63 shows in America, culminating in two big blowout performances at the 18,000-capacity Pacific Amphitheater in Costa Mesa, in Orange County, southern California, on 14 and 15 November 1992. As ever, Ozzy's US dates would be supplemented by the addition to the bill of strong, headlining acts in their own right: Ugly Kid Joe and Slaughter for the early shows, both of whom had big chart albums in the US that summer; then later, Alice In Chains, blue-chip Seattle grunge stars whose second album, *Dirt*, was then on its way to quadruple-platinum status in the US; plus, along the way, various marquee-name third-stringers like Blind Melon and Motörhead.

Sharon Osbourne, however, had plans for an even bigger act to join the bill and help send Ozzy off in a blaze of glory at that final Costa Mesa show: Black Sabbath. It was an idea worthy of all her shrewd cunning as a music businesswoman and emblematic of her fiercely protective attitude towards her husband, whom she had dragged from the career grave Sabbath had left him in a decade before. With the Dio–Iommi–Butler–Appice line-up back in business, they would be the opening act that night – thereby showing both how benevolently Ozzy felt towards his old gang

– good old Ozzy – but also putting the Dio era into a lasting perspective: as beneath Ozzy to the very end. Then to cap it all, for the encores the original – and by implication, still the best – Sabbath line-up of Ozzy, Tony, Geezer and Bill would be reunited for one last, glorious, night-to-remember moment.

That was the official line anyway. But of course Sharon was already looking far beyond that. Once Ozzy's misdiagnosis had been confirmed, and she knew his career as a live performer was far from over, she nevertheless maintained the party line that these would be Ozzy's final dates, thereby boosting ticket sales for the No More Tours tour considerably. Nor had she been coy about the 'kind' invitation Ozzy had extended the re-launched Dio-Sabbath to join him at his 'final' show in November. The knowledge that the original line-up would then reconvene for the encore, however, was neither confirmed nor denied, but only in the way 'best-kept secrets' always are in the music business: i.e. everybody knew it was on. Again, sending ticket sales for those final two shows through the roof.

The whole thing was just too perfect. So perfect, in fact, that when Ronnie James Dio baulked at the idea – appalled at the suggestion that *his* Sabbath should open for Ozzy, and that Ozzy's Sabbath would then close the show *without Dio* – and refused to comply, threatening to walk out on Sabbath if they did not stand by him, Sharon saw it as the delectable icing on an already magnificent cake. For the final part of her plan was to use the final Costa Mesa show as the launchpad for a full-blown Ozzy-Sabbath reunion. Knowing full well that Tony and Geezer would not be able to resist one last, huge payday by getting back together for a world tour with Ozzy and Bill, the only snag would have been finding a way to drop Ronnie without Ozzy and the others appearing to be cold and ruthless. Dio dropping himself before the circus had even come to town was just too good to be true: the perfect answer to this problem. Sabbath, as usual, would simply bring someone in at the last minute to fill Ronnie's role at the Costa Mesa show: when their usual standby, Tony Martin, couldn't get an American visa in time, they turned to Judas Priest singer Rob Halford, yet another Midlands crony who had recently left Priest and was delighted at the extra profile the Sabbath show might lend his new solo career. Rehearsing during a day off from the Dio-Sabbath tour in Arizona, a week before the Ozzy dates, the band dropped most of the Dio-era set they were then performing and turned it into more of an Ozzy-era set, specifically attuned to songs like 'Symptom Of The Universe' which were now beyond Ozzy's vocal range.

What Ronnie James Dio did during this day 'off', no one thought to ask – or care. A highly intelligent man who felt he already knew everything about the ways the minds of old-school music biz movers like Sharon Osbourne work, Dio was hip to everything that was going on – including the blind spot the others appeared to have about how demeaning his line-up of Sabbath opening for Ozzy would be – and he wasn't going to stand still for it. What added insult to injury, in his mind, was how easily the others rolled over at Sharon's offer: and how little they cared where it might leave him. He would never forgive them.

In an interview he gave less than two years after the Costa Mesa show, filmed on his tour bus for a European music TV channel, he was clearly still angry about the whole thing. 'We all geared things up to make another Black Sabbath album with [the Vinny and Geezer line-up]. Then when they felt it was more important to make whatever money that was offered from Ozzy to be the opening act for him, I totally disagreed,' he explained. When they went ahead and did it anyway, bringing in Rob Halford, 'That showed me how important they must have thought I was as a person. But it didn't matter what they thought. I did not want to be part of the circus that was gonna happen that night.' He went on to claim that the subject was never even properly discussed with him. 'No matter what they tell you, it was never *once* discussed. "Ronnie, why don't you wanna do this?" Never even asked me so I didn't tell them ... All they had to do was say that this band [the Dio-Sabbath line-up] was more important to us, for this band to last for two or three more albums, or until the end of our careers, than two waste-of-time shows with Ozzy Osbourne. So we can have a reunion and make millions of dollars ... so yes, it could have been solved. But it wasn't,' he went on, his anger gathering. 'No matter what stories Tony Iommi or Geezer Butler have made up for themselves now, we never talked about this. We were on a [tour] bus just like this. They stayed in the back and I stayed in the front. Sorry, I didn't want to do that but that's the way they chose to do it ... They blew the best band there could have been on the face of the Earth. You stupid assholes.'

The Costa Mesa show itself, featuring Rob Halford and the Dio-era line-up of Black Sabbath, followed by Ozzy and his solo band – followed by the big reveal of the four original members coming on to blast through a 30-minute encore – was something of a damp squib. The set with Halford was perfunctory, the singer forced to use teleprompters to sing the lyrics, which then broke, forcing him to improvise. The Ozzy set with Sabbath was much better but no more than a glorified encore, with little said publicly about what the next move might be, other than sticking to the party line about this being Ozzy's last show. It was a nice climax to a good show, which went down tremendously well with the audience, but offered no lasting resonance beyond that. The next day the four were driven together for another big PR event: pressing their hands and signature into wet cement at the Hollywood Rock Walk, alongside such legends as James Brown and Jimi Hendrix – all of which, along with the 'reunion' set, was faithfully reported by MTV and similar dedicated-music channels around the world. Then that was it. Once again the story of Black Sabbath was allowed to subside into gossip and misinformation, with only the occasional, more hopeful than helpful, hints of what might or might not be happening coming from various members of the camp.

When, nearly a year later, there was still no word on the implied reunion, and an announcement was made on a new Black Sabbath album in the works without either Ozzy or Dio, it seemed the story had plunged once more into chaos. Eventually two strands emerged. The first: that after eight months of negotiations between the four different management companies and various lawyers, Ozzy (and Sharon) bailed out of a reunion tour just 24 hours before final signature, informing the others by fax. 'The tour was definite,' said Geezer. 'We spent six months signing contracts.' Then, 'Ozzy backed out via fax.' Speaking years later, Iommi said: 'At the time, I feel Ozzy let a lot of people down. It was Ozzy that put the idea in everybody's head to do it. And it went on for eight months of negotiations between managers and lawyers and everybody else. We signed our agreements, Bill Ward, Geezer and myself, and it was Ozzy that pulled out in the end.'

When I spoke to Bill a few years later, the hurt was still evident. 'I have no idea,' he said when I asked what happened. 'All I know is that I received a fax from Sharon Osbourne, right at the time when we were going to sign the contracts, and so on and so forth. Ozzy didn't want to do it. And I got no explanation or anything else. I don't know if Tony got an explanation or if Geezer got an explanation. There was no reluctance on my part.' He added: 'I was pretty pissed off. I'd put everything on the shelf with my work for at least six months, you know, to make preparations for the shape that I needed to be in, the order and the discipline of where I needed to be to do a Sabbath tour. Yeah, then I just got a fax saying Ozzy didn't want to do it. So I went, okay, whatever ...'

Their shared mystification at Ozzy's eleventh-hour reversal is not difficult to unravel, though. As far as Sharon Osbourne was concerned, Black Sabbath were finished without Ozzy. Having blown Dio out, they had rendered their one viable alternative to Ozzy impossible. There should have been no need for protracted negotiations, the deal was very simple: come with Ozzy and do what Sharon says, or go back to where you were before, while Ozzy carries on with his highly successful solo career. Sharon had also recently gone through the process of shedding many of her other commitments, divesting herself of the management interests in Lita Ford, the group Bonham, Lemmy of Motörhead and Brit rockers The Quireboys, all of whom were still then hot property. She hadn't done that to now deal with four different management teams all vying for ownership of a Black Sabbath re-union that could not possibly make sense without Ozzy. Privately, however, word was Tony and Geezer had been on board to under-take the reunion, on the terms Sharon offered, but that it was Bill's organisation which had slowed things down to the point of Sharon finally deciding against it. Privately, there was talk of Bill simply being too 'difficult' to accommodate, his insistence on trav-elling in his own tour bus, instead of flying from gig to gig with the rest of the band mentioned, in passing. Or the insinuation that he was simply too ill. But Bill's tour bus foibles were easily accommodated when the line-up did eventually tour together just a few years later. And Bill's health, as he told me, 'has never been an issue for me. If it's an issue for anyone else, they haven't said anything to me.' The problem, as always, was simply down to money. Bill, the downtrodden alcoholic and drug casualty whose self-esteem had once been so low he invited Iommi to set fire to him, had been abandoned somewhere in rehab. The new, clean and sober, Bill wanted to be paid fairly for his work. But what Bill considered fair wasn't necessarily what everyone else considered fair. It was a theme the band would return to, at length, as the years rolled by.

*

What nobody knew was that something had happened in the run-up to the Costa Mesa shows in 1992 that would alter the course of the Black Sabbath story for ever. Forty-eight hours before the first show, Tony Iommi had been arrested in Sacramento, for non-payment of child support: a lawsuit issued on behalf of his former wife Melinda, now living back with her family in Modesto, California. He was taken off Sabbath's tour bus by the arresting officers, placed in handcuffs and leg shackles, and driven to Modesto County Jail, where he spent the night in fear of his life from the other prisoners, while bail was arranged and set at $75,000 – a substantial sum of money Tony Iommi, still then recovering from his recent battles with the British taxman, did not have easily to hand.

In his memoir, *Iron Man*, Iommi writes that it was Gloria Butler who informed Tony's managers, Ralph Baker and Ernest Chapman, of the guitarist's plight, and they who, in turn, sent a local lawyer to the jailhouse with a briefcase containing $75,000 in cash. Thus freeing the terrified guitarist, and allowing him to make the Costa Mesa shows in time. Yet in 1994, around the time Sharon decided not to pursue the Ozzy-Sabbath reunion, she phoned me to tell me she had now acquired legal rights to the name Black Sabbath after helping Tony Iommi out of an embarrassing financial fix which found him briefly incarcerated in jail after, she said, his credit cards had been snipped, sending her own private plane – and lawyer, with bail money – down to rescue him in return for his signing over his remaining rights to the Sabbath name. At the time she had wanted his plight known to the world as payback for all the years of grief he had delivered to both her and, most especially, Ozzy. She urged me to print the story. 'Ozzy was pushed around for years,' she said simply. 'I've made sure that never happens again.' Indeed she had.

'Is this the beginning or the end, then, of any possible reunion between Ozzy and Sabbath?', I asked her later. She treated me to that wonderful, cheeky, told-you-so smile. 'All I can say if there's one thing I've learned over the years is that you're never dead in this business. So many times my old man was supposed to be on the way out the door but here we are, still doing well, still full of surprises. Who knows what might be round the corner?'

As so many times before, panic set in with Iommi and Butler desperately fishing around for a new singer and drummer – Appice, again as before, having decided to go with Ronnie Dio rather than sit out the planned Ozzy reunion tour. The ever-faithful Nicholls was still there on keyboards, Tony's permanent shadow; everyone else had fled. They hurriedly tried to persuade Rob Halford to join on a more permanent basis, but he was on the verge of releasing the first album by his own new outfit, Fight. There was a suggestion of bringing Cozy Powell back in but he was still angry with the way he had been treated after his accident and, besides, he was now holding down a steady gig with Brian May's solo outfit.

All too predictably, they turned to Tony Martin to revive his role as vocal stopgap – something he seemed only too eager to do – his solo album, *Back Where I Belong*, a worthy if unremarkable collection of melodic rock released the previous year, having singularly failed to make any impact whatsoever. They also hired yet another well-travelled journeyman, in New York drummer Bobby Rondinelli, whose previous claim to fame included stints in Blue Öyster Cult and Rainbow, but was then working as a session man. The resulting album, the punningly titled *Cross Purposes* (geddit?), was as good as any of the previous Martin albums, better than most. But the damage to the band's reputation was irreparable. *Cross Purposes* barely touched the UK Top 40 and again flopped miserably in America. There were a string of US dates, to promote the album's release early in 1994, but the band that had last been onstage at the giant Costa Mesa arena was back to playing ballrooms and theatres. In the set they now included no fewer than eight numbers from the Ozzy-era albums, four from the Dio albums, and just two from their own current album with Martin. In New York the tour stopped for one night at the 3500-capacity Roseland Ballroom. The show was not sold out.

Around this time, a journalist from a guitar magazine asked Geezer if he still had any regrets about the aborted Ozzy reunion tour. He replied: 'Since you ask, yes.' While conceding it 'would have been great for the young fans who never saw us', he added, 'and great for us, because we'd have got a couple of million dollars'. At the end of the *Cross Purposes* world tour, which managed just three shows in Britain, and none in London – the first Sabbath tour not to play at least one show in the capital – Geezer walked out, swearing that this time it really was the end for him. Tony Iommi, though he didn't know it yet, would soon follow, only he would have to be pushed. Hard.

It got worse – much worse – before it could get better, of course. There was one further Black Sabbath album, titled *Forbidden*, and released to utter bafflement in 1995. Produced by Ernie C (Cunnigan), guitarist in Body Count, the rap-metal band fronted by rapper Ice-T – the latter sharing 'vocals' with Tony Martin on the opening track, 'The Illusion Of Power' – at a time when 'nu metal' rap-rock acts like Limp Biskit were enjoying their 15 minutes of fame, *Forbidden* was an embarrassing last throw of the dice by a 'band' that had lost their way so badly they were surely never coming back.

With Geezer having vamoosed, Neil Murray agreed to rejoin. Iommi's preferred choice would have been to keep Bobby Rondinelli on drums, but he finally plumped for inviting Cozy Powell back too. As Murray explains: 'Tony thought that it was probably better to have the same rhythm section as in 1989/90, but things were not the same. In 1994, Sabbath was very much Tony's band, and Cozy was expecting that it would be a twin-leader situation as before, but that wasn't the case, which Cozy found irksome.

Musically, Cozy wanted Sabbath to sound like it had on *Headless Cross*, but that was rather dated and Eighties by then.'

Murray recalls how during songwriting rehearsals at Bluestone farm in west Wales, in October 1994, 'Cozy quite often got the beat the wrong way round when learning a new riff, in that he wasn't hearing the riff the way Tony had in his head. This happened enough times to make all parties feel uncomfortable. Geoff Nicholls had taken Cozy's place as Tony's lieutenant, and it also didn't help that myself and Cozy had a few weekend prior commitments to gigs with Spike Edney's SAS Band – basically, the Brian May Band without Brian but with various guest singers. It was implied that we should commit every waking hour to Sabbath, though of course nothing was said at the time. Tony, Tony Martin and Geoff used to generally go home to Birmingham at weekends anyway.'

With IRS urging the band on to a much more post-grunge Nineties sound, 'The idea was to get a producer who would get a more current sound, and for some reason Ice-T was the choice, perhaps because Tony Iommi had met him and got on well. However, Ice-T backed out in favour of Ernie C, who turned out to not have much in the way of production ideas and mostly wasn't on the same wavelength as the band. Cozy particularly didn't care to be told to change the drum patterns he'd worked out.'

But while the production would be blamed for most of the album's shortcomings, it was the very concept that was skew-whiff. Black Sabbath as rap metal overlords? What drugs were they on now? In fact, Iommi's days of burying his head in mountains of coke were coming to an end, yet he had never felt so lost before. The subsequent tour was equally disheartening. After a month of shows in North America and Canada, Cozy quit in disgust.

'Cozy's lack of say in the band's direction, his dissatisfaction with the venues we were playing, which were big clubs some of the time, finding Geoff Nicholls and Tony Martin irritating and childish, which they are, expecting to be paid more etc. led to him quitting,' says Murray now. Bobby Rondinelli was summoned back and duly returned for long tours of Europe, where the band remained significant, Britain, where they did not, and Japan, where most people had no idea who was in the band but expected to at least hear 'Paranoid'. They were not disappointed. There had been an Australian tour scheduled for the end of the year but that was cancelled at the promoter's insistence after it became clear no one was interested enough to buy tickets any more.

'Tony Iommi was much happier with Bobby Rondinelli back in the band,' says Murray, 'and the European and Far East tours which followed were a lot more successful and enjoyable. In the US, people didn't know the songs from *Forbidden*, which was demoralising, though they sounded a lot heavier than on the album.'

For once, though, heavier was simply not enough. Tony Iommi played his last show in Black Sabbath without Ozzy Osbourne at the modestly appointed Sankei Hall, in Osaka, Japan, on 22 November 1995. There would be no more endless fucking around with the Black Sabbath name. Sharon Osbourne would make sure of it.

The angel that would finally swoop down from heaven to save Tony Iommi and Black Sabbath was Sharon Osbourne. She had done it once, spectacularly, with Ozzy. Rescuing him from his own coke-induced pity pot at the Le Parc hotel, to become one of the biggest, most successful, most talked-about rock stars of the 1980s – the decade in which Black Sabbath had lurched from one self-harming crisis to another before finally collapsing in an unseemly heap at the bottom of the rock ladder, as helpless to decide their own fate as a blind beggar at a Roman slave market. She had done this with guile, with cunning and with luck. Now those same qualities would come to her aid again. Together with the sheer bloody-mindedness and thirst for revenge inherited from her father, the only one she had fully vanquished, but whose time was now surely past. And though they would be marshalled initially in the service, as always, of her husband, Ozzy, the knock-on effect would be such that Tony Iommi and the rest of the original Black Sabbath cast would be swept along too.

Infuriated, and not a little embarrassed, to be told by Perry Farrell – the former Jane's Addiction frontman who'd since become organiser of the travelling summer festival Lollapalooza, then the hottest outdoor ticket in the US rock calendar – that Ozzy was 'not cool enough' to be considered for the 1995 version of the festival, she did what she and her father always did in such circumstances, and swore a blood oath of revenge. 'They actually fucking laughed at the idea of Ozzy being on the Lollapalooza bill,' she told me, her face like thunder. 'They said he wasn't cool enough, these fucking little wankers who hadn't been born when Ozzy was inventing heavy metal with Black Sabbath. So I thought, fuck them! We'll do our own festival ...'

The result – Ozzfest, a travelling festival show headlined by Ozzy but featuring dozens of the newest, hottest bands across several stages, as well as secondary features such as 'chill out' zones, 'tattoo and piercing parlours' and all sorts of sidebar stalls dealing in everything from New Age paraphernalia to herbal remedies and hot dogs – became so successful so quickly that by its second year it had totally eclipsed Lollapalooza to become the largest dollar-making show of the American rock calendar, leaving Lollapalooza in the dust. (When it failed to attract a big enough headliner, the festival cancelled its 1998 shows, and lay in abeyance for the next five years, before Farrell, taking a leaf out of Sharon's book, perhaps, reformed Jane's Addiction for a reconvened twenty-first-century Lollapalooza.) 'I was so fucking pleased,' said Sharon. 'I thought: take that, you little cunts! Calling my husband uncool! Who's fucking uncool now?'

But she still had one more trick up her billowing sleeve: getting Ozzy back with the original members of Black Sabbath. Not just for one night either but an entire tour, maybe even an album and DVD too. Ozzy and Sabbath had finally begun making their comeback – not with the big headline-making trumpets previously envisaged, but almost a toe-in-the-water exercise with the Ozzfest tour of America in the summer of 1997. The only missing component had been Bill, who was said to be 'unwell'. His place was taken by Faith No More drummer Mike Bordin: a good fit, fans decided, as FNM were well known for including their own version of 'War Pigs' in their set. Then, in November that year, they headlined their first UK dates for nearly 20 years with a brace of shows at the NEC in Birmingham. This time Bill was there. Inevitably, the shows got huge publicity. In America, it once again made Ozzfest the biggest dollar-grossing outdoor rock show of the year, while in Britain, where the nascent classic rock market was just starting to kick in, it also made a huge splash.

I took the opportunity while they were in the UK to interview them all – again. To try and make sense of what at the time seemed like a weird postscript to their story. I began by speaking with Tony Iommi. So how did it feel to finally be back with Ozzy now after everything that had gone down the past 30 years? 'Absolutely great. I mean, it's unbelievable. It is, it's like a bloody soap opera, really. Like a fairy tale in some ways. We can get together now and really respect each other, I think, a lot more than we ever have. And we can all sit down and talk, and all the crap's gone by now. We've experienced everything that *we* wanna experience and get all that aside and get on with, you know, actually enjoying what we're doing.

'It was so great doing the [Ozzfest] tour because it was really thoroughly enjoyable to be back together again. And I think we all appreciate being able to get up there – and the *sound* when the band started playing together, is just ... you realise how unique it is. I mean, all the line-ups I've had – and the same with Ozzy – it never sounds the same as when you get up there the four of you and start playing. Or in that case, the three of us ...' he added pointedly.

So how was Bill? Tony said he'd just spoken to him on the phone 'about doing these shows at the NEC and Bill's absolutely thrilled. I always talk to Bill a lot anyway, and I've stayed in touch with him over the years.' And he'd got seriously straight? 'He has, yeah he has. He's got himself sorted out now and he's really into playing and he's really into wanting to play. I think for Bill it's a great lifetime thing to be able to get back and play with Sabbath, you know? It's gonna be a great feeling for us all to walk onstage. Cos there's no better feeling, you know? To walk on with the original line-up.'

And if it went well? 'Well, at the moment we're just taking it in stages and we're gonna see how the shows go before ... We're not saying we're getting back together for ten years or anything. We're just taking it in stages and so far it's worked quite good.' What had taken so long? 'I don't think we've ever been that far apart from each other in the heart, it's just that we've all done our own thing and, yes, we have had a lot of disagreements and things haven't all been rosy. But now we can sit down and talk about stuff where we couldn't all them years ago. We were a lot younger then and we didn't appreciate what we have now.'

Sentiments echoed by Geezer, when I spoke to him the following day. 'You can't beat the original line-up. It's the original line-up and it's irreplaceable, as far as I'm concerned.'

Why hadn't Bill been invited to participate in the Ozzfest shows, though? 'Because Ozzy needed a quick decision on it.' According to Geezer: 'Last time, Bill took over eight months to decide about it and it just fell apart. This time, we had just two months to either say yes, and do it, or to say no. Once Ozzy had suggested it and Tony had said yes and I'd said yes, we just couldn't wait to see how long it took Bill to say yes.' He laughed but it struck me how much the story had changed from five years before when the message was that all and sundry had signed on and that it was Ozzy's last-minute change of heart that had scuppered things. This, though, sounded closer at least to the truth.

'It's not just Bill, it's his management,' said Geezer. 'You know, it's erm … difficult. And we had to have a quick decision, so that was it. We did it without him.' And how were things now Bill was coming back for the NEC shows? 'Fine. But then you can never tell with us, we'll probably kill each other at rehearsals and that'll be the end of the NEC. It's that kind of a band. You never can predict what's gonna happen.'

In an ideal world, Geezer said, he'd love to make another album and get the whole shebang back on the road. 'But if there's anything to break us up again it's to be stuck in a studio for two years together. I'm sure at rehearsals we'll know if we could ever do any new stuff or not. If the spark's still there, then yeah, I'd love to do it. But I'd hate to do an album just for the money that totally ruins the name for ever. It would have to be at least as good as *Paranoid* or *Sabbath Bloody Sabbath*. And that's the way it would have to be. If it was gonna be another *Never Say Die*, then no, forget it …'

Finally I spoke to Bill, over the phone, as he still hadn't left for the UK yet, and quite unexpectedly where he called out of the blue one night, to tell me he had no idea what this 'Bill's ill' spiel had come from and that he was actually broken up over not being invited to take part in the Ozzfest dates that summer.

'I think sometimes, I don't know why, but, you know, I've been pulled into a number of situations lately where I feel like I've been blamed sometimes,' he began uncertainly. I told how the rest of the band had been saying they were waiting to see if he was 'well' enough to do the NEC dates. 'I'm fine!' he protested. 'I've been playing concerts in the United States since February with my own band. I'm fine. You know, I don't know where these concerns come from but I do know that they're not my concerns ... Just tell me where I've gotta play and I'll show up and play.'

So why hadn't he done the first Ozzfest dates then? Why had they gone out without him? 'I've no idea. I haven't been given an explanation.' So if they had asked him to do it? 'I'd have been there in a second. I was totally willing. Totally willing to do it! I was very disappointed that I hadn't been asked. I felt discounted, I felt, you know, pretty hurt. I had to experience, for the first time in my life, the original band playing without me, and it felt very painful.' He went further, claiming he was never even asked. 'I was never given a choice. Nobody talked, nobody asked if I would be a part of this, they just went ahead and did it – that's how it went down. And, you know, I've got invited to do the NEC and I've said yes ... I don't know what the fears are, I don't understand it. It's certainly not coming from me. I'd be willing to play in Sabbath, period. In the original line-up. I'm not gonna walk away from that, you know?'

And would he be comfortable with the idea of Sabbath staying together now, maybe even making another album? 'Oh yeah! Oh yeah, of course! For me, if there's opportunities where the original band can do some things together, I would love to continue to work in that capacity ... There are no reservations on my part. It's part of my life. It's always been a part of my life. I would be totally comfortable doing that, you know?'

I ended with a visit to Ozzy's huge mansion in Buckinghamshire. The same place where he'd tried to strangle Sharon nearly ten years before. We sat in his 'play room' while he puffed on a cigar – his only remaining vice, he insisted, though his pockets still rattled with pills.

'I mean, I've dabbled and I've smoked a joint here and there, you know?' he said. 'I've had a fucking Valium here and there and whatever. But the way I look at it, in the old days I used to wake up lying in my own urine and puke every morning, every single morning. And you'd think that after so much of that a normal person would go, "Why am I fucking doing this? Look at me, I'm lying in this shit and puke and piss and whatever." Normal, rational people would go, "I'm not a fucking animal." But I'd get in the shower and when I put clean clothes on I felt new again. The first order of the day would be, fuck me, it's nine o'clock, they'll be opening soon. And that would be my thought. To get out the fucking house to get to the pub. I bought my last house, Beal House, because it had a pub at the end of the drive. I spent millions of pounds on a fucking house not because I liked the house but because I liked the pub at the end of it. I could have bought the fucking pub!' He shrugged. 'For me, there's no such thing as moderation. I have to really watch myself because it's easy to start the whole thing rolling. You know, I don't even like smoking dope [any more], to be honest with you. It freaks me out, you know? I get paranoid.'

What had it been like, finally getting back together with Black Sabbath for the Ozzfest dates that summer? 'I must confess, I was expecting one thing ... because Tony and I never really had a rapport and I still feel a little bit kind of strange. But it's a lot easier working with him now than it ever has been. He's changed so fucking much. Both his parents passed away and he had a little bit of a rough ride with his marriage – his daughter [by Melinda] got taken into care and whatever – and so much water's gone under the bridge. And I can't honestly say I feel the same way towards him now that I used to. And I'm not saying that because of the re-formation because I don't really need the re-formation. I can just as well get another band and go out on tour. But the three questions throughout my career were: did you really bite the head off a bat? Did you piss up the Alamo? And, will we ever see [you with] Sabbath again? And I used to say, yes, yes, no. But, you know, Sharon's very, very clever, she makes you think it's your idea. At first I was like, "No! No! No! No!" But Sharon says, "Give it a shot, see what you think." She's very good, and she's never steered me wrong yet.'

I asked what the deal was with Bill and Ozzy clammed up. 'I don't know, you'd better ask Bill about that. I can't speak for Bill. I'm not being rude or anything, but I can't speak for Bill because I don't know what he's ... I respect Bill for what I respect Bill for but whatever anybody's personal beliefs are, I think you should leave your beliefs – this is just my opinion – whatever beliefs I have, whether they're good, bad, or indifferent, if they're gonna affect the rest of the people on that stage, I should leave them in the dressing room and pick them up again when I get offstage.'

Bill had yet to arrive back in the UK for rehearsals for the NEC shows but Ozzy said he was really looking forward to it. 'Sharon said to me, "Oh you needn't go down for a couple of days." I said, "No, no, I'm gonna be here from day fucking one." Cos when we meet I wanna start to feel comfortable with each other and just spend a couple of hours chatting over ... well, now it's a cup of fucking tea, you know? We've come the full circle.'

Was Ozzy happier now though? 'No, I'm still fucking insecure, I'm still crazy. I still think I'm going to fail at everything I do. I think that's in my make-up. I'm still taking Prozac.' He paused. Then: 'If anybody said to me, "Ozzy in the shortest amount of words, how would you describe Black Sabbath?" I would say awkward. Just when I got a vocal line to go on top of this incredible riff, Tony would fucking change it. Not only the riff but the rhythm and I'd be going, well, how am I gonna get that to fit this? It was like a challenge. But being so young, there was no musical training, it just came natural.'

The two NEC shows would be a revelation. The first time the original line-up had completed a full concert in almost 20 years, it was an occasion to be cherished. Having seen Ozzy through all his various solo permutations – first with the irreplaceable Randy Rhoads, who added lustre to his legend as a genuine music man, then Jake E. Lee, who added glamour to his image at a time when Ozzy was in danger of becoming known solely as the man who bit the head off a bat, up to and including Ozzy's most recent, more convincing return to rock fundamentalism with guitarist Zakk Wylde – it was eye-opening to see him back onstage where he really belonged, not just with Tony Iommi, who had bullied him at school, who had 'put the fear of God into me' in Sabbath's heyday, and who now relied totally on Ozzy's (and Sharon's) largesse to try to live again, but with Geezer and Bill, both of whom came from the same mottled streets he had, who had been through the same bizarre looking glass, from the black-and-white post-war mien of Aston, a town busy dying before it had even been born, to the Hollywood Bowl and beyond as one of the biggest, most famous rock bands of them all. This was Ozzy and Sabbath finally coming home and it was a joyous occasion. The second night was perhaps even more so, the band super tight, knowing the shows were being filmed and recorded for the inevitable live CD and DVD. In the audience were so many ghosts of Sabbath past, from former members – in the hotel restaurant before the first show I ran into Neil Murray and Cozy Powell having dinner together – to friends and former colleagues like Paul Clark and Albert Chapman, even Don's son, David Arden. Yet onstage it was as though time had stopped on a particular night back in 1973, when Sabbath still ruled and rock itself was still young.

Would these current shows with Sabbath be one-off events, I asked Ozzy some days later, or would they lead to more, maybe even an album? 'Well, let's put it this way,' he said, puffing out his cheeks, 'I don't wanna bite off more than I can chew. I don't know what's gonna happen today, which is we're gonna listen to the tapes and talk about releasing a live album. But tomorrow, Bill might say I hate you and get on the first plane back. I may say I don't wanna do this for ever. I don't want to commit myself and say I'm gonna put my own career on the shelf and get back with Black Sabbath. I don't know.'

How about a proper new album, though, with new songs, just like the old days? 'Oh, yeah! [But] I don't know if we could write together again because we've all changed so much. I'm not as forgiving as I used to be any more. I'm not as easy to push over as I used to be, you know? I've learnt a lot in my own way over the years. I know when I've got something good to offer. A lot of chess pieces have changed around on the board, so I don't know if the chemistry's still there but if it was possible, I'd love to do it.'

As it transpired, there would only be the double live album, simply titled *Reunion*, and accompanying DVD, both of which sold well enough to encourage the band to return the following summer for a spate of European festivals. But again, bewilder-ingly, without Bill – Vinny Appice now taking his place. However, at the end of 1998 there was a 22-date US arena tour – with Bill back in the line-up, which they kicked off in October, with an appearance on the David Letterman *Late Night* TV show. Ozzfest would return in the summer of 2001, and with it both Ozzy and Black Sabbath – and Bill Ward. This time, though, there had been plans to follow with an album, produced for them by producer du jour Rick Rubin, a self-confessed Sabbath nut since his youth, then on a hot streak off the back of his award-winning series of albums with Johnny Cash. Six tracks were said to have been laid down in various stages of completion, but when the plug was then pulled, it surprised no one. People had long since ceased trying to keep up with whatever was going on over in the impos-sible-to-follow realm of Sabbath past and present.

Instead, there was now something else looming on the horizon that would throw Black Sabbath onto a very low backburner – at least as far as Ozzy and Sharon were concerned.

It had been back at Ozzy's house in Buckinghamshire when I got my first suggestion of it, though I had no idea what was actually brewing. I had mentioned a TV documentary I had recently watched again on video, a kind of Lifestyles of the Rich & Famous spoof, made on Ozzy – and featuring Sharon – which had been hilarious: Ozzy sticking the head of his pet parrot in his mouth as if to bite it off, Sharon striding through the kingdom of their palatial Hollywood abode like the Queen of Sheba. The pair of them had been like a double-act – naturally funny and of course compelling because of the accompanying glitz – and it reminded me of how funny they always were together whenever you went out with them for dinner or whatever.

'You should forget music and just be on TV,' I joked.

Sharon laughed and said, 'Do you know, that's what someone else said after seeing that programme. We have thought about it. The trouble is, what would we do? Ozzy's hilarious but it's not like he's a joke teller or anything, and who wants to see me?'

'Maybe something like a chat show?' I suggested.

'Naw,' she shook her head. 'Ozzy would be more interesting than the guests.'

It was true. Ozzy on telly *would* be funny; as would Sharon. But what sort of programme could you put them in? Nothing one could easily imagine then, anyway ...

The 1990s had not been so kind for the only other person that had really contributed significantly to the Black Sabbath legend: Ronnie James Dio. Having walked out of Sabbath with his dignity intact, Dio made a much more forward-thinking album than *Forbidden* but without any of his credibility sacrificed. Featuring another new guitarist in Tracy G (Grijalva), a hotshot LA gunslinger who had been in early line-ups of future platinum-sellers

Great White and Love/Hate, Ronnie – along with Vinny Appice back on drums, and former Dokken star Jeff Pilson on bass – produced a truly band-oriented collection called *Strange Highways*, which found him abandoning his signature fantasy song lyrics for a new, dead-eyed realism that reflected his own more general view of his role as rock poet and spokesman.

'The music world has moved on,' he told me at the time. 'It's not enough for me to sing about kings and queens, or dragons and monsters any more. You only have to look at a newspaper to see there is real evil in the world, that humanity is no better than a cancer. As a writer, as someone who takes what he does seriously, I can't let that go by without having my say about it.'

By the time we met again, when I was once again working as his British PR in 1996, he had released a second album with the same line-up, titled *Angry Machines*. An even more brutal collection than its predecessor, yet with an added layer of atmospheric keyboards from Scott Warren, Ronnie was keen to spread the message that he was back and better than ever before. But there were few left in the media that were willing to lend an ear. By the mid-Nineties, grunge had helped restore Sabbath's reputation as innovators, but it was the Ozzy era they were preoccupied with; the Dio era all but written out of the story as a time of flowery, frock-coat metal, far too Tolkien-esque and twee to be taken seriously in an age when bands like Nirvana, Alice In Chains and Pearl Jam wrestled with far more real 'issues'. It didn't matter that *Angry Machines* occupied the same lyrical territory, Dio was about as out of fashion as it was imaginable to be. Never mind that his devil-horn salutes were now de rigueur at all rock shows, grunge or not, I could not get anyone to even come along and interview him. After two days of fanzine writers and pirate radio hosts, we threw in the towel. 'Don't worry about it,' Ronnie told me, his gaunt face hollowed by failure. 'Let's go get a beer.'

'There was some points in the Nineties,' Vinny Appice says

now, 'when I played with Ronnie where I felt bad for Ronnie. I'm thinking, we're in this club somewhere in god knows where, and this is Ronnie James Dio singing in this fucking stupid place with its shitty dressing room, or no dressing room. I was like, he doesn't deserve this, you know?'

Fortunately, for Ronnie, it was a temporary blip. In 2000, he came back with one of the most extraordinary albums of his career: *Magica*. A concept album based on one of his own short stories, which he narrates, it combined all the most potent elements of his classic writing style – portents of doom; sigils from other worlds; dream interpretation and otherworldly nights-capes – with his more contemporary take on a world that barely deserves saving, but individuals that definitely deserve a second chance. No longer over-concerned with making chart-ready albums, it was as if this was the real Ronnie James Dio finally stepping forth. As a result, *Magica* became his first significant independent hit in America, and his biggest European success for years.

Encouraged, he released a follow-up in 2004, which more directly recalled his classic Rainbow and Sabbath catalogue, titled *Master Of The Moon*, and took his band out for their longest tour in years, supported by Anthrax. The plan then was, he said, to write and record two follow-ups to *Magica*: *II* and *III*; work for which he was currently engaged on when, in 2006, came the news that Universal, who now owned both Phonogram in Britain and Warner Bros in America, were putting together a high-profile compilation, to be titled *Black Sabbath: The Dio Years*. The same year, Tenacious D – featuring movie star Jack Black – included the tribute song 'Dio' on their multi-platinum debut album; they also invited Ronnie to appear as himself in the movie *Tenacious D In The Pick Of Destiny*. Suddenly, Ronnie's career was being given a new lease of life.

The *Dio Years* compilation sold well enough in America to

prompt a Canadian promoter to inquire about possible live dates. With Tony Iommi and Geezer Butler unable to tour as Black Sabbath any more, under duress from Sharon Osbourne – who now owned the franchise, and was shrewd enough to realise the big money was no longer in a Dio-Sabbath reunion, but an Ozzy one, and that keeping the name out of circulation, and not having its value distilled by a 'bogus' version of the band going out touring, would ramp up the price of an Ozzy reunion further down the line – the suggestion was made that they tour together simply as Heaven And Hell. There had been two further Ozzfest tours featuring the original line-up of Sabbath, including Bill Ward, in 2004 and 2005. But with the festival now in temporary abeyance, and with both Ronnie and Vinny Appice on board, Tony and Geezer were more than happy to comply. Thus in March 2007, Heaven And Hell, as the Dio line-up of Sabbath must now be known, set out on half a dozen dates in Canada, followed by a riotous in-store appearance at the Best Buy store in Manhattan.

That was supposed to be it. But when, the following summer, they were offered a headline spot on the 17-date US Metal Masters tour, they again accepted and were overwhelmed by the reception they received. It was at this point that the LA-based label Rhino, known for the high quality of their back-catalogue presentations, offered Heaven And Hell a deal to make an album. Suddenly, as if by magic, the old Dio–Iommi–Butler–Appice line-up of Black Sabbath – whatever they were called – were really back in business. No one was more delighted than Ronnie. He would be nearly 67 when the album, warmly titled *The Devil You Know*, was released in April 2009, and he had not sounded more at the top of his game since the original *Heaven And Hell* album three decades before. Nor, for that matter, had Tony Iommi and Geezer Butler.

Iommi, of course, had by now long been recognised as the riffmeister, and on titanic new tracks like 'Bible Black' – the first too-heavy-even-for-rock-radio single – or the splendidly romping

'Eating The Cannibals' – proof that stern-faced Ronnie really did have a sense of humour – he did not disappoint. While Dio was also on top tremble-tremble form. 'Come lie on a bed of nails and slumber,' he exhorts on 'Follow The Tears' in that voice which sounds like a body being dragged from the river. Elsewhere tracks like 'Double The Pain' (featuring Butler's trademark belly-rumbling bass), 'Rock And Roll Angel' (built on the kind of choppy riff Metallica turned into a career) and set finale 'Breaking Into Heaven' (the ultimate in fallen angels attacking paradise-type songs) made fans realise what they'd been missing all these Sabbath-less years.

'It feels like coming full circle,' Ronnie told me at the time. With the album reaching No. 8 in the US – the highest chart placing for a Sabbath album there since *Master Of Reality* nearly 40 years before – it seemed the Ronnie James Dio story – a gothic tale of triumph repeatedly thwarted by tragedy, only for him to win out in the end – would have its happy ever after. Only that really would have been too perfect.

The last time we spoke, Ronnie sounded barely changed from the fiercely proud and determined man I had first met nearly 30 years before. 'I've been very fortunate,' he said. 'To be in one world-famous band is more than most musicians can ever dream. To be in two is almost being greedy. But to find yourself being a success for a third time, especially when it's with your own band this time – well, like I say, I consider myself extremely fortunate.'

Just a few months later the story changed again, as it seemed it always must for Black Sabbath, lest there be any happy endings not worth crying over. On Friday, 13 November, Ronnie was diagnosed with stomach cancer. He had, says Wendy Dio, been suffering from stomach problems for five years. Back in 2004, she recalls, 'He had had this terrible pain in his stomach and I had taken him to a specialist. Now I get really mad about this because I think now, had I known what I know now, I would have insisted the specialist give him more tests and stuff. But the specialist said, "Oh, it's just a gas bubble, he's got."'

Relieved it was no more, though his stomach continued to trouble him, says Wendy, Ronnie took to 'swallowing tons of *Tums*' and other over-the-counter digestive aids. When, in that last year, the stomach pains had grown more severe, Ronnie still thought it was a severe form of indigestion and refused to go to the doctor. 'He would just take *Tums* by the handful all the time, because he thought he had this indigestion, like a hiatus hernia or something like that.'

When, after finally submitting to hospital tests, in November, they got the diagnosis, 'It was devastating. But I hid from him – maybe I shouldn't have done and I feel guilty about it now – but I hid from him how sick he was. [Because] I just didn't believe it. I thought, he's gonna get over it. We'll do everything. I spent the whole weekend on the internet looking for *the* best hospital for stomach cancer, which was MD Anderson in Houston.'

For the next few months the pair would fly to Houston every fortnight for Ronnie's chemo treatments. 'I always told him, "We're gonna beat it. It's a dragon! We're beating the dragon! We're killing the dragon!" And quite honestly, he didn't suffer at all – until that last weekend. He was positive, he was up, he was writing, he was doing stuff. We just considered, we're gonna beat it. It's not gonna beat us. We're gonna beat it. But unfortunately it's a terrible disease.'

When the cancer began to spread, the singer became 'terrified that it was gonna take his brain. That he was more scared about than anything.' He was spared that torture, fortunately, but for a while he lost the sight in one eye. 'I took him to a specialist, they looked at the eye and they said, well, we can laser out the cancer but it won't bring your sight back.' But then an experimental drug named Avastin, prescribed by another specialist, miraculously cleared his vision again. 'This drug was unbelievable! Also he had, like, a shaky thing in his leg. It stopped that! It stopped his hand [from shaking]. The only thing it couldn't stop, and what killed Ronnie, was it went to his liver. Once it went to his liver that was it.'

A month before he died, Ronnie spoke publicly about his cancer with the Artisan News Service on the 'black carpet' of the *Revolver* magazine annual Golden Gods Awards, at Club Nokia in Los Angeles. Asked about how he was dealing with the disease, Ronnie said, 'Well, I feel good and bad at times. It's a long process. Chemotherapy is a … I never realised what a difficult thing it was to go through. It's a real cumulative effect – the more you have, the more it piles up on top and it takes longer and longer to get over it. I find it very difficult to eat. I don't like to eat anyway, so I guess that's okay. But I know I have to. But this makes it very, very hard. But if you're determined to beat it, then you have to go with what you believe is going to beat it for you, and in this case it's that. I go to a great hospital in Houston called MD Anderson, which I think is the best hospital in the world, I have the best doctor in the world, Dr Ajani, who I really trust and I really believe in, so I think I've done all the right things. It makes me feel positive about my life and positive that there is a lot more of it to live.'

Wendy recalls how when, just weeks later, 'the last day came, I was supposed to fly to Chicago, and he called. He said, "I'm not feeling good. My stomach is *really* hurting today." I said, "Well, let's go to the hospital." So we went to the hospital. He said, "You go." I said, "I'm not gonna go. I'll stay." Then he was in so much pain they had to give him the morphine. The pain was so bad, three times they gave him the morphine and after that you couldn't talk to him. He was like in a coma. Then he passed on the Sunday. But that was really the only time he was in real pain – apart from all these bloody treatments and all these

things that you have to do. He was positive, he was fine, everything was good.'

Ronnie James Dio was pronounced dead at 7.45 a.m. on Sunday,
16 May 2010. Wendy issued an official statement later the same
day. As she says now, however, 'The only upside I can think of for
Ronnie is, Ronnie went out at the height of his career. He had
gone … full circle. He had gone back with the Sabbs, which is
something he always wanted to do. To make that good with them
because he always enjoyed the music he played with them. And
he was able to go back and relive that and everybody was on such
a great positive note. Everything was going well for him. He was
at the top again of his career. And he went out then. And I think
that that is probably something that he couldn't have handled if
he had just gone down, getting older and his voice had gone or
anything like that. That's the only possible thing I can think about
it happening. To go back and do it again and be friends with the
guys again, because he always loved the guys, and I think they
always loved him. They're really good to me as well. They always
keep in contact with me. Because we were there at the end and we
were there with Ronnie.'

There had been another summer tour for Heaven And Hell
booked that year. But once again, the Dio era of Sabbath had
come to an unexpectedly early and sad end. The saddest.

THIRTEEN
13

'I went to see Spinal Tap and I didn't think it was funny!' I recall Ozzy once saying to me. 'I thought it was a fucking documentary, I did! I swear to God! Everybody went, "Didn't you think that was hilarious?" I'd go, "No, it was like a documentary about my life." And it was! When they got lost on their way to the fucking stage that happened to me a thousand times! Some cunt didn't change the signs around and you'd end up in the fucking car park with your guitar and your fucking platform boots in the rain.'

By then, of course, it had long since emerged that significant parts of the movie, *This Is Spinal Tap*, really were based on parts of the Black Sabbath story: specifically, the Stonehenge set, which the Ian Gillan-fronted line-up had had so much difficulty with in 1983. But Ozzy wasn't thinking of Stonehenge or Ian Gillan when he brought the subject up. He was simply referring to the fact that the real heart of the movie – one of the most wince-inducingly funny and familiar to anyone who has ever been in or around a successful rock band – could have come from almost any part of the Sabbath story – particularly the Ozzy years, with their tales of vanishing drummers, girlfriends becoming managers, inter-band mendacity and its general none-more-black credo.

Writing this in the late spring of 2013, at the elongated start of yet another, much-hyped Sabbath 'comeback', the most incredible thing to me is that we keep buying it. No matter that the 18 studio albums bearing the Black Sabbath name that have been released since 1970 have featured five different singers, five different bass players, and five different drummers – not counting those other singers and musicians that only made it as far as playing live with them like Ray Gillen and Mike Bordin, or the keyboardists they have used, not least trusty Geoff Nicholls, who was finally let go in 2004, or Don Airey or Gerald Woodroffe before him, and Adam Wakeman and Scott Warren, who have taken his spot since. No matter that their reputation fell into such disrepute in the 1990s that their IRS albums – the ones featuring Tony Martin – were allowed to go out of print. (You can now get them online.) No matter that Ozzy Osbourne is now so familiar to millions of TV viewers around the world, he's more like an eccentric old uncle than a credible rock presence. Because the Black Sabbath story is now in the hands of a true music biz master like Sharon Osbourne, they can come back as often as they like – as long as it's with Ozzy, and under Sharon's control – and it will always feel like the first time: to someone.

This latest 'comeback' cleverly hinges on the fact that it will also feature the first official Sabbath album to include all four original members since 1978. The icing on the cake, another re-visited idea that they promise to make work this time: production by Rick Rubin. Again there is no little suspension of disbelief involved for all concerned. Rubin has already tried and failed with Sabbath once before, when the 2001 sessions were aborted after it became clear that not even Rubin could reignite whatever was left of the spark that had flared into those first five Ozzy-era Sabbath albums. Considering similar failures on the producer's part to do the same for those other blue chip rock legends he professes to have loved so long, AC/DC, whose singularly underwhelming 1995 *Ballbreaker* album laboured under a similar brief; and Metallica, whose 2008 'return to their roots' collection, *Death*

Magnetic, sold well but again failed to live up to the hype, musically. On the other hand, the argument goes, if anyone can breathe life back in Black Sabbath, surely it's Rubin? This, after all, will be the first album from the original line-up since the 1970s.

Except, of course, it won't: Bill Ward having once more thrown a spanner into the works of that particular marketing plan by causing a globe-wide stink over being handed what he describes as 'an unsignable contract' – and telling Sharon Osbourne and the rest of the band what they can do with it.

But to go back to the beginning ...

Officially, the road to Black Sabbath's first album with Ozzy Osbourne for 35 years began on a sunny morning in November 2011, inside a dingy bar on LA's Sunset Strip. Outside the Whisky A Go Go, a queue of grumpy media – gathered there since mid-morning – waited impatiently to be ushered through the front door to report on one of the worst-kept secrets in music. *Why the hoopla?*, they complained to each other. *We all know what this is about.* Nevertheless, one by one, the reporters approached the will-call window and slid their driving licence under the glass. Their name was checked off on the closely held list, their licence returned, and in they'd go, past the menacing glower of the burly security man and into the famous club, where the lights in the main room remained off, leaving it in a blue, inky hue.

The primary source of light was the Sabbath logo shining off a large movie screen that hung in front of the stage. While the screen's obvious purpose was to block off whatever was on the stage behind it, reporters moved by the faintest whiff of curiosity could simply lean forward and see two large folding tables sitting side-by-side across the front of the stage, with a range of name cards across the front: Tony Iommi, Geezer Butler, Bill Ward and Ozzy Osbourne. Also on the table was a name card for Midas-touch producer – and longtime self-proclaimed Sabbath fan – Rick Rubin.

The press conference had been well-publicised with everybody from *Rolling Stone* magazine to snarky little one-man websites reporting that the metal pioneers were preparing to unleash a bombshell of an announcement on 11 November. Officially, Black Sabbath would address the press at 11.11 a.m., with the tatted-up hardcore legend, singer Henry Rollins – another self-avowed Sabbath devotee – serving as the event emcee. Beyond the logistics, little information was offered, although lost on precisely nobody was the fact that Black Sabbath had made their LA debut in that very same venue 41 years earlier. Nor that with Dio laid to rest the year before and Ozzy's solo albums – like everybody else's albums in this post-download age – no longer generating enough sales to pay the rent, if ever there was going to be a full-bore album–tour 're-formation' by the world's most re-formed band, now was it. Conveniently overlooking all the other 'reunions' this line-up had undergone of one variety and another for the past 20 years. With both Ozzy and Tony dropping not-so-vague hints to the media in the preceding months, the only shock would have been an announcement that they were *not* reuniting. By the morning of the conference, the question on everybody's mind was not 'What if?' but simply 'When?'

Up in the Whisky's second tier, black curtains shrouded a flurry of activity, although the unmistakable auburn coif of Sharon Osbourne could be seen flitting back and forth. Then, at 11.11 a.m. on the nose, a movie montage exploded on the screen and behind a deafening soundtrack of clips from Sabbath's biggest hits, images throughout the band's history – minus the Dio or Hughes or Martin years, of course – splashed one after another. Simultaneously, the same movie was broadcast on the band's new website, confirming what we knew: the original Sabbath line-up would indeed be reuniting.

To kick the whole shebang off, Sabbath would be headlining the final night of the 2012 Download Festival, in England, in June the following year. This was to be the curtain-raiser on a world tour and – cue trumpets – the release of a new album, produced by Rick Rubin, every has-been rock band's favourite bearded guru. The last time the original Sabbath line-up had recorded together, everyone was reminded, was in 1978, making this a comeback album in every sense of the word, complete with the suffocating expectations and fire alarm hysteria that such projects generate. Or that it is very much hoped such projects generate by the managers, promoters and record company executives behind them.

As the greatest-hits montage drew to a close, Ozzy, Bill, Tony and Geezer shuffled out and took their respective seats onstage for a Q&A with the media. To a man, each one of the musicians appeared hale and hearty. Tony and Ozzy amicably fielded questions while Bill and Geezer remained silent for the most part. All wearing dark suits, each spangled with a red poppy for Remembrance Day, the four men radiated the kind of charisma only bands who have known each other several lifetimes can. There were grins across the board as they bantered with Rollins about the timing of the album with Rubin. With a measure of astonishment, Ozzy disclosed that they had already written seven or eight songs for it. When Rollins opened the floor for questions, *Classic Rock*'s Joe Daly stepped forward and asked, 'Tony, what are your hopes for this reunion?'

It was a legitimate question. Why now, after all these years? Was it the money, or was it all about the legacy? 'My hopes for the reunion?' Tony replied, before pausing a bit, as if not anticipating such a tricky question. 'It's just great to be back together and to be able to play and write some great music, you know, and be with the guys that I've known … all me life. It's a real special thing, you know? We've known each other so long, it's like a family, and it'd be great to actually know we were actually working together and be in a room and play. It's great fun and we're really enjoying it.'

While the forthcoming new album emerged as the centre-piece of the event, back in Britain news of the Download appearance saw tickets to the festival hit eye-watering premiums. Their Download appearance would be more than the crown jewel of the year's concert schedule; it promised to cement a place in history. Or so everyone fervently hoped. What's more there would be a second high-profile festival event, this time in America, when Ozzy and Sabbath would headline at – another private victory for Sharon – the Lollapalooza show in August. There would also be a 'warm-up' show prior to the Download Festival, at the Birmingham O2 arena, where proceeds would be donated to the Help For Heroes charity. It seemed like all the best stories need a happy ending, even one as black as this.

The 2012 Download Festival – the modern-day three-day descendant of the original one-day Monsters Of Rock festival from the 1980s, and situated on the same Castle Donington racetrack site – promised to be the biggest yet, in terms of both size and quality of the acts. While the festival's branding might have changed, the sonic recipe remained largely untouched, the vast majority of the 2012 line-up hailing from the shores of hard rock and heavy metal, although the first night's headliners offered the head-scratching duo of Chase & Status setting the table for The Prodigy. The second evening would feature Metallica as headliners, playing the *Black Album* in its entirety, with Sabbath closing it all out on Sunday evening. Acts like first-generation Seattle grunge stars Soundgarden (who would 'open' for Sabbath on the final night), Megadeth, Ghost and Slash dotted a truly jaw-dropping rock smorgasbord, showcasing an array of acts from the shit-hot and up-and-coming, to the gaunt, broken-down and 'I didn't even realise they were still together' outfits.

Then there was Black Sabbath. The road to the festival had been impossibly hard. Within weeks of the official announcement of the comeback album and tour, Tony Iommi had been forced into making a more private, less triumphant announcement of his own: he had been diagnosed with cancer; in his case, a form of lymphoma. While subsequent news releases vainly attempted to obscure the realities of his cancerous decline, the writing on the wall was clear: Tony Iommi's battle with lymphoma had taken an aggressive turn for the worse. Plagued by nausea and exhaustion – the merciless side-effects of chemotherapy – Tony's stamina had withered and news of his deterioration accompanied the announcement of the cancellation of the Sabbath world tour, save for Download and Lollapalooza. Originally scheduled as a way station along a triumphant comeback campaign, Download was now shaping up to be a swan song.

Even in the days leading up to their 10 June headlining slot, uncertainty began clouding the band's every move. By the festival's first day, the square jaws and cocksure grins from the Whisky A Go Go were long gone – and so was Bill Ward. Citing contractual problems, Bill had taken his complaints public, specifically blaming Sharon Osbourne for insisting on an 'unsignable' contract, and on his Facebook page outlining a laundry list of grievances that stretched back many years.

In a Facebook posting headed 'Statement on Black Sabbath Album & Tour: Los Angeles, CA – February 2, 2012', Bill wrote:

Dear Sabbath Fans, Fellow Musicians and Interested Parties,

At this time, I would love nothing more than to be able to proceed with the Black Sabbath album and tour. However, I am unable to continue unless a 'signable' contract is drawn up; a contract that reflects some dignity and respect towards me as an original member of the band. Last year, I worked diligently in good faith with Tony, Ozzy and Geezer. And on 11/11/11, again in good faith, I participated in the LA press conference. Several days ago, after nearly a year of trying to negotiate, another 'unsignable' contract was handed to me.

Let me say that although this has put me in some kind of holding pattern, I am packed and ready to leave the US for England. More importantly, I definitely want to play on the album, and I definitely want to tour with Black Sabbath.

Since the news of Tony's illness, and the understanding that the band would move production to the UK, I've spent every day getting to or living in a place of readiness to leave. That involves something of a task, and as I've tried to find out what's going on with the UK sessions, I've realised that I've been getting 'the cold shoulder' (and, I might add, not for the first time). Feeling somewhat ostracised, my guess is as of today, I will know nothing of what's happening unless I sign 'the unsignable contract'.

The place I'm in feels lousy and lonely because as much as I want to play and participate, I also have to stand for something and not sign on. If I sign as-is, I stand to lose my rights, dignity and respectability as a rock musician. I believe in freedom and freedom of speech. I grew up in a hard rock/metal band. We stood for something then, and we played from the heart with honesty and sincerity. I am in the spirit of integrity, far from the corporate malady, I am real and honest, fair and compassionate.

If I'm replaced, I have to face you, the beloved Sabbath fans. I hope you will not hold me responsible for the failure of an original Black Sabbath line-up as promoted. Without fault finding, I want to assure everyone that my loyalty to Sabbath is intact.

So here I am. I lay my truth down before you. I'm good to go IF I get a 'signable' contract. I don't want to let anyone down, especially Black Sabbath and all the Sabbath fans. You know I love you. It would be a sad day in Rock if this current situation fell to the desires of a few.

My position is not greed-driven. I'm not holding out for a 'big piece' of the action (money) like some kind of blackmail deal.

I'd like something that recognises and is reflective of my contributions to the band, including the reunions that started fourteen years ago. After the last tour I vowed to never again sign on to an unreasonable contract. I want a contract that shows some respect to me and my family, a contract that will honour all that I've brought to Black Sabbath since its beginning.

That's the story so far.

Stay safe and stay strong.

I love every single one of you.

Bill Ward.

Two weeks later, there was a follow-up post on Bill's Facebook page:

Dear Sabbath Fans,

I wanted to let you know where things are at, from my point of view, as of today, February 17, 2012.

As my statement of February 2, 2012 indicated, I have not declined to participate in the Sabbath album and tour. At the earliest opportunity, I am prepared to go to the UK and record, and later tour with the band.

Last week, we sent further communication to the attorney handling the negotiations to try to reach an agreement. At this time we are waiting to hear back. I remain hopeful for a 'signable' contract and a positive outcome.

I want to thank everyone who has voiced and posted their opinions, thoughts, support and love through all media, including the newly constructed sites. I applaud your worldwide reaction in support of the original band. And speaking for myself, your intent and truth will always be respected.

While believing in your freedom for expression, keep in mind

that Tony, Ozzy and Geezer are still my lifetime friends, and I
cannot support comments with an objectifying or derogatory
theme towards them or their various representatives.

Many thanks to all of you. You are truly phenomenal.

Stay safe, stay strong.
Bill Ward

He received hundreds of comments back. Thousands more arrived on forums and chat rooms around the world, yet Sharon never gave an inch. Why should she? Bill could have what he considered his fair share of nothing, or what she dictated. Bill chose nothing. Once again, the original line-up reunion was off. Not that the band appeared to care, merely papering over the cracks. It wasn't like Ozzy had been given an 'unsignable contract', was it?

Finally, on 15 May 2012, Bill made it official, again via a message on his Facebook page:

Dear Sabbath Fans and Fellow Musicians,

I sincerely regret to inform you that after a final effort to
participate in the upcoming Sabbath shows a failure to agree has
continued. At this time I have to inform you that I won't be playing
with Black Sabbath at the Birmingham gig dated May 19th, 2012,
nor will I be playing at Download on June 10th, 2012. Further, I will
not be playing at Lollapalooza on August 3, 2012.

It is with a very sad heart that I bring you this news. I am
sincerely passionate in my desire to play with the band, and I'm
very, very sorry that it's fallen to this. This statement is even more
painstaking to write, as I was particularly excited to play alongside
Tony Iommi after the recent treatments he underwent. I wanted that
to become a reality.

He then referred readers back to his original comments for further details on his position.

Geezer Butler then took it upon himself to respond to Bill's latest postings by making a statement of his own, on the band's official Facebook page, dated 19 May 2012. Geezer wrote:

I feel sad to see the Sabbath reunion becoming a bit of a soap opera on the internet. It has been a very tough year for us as a band, having announced our reunion plans, only for Tony to be diagnosed with lymphoma, leaving us no choice but to postpone the proposed Sabbath tour, and then for Bill to go public on his site about an unsignable contract. None of us knew how Tony was going to respond to his intensive chemotherapy, and radiotherapy. Ozzy and myself flew to England to be with Tony, and on his 'good' days, we'd meet at his home studio and put ideas together for the upcoming album, all sitting down together, no drummer involved, just three of us quietly putting together ideas. We thought that when we had enough songs together for a full band rehearsal, we'd move back to LA and put the whole thing together with Bill. Unfortunately, to our surprise, Bill issued a statement on his site saying he'd been offered an unsignable contract. He hadn't told any one of us he was having contractual problems, and frankly those things are worked out between our representatives, and never between the four of us let alone in public. We had the idea of keeping just one show in this year, hoping that Tony would be well enough for that show, and that things with Bill would be sorted. As you may expect, a one-off show at Donington Festival (Download) costs an absolute fortune to stage, involving over 50 people, transport, air fares, hotels, meals, agents, promoters, accountants, lawyers etc, so none of us expected to make much money from it – it was a one-off Sabbath show for the fans, before we go into recording the new album. Apparently, this wasn't acceptable to Bill's representatives, they wanted an amount that was so unrealistic that it seemed to have been a joke. So we resigned ourselves to doing

Download without Bill, hoping he'd change his mind and at least make a guest appearance. We started rehearsals a few weeks ago with Tommy Cluefetos, the drummer who will be on the Ozzy and Friends Tour. Brilliant drummer and good bloke. It was decided we'd better do a warm up show, to break the ice since we haven't played together live. The O2 Academy was available in Birmingham, where we were rehearsing, so we decided on that, and to make a donation to Help For Heroes Charity, since we'd be ironing out any glitches we may have. Then Bill put out a further statement saying he'd been ready to play the Birmingham show, but he was expected to have to do it 'for free'. Well, I think that's basically how you raise money from gigs for charity – you play them 'for free'.

All I am saying is that there are two sides to everything. I do hope to play with Bill again some day. For whatever reason; it wasn't meant to be this time. Bill's made his decision, and I have to respect that. Hopefully this painful year will be worth the wait for the new Sabbath album and end in joy and happiness for all.

Stay frosty,
Geezer

Bill's immediate Facebook response, posted within hours of Geezer's, went as follows:

Dear Sabbath Fans and Musicians,

I have read Geezer's statement of May 19, 2012 titled 'Heavy Heart'. Out of respect for the Birmingham gig, I wanted to wait 24 hours before releasing this statement. There are some points he brought up which I want to respond to.

1) I had indeed notified Ozzy, Tony and Geezer, well before my first public statement, that I was having contractual difficulties.

2) I came out into a public forum to be accountable to the fans

*primarily, and to say at a public level there's a problem. The band
members stopped talking and corresponding with me some time ago,
with the exception of a nice letter from Tony on my birthday. Prior to
that, Geezer and I were corresponding, but that stopped abruptly in
late February after I emailed a specific question to him.*

*3) In my statement of May 15, I clearly stated I would play
Birmingham for free. That was not a problem – charity or otherwise.*

*4) My Download fee was not an extravagant amount. Originally,
when Download was part of a full tour, I had asked for a decent fee.
More recently, as we were negotiating just Download/Birmingham
and Lollapalooza, I told my attorney that I would accept the
proposed small Download fee, but there were other parts of the offer
that were unsatisfactory.*

*I will continue to be honest and respectful towards the band and
our fans. I will also confront any untruths about me, and any fault
finding missions aimed at me that come to my attention.*

I hope the band and the fans had a good gig in Brum.

Stay safe/stay strong.
Bill Ward

Given the towering egos in play, not the least of which belonged to the Osbournes, Bill surely knew that his public airing
of the laundry would mark a point of no return. But these resent-
ments had burned in Bill's mind for years and with the freshly
stoked flames at an all-time high, his shockingly public accusa-
tions squashed any realistic chance of reconciliation in time for
Download. The word among the backstage scene makers was
that Bill was unable to get his head around the fact that Ozzy –
understandably, given his continued status as one of the most
recognisable rock stars on the planet – would again be taking the
lion's share from the proceeding millions, with the other three
left to share out what was left over. Even if what remained might

have given him several million dollars. That Bill, in his bizarrely archaic way, still held fast to the belief that Black Sabbath was, somehow, despite everything, still a band of four equals. Something that, in reality, they had never been. Certainly, Bill, of them all, had always been treated like the court jester, the willing fool, there to hit things and be hit. It wasn't really so, but the fact remained: Bill had destroyed his own career. From Sharon's point of view, what she was offering was little more than a glorified handout. Did Bill want a small percentage of a large take, or nothing at all? Very publicly, right or wrong, Bill chose the latter.

Bitter caterwauling from the loyal ranks exploded as the online feud gathered momentum, with a vocal majority insisting that the word 'reunion' was now inapplicable without Bill behind the kit. Since 1969, Sabbath had seen 25 musicians pass through its ranks, with Tony as the only constant, yet purists understandably seethed. How could there be a bona fide reunion without Bill? Were Sabbath fans yet again being sold a bill of goods?

Beyond the semantics of the word 'reunion', Bill's absence implied a more substantive issue. His style, richly influenced by jazz and other progressive stylings, invested Sabbath's signature sound with a unique, free-flowing cadence; it was not the strength of the hits that defined Bill, but the spaces between them. While Tony's riffs were generally acclaimed as the essence of the Sabbath sound, equally important was the backbone of the band's essential mien – eventually the sound of heavy metal as it is now understood – the interplay between Bill and Geezer.

As Download approached, the story of Bill Ward's refusal to play along became the fly in the ointment of the hoopla surrounding this latest Sabbath 'reunion'. Meanwhile, it was finally confirmed that, as Geezer's Facebook posting had suggested, Ozzy's regular drummer in his solo band, Tommy Clufetos, was tapped to join Sabbath for their live appearances. Tommy had earned a fearsome reputation as one of the planet's most powerful drummers, laying down beats for Alice Cooper, Ted Nugent and, more recently, Rob Zombie. Tommy's style was ferocious, bordering on violent; he would often spring off his drum stool to bring the weight of his entire body behind his strikes. As a professional, Clufetos was seasoned enough to appreciate how to best serve the material and, by common consent, he was an elite timekeeper. Yet there was little chance his aggressive style wouldn't profoundly alter Sabbath's sound; the difference between Bill and Tommy like that between English and American football.

At the warm-up show at the Birmingham O2 Arena, with Clufetos behind the drums (unacknowledged by Ozzy), the band delivered a bracing set of classics to the audience of 3000, who flooded the Internet with effusive reviews and mobile phone photos and videos that revealed the band to be in far better form than anyone had imagined. Perhaps the Download show still had a shot at the history books. Beyond that, no one knew.

The weather on the first day of the Download Festival rivalled the torrential rains that had battered Glastonbury the year before. The organisers delayed the festival opening until 2.00 p.m. in order to lay down more hay across the muddy soup that was once a fairground, even as the skies poured forth. Howling winds had turned festival banners into dangerous giant sails, so the operations crew removed a number of potentially lethal signs and banners lest they impale some poor, unsuspecting camper. Certain acts that had been scheduled to appear early in the day were scratched altogether, the mind-numbing level of precision required for orchestrating the sets of over 100 acts on five stages across three days of wind and rain yielding little room for make-up slots.

By the second day, the rains had ceased and the fields had dried somewhat, although punters crossing the grounds repeatedly found themselves mired in mud so deep that many lost their shoes in Britain's version of quicksand. As Sunday arrived and the afternoon acts began their sets, the only thing threatening Sabbath's big moment now was Sabbath themselves. Of course, what made their slot so prestigious – playing the final night of a three-day festival – also meant that they would be facing a city of music fans who had been occupying a field for three days, drinking and eating themselves into a stupor, while getting shell-shocked by literally hundreds of heavy metal anthems. In such circumstances, there's no room for warming up the crowd; you either grab them by the short hairs in the very first song, or you'll be singing to the backs of thousands of jackets heading for the car park.

The Jim Marshall Main Stage (named after the amplification pioneer who passed away earlier in the year) stood tall in the countryside, with massive movie screens on either side and towers of monitors rising up from the stage like gigantic black tusks. Throughout the day, it held sets by Lamb Of God, Megadeth and a surprisingly listless one from Soundgarden before the stage was cleared for the main event. Just before the Sabbath set began, an unwanted guest arrived in the guise of a bone-cracking chill blowing across the fairground. Despite the body heat of 100,000 people, even the most menacing-looking of leather-clad metalheads jumped up and down to fend off the toe-curling temperatures.

And then it was on. Like the Whisky press conference, Sabbath's appearance began with a sprawling video montage of the band's storied career before the four musicians stepped out into a hail of applause, opening with – what else? – 'Black Sabbath'. Despite the acoustic challenges presented by an outdoor venue on a cold, windy day, the band sounded polished and robust through Download's NASA-sized PA system. Those first chilling, shimmering notes sounded majestic and, in that instant, all the anticipation and uncertainty evaporated. Even from the back of the field, the quartet appeared sturdy and confident. The crowd lunged forward.

At 63, Ozzy's days of storming across a stage are long over. Instead, he shuffled about and banged his head in communion with the music. There was, however, a certain purity in it all. He appeared lost in the sounds, revelling in every note, at times oblivious to the legion of overwrought fans at his feet. Ozzy wasn't interested in playing Simple Simon with his audience; he was there to bask in being part of one of the greatest catalogues in rock history. He made this music and he was damn well enjoying himself playing it again.

If doubters looked for cracks in the veneer, it was a fool's errand; Sabbath were in top form from the first thunderous note, and while by this point the band had already amassed upwards of fifteen new songs for the forthcoming album, this was no night for new material. Only bands with something to prove worried about tawdry impositions such as previewing new material. Tony, his fretboard adorned with crucifixes matching the one hanging from his neck, appeared largely unaffected by his battle with lymphoma, although his movements were few, as always, placing musicianship before showmanship. In fact, with the exception of the raging, shirtless Tommy Clufetos, the band indulged in precious few theatrics, generally staying close to their monitors, occasionally walking to the front of the stage before retreating back to their corner.

Meanwhile, Ozzy was turning in a performance that was in many ways the polar opposite of the foul-mouthed clown he had become on TV throughout the previous decade, and returned instead to being a proper rock star, propelling the set from one song to the next with a weird intensity. He commented little between songs and in doing so he allowed the music to enjoy centre stage. Occasionally taunting or baiting the audience, Ozzy was all business. Gone was the boorish caricature of his reality TV show; here was the consummate frontman, masterfully working the crowd by feeding them just enough banter, just the right blend of moves, to keep them nibbling contentedly from his hand. Menacing, defiant and at times chippy, Ozzy Osbourne didn't need pyrotechnics or gymnastics to remind the world of who exactly started heavy metal.

During the third number, 'Behind The Wall Of Sleep', Ozzy introduced 'Mr Geezer Butler' for his bass solo; a sonic interlude that predictably inspired a field of Dio's devil-horns from the fans. Behind Clufetos' steroidal skins assault, Sabbath sounded more alive than ever. No mercy, no sentimentality; just pure musical Armageddon. At one point Ozzy gestured to Tony and said, 'The guy on the stage I've known for most of my life, and he's one of the strongest guys I know. Let's hear it for Mr Tony Iommi.' The crowd, well aware of Tony's situation, responded accordingly. The applause shook the very earth beneath them.

'War Pigs' elicited its requisite singalong before the band swung into 'Electric Funeral', 'Wheels of Confusion', 'Sweet Leaf' and 'Symptom Of The Universe', followed by an exhilarating drum solo. The 32-year-old Clufetos beat, howled and jumped out of his seat, as he filled the British countryside with drums loud enough to tip Stonehenge. Bill Ward might have been missed, but the crowd's explosive approval suggested his absence was not diminishing their enjoyment of the show. Not this time anyway.

The sound was *immense*. 'The Wizard' came on like rolling thunder as Iommi lingered behind Ozzy firing from the hip. So simple in its brutality. The minor pentatonic and fifth chords; that's it. The building blocks of the band to which every single band that preceded them this weekend owes a debt. Geezer turned in a performance right from the top of his game. He locked on to Tommy Clufetos' twin kick drums like a guided missile. Clufetos was *astonishing*. Thunder and fury and power and glory raining down like hammers of the gods. The double-kick flourishes, tastefully and sparingly applied, added a real gloss to the mix, bringing a pleasingly contemporary edge to the sound that spawned heavy metal.

As the set neared its close the audience were primed, howling for more, and when Ozzy yelled, 'You have to do something for me on this last song, go fucking nuts!' most were only too happy to oblige. The ending to the set was the same as it was 40 years before: a romping, breathless 'Children Of The Grave', followed by the victory lap of 'Paranoid'. When it was finally done, they gathered at the front of the stage for their bows as fireworks exploded above them. Nobody else moved when Sabbath walked offstage. There might not be ten more years in the tank, but, for now, Black Sabbath were once again masters of their own reality. Would this be the last time they played this song in their homeland? Not while Tony Iommi still draws breath.

Since then the band's news management has fed out a trickle of information about the new album. It is to be called 13. No, that may not be the case. Actually, 13 is the title. Well, we'll have to see. Etc. What is certain is that with a new deal with Universal under their belts, and Japanese, Australian and New Zealand tour dates locked in for early summer, 13 – as it was eventually called – will be released in June 2013.

Speaking to the *NME* Online site, Ozzy commented: 'We've written about fifteen songs so far, whether they'll get on an album [I don't know] … You just keep on writing. I was trying to [work out]: where would we be now musically if we'd have stayed together?' Regarding how Rubin approached the writing sessions with the band, Butler said, 'He sat us down, put the first album on and said "Listen to this, imagine it's 1969, you've just done that, what would you do next?"' Iommi also discussed his battle with cancer and how playing with the band last summer gave him a 'boost'. He said: 'It was great. Going through what I've gone through over the past year has been like living in a different world – being onstage and to get that [reaction from the fans] is just fantastic, it really boosts you up.'

I tried to speak to Bill again, one last time, for this book, at the start of 2013, but while he remained cordial and thanked me for my interest, he made it clear he'd 'said all I have to say' on the subject of Black Sabbath – for now. That he was, in fact, considering writing his own book on the subject.

His pain, though, clearly remains considerable. The one who always fell prey to the worst of Tony's 'pranks', while being the one who Ozzy always remained closest to, and without whom Geezer's grumbling bass would simply never had anything to lock tentacles with, whatever the rest of them say now, he will be sorely missed on both 13 and the forthcoming world tour, which they planned to announce dates for once the album drummed up the requisite amount of publicity again.

The last time I spoke properly to Bill was during his last tour with Sabbath, in the summer of 2005. We were discussing the imminent anniversary of the death of his friend John Bonham – and of all his other drummer friends that have passed away. Most poignantly, Cozy Powell, one of the many drummers that tried – and failed – to replace Bill in Sabbath, and who died in a car crash in April 1998. According to a BBC report, at the time of the crash, Powell's blood-alcohol reading was over the legal limit, he was not wearing a seatbelt, and he was talking to his girlfriend on his mobile phone. It sounds crass but it's hard to imagine the fast-living, car-crazy Powell finding a better way to die – had it not happened too early. He was just 50.

We spoke of this and Bill told me about the things he takes with him on the road that he doesn't normally share. Right next to him in a box that he keeps next to the bunk he sleeps in on his own personalised tour bus, 'I carry different belongings from all my friends that have passed away. I have Cozy's gloves,' he said tenderly. He kept mementoes of the others which he asked me not to share the details of. Partly, he said, because in a strange way he feels almost guilty for being the one who didn't die young. 'They're just pictures from our time together and other private things,' he said. 'But I keep all these guys close to my heart and just know that they were the best. Each man, I owe a lot to.' He sighed heavily and added, 'They're all my guardian angels. This might sound really silly maybe but I'm being very vulnerable about this right now, Mick. But I often talk to Cozy, Bonzo, Mick Evans, [Jim] Capaldi ... guys that have passed away that are no longer here. I talk to them before I do a show or if we're on the road. I have a little bag that I carry with something of all of them in it. They're always with me on the road. And I joke about it. When I'm at home, before I pack my bags, I'll say, "Come on, you lot. We're going back out on the road, lads!"'

He said how his last conversation with Cozy took place just a few days before he died, and that he 'felt resolved, even though there was nothing to resolve'.

And was that how he felt now about the guys in Sabbath? 'Erm ... I don't know about resolved. But we've forgiven each other, I think. And we love each other. Despite everything ...'

By the end of the first decade of the twenty-first century, despite his frequent appearances onstage again with Black Sabbath, his steady stream of ever less interesting solo albums – four in that decade, most of which continued to play well with each emerging generation of heavy metal kidz, but none of which capture the spark or energy or interest of his best work with Randy Rhoads or Tony Iommi – Ozzy Osbourne was no longer considered a mere rock star, with or without the band who had once kicked him out yet now relied on him for their continued half-life exist-ence. He was a TV star. Moreover, a 'reality' TV star. One of the first and still the best, yet nothing more, really. And not just Ozzy but Sharon, too, and two of their three children, Kelly and Jack

(Aimee, their eldest, having somehow avoided the ignominy of becoming a fellow star of *The Osbournes*, or *The X Factor*, or any of the other brand-extending shows her parents and siblings have subsequently entrusted their reputations to).

The Osbournes, which had begun airing in America in February 2002, had seen to that: an overnight broadcasting phenomenon that would be the progenitor of dozens of copycat shows, not nearly as good but still floating around on terrestrial TV like abandoned rusty satellites over a decade later. As Don Arden himself had told me more than once, 'It ain't about who's right or who's wrong, kid. It's about who wins. And I was always a winner, whatever anyone says about me.' Another lesson his daughter had plainly learned well. For if there is to be any real winner in the Black Sabbath story it is surely Sharon Osbourne, who was not born poor in Aston, did not write or record any of their songs, nor appear at any of their shows (at least, not on-stage), but whose dreams and desires have decidedly driven their career to its current conclusion as surely as if they had been dolls in her pram.

The last time I sat down for a proper conversation with Ozzy was at the Dorchester hotel, not long after *The Osbournes* had aired its final episode, and Sharon's own TV career had now gone into overdrive with her about-to-get-serious appearances on first Britain's *X Factor*, then *America's Got Talent*.

Who had the original idea for a TV show? 'Journalists would come round to the house and it would be like trying to do an interview in a shopping mall. Always a fucking drama or a calamity going on. They'd say, "Is it always like this? What is it with you guys?" So I said to Sharon, you know what we should do, film these fucking things. I mean, sometimes things happened, you'd go, "That had to have been worked out! It just wouldn't happen like that in real life." But to us it's a *daily* occurrence. Cos of that I can't even watch it.'

What had been his initial reaction to the instant success of the show? 'It was like going to bed one night, getting up the next day and opening the door and it's a completely different world out there. I was like, "Is it me, or is this just really fucking weird?" All these TV guys jumping for joy. In the end I asked them, "If the show had been an album, how many records would we have sold?" This guy goes, "You know *Thriller*? Well this is like eighteen *Thrillers*." I'm going, *what!?!* Then I was the one jumping for joy!'

And now? 'One thing I did learn about TV, you think the music business is weird, in TV they really are all fucking mad. I mean, they get up, probably have a bonk or a row, or tread in dog shit or whatever. Then they've got to go on television and go, "HI FOLKS, IT'S JIMMY AND SUE!!" They can't go, "Fucking hell, it's raining and I feel like shit ..." On a personal level, it's been weird. Like, I just went to an AA meeting. Nobody used to bat an eye when I walked into a meeting, now they all come up to me. It's the same everywhere I go now. People think they *know* me ...'

Where did Black Sabbath fit into things now for him, I wondered? Did he even care any more? 'I care as much as I ever did,' he replied in that singsong voice, part Brummy, part LA. 'But I don't wanna push my luck. I went from absolutely hating them – how many thousands of times must you have heard me say I would *never* play with them again – to putting that all behind me. We've all grown up, we've all changed. But whether we could ever make another album together ... Listen, if we started writing and came up with the next *Master Of Reality* or *Sabbath Bloody Sabbath*, I'd be a fucking idiot not to put it out. But I will not do a new Sabbath album just because of the name. I don't wanna do something half-arsed and have everybody go, "Oh, they only did it for the money ..."'

Did he ever get to the bottom of his medical condition? If it wasn't multiple sclerosis, did he ever find out what it was? 'Yeah.

I always assumed it was the booze and stuff. Turns out I was wrong. I only just found this out, actually, but it all stems from the family again. A few years ago, I started to develop this really bad tremor. I thought it was from detoxing. I'm thinking, is it the shock? Am I having a nervous breakdown? Now I find out I've got ... it's called Parkin, but it's not Parkinson's. Anything to do with the central nervous system, it has the word Parkin in it, apparently. What I've got is called a Parkin Hereditary Tremor and I have to take medication for it on a daily basis for the rest of my life. When I found out, I phoned my sister. She goes, "Not you as well!" I said, "What the fuck do you mean, not me as well?" She says, "Oh, mum had that, so did Auntie Elsie and your grandma ..." I'm like, "Thanks for fucking telling me!" Me walking around for years thinking I'd got some sort of drug paralysis.'

Does he see himself as a survivor? 'I don't know about "survivor" so much as blessed or just lucky. I was out there using and abusing for years. I should be dead. They talk about money but, honestly, the most valuable thing to me right now is my sobriety. I've never had this much time to *think* with a clear head.' Had he ever considered why he had become such an addict? 'What I recognise now is that I have certain feelings – certain fears to do with my childhood – that I don't know how to deal with. When I was a kid, we did a lot of shouting but we never communicated big things. My old man would have a row with my mum then go down the pub, then come home later happy and singing. I used to think the pub must be a fantastic place. Drinking and smoking was normal in our house. When I couldn't sleep my dad would give me a bottle of beer. So for a long time, alcohol was great for me. I loved it and had some great times on it. But then, like everything does, it came to an end. It stopped working, but I still had the fear and the voices in my head telling me to do it.'

He had talked to me before many times about the voices in his head. I had always assumed it was a drug thing. Did he still get them now, even though he was straight? 'Yeah. The thing is, it's an illness of the mind, and of the body and the spirit, so you're spiritually sick. And I've got no choice but to accept that, because when I do what's suggested I do, the voices turn down. Cos I used to have a fucking football crowd in my head, you know? Plus, I'm just compulsive. Sharon will ask for a glass of Château De Fuckwit or whatever, but to me it's either red or white and you wake up the next day having pissed the bed. These days I've learned how to turn the voices down. I believe that everything is a balance. You can't have good without bad, you can't have day without night, you can't have light without shade. It's all yin and yang. It's all balance.'

Is that how he felt these days, then: more balanced? 'No, no! I'm still the most unbalanced fucker you'll ever meet. But I'm working on myself. It's a really weird process but suddenly ... I don't know whether I grew up or if one of my commonsense valves finally unlocked itself, but I don't even get wound up by other people having a drink now. I have become one of those terrible ex-smokers now, though. They say an ex-smoker is worse than a non-smoker and it's true. I can't stand to be around it. Luckily, in California you can't even smoke in a fucking chimney now. But I was in a restaurant in London recently with Sharon, and there was this woman at the adjacent table smoking one after another right through her meal. Then I look again and she's got a fucking cigar in her trap! Sharon goes, "She probably goes to bed with a fucking pipe up her cunt!"'

He was now in his sixties. If he didn't want to, he wouldn't have to work again, surely? 'Well, that's not quite true, because the more money you make the more people you've got to employ to keep everything going. Bigger office suddenly, more security. And then you've got to live in Beverly Hills ... I mean, I *could* retire but what the fuck am I gonna do? Look out the window all day? It's hardly a fucking job what I do ...'

So what was left for Ozzy Osbourne now? Did he have a life plan, as such, at this point? '*The Osbournes* is finished now, thank God, so at least I can fart and walk around naked in me own home again without no one laughing at me. And I'm touring again this summer. But where I'll be this time next year or any of that … You've got to remember who it is you're talking to. Cos of the [AA] programme I'm on, my whole thing right now is to try and take it all one day at a time. And considering some of the days I have, if I can manage that, then I really am a fucking star …'

By chance, I happened to speak with Wendy Dio just prior to finishing this book. Wendy, who remains close friends with Gloria Butler, and stayed in touch with Tony and Geezer. She talked about how she burst into tears when she heard of Tony's diagnosis, how it brought painful memories of Ronnie's illness back to her. How Geezer was one of the last people Ronnie said goodbye to before passing.

This time, though, there was better news ahead, she hoped. 'Tony's been going through it, but now he's doing fantastic. I know Tony's gonna beat it. Unbelievable. He's doing really well. You know, I think because of Ronnie dying he went and got checked. Because he's got the lymph nodes in the groin and I think instead of just leaving it and thinking, oh, you know, whatever, I think he went and he got early detection. And he looks great. He's doing fantastic again.'

The proof of that was when Tony, Geezer and Ozzy arrived in London in March 2013, to give a series of interviews to promote the imminent release of 13. They also brought with them three of the tracks from the album: the monolithic, nine-minute opus 'God Is Dead', which, rather incredibly, sounds like it might have been recorded for either of their first two, now classic albums, complete with some classic Geezer 'great brain' lyrics. 'With God and Satan at my side,' sings Ozzy in the same deep, doleful voice of days of yore, 'from darkness will come light …' Even more evocative of their earliest days is 'The End Of The Beginning', which begins very much like the original 'Black Sabbath' track, at the slow, sullen speed of the very darkest night falling, before gradually ovulating into the kind of deeply trippy groove which reminds one that Sabbath didn't just invent the peculiarly eerie sound of British heavy metal, they also instigated what is now recognised as full-on, eye-to-the-ground American stoner rock.

On tracks like 'Age Of Reason', with its magnificently over-the-top coda, it sounds like something prime-era Sabbath might have concocted for *Sabbath Bloody Sabbath*, still their landmark album, as far as this writer is concerned. Could it be that Rick Rubin has managed to do what he could not with AC/DC and really bring Black Sabbath back full circle to where they were before they lost what they never knew they had until it was all too late?

Maybe.

The missing link, of course, is and will remain Bill Ward. But the drummer they brought in to replace him on the album, at Rubin's suggestion – Brad Wilk of Rage Against The Machine – does, it has to be said, a fantastic job filling in. 'Brad was very nervous,' Iommi conceded. 'He's a big Sabbath fan, but he's done a great job.' And so, it should be added, does Ozzy. He still can't really write, but his voice hasn't sounded so good – so natural – since, yes, those early Sabbath classics; another innovation by Rubin, who, says Tony, forced Ozzy to sing 'in a lower range. Rick enforced that.'

The elephant in the room was Tony's illness, which he is still receiving treatment for, but which he suggested would not prevent the band undertaking a world tour – but in stages.

'I have to have the chemotherapy every six to seven weeks.' Or as Geezer, for once getting the final word, grimly joked: 'We want to tour as much as possible. But really, it all depends on, you know, if we're still alive. And at our age that goes for all of us.'

Amen.

NOTES AND SOURCES

Having worked with Black Sabbath, Ozzy Osbourne and Ronnie James Dio, on and off, for nearly 35 years, both as a writer and a press agent, I have been fortunate enough to interview them all formally on many occasions, as well as get to know them personally. Therefore, the majority of quotes in this book are taken from those times. I was also assisted, however, by the excellent work of Joel McIver, the doyen of underground metal writers, whose own biography, *Sabbath Bloody Sabbath*, is well worth a read. Thanks also to my brilliant researchers, Joe Daly and Harry Paterson.

There are also some other excellent books that I found useful in helping me put the pieces of the Sabbath story together, and which I have occasionally quoted briefly from. Most noteworthy, *Iron Man*, by Tony Iommi (Simon & Schuster, 2011), *Never Say Die* by Garry Sharpe-Young (Rock Detector, 2004), *Extreme* by Sharon Osbourne (Time-Warner, 2005), *Child in Time* by Ian Gillan (Smith Gyphon, 1993), *Off the Rails* by Rudy Sarzo (Tod Smart, 2008), *Love, Crime and Rock 'N' Roll* by Paul Clark (unpublished), and my own previous books, *Diary Of A Madman* (Zomba, 1986), *Paranoid* (Mainstream, 1999) and *Mr Big* (Robson, 2004).

I was also assisted by my regular subscriptions to the following magazines: *Classic Rock, Mojo, Rolling Stone, Creem, Billboard, Metal Hammer*, and from the archives, *NME, Melody Maker, Sounds, Record Mirror, International Times, Kerrang!, Let It Rock,*

Guitar Player, Disc & Music Echo, Trouser Press, The Rocket, Rag, Phonograph Records, Circus Raves, Guitar World and several others.

There are also some online resources definitely worth a mention that were always interesting, even when they didn't yield quotes, but certainly in terms of colour and background: Bob Nalbandian and Mark Miller, whose 2002 *Shockwaves* podcast was great, plus www.blacksabbath.com and www.black-sabbath.com, www.ozzyhead.com and www.sabbathlive.com. If I have inadvertently missed mentioning and giving credit to any others, I will happily correct, with thanks, in future editions.

INDEX